COMPARING PUBLIC SECTOR REFORM IN BRITAIN AND GERMANY

Comparing Public Sector Reform in Britain and Germany
Key traditions and trends of modernisation

Edited by

HELLMUT WOLLMANN
Humboldt-Universität zu Berlin

ECKHARD SCHRÖTER
Humboldt-Universität zu Berlin

LONDON AND NEW YORK

First published 2000 by Ashgate Publishing

Reissued 2019 by Routledge
2 Park Square, Milton Park, Abingdon, Oxon, OX14 4RN
52 Vanderbilt Avenue, New York, NY 10017

Routledge is an imprint of the Taylor & Francis Group, an informa business

© Hellmut Wollmann and Eckhard Schröter 2000

All rights reserved. No part of this book may be reprinted or reproduced or utilised in any form or by any electronic, mechanical, or other means, now known or hereafter invented, including photocopying and recording, or in any information storage or retrieval system, without permission in writing from the publishers.

Notice:
Product or corporate names may be trademarks or registered trademarks, and are used only for identification and explanation without intent to infringe.

Publisher's Note
The publisher has gone to great lengths to ensure the quality of this reprint but points out that some imperfections in the original copies may be apparent.

Disclaimer
The publisher has made every effort to trace copyright holders and welcomes correspondence from those they have been unable to contact.

A Library of Congress record exists under LC control number:

ISBN 13: 978-1-138-71757-2 (hbk)
ISBN 13: 978-1-138-71754-1 (pbk)
ISBN 13: 978-1-315-19629-9 (ebk)

Contents

List of Contributors vii

Preface ix

1 Comparing Institutional Development in Britain and Germany: (Persistent) Divergence or (Progressing) Convergence?
 Hellmut Wollmann 1

2 State and Society in Britain: Some Contrasts with German Experience
 Nevil Johnson 27

3 The Administrative State in Germany
 Klaus König 47

4 Regionalism in the United Kingdom: The Role of Social Federalism
 L. J. Sharpe 67

5 The Institutional Framework: Federalism and Decentralisation in Germany
 Gerhard Lehmbruch 85

6 The Development and Present State of Local Government in England and Germany – a Comparison
 Hellmut Wollmann 107

7 The Public Service in Britain: From Administrative to Managerial Culture
 Frederick F. Ridley 132

8 Actor Constellation, Opportunity Structure and Concept Feasibility in German and British Public Sector Reforms
   Hans-Ulrich Derlien — 150

9 Local Government Services in the United Kingdom and Germany
   Eckhard Schröter and Manfred Röber — 171

10 Culture's Consequences? In Search of Cultural Explanations of British and German Public Sector Reform
   Eckhard Schröter — 198

11 Regressive Modernisation? The Changing Patterns of Social Services Delivery in the United Kingdom
   John Clarke and Paul Hoggett — 224

12 Social Administration in Germany: Basic Structures and Reform History
   Dieter Grunow — 244

13 Privatisation of Social Services in the United Kingdom
   Brian Munday — 264

14 Social Service Delivery by Private and Voluntary Organisations in Germany
   Rolf G. Heinze and Christoph Strünck — 284

15 Trends in the Marketisation of British Social Services
   Michael Hill — 304

16 The Rise and Fall of a Social Service Regime: Marketisation of German Social Services in Historical Perspective
   Frank Bönker and Hellmut Wollmann — 327

17 Explaining Success in Administrative Reform
   B. Guy Peters — 351

Index — *363*

List of Contributors

Frank Bönker is Lecturer in Economics at the European University Viadrina Frankfurt (Oder).

John Clarke is Professor of Social Policy at the Open University.

Hans-Ulrich Derlien is Professor of Administrative Science at the University of Bamberg.

Dieter Grunow is Professor of Government and Public Administration at the Gerhard-Mercator University Duisburg.

Rolf G. Heinze is Professor of Sociology at the Ruhr-University Bochum.

Michael Hill is Visiting Professor of Social Policy and Politics at Goldsmiths College, University of London.

Paul Hoggett is Professor of Government at the University of the West of England Bristol.

Nevil Johnson is an Emeritus Fellow of Nuffield College Oxford.

Klaus König is Professor of Public Law and Public Administration at the Postgraduate School of Administrative Sciences Speyer.

Gerhard Lehmbruch is Emeritus Professor of Government at the University of Konstanz.

Brian Munday is Director of the European Institute of Social Services (EISS) at the University of Kent at Canterbury (UKC).

B. Guy Peters is Maurice Falk Professor of Government at the University of Pittsburgh.

Frederick F. Ridley is an Emeritus Professor of Government at the University of Liverpool.

Manfred Röber is Professor of Public Management at the Fachhochschule für Technik und Wirtschaft Berlin.

Eckhard Schröter is Assistant Professor of Government and Public Administration at the Humboldt-University Berlin.

L. J. Sharpe is an Emeritus Fellow of Nuffield College Oxford.

Christoph Strünck is Assistant Professor of Political Science at the University of Düsseldorf.

Hellmut Wollmann is Professor of Government and Public Administration at the Humboldt-University Berlin.

Preface

During the last two decades public sector reform has ranked high on the political agenda throughout Western Europe. In particular, there has been an explosion of reform initiatives associated with the New Public Management (NPM) movement. The British and German cases are no exception to this rule, but whereas the United Kingdom has been swept by a tidal wave of administrative change, Germany has so far only seen comparatively faint ripples. Many reports on public sector modernisation portray NPM-driven changes as a secular trend, yet there is also good reason to suggest that deeply rooted political and institutional structures, as well as of entrenched administrative cultures have had a crucial impact on the numerous reform programmes for public bureaucracies. In this context, country comparisons often run the risk of only looking at the face value of ongoing public sector changes without reflecting on how much the current reform discourses are embedded within specific institutional and cultural traditions. Furthermore, progress of comparative research in this field may be severely inhibited by an unfortunate split amongst various scientific communities, thus keeping 'generalists' with their broad dimension of expertise apart from 'specialists' who focus on developments in particular policy areas. Similarly, this research field has become an increasingly contested area for public management experts on one side and political scientists on the other.

Starting from the assumption that a clear understanding of each country's key political and administrative traditions is necessary in order to overcome the problem of possible 'ecological fallacies' and to promote mutual learning processes, this volume applies a pronouncedly political science approach to the study of public sector developments. At the same time, it brings together political scientists, public management experts and policy specialists. In doing so, this work pursues a twofold objective. First, it seeks to examine in the light of the New Public Management discussion those key institutional and cultural factors which are most likely to shape current public sector reform policies in Germany and the United Kingdom. Second, the volume sets out to link the results of these discussions to actual reform trends in the fields of social policies and social administration in order to generate applicable and problem-oriented results.

In view of the characteristic traits of the British and German state traditions, we suggest that (at least) four broadly defined factors can be identified. The first category is concerned with the underlying notion of the state and state-society relations in historical perspective. Whereas *Klaus König* highlights the pervasive German tradition of the administrative state, *Nevil Johnson* contrasts this continental concept of the state with the Anglo-Saxon 'civil society' tradition. Second, the structural features of the government systems and the peculiar type of intergovernmental relations are most likely to have a lasting impact on the substance and course of reform processes. As a consequence, the influences of the unitary and federal state models, i.e. the way in which administrative functions and political power are distributed among the various tiers of government, deserves our closer attention. While *Hellmut Wollmann's* chapter focuses on institutional developments at the local government level and national variations in central-local relations, the contributions by *Jim Sharpe* and *Gerhard Lehmbruch* are mainly concerned with the social and historical foundations of the federal or meso-level of government. A third cluster of influential factors concerns the public sector workforce and concepts of the public service which underscore the particular conditions of service and codes of ethics. We also scrutinise closely the underlying ideas of a professional 'public' or 'civil service' at both the national and local government levels and the practical implications of envisaged moves towards a more business-like managerial culture in the public sector (see the chapters by *Frederick F. Ridley* and by *Eckhard Schröter* and *Manfred Röber*). Starting from the concept of the public service, *Hans-Ulrich Derlien* widens the perspective and presents a comparative reform history of the British and German cases. Finally, the cultural patterns which guide political and administrative behaviour are given the close attention they deserve. Does a greater civic assertiveness and stronger consumerism in the United Kingdom account for the search for public sector efficiency and the rise of market-driven reform measures in the 1980s? Does a political culture in Germany that is still state-centred help to shield the public sector from pressures for fundamental change? Looking at empirical data on political values and attitudes *Eckhard Schröter* seeks to shed some light on the political support for public sector reform programmes in both countries.

Looking at the changing fabric of the welfare state in the production and delivery of social services, our volume further sets out to analyse and evaluate recent reform steps in the light of basic institutional and cultural idiosyncracies of the British and German administrative systems. The first set of papers by *Dieter Grunow* and by *John Clarke* and *Paul Hoggett* present an overview of the basic architecture of the welfare systems and the dominant patterns of service delivery, with particular emphasis placed on the social security systems. The following chapters deal in greater detail with personal social services which can also be grouped under the social care heading. In keeping with the country-specific reform profiles, the privatisation of social services is placed in the foreground of *Brian Munday's* chapter, whereas *Rudolf G. Heinze* and *Christoph Strünck* mainly address the (changing) role of the traditionally strong non-profit welfare associations in the German system. Finally, *Frank Bönker* and *Hellmut Wollmann*, for the German case, and *Michael Hill*, writing on the British case, put the more recent changes into a wider, policy-oriented perspective and present longer historical analyses of the development of national welfare systems. In the concluding chapter *B. Guy Peters* steps back from the bilateral country comparison and seeks conditions for successful public sector reforms by drawing on examples from the wider international community.

This volume has its origins in two conferences held at the Institute of Social Sciences of the Humboldt University, Berlin. With a few exceptions, the studies collected in this book were first presented at the 1997 Anglo-German Workshop, and subsequently revised and updated for publication. Most of the contributors to this volume had the opportunity to discuss their revised chapters with one another again at the 1998 Anglo-German Workshop on 'Public Sector Modernisation in the UK and Germany'. This second meeting, focusing on current reform initiatives and aiming at an assessment of the New Public Management in practice, was meant as another step in the systematic investigation of British-German public sector comparison, and we as organisers are looking forward to seeing the results of this meeting documented in print.

We are indebted to a number of institutions and individuals and would like to take this opportunity to extend our grateful thanks for their support. Above all, our thanks go to the Anglo-German Foundation for the Study of Industrial Society, London, which made both conferences possible by giving generous financial support. In particular, we owe our thanks to Dr Ray Cunningham, research director at the Anglo-German Foundation. Furthermore, we wish to express our gratitude to the British Council, Berlin and the Hans-Böckler-Stiftung, Düsseldorf, for further financial assistance.

We would also like to pay tribute to those workshop participants who have given freely of their expertise as discussants and commentators. Among the many others who have been important sources of advice, the contributions which particularly stand out are those of Klaus H. Goetz, Christopher Hood, Werner Jann, and Christoph Reichard. At Ashgate Publishers we were extremely lucky to have an understanding editorial team. The final product also owes much to Martin Lodge who was an invaluable help in copy-editing the final manuscript. Thanks go also to our research assistant at Humboldt University, Heinrich Wollny, for his help in preparing the camera-ready copy. Finally, of course, the completion of this book would not have been possible without the excellent collaboration of its contributors whom we thank for their co-operation and patience during its production.

Hellmut Wollmann
Eckhard Schröter

Berlin, August 1999

1 Comparing Institutional Development in Britain and Germany: (Persistent) Divergence or (Progressing) Convergence?

HELLMUT WOLLMANN

Introduction

This chapter is meant to achieve particularly two aims: In order to prepare the ground for a comparative analysis of institutional development in Britain and in Germany the article will, first, highlight some of the basic factors that have historically shaped the institutional fabric of the two countries and eliciting their institutional *divergence*. Second, by, in brevity, drawing on material and conclusions put forward in later chapters of this volume the question will be addressed as to whether, particularly in their more recent development, the two countries have exhibited institutional *convergence* and, if so, *why*.

The (Early) Political, Institutional and Cultural Development of the Two Countries: a Case of Extraordinary Divergence

Political Continuity vs. Political Rupture

Britain has experienced a conspicuously continuous development, marked by the gradual emergence of a parliamentary monarchy. Parliament, with its feudal origins in the 13th century, 'is a particularly important example of continuity' (Rose, 1982, p.39). She has not suffered any disruption and trauma of a successful foreign invasion since 1066. By contrast, Germany has lived through a history of political and territorial ruptures. She was a latecomer to national unity, with the German States being finally united under Bismarck in the *Kaiserreich* of 1871. As a result of the revolution of November 1918, Germany became a parliamentary democracy which staggered under the political and economic pressure of the inter-war years and was terminated by the Nazi seizure of power. Following Germany's liberation from the totalitarian Nazi regime, her occupation by the four Allies and her division by the Iron Curtain, the Federal Republic of Germany which, in 1949, was established in the Western Occupation Zones became the first politically and economically viable and stable parliamentary democracy in German history. In the Soviet Zone, the German Democratic Republic was set up by the Soviet Union and was turned into a dictatorial communist regime. Finally, in 1990, the two German States were united.

(Formally) Unlimited vs. (Constitutionally) Restricted Power of Parliament

The development of British modern parliamentary monarchy and democracy has been marked by the concept of *Parliamentary Sovereignty* according to which, in a famous dictum of *Blackstone*, 'Crown in Parliament can, in short, do everything that is not naturally impossible' (quoted from Rose, 1982, p.52). The traditional formula 'Crown in Parliament' reflects the historical compromise and 'negotiated' constitutional transition between the Crown and the Commons which still formally recognises the Crown as representing government (Rose, 1982, p.50 ff.). Real power lay for a long period with the two Houses of Parliament but has rested, since the abolition of the veto power of the House of Lords in 1911, solely with the House of Commons, that is, in the last resort, with the simple majority of its members. In the absence of a written constitution, Britain's constitutional history has been shaped and carried by (often centuries old) conventions, precedents and practices. While the absence of a written constitution and the very principle of Parliamentary Sovereignty has amounted virtually to what has been called an 'elective dictatorship', in reality the Britain, in her entire political history, has never fallen victim to a parliamentary majority blatantly abusing these formidable formal powers.

In *German* constitutional history, the struggle for parliamentary supremacy and the function of the written constitution have taken an almost entirely opposite course. The abortive liberal Revolution of 1848 ended with a constitutional compromise through which, throughout the German States, parliament, elected by property-dependent suffrage, had woefully limited powers, while the government was appointed by the ('constitutional') monarch and not responsible to parliament. After the revolution of 1918, the Weimar Constitution of 1919 was enacted in the Continental European tradition of a written constitution which laid down the organisational and procedural ground rules of the new republic (as well as fundamental rights of the citizens) and could be amended only by a qualified (two-thirds) majority. Reflecting the traumatic experience that crucial provisions of the Weimar Constitution were suspended by the national parliament (*Reichstag*), on coercion by the Nazis in a seemingly procedure, the new federal constitution (*Grundgesetz*) of 1949 went as far as laying down that a number of basic constitutional principles (such as the democratic order, rule of law, federalism, judicial review, certain fundamental rights) can never be changed, not even by a unanimous vote of Parliament.

Majority Rule vs. 'Semi-Sovereign' Decision Making

In Britain the majoritarian electoral system lends itself to generate clear-cut parliamentary majorities and to produce landslide victories which put the winning party in government and the loser in opposition. Hence, the stage seems to be politically and institutionally set for having a *majoritarian* and *competitive* style of political decision-making rather than a *consensual* and *consociational* one,[1] thus making for relatively sharp policy shifts in the wake of party majority and government shifts. Yet, somewhat belying such conclusions, the sequence of government changes in Britain's recent political history reveals a 'moving consensus' (Rose, 1984; Page, 1991) in that incoming government has largely accepted and built upon the policy changes introduced by its predecessor.

In the Federal Republic, the electoral system of proportional representation, in combination with the 5 per cent hurdle (*Fünfprozent-Klausel*), has favoured a political party system made up of two major parties (Christian Democrats, CDU, and Social Democrats, SPD) and two or more minor parties which manage to overcome 5 per cent barrier (such as the Free Democrats, FDP, throughout the existence of the Federal Republic, more recently the Greens, Die Grünen, and, since 1990, the post-communist Party of Democratic Socialism, PDS). As the electorate has been conspicuously wary of providing a political party with an absolute majority of the parliamentary seats, the Federal Republic has been ruled by coalition governments which, depending on compromises, tend to settle on the lowest common denominator and, hence, on incremental rather than large-scale policy change. Another important peculiarity of the decision-making process relates to the Federal Council *(Bundesrat)* which is the Upper Chamber in federal legislation and policy-making. As it is made up of representatives of the *Länder* governments, its decision-making is strongly shaped by *Länder*-specific concerns, but also by party political interests. The latter becomes particularly salient in a political constellation in which either of the two major political parties is in a minority and opposition situation in the Federal Parliament while it controls a large enough number of *Länder* governments as to command a majority of the votes in the Federal Council – in German variant of what in France is politically called *cohabitation*. Furthermore, a number of institutions, such as Federal Constitutional Court *(Bundesverfassungsgericht)* and, until recently, the Federal Bank *(Bundesbank)*, have been formidable players in the decision-making arena. Such (and other factors) have led observers to call the Federal Republic a 'semi-sovereign state' (Katzenstein 1987) and to identify its long-term decision-making pattern as essentially *incrementalist* and *middle of the road* (Schmidt, 1993; Wollmann, 1991).

State-Less vs. State Tradition: Common Law-Based vs. Roman Law-Based Political Thinking

The idea of the 'State' as a separate legal entity ('moral person') has remained 'alien to English political thinking' (Rose, 1982, p.47), while it has been dominant in Continental European political thought (Dyson, 1980, see also the articles by Johnson and König in this volume). Continental legal thinking, rooted in the Roman Law tradition, has conceived the State as separate legal entity endowed by constitution with certain competencies and acting through 'organs' (parliament, government, etc.). English thinking, ingrained in the Common Law tradition (Dyson, 1980, p.53), is oriented on individual *institutions*, ranging from the Crown to the other institutions in the land (such as local councils) upon which, by parliamentary act, concrete powers are conferred.

Besides the distinct legal traditions, in Britain the advances of parliamentary government were embedded in and actually driven by the emergence of a bourgeois ('civil') society (for the civil society tradition of Anglo-Saxon countries see Heady, 1996; Stillman, 1991, p.19 ff. and König and Füchtner, 1998, p.8 ff.). Imbued with philosophical (Benthamite) utilitarianism, the views and thoughts on government were ensuingly pragmatic in seeing it as being instrumental, if not ancillary, to the needs and demands of the emergent bourgeois society and capitalist economy rather than as constituting a self-standing 'State' in its own right. By contrast, the concept of the State developed in Germany with the rise of the absolutist territorial rulers for whom Roman Law was a useful legal expedient for construing the State as a self-standing legal and as opposed to late-feudal institutionalism. During the 19th century, with the emergence of a bourgeois society largely fostered by the 'enlightened' late-absolutist state bureaucracy, political thinking hinged on juxtaposing State and Society, the former being seen as representing the common good[2] and standing above and beyond partisan interests (*Überparteilichkeit*), while Society was viewed as the realm of individualistic egoism and partisan strife. With the advances of the Welfare State, in yet another important twist in political thinking, the State was perceived, particularly in the 'social democratic' welfare state model dominant in the 1970s, as the guardian of democratic government and social justice.

It should be noted, though, that, notwithstanding these important, if not fundamental differences in the conception and perception of the 'State', the two countries have exhibited significant commonalities in the real world of public sector development as surfacing in a number of scores. As measured by the public sector share of the GNP (for the following data until 1990 Kohl, 1995, p.726; for comparative data see also Alber, 1998, p.210 ff. and Naschold, 1995, p.50), in 1870 Germany's public sector was larger (14.2 per cent) than that of the UK (8.7 per cent). In the following years the public sector share rose in both countries at a similar rate. At the turn of the century both countries had a public sector share of some 15 per cent. At the end of the 1920s, during the worsening economic crisis, the public sector share reached around 25 per cent. After 1945, with further advances of the modern welfare state, the public sector continued to grow in both countries towards 40 per cent by the end of the 1960s and towards 45 per cent (and beyond) by the end of the 1970s. Since the early 1980s the public sector profiles of the two countries have noticeably deviated from each other. Whereas, as an obvious result of Conservative retrenchment policies, the public sector share in the UK was reduced to 39.9 per cent in 1990, in Germany, reflecting the enormous public spending demanded by German unification, it soared after 1990, reaching a record of 50.6 per cent in 1993 and 1995 before falling to 48.8 per cent in 1997 (Homeyer, 1998, p.347).

Another facet of the picture is provided by looking at the percentage of public sector employees as compared to the total number of employees in the national economy. In recent years the percentage has been remarkably higher in the UK, fluctuating around 20 per cent in the UK as compared to 15 per cent[3] in Germany. It should be noticed that, that notwithstanding its neo-liberal 'lean state' concepts (and rhetoric), the Tory governments have not significantly sized down the percentage of public employees. (Alber, 1998, p.218). One reason for this comparatively high percentage of public sector employees is certainly the fact that most of the personal social services have been delivered by public sector personnel whereas in Germany they have primarily been supplied by non-profit-making welfare organisations (see Grunow, Clarke and Hoggett, Heinze and Strünck, Munday, Hill as well as Bönker and Wollmann, all in this volume).

Thus, under the 'State' versus 'State-less' rubric, the situation in the two countries is somewhat ambivalent and contradictory. While Germany has a 'strong' State tradition, some crucial areas of 'social services' have been traditionally marked by the conspicuous absence of direct public delivery and, instead, by the operation of non-governmental organisations (NGOs). By contrast, Britain has lived conceptually in a 'stateless' tradition, the provision of public services, however, has traditionally been characterised by the predominance of direct public delivery.

Rule of Law

In Britain's Common Law tradition judge-made law as an time-honoured body of judicial precedents has been prevalent as the source of law, while parliamentary statute law was rather the exception. It appears as one of the paradoxes of English constitutional history that Parliament showed great reserve and restraint in exerting its legislative power. Thus, Britain has no legalistic tradition in the Continental European meaning (Jones, 1990, p.171). As a result of the Parliament's restraint in enacting detailed statute law and also because of the absent distinction between public and private law, Britain has not developed an elaborate system of *administrative law* as a self-standing body of law geared to the public sector (see Ridley in this volume). Against this historical background it is not surprising that a separate system of administrative courts has not been established. Instead, complaints against 'public' actions can be brought before the ordinary courts (or special tribunals). Hence, legal skills and legally trained personnel are hardly needed in the conduct of government matters, neither at the lofty central government level to which preferably Oxbridge-educated generalists have been recruited nor at the local level where, in order to handle the earthly tasks of local government, technical and professional skills are demanded (see also Ridley in this volume). Concomitantly, in Britain's educational and vocational training system no special institutions or curricula geared to public administration have caught roots (see Schröter and Röber in this volume).

By contrast, the evolution of Germany's legal system, from the late 18th century onward, strongly influenced by the ideas of the French Enlightenment with its emancipatory and egalitarian impetus to abolish feudal privilege and to propagate the principle of *codification*. This made the as comprehensive as possible legislative regulation by parliament, that is statute law, the prime, if not the sole source of law, while, in Montesquieu's concept of the separation of powers, the judge was limited to authoritatively interpreting the legislative provisions (as the 'mouth of the law', *bouche de la loi*). In its (largely abortive) struggle with the still semi-authoritarian monarchic powers, the liberal bourgeoisie regarded legislation, passed by the bourgeoisie-dominated parliament, as the crucial instrument for exerting some control over the State bureaucracy still – like the Army – firmly in the hands of the monarch. This thrust at securing the rights of (bourgeois) citizens against infringement by the still semi-authoritarian monarchic state authorities and at pertaining a 'codified' comprehensive legal coverage of such protect lies historically at the heard of the German 'State of Rule of Law' (*Rechtsstaat*). Largely drawing on French experience, the elaboration of administrative law designed to regulate citizen/state relations in all sectors of state administration became a separate body of ever more detailed legal provisions and also ushered in an corresponding self-standing system of administrative courts. While in the latter part of the 19th century the *Rechtsstaat* was tinged with legal positivism, a strongly normative underpinning surfaced after 1945, when, in view of the past the criminal excesses and atrocities of the Nazi State, the reestablishment and guarantee of the *Rechtsstaat* was given the highest constitutional salience.

With the advance of *legalism* in the regulation of public administration towards the end of the 19th century, legal skills and legally trained state officials were increasingly required by public administration (see also Wagner and Wollmann 1991, p.59). As a consequence, the 'lawyers' monopoly' (*Juristenmonopol*) took root and has dominated public administration to this day (Wollmann 1997a, p.84).

Unitary/Centralist vs. Federal/Decentralist Structures

In the country's political development Britain moved early to extend 'unitary government' within the British Isles by the annexation of Wales by England to form Britain (in 1536), by forming Great Britain by uniting Britain and Scotland (at first, in 1606, under a common monarch and then, in 1707, by abolishing the Scottish Parliament) and finally by creating the United Kingdom by adding Ireland in 1801. Again, the UK's constitutional development harbours some paradox. On the one hand, there are good reasons, particularly when comparing the UK with federal countries such as Germany to see in the UK almost the epitome of a unitary government (for analyses of the contrasting traditions see Sharpe and Lehmbruch in this volume). On the other hand, one needs to recall that, constitutionally speaking, the Crown came to 'preside over a multi-national kingdom' (Rose, 1982, p.6 ff.). Probably in reflecting its territorial basis of the 'four nations under one Crown' (Rose, 1982), the UK has not created an explicit operative regional (*meso*) level (Sharpe, 1993); instead, the four 'nations' have remained to be the 'frame of reference' for institutional differentiation, let alone the 'national' (quasi-regional) differentiation through what has been called 'social federalism' (see Sharpe in this volume). Thus it seems more than warranted to take a more balanced interpretation of the Britain being a *unitary* government thesis (Keating, 1999, p.3).

After a first attempt by central government in the late 1970s failed to 'regionalise' the UK by the establishment of Scottish and Welsh Parliaments and the devolution of powers,[4] its regionalisation has recently taken a historic step ahead by the creation of the Scottish Parliament and the Welsh Assembly as proposed by the incoming Labour government and approved by referendums in September 1998 (see Keating, 1999, p.3).

In a similar vein, Britain's central/local government relations have been marked, particularly in the 19th century, by a peculiar paradox (Sharpe 1993, p.250). On the one hand, it was deduced from the principle of Parliamentary Sovereignty that any institution in the land could act only if and when explicitly permitted and empowered by Act of Parliament to do so (*ultra vires* doctrine). By constitutional convention and *factually*, however, the central government in London chose to primarily deal with foreign policy, running the Empire and making key decisions in domestic policy-making, while leaving the mundane domestic matters largely to the local councils in what has been termed a 'dual polity' (Bulpitt, 1983). With the advances of the modern welfare state, however, the interventions and the involvement of central government in the local government level have intensified and culminated in the onslaught of centralist policies under the Conservative government in the 1980s and 1990s. (This development will be taken up on more later in this article and in a comparative intent in more detail in the article by Wollmann in this volume).

Germany's constitutional and institutional development has been fundamentally shaped by her decentral structures which have their roots in early medieval history (see also Lehmbruch in this volume). When Germany was finally united to became a nation state in 1871, it was the monarchs and princes that formally signed the Unification Treaty and remained the politically dominant forces in the Federal Council (*Bundesrat*) which, acting as an Upper Chamber, was much more powerful than the elected Reich Parliament (*Reichstag*). After the defeat of Nazi Germany in 1945, first the *Länder* were (re-)established by the Occupation Forces with the foundation of the Federal Republic, in 1949, following suit. Mirroring the political and institutional primogeniture of the *Länder* and carrying the handwriting of the Western Allies, the Federal Constitution (*Grundgesetz*) of 1949 passed by the Constituent Assembly *(Parlamentarischer Rat)* gave the Federal Republic a pronouncedly federal and decentral design. Skipping further details at this point, it should suffice to call to mind that the Federal Republic has, experienced a process of 'unitarisation' and (re-)centralisation in defiance of the original constitutional intent. Partly falling in line with the 'centralist' feature of the (constitutionally, to be sure, federal) Weimar Republic and partly responding to some inherently centralising factors, including constitutional provisions (such as the 'homogeneity imperative' – *Homogenitätsgebot* – of art. 28 paragraph 1 of the Federal Constitution), the Federal Republic has developed towards what has been termed a 'unitary federal state' (*unitarischer Bundesstaat*, Hesse, 1962).

The position of local government is somewhat ambivalent and contradictory as the bottom level in what, constitutionally speaking, is a two layer federal system consisting of the Federation and of the *Länder* with local government being seen as a constituent part of the latter (for details see Wollmann later in this volume). On the one hand, the autonomy of the municipalities and of the counties (*Kreise*) is guaranteed by the Federal Constitution as well as by the *Länder* constitutions; local government in the Federal Republic probably has a wider scope of tasks and responsibilities than in any other European country. On the other hand, local government is institutionally embedded in and politically confronted with the *Länder* jealously defend their constitutional status and cherish their traditional 'quasi-sovereignty' (*Eigenstaatlichkeit*). While they are fervent *de*centralists in their relation to the federal level, the *Länder* tend to take a *centralist* stance with regard to 'their' local level government.

However sketchily presented, the preceding paragraph should have served its purpose to highlight some of the key elements that make up the in part glaring difference in the political and institutional profiles of the two countries and mark the different *starting points* and different *path-dependencies* of the further institutional developments.

Comparative Outline of Institutional Developments

In focusing on institution building in the two countries (methodologically speaking as a dependent variable) and in trying to identify the factors that have shaped it (explanatory variables), the following analytical sketch does not claim to provide a coherent and consistent hypothetical model for comparative analysis. By drawing on current conceptual debates, on the discussions pursued in the articles and among the authors, the following factors should, however, be singled out as salient factors:[5]

- The *socio-economic* context impacting on decision-making.
- The *policy concepts of the relevant actors* and the ensuing policy regimes which are likely to shape the decisions on policy as well as on institutional (polity) choice to be taken, for instance, the ('social democratic') welfare state or the (neo-liberal) cutting back the welfare state/minimal state concepts.
- The *power constellation, interests and will and skill of the relevant actors*, particularly of the political parties (for actor constellation and opportunity structures, see also the chapter by *Derlien*).
- The *decision-making system*, such as its unitary versus federal, controversial/competitive versus consensus/consociational etc. features.
- The (national as well as international) *discourses* and *discourse*

regimes (Wittrock, Wagner and Wollmann, 1991; see also Sabatier, 1993, for advocacy coalitions) which impinge upon and legitimate decision-making in the (national) arenas.

- The (political) *culture* in which such policies are embedded and generated, such as the cognitive and normative frame of the (central) political elites as well as the cognitive and normative orientations of the general population (for a more detailed discussion, see Schröter in this volume).
- Processes of (national as well as international) *learning* and *diffusion* influencing decision-making (Ikenberry, 1990).
- The *inertia of existing institutions* and their ('structurally') constraining effect on the discretion and of institutional decision-making. The effect of such institutional *legacies* of the past is captured in the concept of *path-dependency*.[6]

In the following, this list of factors will be applied to the institutional development in the two countries. To achieve some analytically viable 'bench marking', an explicitly historical approach will be pursued in order to identify the situation and state from which the institutional development in question historically departed. The periodisation which underlies the following comparative interpretation roughly distinguishes (Bennett, 1993, p.12): the historical take-off period of modern local self-government in the 19th century; the emergence of the modern welfare state (roughly since the First World War and climaxing in the 1960s and early 1970s); the crisis of the welfare state (since the mid-1970s and well into the 1990s), and eventually the current period. Although the author is aware of the 'threat to validity' that is invited by limiting this comparative exercise to just a few policy fields, the focus in the following will be on the development of local government and the provision of social services (i.e. personal social services and social housing). By largely drawing on the articles in which these policy fields are treated in more detail (see Hill, Bönker and Wollmann, Wollmann in this volume), the following account proceeds by briefly characterising the institutional development and attempts to make a 'causal interpretation' by applying the analytical scheme outlined above. (The constellation of variables is shown in italics.)

Local Government I: The Status of Local Government

As was already hinted at in the introductory chapter, in 19th century Britain the development and status of local self-government was marked by a 'dual polity' (Bulpitt, 1983). Acting on a general (male) suffrage, with broad local autonomy and financially independent (on the basis of locally levied property taxes), Victorian local self-government, until well into the 1930s, was called the 'golden age of local self-government'. It was based on a *power constellation* in which Parliament decided to let Britain be run as a 'decentral' country. With this combination of political (democratic) strength and functional (multi-purpose) salience, English local government was an exceptionally advanced case of local self-government in contemporary Europe.

In 19th century Germany, divided into a multitude of large and small States, the development of local government was characterised by a *power constellation* in which the introduction of local self-government was, after 1808, the work of the enlightened bureaucracy of late-absolutist States and, after the failure of the liberal Revolution of 1848, the outgrowth of the political compromise between the urban bourgeoisie and the still semi-authoritarian monarchic powers. While the latter retained control over the State authorities, the former were granted local self-administration, based on a extremely limited (male) suffrage (meant to politically exclude the growing working class). While local self-administration reached significant strength and a wide spectrum of responsibilities, it remained politically weak because of its extremely narrow political base.

In Britain, with the advances of the welfare state, central government proceeded to make local government an instrument of the welfare state by adapting the local government levels territorially as well as organisationally to what was seen as central government requirements. While important functions were transferred to national agencies, other functions (education, housing, social services) were expanded. In emphasising these functions, the 'exceptionalist' independence which characterised the 19th century 'dual polity' model was reduced and in a way adapted to the needs of the modern ('national') welfare state. This development reached a climax after 1945 with the Labour government taking power and in the 1970s. In Germany the development of local government was shaped by two strands. First, after the Revolution of 1919, universal suffrage was finally introduced in local elections. Second, beginning in the turbulence of the 1920s, again after 1945 and culminating in the 1970s, the responsibilities of local government in one way were extended while integration into the federal system was intensified.

Against this background, the development in the two countries has shown noticeable *convergence*. Whereas in both countries the overarching factor impinging on local government development can be seen in the dominant *policy concept* and *dominant discourse* of the advancing welfare state, institutional differences came from national specificities. One major national specificity was the *decision-making structure* which in the UK was largely unitary and central, while in federalist Germany it was decentral and fragmented, giving the *Länder*, *inter alia*, legislative and political power to decide on local government matters. Examples are the territorial reforms which in Britain were carried out as early as 1888 and 1894 and again in the early 1970s and in the *Länder* of the Federal Republic between the mid-1960s and the mid-1970s. The 'radicalism' of these reforms in Britain illustrates the dominant instrumentalist and efficiency orientation. By contrast, in some of the German *Länder* more consideration was given to retaining small-scale democracy, probably for reasons of *political culture* which, in view of Germany's political past, is given greater attention. Also, the local population in Germany appears to have a stronger allegiance to their locality.

In Britain, local self-government was fundamentally reshaped after the Conservative government came to power in 1979. In a barrage of measures it was remoulded in several crucial aspects: by the privatisation of council housing, by compulsory competitive tendering (thus pushing local government into an 'enabling' instead of a 'direct delivery' function) and by the transfer of local government tasks to a multitude of autonomous organisations (with financially dependent boards appointed by central government). As a result, the local government model has been reversed with the central state being now 'more powerful in relation to the localities than it has ever been in the past' (Sharpe, 1998, p.1). So, the comparative position of English local self-government has been historically reversed. In fact, it has been argued that English local government has fallen 'out of step with the rest of Europe' (Stoker, 1991, p.14).[7] In Germany, however, the challenge to the welfare state has not had a noticeable impact on the intergovernmental status of local self-government.

The recent development in Britain which has produced *divergence* can be explained by a constellation of factors. When the neo-liberal *policy concept and discourse* became politically dominant in the UK after 1979, it was *party political* zeal that turned this policy almost into a 'war' against local government and its entrenched Labour majorities. On top of that, *the decision-making mechanisms* of English government fostered the passing of politically and institutionally incisive legislation. In Germany, by contrast, the federal *decision-making structure* would have made such an all-out attack on local government impossible, had there ever been such an intention at the federal level. Also at the *Länder* level no such attempt is known to have been undertaken, as the *political parties*, including the Christian Democrats who generally side with neo-liberal *policy concepts* would never have gone so far as to remould local government.

Local Government II: The Case of Local Democracy

In Britain, universal (male) suffrage was first introduced in 1835 (to the town and parish councils) and in 1888 and 1894 (to the county and the newly created district councils). Suffrage was extended to women in 1918. In Germany, i.e. in the German States, the introduction of local self-government at the beginning of the 19th century was the basis of an extremely limited (male) suffrage subject to narrow property and income requirements. This 'plutocratic' election formula remained in force until 1919 when finally universal (male and female) suffrage was enacted.

Since this period both countries have been largely convergent in the dominance of representative democracy and consequently of the election of local councils. More recently there have been moves in both countries towards curbing the traditional preponderance of the principle of representative democracy by introducing direct democratic procedures.

This is particularly the case in Germany where, in the early 1990s, the *Länder* proceeded to introduce local referendum procedures and the direct election of municipal mayors (and also of the head of county administration, *Landrat*), as well as referendum procedures in some *Länder* for 'recalling' them. In a conspicuous reversal of the historical development in which Germany was a blatant latecomer to full-fledged local democracy, Germany has now become a European frontrunner in direct democratic local level procedures (see for details Wollmann later in this volume).

In Britain, following its election in 1997, the new Labour government also put forward proposals meant to revive local democracy. For example, (consultative) referendums were proposed for more direct involvement of the local population (DETR, 1998, p.8). In a first application of such a procedure, Londoners were given the opportunity on May 7, 1998 to vote on having a directly elected (executive) Mayor with a London-wide assembly (Schröter, 1998). Similarly, it has been proposed to politically and functionally revitalise the parish councils which have recently been referred to as 'an essential part of the structure of local democracy in our country' (DETR, 1998, p.19).

In (west) Germany, when democracy was restored after 1945, the principle of representative democracy was given almost complete priority in the Federal Constitution of 1949, in most *Länder* constitutions and in municipal legislation. Referendum procedures were almost entirely ruled out, largely because of the *legacy* of the late Weimar period, when referendums were misused by extremists in the early 1930s to destabilise and finally destroy democracy. An important impulse for the upsurge of direct democratic procedures in the early 1990s was the fact that the (basic democratic) protest movements of the East Germans in the autumn of 1989 were instrumental in toppling the Communist regime and acted as a political *legacy* which influenced the GDR's 'post-revolutionary' Municipal Charter of May 1990 to include local referendum procedures and other legislation in the same mould. In addition, the new *Länder* legislation was probably also carried by a *political discourse* in which it was argued that in view of more than 40 years of stable German democracy, it was time, at least with regard to local democracy, to rectify the predominance of the representative principle. A process of *learning*, *diffusion* and competition between the west and east German *Länder* has probably also been at work.

In Britain, the discussion about strengthening local democracy has obviously been promoted by the mounting *political discourse* concerning the fact that the local election turn-out in the UK has fallen below 40 per cent (i.e. almost half the turn-out in France or Germany), which is interpreted as indicating the alarming degree of erosion which local government has suffered in the perception of the local population.

The 'Executive' Function in Local Government

With regard to carrying out its functions, the English local government model was based on the assumption that the deliberative (*inter alia*, rule setting) as well as the executive functions in all local government matters lie solely with the elected council and its committees ('government by committee'). It has been increasingly realised, however, that the collegiate voluntary conduct of the executive leadership has become more and more incapable of coping with the complex problems of modern city administration. Consequently, in the more recent English reform debate (e.g. DETR, 1998) alternative institutional options have been put forward which have in common the idea of a certain separation of functions and roles moving towards a dualistic distinction between the deliberative competence of the elected council (as a collegiate body) and an executive function (resting with a 'strong' mayor or with a cabinet with a leader) (see for details Wollmann later in this volume).

In Germany, the question of how to regulate the executive function of local government has long been a problem both conceptually and institutionally. In the plethora of municipal legislation enacted after 1945, some of the *Länder* opted for the basically monistic design, following the English local government model. Others went dualistic in having the (executive and monocratic) mayor either elected by the council or directly elected by the local population. In the most recent development, the basically monistic municipal charters have been finally discarded and the directly elected ('executive') mayor has been extended to practically all *Länder*.

In Germany, this most recent reform move was furthered by two *discourses*. On the one hand, in discussions which gained momentum in the 1980s the viability of the basically monistic model (e.g. in North Rhine-Westphalia) was increasingly questioned and the directly elected (strong) mayor model (in force in Baden-Württemberg and Bavaria) was hailed as enhancing the 'governability' of the municipalities. On the other hand, direct election was welcomed as strengthening the democratic rights of the citizens. The swiftness of the most recent change is also accounted for by a *learning and diffusion* process among the *Länder*.

In Britain the recent move away from the time-honoured 'government by committee' model and towards some form of dualistic and executive model has been encouraged by a *discourse* in which the incapacity of the traditional model to face the current administrative challenges of local government is increasingly expressed. The recent debate shows a large measure of *international learning and diffusion* (particularly from studying the US experience).

Administrative Reforms and Modernisation in Local Government

During the late 1960s and the 1970s local administration in both countries underwent a period of administrative reform which, somewhat 'technocratically', was first of all directed at improving the internal organisational and professional capacity of municipal administration. While, in Britain, this round of reform seems to have been largely triggered by *central government legislation* stipulating institutional organisation through departments, in Germany it was promoted by the expansion of urban policies by *federal and Land legislation* as well as the national and international *discourse on planning* that was dominant at that time. The lasting effects of this bout of administrative reform have been significant in German municipalities and counties.

Since the early 1980s English local government has seen a wave of administrative modernisation under the catchword of New Public Management (NPM). It was instigated by *central government legislation*. (e.g. the prescription of compulsory competitive tendering) as well as by the national and international *discourse on NPM modernisation* which hinges on the concept of transferring basic organisational and managerial principles from the private business sector to the government sector. The disposition of central government to impose NPM in governmental reforms and the readiness of (local) government personnel to accept it is probably *culturally* nurtured as in English thinking the borderline between the governmental and the private business sectors is, at least in organisational matters, blurred.

In Germany, by contrast, the concepts of NPM emerged in the debate on pubic sector modernisation as late as at the beginning of the 1990s. Since then, however, they have spread rapidly through the municipalities and counties. Various reasons may account for this delay in joining the *international NPM discourse*. First, there was a widely shared self-assured assessment among administrative practitioners and experts, bordering on complacency, that German administration, particularly local administration, had in the past performed well by international standards, which may also be seen as the result of the administrative reform activities pursued especially since the 1970s. Second, some key concepts of NPM, such as challenging the monopoly-like provision of social services by the local authorities themselves (see Munday in this volume), are not greatly relevant to German local government, because it has been 'contracting out' social service delivery to non-public non-profit-making welfare organisations for a long time (see Heinze and Strünck in this volume). Third, the acceptance of managerialist modernisation concepts taken from the private business sector and its economic rationality is *culturally* more difficult in the State and public sector tradition of Germany than in Anglo-Saxon countries.

Social Service Provision and Social Housing

During the 19th century, local government in both countries, in line with the medieval poor law tradition of the municipalities and also ordered by central or state government, provided social assistance to the needy in elementary forms. With the advances of the *policy concept* of the 'national' welfare state, local government came to play an enhanced role in the provision of subsidised (social) housing, of personal social services and, in Britain, but to a much lesser degree in Germany, of health care (see Hill as well as Bönker and Wollmann).

While, regarding social housing and personal social services, the development of policy was fairly similar in Britain and Germany, the institutional modality of delivering these services was quite different from an early date. In Germany it became the 'style' to have these services provided by non-profit organisations. In Britain it was increasingly the 'style' to have them directly provided by the local authorities and their personnel. This was true from the outset in the provision of social housing as 'council housing', but especially after 1919, and in the case of almost all social services, but particularly since the 1970s.

In Germany, the non-public delivery 'style' was rooted in a *culture* of 'subsidiarity' which in turn reflected the *political strength* of the welfare organisations and their socio-cultural 'patrons' (churches, trade unions). In Britain, local 'self-production' 'style' was probably the outgrowth of the *political and institutional strength* of the local councils and of the absence of socio-cultural organisations that could noticeably challenge them.

Since the 1980s, the provision of social housing and of personal services came under attack in both countries along similar lines with convergent outcomes. Both in the UK and in Germany the owners of social housing were legally obliged (in the UK) or were encouraged (in Germany) to privatise their social housing stock, preferably to sitting tenants. Likewise, conceptually largely congruent changes were effected with regard to the provision of personal social services (see also Clarke and Hoggett and Hill in this volume). While in the UK the criticism was directed against the quasi-monopoly which the local authorities held in the 'self-production' of services, in Germany the 'quasi-monopoly' of the welfare organisation and the quasi-public and 'big bureaucracy' type of service provision came under attack. In both countries the marketisation of services was introduced – in the UK in the form of compulsory competitive tendering which legally obliged the local authorities to expose the provision of services to market competition, while in Germany the change has been much more limited. For example, under the Nursing Care Insurance Act of 1994 *(Pflegever-sicherungsgesetz)*, the market for the provision of nursing homes has now been opened to all providers, including commercial ones.

In the UK the privatisation of council housing and the marketisation of personal social services was part of the more comprehensive political strategy by which the Conservative governments wished to carry through their neo-liberal *policy concept* of cutting back the public/municipal sector in favour of the market, together with the *party political* goal of weakening local government as a Labour stronghold. Sweeping legislation was again facilitated by the UK's centralist *decision-making structure* with Parliament and its government majority playing the major role.

In Germany, the legislative process to introduce change was typically much more arduous and its results were much less radical. As the result of an almost clandestine legislative manoeuvre by the neo-liberal opponents of social housing, the tax benefits of the non-profit housing corporations were abolished, thus freeing them and encouraging them to sell off their housing stock. Regarding the marketisation of personal social services, the breach in the oligopolistic fortress of the welfare organisations has so far only affected home care. While finally translating neo-liberal *policy concepts* into legislative provisions and political reality, these two legislative outcomes reveal the complex and oblique ways of the Federal Republic's *decision-making structure* (see also Bönker and Wollmann, 1996).

Conclusion

In order to address more generally the question as to whether, to what extent and why the two countries converge, considering the conspicuous differences in their political, institutional and cultural structures, the following general trends and most salient constellations of factors are highlighted.

The strongest rate of institutional convergence in the fields looked at in this paper occurred with the advances of the democratic welfare state when, on the one hand, central government in the UK made English local government give up its 19th century 'dual polity' type of exceptional functional and financial autonomy by integrating it into nation state welfare policy, while in Germany the most significant change was brought about by finally democratising local government and further integrating it into the nation's welfare state policy. Whereas the exigencies of the advancing democratic welfare state and the redefinition of the intergovernmental status and function of local government served as the lever common to both countries, the rate and details of institutional change were significantly different, as were the factors and constellations of factors influencing them. For instance, in both countries central government made large-scale congruent *policy* moves in the fields of social housing and social services. The *institutional (polity)* arrangement at the local level to deliver these services, however, was quite different (in Britain: 'self-production' by the local authorities, in Germany: Delivery largely through non-public non-profit-making organisations and corporations). Such differences in the rate and in the institutional modality amounting to specific national styles or regimes (see Bönker and Wollmann in this volume) are largely accounted for by country-specific pre-set conditions. These range from the different *policy concepts* and *power positions* of the relevant actors to historical and entrenched political and institutional arrangements which impose themselves as set *structural (path-dependency producing)* factors in the decision-making process. Thus, while the advancing *democratic welfare state* as an increasingly *international policy regime* was marked by a high degree of convergence between the two countries, in main welfare state *policies* as well as in basic *institutional* adjustments, the rate and modality of institutional change in each country largely remain a product of the 'national state' and its country-specific political, institutional and cultural parameters.

With the *crisis of the welfare state*, the most conspicuous change, in the fields observed in this chapter, pertained to a markedly increased *divergence* since the Conservative government, which by coalescing its neo-liberal beliefs, its party political determination and the decision-making mechanisms of the UK government system in a unique way, seriously weakened local government functionally as well as politically. At the same time, in some other policy areas (social service provision through forms of marketisation and also administrative modernisation through New Public Management) there has been some *convergence* between the two countries in a common response to neo-liberal policy concepts. Whereas the *neo-liberal policy regime*, which with the deepening crisis of the welfare state became increasingly dominant internationally, impacted profoundly upon English local government due to a single constellation of factors, the rate and kind of institutional change it brought about in other policy fields again significantly depended on country-specific conditions, including institutional and cultural *legacies*.

Most recently, the most significant and consequential change in the intergovernmental relation is being effected as a major development of *convergence* by the 'regionalisation' of the UK, probably chiefly prompted by progress in European integration and its mounting institutional pressures. With regard to local government, the *divergence* between the two countries seems to be widening, as the German *Länder* have almost uniformly been moving towards introducing direct democratic procedures and installing directly elected (executive) mayors. This surprisingly fast institutional shift in the local government legislation of the *Länder* can be seen as the combined effect of a mounting international discourse on the further democratisation and, at the same, managerial strengthening of local government on the one hand, and of country-specific experience as well as single events (the direct democratic *legacy* of 'rebellious' East Germany) on the other hand. Again, while *international policy and discourse regimes* provide important impulses, the pace and rate of the changes actually taking place have been largely shaped by country-specific factors and *legacies*.

Finally, these findings are briefly discussed in the context of the debate conducted in comparative political science as to whether there is similarity across policies and across polities in a given country or rather whether there is similarity across countries in a given policy.[8] The findings in this article seem to corroborate, under certain conditions, either of these theses. On the one hand, it may well be argued that with the emergence of the welfare state an apportioning between the central and the local government levels was functionally required. From this followed an increasing integration and incorporation of local government into the welfare state policy of the national state, i.e. a convergent central level policy with regard to local government 'across countries'. In the same vein, the convergent move in both countries towards having some form of distinct political 'executive' function (still incipient in Britain, further advanced in Germany) may be seen as functionally mandated ('across countries') by the need to redefine and 're-institutionalise' the relation between the elected council/local politicians and the professional administration. On the other hand, there are examples where in order to fulfil the same function, institutional modalities have been put in place which have commonalities within the given country ('across polities'), while differing between countries. A case in point is the delivery of social services (personal social services and social housing), where country-specific delivery styles or regimes can be identified. As has been shown, the emergence of such styles or regimes can be traced to institutional and cultural specificities, if not 'path-dependencies' in the two countries. At the same time, the empirical evidence drawn on suggests that even where the similarity of policy/polity across countries thesis seems to apply in principle, country-specific political, institutional and cultural factors, legacies etc. significantly shape the rate and pace of such institutional developments that are mandated functionally across countries.

So while the internationalisation of the socio-economic problems and political contexts (the fashionable term 'globalisation' has been intentionally avoided in this article) may act, in the long run, as a powerful lever to bring about far-reaching institutional convergence, it is fairly safe to predict that, in the short and in middle term, the rate, pace and also path of the institutional development of the two countries will continue to be strongly shaped by their specific political, institutional and cultural features and 'path-dependencies'. This should prove particularly true for Britain and Germany in view of the many distinct institutional and cultural features deeply entrenched in their histories.

Notes

1   For the conceptual and terminological distinction between competitive/ *konkurrenzdemokratisch* and consociational/*konkordanzdemokratisch* (see Lehmbruch, 1992).
2   Hegel went as far as philosophically extolling the State as the 'real world embodiment of the moral idea' (*Wirklichkeit der sittlichen Idee*).
3   In 1974: Federal Republic 13 per cent, UK 19.6 per cent; in 1991: Federal Republic 14.8 per cent, UK 19.9 per cent (figures from Naschold, 1995, p.51; see also Alber, 1998, p.218).
4   In 1978 Parliament endorsed a Devolution Act that authorised representative Assemblies for Scotland and Wales. However, in the referendums of 1979 the Welsh electorate rejected devolution, while the Scottish electorate failed to give it a clear endorsement (Rose, 1982, p.3).
5   Some of these factors may be classified as actors-related, while others largely lie outside the ('voluntarist') reach of the actors and make them in a way 'dependent' on the previous and existing 'path' of institutional development (see for an overview of these different conceptual strands Schmidt, 1993).
6   The concept path dependency was introduced into the social science debate from different fields of science, such as technological development and institutional economics (North, 1990). Before being generally employed in institutional analysis, it was introduced into the research on the (institutional) transition and transformation in former socialist countries, particularly by Karl and Schmitter, 1991. For an application of the concept

in comparative analysis (see Wollmann 1997c). For an excellent recent (critical) assessment of the concept (see Beyer and Wielgohs, 1998).

7   This harsh assessment deserves to be treated with caution. Comparative 'bench marking' brings to mind that at least in two areas essential to local autonomy where English local government has until recently preserved crucial elements of a 'dual polity' system. First, the local rate to be levied by the local councils at their political discretion and, second, (primary and secondary) education which, including the recruitment of teachers and the setting of curricula, was in the hands of the local councils. In both aspects Britain was by far more decentral than, for instance, Germany where the tax-levying powers of local government have, in recent history, been much more limited and the education system has always firmly been the domain of the State. So what, seen through English eyes still accustomed to seeing traces of the conspicuously decentralist 'dual polity' model, looks like a virtually revolutionary change, may be perceived from a more general and comparative perspective as a further step in the (over?) adjustment of decentralist structures to the exigencies of the modern (welfare) state and thus a 'normalisation' rather than a move towards (centralist) 'exceptionalism'.

8   For the similarity across policies/polities in a given country thesis, see in an early formulation (Heidenheimer et al., 1982, p.317), for the policy style (across policies in a given country) (see Richardson et al., 1982), for the similarly conceived administrative culture (in a given country) thesis (see Jann, 1983); for the opposite similarity across countries in a given policy/polity thesis (see Rose, 1984b), for a similarly construed functional imperative thesis (see Hood and Schuppert, 1988, p.17).

References

Alber, J. (1998), 'Der deutsche Sozialstaat im Licht international vergleichender Daten', *Leviathan*, vol. 26, pp. 199-227.

Bennett, R. J. (1993), 'Local Government in Europe: Common Directions of Change', in R. J. Bennett (ed.), *Local Government in the New Europe*, Belhaven Press, London, pp. 1-27.

Beyer, J. and Wielgohs, J. (1998), *Path-Dependency Approaches and National Differences in Post-Socialist Institution Building. The Case of Large Privatization Policies*, unpubl. ms., Humboldt University, Berlin.

Bönker, F. and Wollmann, H. (1996), 'Incrementalism and Reform Waves: The Case of Social Service Reform in the Federal Republic of Germany, *Journal of European Public Policy*, vol. 3, pp. 441-60.

Bulpitt, J. (1983), *Territory and Power in the United Kingdom*, Manchester University Press, Manchester.

Department of the Environment, Transport and the Regions (1998), White Paper, Modern Local Government in Touch with the People, London.

Dyson, K. (1980), *The State Tradition in Western Europe*, Robertson, Oxford.

Heady, F. (1996), *Public Administration – a Comparative Perspective*, 5th ed., Dekker, New York, Basel.

Heidenheimer, A. J., Heclo, H. and Teich, A. C. (1982), *Comparative Public Policy, The Politics of Social Choice in Europe and American*, 2nd ed., St. Martin's Press, New York.

Hesse, J. J. and Sharpe, L. J. (1990), 'Local Government in International Perspective: Some Comparative Observations', in J. J. Hesse (ed.), *Local Government and Urban Affairs in International Perspective*, Nomos, Baden-Baden, pp. 603 ff.

Hesse, K. (1962), *Der unitarische Bundesstaat*, C.F. Müller, Karlsruhe.

Homeyer, I. von (1998), Die Ära Kohl im Spiegel der Statistik, in G. Wewer (ed.), Bilanz der Ära Kohl, Leske + Budrich, Opladen, pp. 357-80.

Hood, C. and Schuppert, F. (eds) (1988), *Delivery Public Services in Western Europe. Sharing Western European Experience of Para-Governmental Organizations*, Sage, London.

Ikenberry, G. J. (1990), 'The International Spread of Privatisation Policies: Inducement, Learning and "Policy Bandwagoning"', in E. N. Suleiman and J. Waterbury (eds), *The Political Economy of Public Sector Reform and Privatisation*, Westview Press, Boulder, pp. 88-110.

Jann, W. (1983), *Staatliche Programme und "Verwaltungskultur"*, Westdeutscher Verlag, Opladen.

Jones, G. W. (1990), 'Local Government in Great Britain', in J. J. Hesse (ed.), *Local Government and Urban Affairs in International Perspective*, Nomos, Baden-Baden.

Karl, T. L. and Schmitter, P. C. (1991), 'Modes of Transition in Latin America, Southern and Eastern Europe', *International Social Science Journal*, vol. 43, pp. 269-84.

Katzenstein, P. (1987), *Policy and Politics in West Germany. The Growth of a Semi-Sovereign State*, Temple University Press, Philadelphia.

Keating, M. (1999), *Reforging the Union. Devolution and Constitutional Change in the United Kingdom*, unpubl. ms.

Kohl, J. (1991), 'Staatsausgaben', in D. Nohlen (ed.), *Wörterbuch Staat und Politik*, Piper, München, pp. 724-9.

König, K. and Füchtner, N. (1998), 'Von der Verwaltungsreform zur Verwaltungs-modernisierung', in K. König and N. Füchtner (eds) *"Schlanker Staat" – Verwaltungsmodernisierung im Bund*, Forschungsinstitut für öffentliche Verwaltung, Speyer, pp. 5-122.

Lehmbruch, G. (1992), 'Konkordanzdemokratie', in M. G. Schmidt (ed.), *Die westlichen Länder*, Beck, München, pp. 206-11.

Lehmbruch, G. (1993), 'Institutionentransfer. Zur politischen Logik der Verwaltungsintegration in Deutschland', in W. Seibel, A. Benz and H. Mäding (eds), *Verwaltungsreform und Verwaltungspolitik im Prozeß der deutschen Einigung*, Nomos, Baden-Baden, pp. 42-66.

Naschold, F. (1995), *Ergebnissteuerung, Wettbewerb, Qualitätspolitik*, Edition Sigma, Berlin.

North, D. C. (1990), 'Institutions, Institutional Change, and Economic Performance', *Journal of Institutional and Theoretical Economics*, pp. 11-23.

Page, E. C. (1991), 'Die "do parties make a difference"-Diskussion in Großbritannien', in B. Blanke and H. Wollmann (eds), *Die alte Bundesrepublik*, Westdeutscher Verlag, Opladen, pp. 239-52.

Richardson, J. J., Gustafsson G. and Jordan, A.G. (1982), 'The Concept of Policy Style', in J. J. Richardson (ed.), *Policy Styles in Western Europe*, Allen & Unwin, London.

Richardson, J. J. and Watts, N. S. J. (1985), *National Policy Styles and the Environment. Britain and West Germany Compared*, IUG Discussion Paper, WZB, Berlin.

Rose, R. (1982), *Understanding the United Kingdom*, Longman, London.

Rose, R. (1984), *Do Parties Make a Difference?*, Chatham, N.J.

Schmidt, M. G. (1993), 'Theorien in der international vergleichenden Staatstätigkeitsforschung', in A. Héritier (ed.), *Policy-Analyse*, Westdeutscher Verlag, Opladen, pp. 371-93.

Schröter, E. (1998), 'Ein Bürgermeister für London: Neue Pläne und alte Probleme der Metropolenverwaltung', *Verwaltungs-Archiv*, vol. 89, pp. 505–25.

Schröter, E. and Wollmann, H. (1997), 'Public Sector Reforms in Germany: Whence and Where? A Case of Ambivalence', *Hallinnon Tutkimus/Finnish Administrative Studies*, vol. 16, pp. 184-200.

Sharpe, L. J. (1993), 'The United Kingdom: The Disjointed Meso', in L. J. Sharpe (ed.), *The Rise of Meso Government in Europe*, Sage, London, pp. 247 ff.

Sharpe, L. J. (1998), *British Centralism Re-visited*, Paper presented at the Anglo-German Workshop 'Public Sector Modernisation', Humboldt University at Berlin.

Stillmann, R. J. (1991), *Preface to Public Administration: A Search for Themes and Directions*, St. Martin's Press, New York.

Stoker, G. (1998), 'English Local Government. Under New Management?', in D. Grunow and H. Wollmann (eds), *Lokale Verwaltungsmodernisierung in Aktion*, Birkhäuser, Basel etc., pp. 372 ff.

Wagner, P. and Wollmann, H. (1991), 'Beyond Serving State and Bureaucracy: Problem-Oriented Social Science in (West) Germany', *Knowledge and Policy*, vol. 4, pp. 56-88.
Wittrock, B., Wagner, P. and Wollmann, H. (1991), 'Social Science and the Modern State', in P. Wagner, C. Weiss, B. Wittrock and H. Wollmann (eds), *Social Sciences and Modern States*, Cambridge University Press, Cambridge, pp. 28 ff.
Wollmann, H. (1991), 'Vierzig Jahre alte Bundesrepublik zwischen gesellschaftlich-politischem Status quo und Veränderung', in B. Blanke and H. Wollmann (eds), *Die alte Bundesrepublik*, Westdeutscher Verlag, Opladen, pp. 547-76.
Wollmann, H. (1996), 'Verwaltungsmodernisierung: Ausgangsbedingungen, Reformanläufe und aktuelle Modernisierungsdiskurse', in C. Reichard and H. Wollmann (eds), *Kommunalverwaltung im Modernisierungsschub?*, Birkhäuser, Basel etc., pp. 1-49.
Wollmann, H. (1997a), 'Modernization of the Public Sector and Public Administration in the Federal Republic of Germany - (Mostly) A Story of Fragmented Incrementalism', in M. Muramatsu and F. Naschold (eds), *State and Administration in Japan and Germany*, deGruyter, Berlin, New York, pp. 79-101.
Wollmann, H. (1997b), 'Transformation der ostdeutschen Kommunalstrukturen: Rezeption, Eigenentwicklung, Innovation', in H. Wollmann *et al.* (eds), *Transformation der politisch-administrativen Strukturen in Ostdeutschland*, Leske + Budrich, Opladen, pp. 259-327.
Wollmann, H. (1997c), 'Institution Building and Decentralization in Formerly Socialist Countries: the Cases of Poland, Hungary and East Germany', *Environment and Planning C: Government and Policy*, vol. 15, pp. 463-80.

2 State and Society in Britain: Some Contrasts with German Experience

NEVIL JOHNSON

Introduction

The principal concern of this paper is with the manner in which the state and its relationships with the society it serves have been understood and conceptualised in Britain. This will require some attention to be paid to the earlier history of thinking about the state, and this should in turn help to explain why in the contemporary context public sector reforms in Britain do not generally run up against obstacles generated by an established and entrenched view of the state.

It will also be helpful to look at these issues comparatively and so it is proposed in this presentation of some of the main features of British thinking about the state and its impact on the methods and structures of government to draw a number of explicit contrasts between British views and practices and those familiar in Germany. It is hoped that such comparison will contribute to a better understanding of some of the differences between the two countries in respect of thinking about the state. This discussion opens with a short summary of what are generally held to be some of the main differences between the British and German approaches to the state both as a concept and a set of practices and institutions.

The British have never really adopted the term 'state' either as a guiding concept in their political thinking or as a shorthand expression for their methods and structures of government and the manner in which their society is politically organised. Thus it has been frequently held that the word 'state' amounts to a solecism or category mistake when applied to British experience (Hughes, 1957), and indeed there are early judicial pronouncements which reject the term as without meaning in English law.[1] Instead the British approach to the structure of government and the political conditions under which governance occurs has been functional, pragmatic, and institutional. The country always has been and still is governed through a variety of institutions, each performing particular functions and having specific powers to enable its officeholders to act. In so far as these institutions have been legally and politically unified it has been through the Crown and Parliament, the two crucial political institutions most deeply embedded in British history and through which the continuity of the country's political development has been most clearly expressed.

In contrast, Germany has from the late 18th century onwards been strongly influenced by views of the state which have been both holistic and teleological. In the early part of the 19th century the word 'state' came to be widely used as a unifying political concept with both normative and descriptive application. Normatively, the state symbolised a political and perhaps a moral unity which the society was urged to achieve: the state so conceived necessarily lay in the future. Descriptively the state had to mean (as it did in England) the particular institutions through which the society was governed, and that meant in the German *Länder* the executive authorities. Chiefly in the second half of the 19th century this account of the state also gained a dimension of unity and uniformity absent in Britain through the desire to set the powers and duties of the institutions of the state within a comprehensive overarching public law framework. Furthermore, it was widely believed that if the actual state could be defined exhaustively in legal categories, this would confirm its character as a genuine *Rechtsstaat*. Despite the great institutional discontinuities suffered by Germany in the present century (and indeed perhaps largely on account of them) this preference for legal formalism in defining the actual state has persisted into the present. Particularly as a result of the emphasis on the protection and development of human rights in the constitution of the Federal Republic the teleological element in the German approach to the state has been reinforced. From one perspective, therefore, the state is a system of actual legal norms, from another of potential values to be realised through the consistent application and development of constitutional norms. It is not, therefore, surprising that in contrast with British reluctance to invoke the term 'state', it remains pervasive in German discussions of politics, government, public policy and law. The 'state' is still an enduring point of reference.

The Origins of the Negative View of the State in Britain

The British view of the state is predominantly English in origin and its basic elements were really determined in the course of the political conflicts of the 17th century. England was by then already fully aware of itself as a nation state: it was the nation that underpinned the strong monarchical state as it had been fashioned under the Tudor monarchs. The conflict between the Crown and Parliament which led to the Civil War and the Commonwealth established once and for all the principle that the executive powers of government – still vested in and for the most part exercised directly by the Crown – should be subject to limits. What these limits should be was still in dispute, but it was clear that they involved acknowledgement of the rights of Parliament and of a rule of law as interpreted by the courts. These developments were conclusively confirmed again in the 'Glorious Revolution' of 1688-89 which expressly subjected the Crown to the consent of representative parliamentary institutions and to respect for both statutes and the traditional Common law of the land as applied by an independent judiciary. The Crown was forced to recognise that it had to govern with the goodwill of Parliament, and this was to lead gradually in the course of the 18th century and later to a mature form of parliamentary government by ministers responsible to Parliament.

The political struggles of the 17th century were also accompanied by radical changes in moral and political argument which laid the foundations for nearly all modern thinking about representative government. A perennially powerful tradition of individualism was established in British political thinking – Hobbes, Locke, Hume, J.S. Mill, to mention only some of the most famous names. This individualist tradition served to reinforce objections to arbitrary powers and hostility to restrictions on individual liberty already strongly expressed in political life and action. It was a negative view of liberty – the maximum freedom from external restraints on an individual's actions and the autonomy of society in relation to the state – which became the dominant philosophical element in the British liberal tradition. To a significant degree it has remained so to this day (Berlin, 1958). This mode of individualism was underpinned and nourished by a widespread endorsement of utilitarian values. This found expression in Hobbes and the very early pioneers of utilitarianism and economic discourse (de Mandeville, 1705). Pragmatism and an emphasis on individual human satisfactions in utilitarian thinking came to full fruition in the emergence of classical economics at the end of the 18th century and soon after in the influential political writing of the utilitarian school of moral philosophers, notably Jeremy Bentham, James Mill, and then his famous son, John Stuart Mill.

The broad effect of these decisive experiences long ago was that the British came to see the state (though they rarely used that word, and when they did it was often pejoratively) as a power external to individuals, subversive of their freedoms and, in particular, of their right to seek their own advantage in their own way. They preferred a negative state with limited powers carefully defined and specified. When, however, public powers were clearly stated and generally held to be necessary and desirable, then as a rule the British were ready to accept that and to uphold a strongly positivist view of the requirement that the law be obeyed. To this extent they remained sympathetic to the insights of Thomas Hobbes and his account of law as the commands of the sovereign, a view which was in its essentials restated by leading jurists of the mid-19th century (Austin, 1832). As the reform of governmental institutions got under way after 1832 it gradually became the standard practice to confer statutory powers directly on ministers rather than as previously on a haphazard range of corporate bodies and official agents (Chester, 1981), chiefly in order to ensure that executive action was undertaken by officeholders directly responsible to Parliament. By the application of this principle of ministerial responsibility governmental actions could be subjected to parliamentary scrutiny and criticism, and in the last resort ministers could be removed from office. The counterpart of ministerial government was that the administrative services which took shape in the middle of the last century were rigorously subject to the authority of ministers and kept out of politics (Barker, 1930; Dyson, 1980). All this was in harmony with a strong popular dislike of functionaries and bureaucrats, a sentiment still very widely found in Britain (Bagehot, 1867).

It is hardly surprising that these experiences allowed no place for the state as some kind of abstract entity or legal unity. The status of public bodies was in principle no different from that of private individuals, since the Common Law did not recognise an area of public law distinct from the law governing the actions of private persons. It followed that public bodies were not privileged in any special way, though procedurally it was often difficult to establish their legal liability and to gain redress. Nevertheless, in proceedings before the courts the Crown sometimes had to fill the role occupied elsewhere by the state, and indeed in that capacity possessed a range of immunities which protected and strengthened ministers as its executive agents.² But as a rule in legal terms the state has consisted of nothing more than the particular institutions through which the society has been governed along with the powers vested in them and the duties conferred on them. The primary purpose of the state so conceived was to protect its citizens so that they could go peaceably about their own business. This in turn assumes that society consists of vigorous, independent and responsible individuals who actively wish to shape their own lives and seek their own advantage (Oakeshott, 1961). In such a context there is literally no place for the state: it is a superfluous category. It was doubtless some insight into this very fact and into the dominance of invidividual interests implied by it which made Hegel so critical of the English approach to political institutions (Hegel, 1831). Furthermore, the British came to see the continuity of their institutions and their capacity to reform and adapt them to new circumstances as providing a far better guarantee of essential freedoms and effective government than would any formalised written constitution. Until quite recently the wisdom of this attachment to an unwritten and, therefore, supremely flexible constitution was highly regarded and admired in many parts of the world, including the continent of Europe.³

German political experience was plainly very different. There was no nation in the political sense until the late 19th century. The basic experience of the preceding century was of absolutist government practised in numerous separate states of very different size and shape. Society was generally far more rigidly structured and hierarchical than it was in England and subject to the authority of numerous dynastic rulers. Some of these were no doubt by the standards of the time progressive and enlightened, but few of them did anything to encourage ideas of limited and representative government. Benevolent despotism remained the order of the day right down to 1848.

It was in circumstances of this kind and under the continuing impact of ideas bequeathed by the French Revolution that modern German thinking about politics and the state took shape. To this process the Idealist school of philosophers made an influential contribution. Given that Germany was still little more than a geographical expression it is not surprising that their main concern was not so much with actual states, but with how the state should be conceived as an ideal to be realised at some time in the future. This preference for stating the problem in abstract and theoretical ways was reinforced by the manner in which Germany as a collection of states came through the period of the French Revolution and its Napoleonic aftermath. Political revolution did not occur, and indeed after the settlement of 1815 was feared by many liberals and those sympathetic to political reform. Consequently, political progress was seen by many primarily in formal terms – the achievement of charters of rights, perhaps even a constitution, the modernisation and codification of legal systems and so on. True, there was a rising demand for parliamentary representation and responsible government, but this had only limited effects. Nonetheless, despite the setbacks of 1848-49 representative political institutions were widely established by the time that German unification took place in 1871, though the political reality of the new Empire was far removed from genuine parliamentary rule.

The whole process of political development in Germany during the 19th century was favourable to the notion of the state, and in two senses of the term which unfortunately have often been dangerously muddled up. The state as it steadily developed in practice was in essentials an administrative state, a legally sanctioned set of executive instruments intended to provide the range of services regarded as necessary and desirable in the epoch of growing industrialisation. Of great importance amongst these was education where many of the German states (most notably Prussia) took steps to provide compulsory school education and a network of state managed and funded institutions of higher education well in advance of similar measures in Britain. The state as the means of executive action became increasingly subject to legal definition of its powers, and eventually to a degree of judicial control as a result of the emergence of administrative law jurisdictions.[4] But, of course, the state as the executive power had less benevolent aspects – the army, the police, the tax administration, for example – and here the subjection to legal requirements was sometimes far less complete. For some time these more obviously coercive features of the state gained much of their legitimacy from the part they had played in helping to create the political nation. Whereas in England the nation was consolidated before its modern political form was determined, in Germany the process occurred roughly in reverse order: the state as executive power (or more correctly, several states in the same guise) established the political nation.

The state also marched forward in the realm of ideas. No matter how limited was the practical impact of the Hegelian view of the state, there can be little doubt that the core concept of the state as the realisation of a rational ideal of freedom which would facilitate reconciliation of the individual with his society had an enduring influence on German thinking on these matters. It meant that the state had to be far more than a nightwatchman and keeper of the peace. It had to be active in drawing society forward to a better understanding of all the dimensions of citizenship. In parallel with this consolidation of what can be called an ethical model of the state, there was a marked shift towards a purely formal account of the state in legal categories: in the late 19th century we move into the era of the magisterial legal theorists, the *Staatsrechtslehrer* who present the state as a totality or unity expressed in a hierarchy of legal norms (Laband; Mayer; Jellinek; Anschütz; Thoma). In reality much of this was no more than legal dogmatics, complex statements of what according to positive legal norms ought to be the state of affairs. Despite the tensions between legal positivism and the Hegelian heritage, these two strands of thinking co-existed in some degree of harmony before 1914: the state was positive law and, therefore, power, and yet it was equally the bearer of an ideal to be realised.

Yet there was in this way of thinking a high risk of confusion. When referring to the state intellectuals, politicians, lawyers and administrators, and many others moved uncertainly and often unpredictably between the ideal level and that of the actual instruments of executive power. Often enough the language of the ideal and of normative legal commitment simply served to disguise the crude political interests of the holders of executive power and the coercive resources they controlled. Whilst the *Rechtsstaat* was an ideal for some, the *Obrigkeitsstaat* was generally the reality for the majority. By this route the term 'state' became a piece of dangerous mystification which was to be used with disastrous effects, especially after 1918, to manipulate a naive public that had little experience of genuine political responsibility.

To summarise the different historical heritages in a few words, Britain has no conscious and received tradition of the state. Against the background of strong support in the society for individualist values the public domain has been understood in functionalist and institutional terms. Powers became predominantly statutory, conferred by Parliament and vested generally in specific bodies and agents. In so far as unifying ideas were required this need was met by Crown and Parliament at the institutional level, by an independent judiciary interpreting both statute and Common law in the sphere of law, and by nation, political community, even commonwealth or common weal when it was desired to refer to the people as a whole and their political arrangements. Germany acquired and has retained a political tradition which makes greater use of the term 'state'. The state appeared in various guises – as the sum total of executive powers, as a legal unity composed of legitimately conferred public powers, and as the political expression of public responsibility for internal peace and social progress. At a more abstract level the state took shape as an ideal of moral improvement and social harmony to be realised through appropriate policies and an adequate legal order. Whatever may have been the varieties of interpretation of the state, there can be little doubt that the use of the term 'state' became pervasive, so that even when activities in the public sector could be stated in concrete institutional terms there was something like a compulsion to tie them back to 'the State'. In this way the term 'state' often became no more than a convenient legitimating device in political rhetoric: people ceased to ask what it really meant and what was the rationale for using it.

Re-building the State after 1945

So much for the historical foundations. The state as we now experience it in both Britain and Germany owes much to more recent history, and in particular to the way in which the powers and responsibilities of government have been shaped and extended since the end of the Second World War.

The challenge of reconstruction after 1945 was quite different in Britain from that which had to be faced in Germany. In Britain political reconstruction was not on the agenda (Morgan, 1984). Indeed, on the contrary it was widely believed that wartime experience had demonstrated the essential vitality of traditional political institutions and methods, and there was a deeper sense of national pride in those institutions than perhaps at any previous time in British history. But there was clearly a strong desire for big changes in economic and social policy, some of which had already been outlined in the plans for reconstruction prepared under the wartime Coalition Government.[5] The Labour Government elected in 1945 put through an extensive reform programme. Part of this focused on welfare reforms, including the establishment of a National Health Service funded out of taxation, a comprehensive national pensions scheme, and a big extension of social housing provision. The other leg of the programme was directed to strengthening the role of the Government in the management of the economy and *inter alia* involved taking into public ownership virtually all the basic utilities in the country as well as the coal and steel industries. Additionally, many of the powers of intervention in economic affairs acquired by the Government during the war were retained, and in theory at least the Government became committed to something which looked like economic planning (Jewkes, 1948).

This period of reconstruction in Britain will always be associated with the terms 'welfare state' and 'Keynesian economic management'. Both seem to suggest that 'the state' might have assumed a decisive role both in the provision of social services and in the shaping and steering of the economy. But this would not be an accurate view of what happened. Whilst many wartime controls over the supply and use of raw materials remained in force, the state did not greatly extend its powers to intervene directly in the running of the economy or to assume responsibility for the provision of services. Instead most executive responsibilities in the public sector were left with local authorities, public corporations or other public agencies, and with private bodies acting with government support and subsidy. What the social and economic measures of the postwar era did above all was to impose potentially very great financial liabilities on the central Government and to stimulate amongst the public greatly increased expectations of what the Government could and should do to ensure the delivery of benefits and prosperity for all. These expectations continued to be encouraged by the Conservative government which took over from Labour in 1951. It reduced to a considerable extent the *dirigiste* powers affecting the private sector of the economy and still held by the Government, but for the most part maintained continuity in relation to the newly established welfare services, levels of public expenditure regarded as tolerable, and public ownership of utilities, including the coal industry. In part as a result of general trade liberalisation and a favourable rate of economic growth in many parts of the world during the 1950s the British economy began to flourish and it looked as if the financial burdens of the welfare state and of a large public sector of industry could be sustained. Yet by the mid-1960s none of this any longer looked plausible (Shonfield, 1958, 1969).

The evolution of the state in Britain during the two decades and longer after 1945 can be summarised as follows. The powers and responsibilities of the central Government and of many other public authorities (including notably the local authorities) certainly increased and on a substantial scale. This was held to be necessary in order to meet the demands of both the welfare state and the managed economy. But there were few fundamental changes in how these powers were defined and exercised: it remained a matter of particular bodies set up by statute and charged with particular functions and powers, often exercised under the supervision of the responsible minister, though this was not always the case. In so far as there was an overarching authority it was chiefly the Treasury with its responsibilities for the control of public expenditure and taxation, and for the management of the economy. But there was no effective coordinating agency charged even with indicative planning at this time. It is not surprising that there is no evidence suggesting that the term 'state' became any more prominent in the popular consciousness than it had been in the past.

Indeed, in most spheres of economic and social policy the political and administrative authorities were expected to proceed as far as possible by persuasion, consultation, the offer of financial inducements and the exercise of influence. What they were not expected to do was to command or to express their policies too openly in the language of legal enforcement. The values of an individualist society and of a pluralist view of democracy remained largely unchallenged.

The postwar German reconstruction – in the West alone, of course – proceeded in a somewhat different way. The Federal Republic was dedicated to the re-establishment of the basic political institutions of a democracy, the rule of law, and pluralistic politics. It started off with the inestimable advantage of a high degree of internal commitment to making the new start a success, and firm external support from the three Western states which retained until 1955 many of the rights of occupying powers. The fact that the constitutional and political settlement was underpinned in this way made it easier to focus on the extensive programmes of economic and social reconstruction which were necessary in order to deal with the great problems left by defeat and wartime destruction. In the economic sphere the principal commitment was to the restoration of an efficient and liberalised market and, somewhat paradoxically, this implied less state intervention in the economy than was generally accepted at that time as desirable in Britain (Löwenthal and Schwarz, 1974; Nicholls, 1994). On the other hand, there were many measures of economic reconstruction which inevitably involved public support and finance, much of this provided by the *Länder* governments and local authorities. But above all the tasks of economic and social reconstruction called for the provision of new legal frameworks for a wide range of activities and services. The legislative achievements of the first decade or so of the Federal Republic were formidable in scale and left enduring marks on the whole social infrastructure of modern Germany. How then did the state re-emerge in and after this huge effort of reconstruction?

The course of development can perhaps best be characterised as follows. Gradually, as the political, judicial and administrative institutions of the new West German state were consolidated, the idea of the 'state' as a unifying point of reference was revitalised and by the early 1960s was coming back into common use. In the economic sphere, though the powers of governments to intervene in the management of the economy remained limited, the state was assumed to have a responsibility to provide a stable framework of order within which market rules could apply. This explains why *Ordnungspolitik* was such a major preoccupation of the reconstruction years. Yet at the same time the state became steadily more involved in the provision of subsidies and incentives for many types of economic activity, whilst in some fields (e.g. transport) public monopolies were the norm. As in Britain the state became identified as a source and guarantor of a wide range of material benefits. In the sphere of social services there was a great expansion of support services of all kinds, including pensions, the totality of which came to be referred to as the *Sozialstaat*, the nearest equivalent in German to the 'welfare state' in English. But despite the diversity of types and sources of provision within the 'social state' (e.g. in the health services and in pensions) and the large part played by insurance schemes, there emerged a marked tendency to see the whole network of services as some kind of totality sanctioned by constitutional imperatives (the 'social and federal state')[6] and operating under nationally determined legislation (Hartwich, 1977). The general responsibility of the *Länder* for the provision and administration of so many services meant that they too appeared collectively as 'the State'. This was particularly obvious in relation to education where the actual provision of services is highly dispersed and fragmented, but where there has long been a range of unified conditions, especially in the schools, which was without parallel until very recently in Britain.

Of widest influence was the strengthening of the theory and practice of the *Rechtsstaat* under the impact of judicial interpretation, especially that of the Federal Constitutional Court in Karlsruhe. Broadly speaking, the effect of the Federal Constitutional Court's interpretation of the Basic Law has been to equalise legal conditions in very many spheres of social life and public activity, and above all to encourage the idea that the equalisation of living conditions (a requirement of the Basic Law any way)[7] and the unification of legal norms are both goods in themselves[8] and the most appropriate contemporary manifestation of the State. Various consequences have followed: the exercise of political judgement and discretion by officeholders has gradually become more difficult; the institutional pluralism which is certainly present in the Federal Republic has lost some of its earlier vitality and effectiveness; acquired rights and benefits enjoyed by individual citizens, organised groups and even public bodies are widely viewed as legally protected claims and are hard to change on that account; and there has been a general strengthening of the belief that legally defined and enforceable solutions represent the best, perhaps the only way of tackling most problems in society. Against such a background it is not surprising that the language of the state experienced a revival and now features prominently in German political and legal argument. Instead of referring concretely and specifically to the institution, officeholder or person who is empowered to act or required to do so, people talk about the state doing this or being required to do that. It is the ground of particular public activities or policies which is invoked rather than the agents themselves. In this context the practice of political responsibility is inevitably weakened, whilst the tendency to resort to judicial arbitration and legally binding decisions is strengthened.

Re-thinking the State: (A) Recent Developments in Britain

The years after 1979 witnessed radical changes in the theory and practice of government in Britain. Under the strains stemming from economic decline and a resultant degree of social tension the postwar consensus on the role of government in the economy and more generally in the provision of comprehensive social support services was broken after the Conservative party under the leadership of Margaret Thatcher came to power in 1979. Policies were developed and applied which reaffirmed market principles and pointed towards a substantial reshaping and reduction of the public sector (Letwin, 1992). Simultaneously the need for individuals to accept responsibility for their own lives and their families was put in the forefront of political argument. As the Thatcher 'revolution' was consolidated virtually all the nationalised industries were privatised and a wide range of other previously public services were put on a self-funding basis and their management subjected to market criteria. Of the major components of the old welfare state only health care and education remained substantially within the responsibility of public authorities, and even in these spheres there is now a greater degree of private provision and non-public service management than there was twenty years ago. Subsidisation of loss-making public services has been greatly reduced and there has generally been a marked shift towards the application of market conditions to their provision. The rate of growth of public expenditure as a proportion of GDP was curbed (though by no means at a consistent rate over the past two decades)[9] and in proportionate terms now stands at a level considerably below that of the Federal Republic. A similar comment could be made on the size of the public sector as measured by the number of people employed in it. Indeed, the Civil Service which works on behalf of the central Government stands at about 480 000, its lowest level since 1945. Moreover, its activities and functions have been dispersed and diffused to numerous semi-autonomous agencies, so that the administrative structure at the centre of the governmental system really is now on a remarkably modest scale.

A number of comments need to be made on these developments. From one perspective they have undoubtedly reduced the functions and powers of the central Government: the state has been in some degree rolled back as the protagonists of change in the 1980s demanded. But from a different perspective it has to be acknowledged that the attempt to redefine the state and the scope of its functions has been accompanied by an increase and intensification of powers. A striking example is provided by the interventions of the central Government in the sphere of school education in recent years. In order to raise standards and to introduce greater equality of provision the earlier autonomy of local education authorities has during the past decade been much reduced. A national curriculum has been brought in, the regular testing of all pupils along with publication of the results of such tests has been introduced, the powers of school governors and parents increased, new methods of school management outside direct local authority control have been established and so on. Clearly such developments (most of which, subject to some adjustments, are being developed further by the Labour government which came into office in May 1997) required new legislation: the central authority was perceived as taking almost unprecedented powers to impose its will on the local education services and the teaching profession.

Other examples of a reinforcement of the central Government's right to set operating conditions can be cited. The local authority finance system was radically revised by the Conservatives, so that the proportion of revenues raised locally is now very small, barely 20 per cent of total spending. All this required legislation, and on more than one occasion. True, there was a remarkably comprehensive programme of industrial privatisation, as a result of which ministerial powers appeared to be much reduced. But this was followed by the establishment by statute of numerous public regulatory bodies with the function of trying to ensure that these monopoly utilities are exposed to competition and prevented from abusing the dominant market position they usually enjoy. So a new layer of control was developed and there are signs that this may be strengthened by the Blair Government.

Within the National Health Service measures intended to improve the management of resources and to generate something like an internal market in the purchase of services by general practitioners were widely criticised as leading to 'more bureaucracy' and the Blair Government is committed to modifying in some degree the market orientation of these internal reforms in the NHS. But it is unlikely that a radical reversal of policy will occur. Instead there is the prospect of continuing incremental adaptation of the changes already made rather than of a return to earlier methods of running the NHS as a protected public monopoly under the direct control of the Ministry of Health.

There are three important conclusions to be drawn in respect of the reform of the public sector and the reduction in governmental responsibilities in recent years. The first is that there has been a genuine realignment and redefinition of what the central Government should be doing and how. It is seen (and sees itself) much more as a facilitator of social and economic activities than as a direct provider and manager of services. This reflects the much greater emphasis on private initiative, private finance and the mechanisms of the market in the provision of a high standard living for the people than was present twenty-five or more years ago. To adopt German terminology, the state has certainly become '*schlanker*', even though its powers remain substantial. The second is that much greater importance is now attached to the efficient management of resources in the public sector than ever before. Constraints on public budgets are tight, and the discipline of efficiency criteria and performance measurement is widely seen as the best route to better services. This shift has been associated with changes in the administrative culture of Britain leading to far more emphasis being put on managerial techniques and competence than formerly at the expense of traditional administrative skills with their emphasis on policy-making advice, the presentation and exposition of policy, and negotiation and diplomacy. All this is likely to be maintained in the future. Finally, the experience of the past twenty years or so has underlined once again the importance of political will if reforms are to be made, a lesson underlined by the 1997 General Election result and by 'New Labour' under Mr. Blair. This lesson reinforces the traditional British preference for a strong and decisive Government, capable of overcoming the rigidities and obstacles likely to be found in any established structure of public services. This view need not conflict seriously with the familiar suspicion of the state and its encroachments on individual and group freedoms.

Re-thinking the State: (B) Recent Developments in Germany

The process of reform within the structures of government and the methods of public service provision has been more difficult in Germany than in Britain, and so far has made less progress. This is no doubt in part because the impulse to put through radical changes has been less sharply focused than it was in Britain twenty years ago when a stark threat of irreversible economic decline was widely perceived, along with accompanying signs of social dislocation. The pressures which the Federal Republic now faces remain more intangible and diffuse, and stem in large measure from changes in the world economy threatening Germany's hitherto strong position in it. A complicating factor was the achievement of reunification in 1990 which brought with it heavy additional costs and burdens at a time when overall economic prospects were already beginning to deteriorate. The situation has also been made more difficult during the past year or so by the need to try to meet the criteria set for entry into European Monetary Union which was only launched at the beginning of 1999. In this complex situation there is a fairly wide agreement on the nature of the problems facing the country and on the kind of measures that are needed: the overall demands of the public sector in terms of financial costs and human resources have to be reduced, the rate of growth of public expenditure commitments, especially on social benefits, has in the future to be effectively controlled and cut back, and the public sector itself has to be made more efficient and effective both in its methods of operation and structures. More generally an effort to re-think the terms on which the state is performing its functions is called for. It has become necessary to ask fundamental questions about what the 'state' needs to do and what can and should be left to private initiative and responsibility. But the obstacles to change and adaptation across the whole range of public services are substantial and there are few signs so far indicating that a fundamental reappraisal of the functions of the state is regarded as practicable or even desirable. Some of the obstacles to change are purely political and stem from the conditions under which governments are formed and act. As the 1998 federal election results show, even after a marked swing in public opinion from one major party to another, the outcome remains a negotiated coalition. And such coalitions are rarely conducive to decisive action and reform. Other obstacles derive from public sentiments and a widespread reluctance to contemplate serious changes in the kinds, volume and quality of many of the services currently provided. But the way in which the state is understood and defined as well as the complex institutional structures in which it is embodied also stand in the way of rapid adaptation to new constraints and pressures. A few remarks will be made specifically on this aspect of the matter.

The contemporary German state is largely embodied in legal norms. Much of this consists of ordinary public law defining powers and duties, for example the corpus of *Beamtenrecht* at both Federal and *Land* levels, or the legislation governing the *Bundesbank*. There is in addition the dimension of constitutional norms to which all ordinary law is subordinate, and the interpretation of which falls to the Federal Constitutional Court. Here there is an accumulated body of interpretation together with what is often called 'ruling doctrine', and it is this which often makes legislative change and the exercise of political discretion difficult. Quite clearly there are changes in public service law which are impossible without amendment of Art.33 of the Basic Law, or which would conflict with earlier decisions of the Constitutional Court. Similarly, there are matters falling within the competence of the *Länder* on which the Federal authorities can do nothing without getting into constitutional law difficulties or facing the need to amend the constitution, something which on matters affecting competences is then likely to be difficult or even impossible. Or yet again it is not difficult to envisage policy issues on which action is impeded by the risk of challenge in the courts, perhaps on human rights grounds or because it is alleged that there is a failure to maintain equality of social opportunities as between one area and another. In short, any programme of change which seriously affects the existing principles and structure of the state with everything that that implies in terms of established interests and claims can be carried out only after surmounting a number of serious and substantial obstacles.

There are at least three levels at which these obstacles exist. First, there are the legal impediments to change which have to be overcome. Here the most serious difficulties stem from the constraints imposed on political and practical discretion by constitutional norms and their interpretation over the best part of half a century. It is now by no means easy to find loopholes in the dense web of constitutional law interpretation enshrined in well over ninety volumes of decisions issued by the Federal Constitutional Court. In theory amendment of the constitution is not too difficult – a two-thirds majority in the *Bundestag* and *Bundesrat* suffices. But even when that condition can be met, there is no guarantee that the executive and legislative arms of the state can avoid the restrictions stemming from established legal doctrine and a deductive manner of reasoning from first principles. Second, there is the level of institutional complexity. All modern states are in some degree 'complex', but the Federal Republic offers an unusual degree of internal complexity and institutional interdependence. It is not without reason that the concept of *Verflechtung* – interweaving – has played a considerable part in the discussion of the dynamics of the German system of government (Scharpf, Reissert and Schnabel, 1976/77). But the price to be paid for so much interconnection of concrete political interests and institutional claims and privileges is that it has become very hard to achieve significant changes. Finally, there is the desire, so widely diffused throughout society, to maintain existing benefits and privileges, the attitudes summed up in the term *Besitzstandsmentalität*.

The existence of these conditions does not mean that changes in the public sector and in public policy can never be made. But as a rule it does mean that the costs of achieving change are high on account of the time, energy and resources that have to be invested in bringing it about. And in any event experience so far suggests that most change has to be carefully qualified in order to minimise the objections to it that are certain to be expressed within the established pattern of interests and relationships. What is more, this situation stretches out from the many different sectors of the state structure to embrace much of society. This is simply because the system of state sanctioned services and privileges has so many beneficiaries who are understandably keen to maintain the benefits they enjoy and to treat them as guaranteed by the state.

Concluding Remarks: A Myth to be Dispensed with?

The British view of the state has been and remains essentially political and pragmatic. On certain occasions the state steps forward as the organised political community, the nation state in fact, with its governing institutions and the responsibilities they have for the welfare of its citizens. But for the most part 'state' is a term that can be dispensed with and we talk instead of particular institutions and officeholders, the powers and duties they have, and the conditions under which they perform their functions. The great advantage of this approach is that it is transparent and allows questions of public policy and needs to be considered separately and on their merits. It works against that confusion of executive agents and actions with the pattern of legitimate authority as such which is the danger always inherent in the continental European state language. What is more, the constitutional tradition of the United Kingdom along with its political understanding of the state as the instruments of government allows for change and variation in the range of state powers and responsibilities in accordance with society's preferences as expressed in the ballot box. The 'state' has not so far been seen as resting on a body of norms which are hard to change or withdrawn from political discretion as a result of their interpretation being entrusted to judges. What is more, the British tradition of the state continues to regard public officials as the servants of political, i.e. elected, masters: it has no place for a bureaucracy which in some mysterious way claims to embody the public interest.

All this still stands in rather sharp contrast to conventional German views of the state. The state is still regarded, at least ideally, as a coherently integrated body of norms expressed in the language of constitutional law. How this conception of the matter can be convincingly related to or reconciled with the moral, cultural and social diversity of an increasingly individualised and pluralistic society is often hard to discern. After all, there are over 7 million ethnically diverse immigrants in the Federal Republic. Equally problematic is the continuing impact of such a view of the state on the political capacity to adapt the society to new demands and pressures, many of them generated by external circumstances and developments. And there is a further puzzle or paradox which deserves mention. The major political commitment of the Kohl Government was to what is usually referred to as 'ever closer union' in Europe, and it is clear that the new Government under Chancellor Schröder will maintain this policy. Repeatedly it has been asserted that the nation state is obsolete and should be transcended as soon as possible within some still undefined wider European union. Yet in principle at least, the German idea of the state and its embodiment in constitutional law might be expected to be highly resistant to such an erosion of the nation state, particularly one which has hardly yet absorbed all the strains of political reunification. The contradictions inherent in the maintenance of the prevailing German idea of the state as seen from an internal perspective alongside a political commitment to the gradual replacement of that state by a complex European Union construction are far from resolution. Indeed, it is not beyond the bounds of political possibility that German society may one day challenge its own state by explicitly opposing a process which appears to be directed towards an outcome in which that very state would be superseded by a yet higher body of externally established norms.[10] At that point the myth of the state in its dominant modern form of a commitment to the achievement of legal coherence within Germany as a territorial entity would surely have to be abandoned.

Notes

1 Most notably *Entick v Carrington* 1765, a case in which all arguments of 'state necessity' were rejected by Lord Camden.
2 The extent of privilege or public interest immunity as it is now called has been significantly reduced as a result of court decisions during the past twenty years or so (see Tomkins, 1998, Ch. 5).
3 German and Austrian admirers of British constitutional principles in the last century included R. von Gneist, O. von Gierke and J. Redlich.
4 An important stage in this process was marked by the establishment in Prussia of the *Oberverwaltungsgericht* in 1875, regarded by many as the precursor of the present-day *Bundesverwaltungsgericht*.
5 The founding charter of the post-war welfare state was the Beveridge report, published in 1942 as Social Insurance and Allied Services: a Report by Sir W. Beveridge. Also important was the White Paper on Employment Policy, Cmd 6527, HMSO 1944.
6 Art 20 (1), GG.
7 Equality of living conditions is now regulated by Art 72 (2) GG. Art 3 is also relevant.
8 There is in English no equivalent for the German term '*Rechtsgut*', a fact which is itself an interesting comment on differences of perception and understanding as between the two legal cultures.
9 Recession in 1990 and after led to an increase in benefit payments and higher public borrowing which meant that the British public sector expenditure quota increased. It remains, however, well below the present German level.
10 The decision of the Federal Constitutional Court of 12 October 1993 in the case brought against the ratification of the Maastricht treaty upheld the decisions of the Federal authorities, but did express certain reservations in relation to the future development of the European Union and its implications for German constitutional autonomy.

References

Anschütz G., Thoma, R. (1930-32), *Handbuch des deutschen Staatsrechts*, 2 vols, Mohr Siebeck, Tübingen.
Austin, J. (1832), *The Province of Jurisprudence Determined*, London.
Bagehot, W. (1867), *The English Constitution*, Chapman and Hall, London.
Barker, Sir E. (1944), *The Development of Public Services in Western Europe 1660-1930*, Oxford University Press, Oxford.
Berlin, I. (1958), *Two Concepts of Liberty*, Clarendon Press, Oxford.

Chester, D. N. (1981), *The English Administrative State 1780-1870*, Clarendon Press, Oxford.
Dyson, K. H. F. (1980), *The State Tradition in Western Europe: A Study of an Idea and Institution*, Martin Robertson, Oxford.
Hartwich, H.-H. (1977), *Sozialstaatspostulat und gesellschaftlicher Status quo*, Westdeutscher Verlag, Opladen.
Hegel, G. W. F. (1831), *Über die englische Reformbill*, Berlin.
Hughes, C. J. (1957), *The British Statute Book*, Hutchinson, London.
Jellinek, G. J. (1900), *Allgemeine Staatslehre*, Häring, Berlin.
Jewkes, J. (1948), *Ordeal by Planning*, Macmillan, New York.
Laband, P. (1876-82), *Das Staatsrecht des Deutschen Reiches*, 3 vols.
Letwin, S. R. (1992), *The Anatomy of Thatcherism*, Harper Collins, London.
Löwenthal, R. and Schwarz H.-P. (eds) (1974), *25 Jahre Bundesrepublik Deutschland: eine Bilanz*, Seewald.
de Mandeville, B. (1705), *The Fable of the Bees, or Private Vices Made Public Benefits*.
Mayer, O. (1895/96), *Deutsches Verwaltungsrecht*, 2 vols, Duncker Humblodt, Leipzig.
Morgan, K. O. (1984), *Labour in Power 1945-51*, Clarendon Press, Oxford.
Nicholls, A. J. (1994), *Freedom with Responsibility: The Social Market Economy in Germany, 1918-1963*, Clarendon Press, Oxford.
Oakeshott, M. J. (1961), 'The Masses in Representative Democracy', in A. Hunold (ed.), *Freedom and Serfdom: An Anthology of Western Thought*, Reidel Publ. Co., Dordrecht.
Scharpf, F. W., Reissert, B. and Schnabel, F. (1976/77), *Politikverflechtung. Theorie und Empirie des kooperativen Föderalismus in der Bundesrepublik*, 2 vols, Scriptor-Verlag, Kronberg.
Shonfield, A. (1969), *Modern Capitalism: The Changing Balance of Public and Private Power*, Oxford University Press, Oxford.
Shonfield, A. (1985), *British Economic Policy since the War*, Penguin Books, London.
Tomkins, A. (1998), *The Constitution after Scott*, Clarendon Press, Oxford.

3 The Administrative State in Germany

KLAUS KÖNIG

Administrative State Traditions

Any discussion of public sector reforms in German government and administration has to consider – given the usual emphasis on economic efficiency criteria – the particular German tradition of the administrative state. In reference to the 300 years' history of the modern state on German soil, it has been said that this state was a creation of the continuous existence of the administration (Forsthoff, 1973). This statement can be qualified by pointing to multiple historic factors such as the enlightened monarch as the 'first servant of the state', the role of the aristocracy, the church and the military as well as the 'state-preservation' interest of the 'intelligentsia' based in the universities. Yet, it is the administrative state that has shown the greater extent of continuity in German society. State bureaucracy in Germany is older than democracy; its regulative idea, namely the constitutional state based on the rule of law, is older than the republic.

This initial position of a classical administrative system – comparable to other Continental European countries – differs from a Civic Culture Administration such as that found in Great Britain. There, the political regime has guaranteed continuity in modern times, establishing public administrations, defining their parameters, and strengthening their role in a lasting democratic and participatory civic-culture system of order. It is from the values of this regime that the public bureaucracies obtain their identification patterns (König, 1996/97).

In Germany, the very necessity of the functionability of public administration continuing in spite of political change required a regulative idea which allowed the politico-administrative system to define itself irrespective of the prevailing regimes. Initially, this regulative idea was that of the state. Accordingly, officials are said to be *Diener des Staates*, i.e. 'servants of the state'. This regulative idea is what regulates power, but it still does not check it. So, a protective corollary emerged with the notion of a state governed by the rule of law. Thus a legal order is incumbent upon the administrative state. Public administration is bound by law. It must abide by the proportionality of means and ends. It has to respect the individual's rights. Yet, it is precisely in international discussions that the characteristic nature of this constitutional-state pattern of identification needs to be emphasised. It does not strive for a unity of constitutional state and form of polity. Thus far, it is apolitical, aiming at a modification and moderation of state power (Hesse, 1968).

In contrast to this specific perspective of the state as a legal subject (*juristische Person*), going back to Roman Law and the historic epoch of civil war and absolutism in Continental Europe, the development in Britain has been different. As emphasised, the British have never really adopted the term 'state'. One can refer to the year 1295 as the beginning of the influence of the separate institutions, the Crown, the House of Lords and the House of Commons, in the government of society. Additional institutions like the Bank of England with its influence on public finances have been evolving since the late 17th century. Jointly with the rule of law, institutions displayed a much more procedural character in governing society than in Germany and other countries such as France and Spain.

It is above all the concept of the professional civil service that has made its mark on the constitutional and administrative state. The premises of the civil service are seen in the need of the state to provide a counterpart to the pluralism of social interests, a counterpart without the antagonism inherent in these interests, while not identifying itself with any particular interest, i.e. an objective instance. Accordingly, the specific characteristic of state bureaucracy is the exercise of power through the enforcement of public law (Forsthoff, 1973). Opinions which reject this contrariness between state and society, the concept of a civil service personifying the notion of the State and dedicated to it, and which regard the public service as a social occupation like any other are inapplicable in this case.

This administrative state assumed more and more functions. Germany developed into one of those industrialised technological countries which, in the process of modernity, acquired a multiplicity of public functions in phases reminiscent of growth rings. At their modern core they still continue to protect territorial integrity, maintain internal order and safeguard public finances. Furthermore, they promote economic prosperity including trade, industry and agriculture as well as the development of public infrastructure. Finally, they embrace the wide variety of social functions characteristic of western welfare states. In some respects, Germany was among the pioneers of this development: for example, regarding social security in case of sickness, invalidity or old-age.

With the end of the First World War, the administrative state's political regime changed, from absolute and constitutional monarchy to a parliamentary republic. When publishing the third edition of his famous textbook in 1924, Otto Mayer, one of the founders of modern administrative law in Germany, looking back on the previous editions, stated that 'there were no important new developments to be recorded since 1914 and 1917' (*'Großes Neues ist ja seit 1914 und 1917 nicht nachzutragen'*). He coined the formula: Constitutional law passes, administrative law persists (*'Verfassungsrecht vergeht, Verwaltungsrecht besteht'* [Mayer, 1924]). In fact, the administrative state and the administrative law survived after 1919. At the same time this remark demonstrates the importance of administrative law as the legal form of steering the relationship between the state and its citizens.

In the Weimar Republic, the problematic nature of the *Rechtsstaatsprinzip* allowing for a modification and moderation of state power, but disregarding further political elements became obvious. The administrative state's constitutional self-regulative idea did not involve a systemic incompatibility with the parliamentary republican regime, but nor did it lead to identification with democracy. However, there were no traditions of a free political order such as in Anglo-Saxon countries, which could master the problems of political freedom and democracy without requiring the concept of a constitutional state. Civil servants may not have done more harm to the Weimar Republic than other groups in society, but they were not among the defenders of democracy, either (Süle, 1988).

The work of destruction by National Socialism did not stop at the civil service. Furthermore, large numbers of civil servants were devoted to that regime. Too often it was the public administration that executed prescribed injustice. Yet even National Socialism could not reshape the traditional public administration to its own evil image. The Third *Reich* only lasted twelve years. A war administration could not do without bureaucratic mechanisms. Totalitarian interference under the aegis of the *Führer* principle, unity of party and state, national community, and the like, did not produce a complete and persistent administrative structure of its own. So the antecedents of public administration were not distant enough after 1945 to prevent a revitalisation of the continuity of a constitutional and administrative state (Ellwein, 1996/97).

The Administrative State in West Germany

After the war and the collapse of National Socialism, the public administration tried, without a historical pause, to do what it was used to doing, namely to function as well as possible, now facing the challenge of not only infrastructural but also social, political and economic destruction, at least in West Germany, and also under the control of the Western occupying powers. This began at the local level, then continuing on a regional scale, and later, reaching national dimensions with the foundation of the Bonn Republic. This historical process fitted into the decentralised nature of the German politico-administrative culture. The occupying powers exercised influence also on the structures of administration, for instance by installing separate political and administrative heads of communal administrations in the British occupation zone. This separation was abolished only recently, curiously enough not least at the instance of reformers, who at the same time discovered the ideas of New Public Management and are now looking for systemic ways of separating politics and administration (Banner, 1988).

Nevertheless, the structural interventions by the occupying powers did not affect the continuity of the administrative state. Here again, the symbolism inherent in the professional civil service cannot be ignored. Not only was it continued to a large extent with the old staff, together with officials expelled from the eastern territories of the German *Reich*, but as an institution, it also remained untouched (Bundesverfassungsgericht, 1953; Quaritsch, 1970). Finally, the professional civil service system was made part of the new constitution. The Basic Law stipulates that the exercise of state authority as a permanent function shall as a rule be entrusted to members of the civil service whose status, service and loyalty are governed by public law; besides, it lays down that the public service law shall be regulated with due regard to the traditional principles of the professional civil service (Bundesverfassungsgericht, 1975).

One may see this as a case where a constitution has been shaped to a pre-constitutional notion of the state. Also, this ruling has led to some degree of petrifaction in public life. Yet, once made part of the constitution, the institution is subject to general constitutional reasoning. And, for the Federal Republic of Germany, this no longer means 'constitutional law passes, administrative law persists' but that 'administrative law is constitutional law in concrete form' (Werner, 1959). A strong constitutionalism – reflected in the concept of constitutional patriotism – also led to a revision of the constitutional state's self-regulative idea for public administration. The old notion of the *'Rechtsstaat'* has been imbued with political elements.

This, in turn, becomes evident in the professional civil service system. Starting from the experience of the Weimar Republic, the Basic Law has taken precautions to ensure a 'combative democracy' (*streitbare Demokratie*) (Jesse, 1980). In the professional civil service context, this means that a constitution-related political loyalty, in German *Verfassungstreue*, is expected of civil servants. Furthermore, only those may be employed as permanent civil servants who can guarantee to uphold a free and democratic basic order at all times. Some of the conditions for admission applied on these grounds during the Cold War met with severe criticism in the West. Although certain modes of procedure are open to argument, after Germany's historical experience with two totalitarian states, namely National Socialism and so-called 'actual existing Socialism' (*real existierender Sozialismus*), the fundamental position should be comprehensible even to those upholding different politico-liberal traditions. The old constitutional self-regulative idea of the administrative state has been revised with patterns of identification which also include political freedom and democracy. The fact that these patterns have become central brings West Germany's classical administrative system closer to the Civic Culture Administration of the Anglo-American sphere.

Although the liberal political and democratic constitutional order took concrete shape in public administration in post-war West Germany, the administrative state was preserved, subsequently reforming itself in accordance with its own terms of development (Ellwein, 1996/97). This included *inter alia* territorial reform (von Unruh, Thieme and Scheuner, 1981) at the level of communes, municipalities, counties (*Kreise*) and districts (*Regierungsbezirke*) which led to a drastic reduction in the number of local and regional administrative units, for example, reducing the number of communes from over 24,000 to fewer than 9,000 communes. This reform was meant to achieve territorial units of optimum size for the supply of public goods and services. The territorial reform was followed by a functional reform (Thränhard, 1978), more particularly a 'communalisation', shifting public tasks in accordance with the concept of subsidiarity to the lower levels of administration. This, however, also entailed financial problems.

The characteristic feature of the administrative state in West Germany up to 1989 may be said to be its manifold reform efforts: reforms in specific sector-oriented planning, regional planning, financial planning, reforms in the internal administrative organisation from communal to Federal level, reforms of legislation, planning and decision-making procedures, reforms in the civil service etc., up to the privatisation and deregulation schemes of the 1980s (Seibel, 1996/97). Of a more fundamental nature for the administrative state, however, was the fact that it became widely and comprehensively open to society to an extent hitherto unknown at least since its bureaucratisation in the 19th century.

Party democracy, too, left its mark on the administrative state. A remarkable number of civil servants, especially in the permanently established administrative grades, have become party members, so that this group is over-represented in the party landscape (Derlien, 1991). Yet the resulting functions are different from the party membership of professional politicians. Civil servants have their career in mind.

For all bureaucratic structures, the administrative state is open to society, i.e. also to the individual citizen. The German administration has, in characteristic manner, translated the demand for democratisation raised in the late sixties and early seventies, into the reformist programme of citizen-oriented administration (König, 1974). From community meetings via citizen information centres, citizen-friendly office hours, easily comprehensible official forms to training of officials to adopt citizen-oriented attitudes, endeavours have been made to change the observed former authoritarian patterns of behaviour.

The German civil service system is not a closed institution. Thus, the administrative state has also opened itself towards its staff. The officials are organised in staff councils, enjoying a multiplicity of information and co-operation rights in their authority in matters of work, organisation and personnel. An important fact is the differentiation of status between permanently established officials, salaried employees and wage earners in the civil service has decreased. Numerous aspects have been changed: job security, working hours, retirement age as well as benefits such as kindergarten, contributions to costs of illness, and the like. With the aid of their trade unions, those employed in the public service under general labour legislation have for years now taken the lead in matters of payment. Meanwhile, they make up the majority of civil service staff (Mayntz, 1985).

All these developments have repeatedly met severe criticism, with epithets such as 'state of unions and associations' (*Verbändestaat*), 'party politicisation', 'democratisation' (Weichmann, 1974), but they did not eliminate the identity of the administrative state. Its patterns of identification are more in danger from two other directions: in the first instance, by the uncoordinated diversification of public products and services and, secondly, by the loss of internal sovereignty. Both facts are related with one another and have been discussed for many years under various headings, from 'ungovernability' (Hennis *et al.*, 1977) to the 'disenchantment of the state' (*Entzauberung des Staates*) (Willke, 1983).

Welfare state dimensions in the Western democracies and industrial countries are an everyday experience. In post-war West Germany, the administrative state also developed into 'big government' (Rose, 1984). The differences were in the degree of differentiation of the spheres of action, in the mode of state control, and in the structural design of the politico-administrative action context in the West.

At the same time this state is highly differentiated. This applies not only to the formulisation of policies but also to their administrative implementation. Differentiation as to the extent of production, instruments of action, functions, media and the like, is reflected in implementation structures, each of them, including as the case may be, public, semi-public, quasi-public, non-profit-making and profit-oriented protagonists. With regard to public administration, criticism has been long levelled at this segmentation. The administrative state must ask itself whether it is still fulfilling the necessary co-ordination functions or has lost its identity in the splitting of products and product groups. The isomorphisms of the administrative state would, as it were, be dissolved in sectoral administrative landscapes of public education, public health and so on.

The problems of the internal sovereignty of a state are also those of its public administrations, from police to pollution control authorities. The various theories on the failure of the state and administration have come to a head in a line of reasoning considering modern society as functionally so highly differentiated that it is now just a matter of the partial systems, such as economy, science and the armed forces, controlling themselves, with the state no longer at the top of a hierarchically ordered society, but itself nothing more than one partial system among many others (Luhmann, 1975). This means that there can no longer be any talk of an interventionist or welfare state that has a direct impact on society. The state cannot claim a privileged role, much less a dominant one. As regards the administrative state, reference may be made here to the problems of renouncing all or some legal-authority modes of action and imperative instruments of rule. Although entering into negotiations with those concerned and jointly seeking solutions is part of the German administrative state tradition, there is a current trend towards a co-operative state and towards co-operative administrative action in general (Benz, 1994). If this were to mean that public administration negotiated without the background of possible legal-authority interventions, that negotiated solutions were not a matter of remedying illegal situations, but a question of somehow achieving socially acceptable results, and if it were to mean that arrangements to replace formal norms, voluntary commitments by private parties, purely monetary incentives or economic instruments even including pollution certificates were characteristic features of the relationship between state and citizen (Schulze-Fielitz, 1993), then the functionally differentiated systems can be influenced from outside only by contextual control (Willke, 1992), if at all, and that we have to do with an 'invisible state', with an administration not detached enough to take binding decisions.

As to the 'disenchantment' with the administrative state, it is not sufficient to highlight the functional differentiation of modern society and the de-hierarchisation of its system of social order. The crucial question is rather whether every society – in order to live together in peace – requires an institution that is capable of taking binding decisions on the establishment and maintenance of values for all its members ranging from legal-authority modes of action to its monopoly of force (Grimm, 1987). This has to be considered the function of a state. Due to the peaceful nature of the revolution in the German Democratic Republic, the state's monopoly over the application of force and its internal sovereignty has not been called into question. Nevertheless, the unification of Germany is a test case of whether the administrative state on German territory possesses sufficient power of co-ordination and authority to subsist in accordance with its modernised self-regulative ideas.

The Administrative State in the Unification of Germany

In East Germany, post-war times did not bring about the administrative state's modernisation with a view to a free and democratic system of order but the liquidation of its rule-of-law tradition. It may be considered symbolic that the Soviet military administration had already repealed the German civil service law of 1937 by its order No. 66 of 17 September 1945. The intention was not to abolish certain bureaucratic dysfunctionalities, but to destroy an agency of the bourgeoisie. The political ruling class, based on Marxist-Leninist ideology, set about establishing a socialist system (König 1993a).

In that process, the state was the 'main instrument' for the implementation of such a programme (Akademie für Staats- und Rechtswissenschaft der DDR, 1984). In line with its central function of economic organisation, a centrally planned economy was established. Work and consumption were controlled in accordance with Marxist-Leninist doctrine. For the state organs, the rule of the party and state leaders was enforced in line with the principle of so-called 'democratic centralism'. Transmission of the party doctrine by the state took place via a command structure – accompanied by 'consultative authoritarianism' – which relegated the classical control mechanisms of a modern state – *viz.* law and money – and was characterised by the planning and administration of scarce materials. This required a cadre-type administration, i.e. by professional administrators, whose qualifications, however, were defined primarily in politico-ideological terms. To those Marxist philosophers, who imagined themselves to be on the march towards a Communist society of the future, where the state was to fade away, the state of the former GDR may not have been easy to explain. However, the rule-oriented, especially Stalinist, legal and political sciences left no doubt about the necessity of state machinery and state functionaries (Balla, 1973).

Instrumental étatism and cadre-type administration led to an economic and social order in East Germany that was, even by its own protagonists, finally termed 'bureaucratic' socialism with a 'centralist administrative organisation' (*administrativ-zentralistisch-organisierter Sozialismus*), terms that were to express that this was not the failure of an idea but of its étatist implementation. While the leadership of the former GDR turned out to be unwilling to reform their socialist system, even compared with the example of the dominating Soviet power, the first democratic government of the German Democratic Republic immediately put forward the old values of German administrative and state traditions, especially federalism and local self-government. The decisive point was that the revolution assumed a formal and legalist character. Change was implemented by way of amendments to the constitution, new acts, ordinances and decisions by vote of parliament. In the short period from the election of a democratic government on 12 April 1990 to the unification vote on 22 August 1990, the People's Chamber passed 164 acts and adopted 93 decisions (Quaritsch, 1992).

Thus, compatibility with the German administrative state's rule-of-law self-regulative idea was established from the beginning. This compatibility was intensified in the treaties on German unification. In this regard, the situation in East Germany differed from that in other countries in central and eastern Europe. On the one hand, state and administration of the GDR had to be transferred to occidental modernity just like their neighbours in the east and south east. It was a matter of administrative transformation everywhere. On the other hand, in the German case, a reference point was available with the Federal Republic. In so far, it was likewise a matter of administrative integration (König, 1993b). With this integration, the scope for changes during the transformation of the former GDR was restricted from the outset, in contrast to the rest of the central and east European countries. By accession to the authority of the Basic Law, a certain constitutional frame was laid out for public administration. The Federal administration as extended to eastern Germany has uniform basic features. Moreover, the administrative authorities of the east German *Länder* and communes are subject to certain constitutional restrictions. In particular, the *Länder* are subject to a rule of Federal homogeneity. Below that level, however, historically developed forms of organisation in public administration have prevailed in the west German *Länder*. In spite of their obligation to adapt themselves in a multitude of material respects – more pronounced in recent years – they have not lost their central importance in administrative affairs. As a result, there was a wide scope for choosing administrative structures in the east German *Länder* and communes.

In general, administration in the new Federal *Länder* and in the new communes has been established in accordance with West German models and practices. There was a broad transfer of institutions from the West, although this was certainly not a particularly strategic process. Considerable influence was exercised by two factors: firstly, the partnerships between individual east and west German *Länder*, as well as between individual east and west German communes, and secondly, the fact that approximately 35,000 west German civil servants contributed to the establishment of an east German administration (Bundestags-Drucksache 13/2280). Thus, it occurred that competing west German models had obstructive effects. In some cases, even perfectly rational administrative organisations were dropped in favour of sub-optimal solutions of Western design, for example in the fields of water supply and waste water disposal. Basically, the east German *Länder* and communes aimed at attaining the same scope of functions and the same degree of organisation as their west German partners (König and Heimann, 1996).

The dominating orientation towards west German models in the establishment of administrative authorities in the new Federal *Länder* needs to be qualified in several respects. Attention must be drawn, above all, to the fact that such orientation was no colonisation under 'direct rule' on the part of the Federal Republic. The establishment of an east German administration was not simply a matter of imitation. Orientation towards West German models does not imply that there was just an exogenous obligation to keep to a specified track (*exogene Pfadabhängigkeit*) (Wollmann, 1996). The mere circumstance that administration in the west German *Länder* and communes is not uniform, but that there is a wide variety in the forms of organisation developed through time and still of importance today, and that one and the same Federal law continues to be implemented by different executive structures at *Länder* level, necessitates selective decisions being made on the spot.

However, it would not be satisfactory evidence of the vitality of the administrative state in its constitutional tradition and its liberal-democratic modernisation, if matters in the field of politico-administrative self-reference had remained the same, namely extension to the east German *Länder*. Decisive were the benefits and services rendered to the east German economy and society and to integration. In this respect, even the drafts worked out by the Bonn ministerial bureaucracy for the legal and financial framework of German unification, showed remarkable degrees of co-ordinating power and authority. In the course of the transformation and integration processes, it became evident that, despite the economic reference system in the West, the dynamic force of the market was not as strong as many had expected. Furthermore, social forces had not been developed in the GDR to such an extent as to allow them to assume the functions of organised interests of a pluralist system. Admittedly, individual pressure groups spread from the west, as could be observed *inter alia* in the field of science. After all, the transformation and integration of east Germany was a state-centred operation. The Western welfare state system had to compensate for the socio-economic deficits. And it was public administration that was responsible for its implementation (König and Benz, 1996).

Enough work remained to be done for the administrative authorities instituted in east Germany in accordance with traditional patterns. A welfare state system of the Federal German kind also meant that tasks neglected by 'actual existing Socialism' had to be taken on, i.e. pollution control, urban redevelopment, public infrastructure, and the like. A multiplicity of state functions unfamiliar and neglected in the GDR had to be developed from scratch and at the same time shaped in accordance with transformation requirements. This started with the institution of social security systems, pension insurance funds, health and unemployment insurance, which had not existed in the GDR in the same way. Social welfare policy and labour market policy had to be newly established. Moreover, the creation of basic pre-conditions for a well-functioning market economy included the provision of an infrastructure. On the whole, infrastructural deficits, one of the causes for the difficult competitive position of the East, are claimed to amount to 500 to 1,000 billion German marks (Biehl, 1993). This magnified the importance of the administrative state. Under these circumstances, the authority of the state and administration could hardly be questioned.

Perspectives of the Administrative State

Accordingly, with regard to the perspectives of the administrative state in Germany, the old dictum that 'there are no important new developments to be recorded since 1989' springs to mind, providing further evidence for the continuity of public administration – had the now unified German welfare state not run into a deep financial crisis (Sachverständigenrat zur Begutachtung der gesamtwirtschaftlichen Entwicklung, 1995/96). One of the reasons is the cost of German unification. Net payments for east Germany total 1000 billion marks. In addition, there is the structural crisis of the German economy. Formerly, locational factors were a problem dealt with by local and regional economic policy. Now, in the light of economic globalisation, we speak of 'location Germany'. This short term evokes the burdens to be borne by the welfare state due to lack of returns and increased expenditures. While it had been possible until 1989 to maintain the ratio of government expenditures to GNP at 45 per cent, in the following years, it exceeded 50 per cent (Bundesministerium der Finanzen, 1995).

At that point, it was inevitable that the growing international argument that, with 'Reinventing Government' and 'New Public Management', provided the key for a more efficient state and more efficient public administration, fell on fertile ground. One encounters a mixture of neo-liberal economic doctrines and management models, enriched with psychologisms from the popular 'business motivation' literature with interesting conceptual contradictions (Aucoin, 1990), which are quite functional in the practice of modernisation. They allow recourse to an ideology and at the same time an opportunistic attitude.

Accordingly, the rhetoric of New Public Management has made its appearance in many public offices in Germany. As in many parts of the world, there is talk of the separation of politics and administration, of contract management, the unity of responsibilities for sectoral subjects and resources, of global budgeting, product segmentation, result-oriented operation, controlling, and so on. (König and Beck, 1997). Yet, there is a notable difference in the methodology of modernisation. In Germany, with its federalist system and local self-government, there is no national leadership in administrative policy and, therefore, no modernisation of administration from above. The municipalities were the first to take up this issue. At communal level, a joint local government centre has been established in Germany, which acts as consultant for administrative reforms (KGSt 1995). This joint agency has developed a 'new steering model' (*Neues Steuerungsmodell*), based on experience gathered in the Dutch municipality of Tilburg and basically – consciously or subconsciously – following the Principal Agent approach (Scott and Gorringe, 1989). From this origin, a certain model conception has spread into many communes, municipalities and counties.

The *Länder* and the Federation, on the other hand, develop their reform concepts in a more inductive way from individual components which, however, are likewise aimed at improving efficiency in state and administration in the sense of New Public Management. Accordingly, budgeting, resource management, cost and results accounting, controlling, and the like are predominant (Bürsch, 1996). The Federation has propagated the political formula of a 'lean state' (Werthebach, 1996). It has to deal with two specific responsibilities and an extra problem. One of the specific responsibilities is due to its extensive legislative competencies in the interest of uniform living conditions throughout the Federal territory. As a consequence, it has to deal with over-regulation in many fields of policy. The Federation is also responsible for the framework legislation for the permanent civil service. Thus, it has to provide the legal basis for the strengthening orientation to performance standards in the civil service. The extra problem is the federal government's transfer from Bonn to Berlin. As a matter of fact, the Federal ministries ought to arrive in Berlin as a lean administration; yet in view of the equalisation measures taken in favour of Bonn, this is hardly conceivable (König, 1997b).

Much of what is currently being said in Germany on New Public Management is more of a proclamation of intent. A number of things have been implemented, but beyond the image promoted by modernisation-eager politicians and administrators, no reliable evaluations are available on their effects and results. This does not preclude that administrative science is making efforts to outline the administrative state's perspectives against the background of its traditional self-regulative ideas. In this context, it is conspicuous that two options from the conceptual tool-box of New Public Management, namely internal rationalisation and managerialism, are widely preferred in Germany.

When looking at the level of performance not only in the German administration, one will doubt that the administrative state offers enough rationalisation reserves to allow the welfare state's financial crisis to be settled in this way. It is not by chance that there is a broad economisation and pruning movement, the policy of down-sizing, that produced measurable rationalisation effects in the United States of America, for instance. In Germany, too, cut-backs in personnel and organisation structures are currently being discussed as topics of economisation (König, 1997c). But as a matter of fact, in view of the burdens to be borne by the welfare state, it has to be questioned whether the division of labour between state, economy and society need not to be modified, allowing efforts for the revitalisation of socio-economic wealth. Too great a share of private savings is going into public budgets, and from there too high a percentage of public expenditures is going into consumption. In Germany, there are still considerable reserves for classical privatisation, especially in the *Länder* and communes.

The extent of production of publicly run manufacture and distribution of both material goods and services should be more fundamentally examined (Naschold, 1996). One might then discover that, except for some core operations, the modern state needs to concentrate more on the functions of guarantor, regulator and co-ordinator instead of attending to the actual production of finished goods. Presumably, restricting public functions in this way would rather strengthen the administrative state in Germany than weaken it.

The second favourite option from the currently discussed package of modernisation approaches is managerialism. There is a special liking for re-organisation and especially for the restructuring of operating procedures.

But this is not the primary weakness of legalist bureaucracies. The thesis has even been evolved that the performances of legalist, 'rule driven' administrative states are superior to those of the new managerialist public sectors. The foremost problem of legalist administrations is the 'cost structures'.

The current modernisation movement is not just a fashionable trend for the administrative state in Germany, it pinpoints a deficit, namely the insufficient economic standards of state action. From this point of view, managerialism leads rather to a side-issue, if not to the wrong track. Private managerialism is designed to control an enterprise, not to rule its environment, namely the market. The formula of Public Sector Management, however, makes it clear that this is not just a matter of public administration. It is intended to 'manage' society in its public sphere of action. This conflicts with law and legislation, political freedom and democracy, uniting state and society in Germany.

As an illustrative example of this, the popular maxim of customer-oriented attitudes may be referred to. Germany no longer has subjects, but citizens. These citizens do not only enjoy political rights and liberal rights to avert state intervention. They are also entitled to claim benefits and services from state and administration. Legalism does not only imply that the executive is bound by legal standards of action, but also that the citizens enjoy individual rights. With these entitlements to benefits and services, citizens have more resources than customers who, on the demand side of the market, depend entirely on their spending power (Bogumil and Kißler, 1995). Accordingly, below the general role of the citizen, there is a high degree of differentiation in terms of rights enjoyed by, for example, pupils, sick persons, tax-payers or people in dealings with the police, in their contact with state and administration (Luhmann, 1966), even extending to the right to welfare benefits in case of poverty. The method of implementing social-welfare schemes is not left to the managerialism of administrative authorities. An extensive system of administrative courts takes care that citizens are granted their rights.

This does not at all alter the fact that the economic control mechanisms in state and administration have to be strengthened. Yet the prevailing conditions may not be just turned upside down by the managerialism of a 'new steering model' nor by economic model concepts of quasi-markets and virtual competition. Instead, economic steering and control must be integrated into the existing patterns of public action at clearly different levels. In many key sectors of politico-administrative decision-making on public goods and services, the only admissible way of control is in compliance with secondary efficiencies (König, 1997a). The protection of human rights, basic research, crime suppression or public aid for subsistence may not be economised upon on the basis of economic principles; only in secondary spheres like numbers of staff, infrastructure, size of organisation or equipment, may the related costs and results be questioned.

If entry into real competitive markets by way of privatisation is not intended, the obvious solution, socially, is the invention of quasi-markets and virtual competition as the functional equivalent for presumed rationality gains (König and Beck, 1997). Yet, if this is to be more than just a comparison, the pre-condition is competition between public organisations in one and the same sector of production and distribution. However, public administration is founded on a fixed order of competencies, precisely intended to prevent competition and rivalries between youth welfare offices, police stations, tax administrations and social welfare authorities or to resolve these by way of rules. This does not preclude certain competitive elements from being incorporated in some case or other into the public health system, the public education sector, or public research organisations (Ranadé, 1995). Here, too, an economic model of Functional Overlapping Competing Jurisdiction (Frey and Eichenberger, 1995) applicable everywhere does not exist. On the contrary, a decision has to be taken for every public commodity on whether and to what extent it should be treated as an ordinary product in a merchandise society (Schmacke, 1996).

These are only a number of comments on how difficult it is to find the 'control mix' appropriate for public affairs. The efficient use of resources is the problem of topical importance in the administrative state's modernisation. With the financial crisis of the welfare state continuing to persist, the relevant reform pressure will lead to further improvements of efficiency in public authorities – though not by inventing a magic formula. But efficiency was not the only problem faced by the administrative state in the Germany of the 1990s. It has to find answers to those questions about its effectiveness that result from the difficulties in ensuring co-ordination and authority in a highly differentiated society. For instance, it cannot organise a stringent segmentation of public goods and services for mere reasons of efficiency. This may allow for an increased transparency of costs, 'client pressure', and the like, but it will aggravate still further the problems of co-ordination that are encountered by a state afflicted as it is with departmentalism. After reconstruction as a constitutional state and legitimisation as a democratic state, the administrative state in Germany may experience, in another historical revival phase, its economic modernisation. But its history will not end in commercialised postmodernity.

References

Akademie für Staats- und Rechtswissenschaft der DDR (1984), *Staatsrecht der DDR*, Lehrbuch, 2nd ed., Staatsverlag der DDR, Berlin (Ost).
Aucoin, P. (1990), 'Administrative Reform in Public Management: Paradigms, Principles, Paradoxes and Pendulums', *Governance*, vol. 3, pp. 115 ff.
Balla, B. (1973), *Kaderverwaltung: Versuch zur Idealtypisierung der Bürokratie sowjetisch-volksdemokratischen Typs*, Enke, Stuttgart.
Banner, G. (1988), 'Der (Ober-)Bürgermeister als Verwaltungschef - ein mögliches Modell?', in D. Fischer, R. Frey, P. Paziorek (eds), *Kommunalverfassung in Nordrhein-Westfalen. Sind unsere Städte noch zu regieren? Beckumer Hochschultage 1988*, Düsseldorf, pp. 59 ff.
Benz, A. (1994), *Kooperative Verwaltung. Funktionen, Voraussetzungen und Folgen*, Nomos, Baden-Baden.
Biehl, D. (1993), 'Die Rolle der EG-Regionalfonds in der Regionalpolitik und ihre Finanzierung in den neuen Bundesländern', in K.-H. Hansmeyer (ed.), *Finanzierungsprobleme der deutschen Einheit*, vol. 1, Duncker & Humblodt, Berlin, pp. 11 ff.
Bogumil, J., Kißler, L. (1995), *Vom Untertan zum Kunden? Möglichkeiten und Grenzen von Kundenorientierung in der Kommunalverwaltung*, Edition Sigma, Berlin.
Bundesministerium der Finanzen (1995), *Finanzbericht 1996*, Bonn, p. 11.
Bundestags-Drucksache 13/2280, 8.9.1995, p. 65.
Bundesverfassungsgericht, 'Decision from 17.12.1953', in *BVerfGE* 3, pp. 58 ff.
Bundesverfassungsgericht, 'Decision from 22.5.1975', in *BVerfGE* 39, pp. 334 ff.
Bürsch, M. (1996), *Die Modernisierung der deutschen Landesverwaltung. Zum Stand der Verwaltungsreform in den 16 Ländern*, Friedrich-Ebert-Stiftung, Bonn.
Derlien, H.-U. (1991), 'Historical legacy and recent developments in the German higher civil service', *International Review of Administrative Sciences*, vol. 57, pp. 385 ff.
Ellwein, T. (1996/97), 'Geschichte der öffentlichen Verwaltung', in K. König, H. Siedentopf (eds), *Öffentliche Verwaltung in Deutschland*, Nomos, Baden-Baden, pp. 39 ff.
Forsthoff, E. (1973), 'Verfassungsrechtliche Grenzen einer Reform des öffentlichen Dienstrechts – Rechtsgutachten', in E. Forsthoff, I. v. Münch, W.

Schick, W. Thieme, C. Hermann Ule, F. Mayer (eds), *Verfassungsrechtliche Grenzen einer Reform des öffentlichen Dienstrechts*, Nomos, Baden-Baden, pp. 17 ff.

Frey, B. S., Eichenberger, R. (1995), 'Competition among Jurisdictions: The Idea of FOCJ', in G. Lüder (eds), *Competition among Institutions*, Macmillan, Basingstoke *et al.*, pp. 209 ff.

Grimm, D. (1987), *Recht und Staat der bürgerlichen Gesellschaft*, Suhrkamp, Frankfurt am Main.

Hennis, W. *et al.* (eds) (1977), *Regierbarkeit*, vol. 1, Klett-Cotta, Stuttgart.

Hesse, K. (1968), 'Der Rechtsstaat im Verfassungssystem des Grundgesetzes', in E. Forsthoff (ed.), *Rechtsstaatlichkeit und Sozialstaatlichkeit*, Wissenschaftliche Buchgesellschaft, Darmstadt, pp. 557 ff.

Jesse, E. (1980), *Streitbare Demokratie*, Colloquium Verlag, Berlin.

KGSt (ed.) (1995), *Das neue Steuerungsmodell. Begründung, Konturen, Umsetzung, Bericht 5/1995*, Köln.

König, K. (1974), 'Öffentliche Verwaltung und Demokratie', in H.-J. v. Oertzen (ed.), *"Demokratisierung" und Funktionsfähigkeit der Verwaltung*, Kohlhammer, Stuttgart *et al.*, pp. 195 ff.

König, K. (1993a), 'Bureaucratic Integration by Elite Transfer: The Case of the Former GDR', *Governance*, vol. 6, p. 386. ff.

König, K. (1993b), 'Entwicklungsverwaltung und Verwaltungstransformation', *Die Öffentliche Verwaltung*, vol. 46, pp. 856 ff.

König, K. (1996/97), 'Öffentliche Verwaltung im vereinigten Deutschland', in K. König, H. Siedentopf (eds), *Öffentliche Verwaltung in Deutschland*, Nomos, Baden-Baden, pp. 13 ff.

König, K. (1997a), 'Markt und Wettbewerb als Staats- und Verwaltungsprinzipien, Carl Hermann Ule zum 90. Geburtstag', in *Deutsches Verwaltungsblatt*, vol. 112, pp. 239 ff.

König, K. (ed.)(1997b), 'Ministerialorganisation zwischen Berlin und Bonn', *Speyerer Forschungsberichte 173*, Speyer.

König, K., Beck, J. (1997), *Modernisierung von Staat und Verwaltung. Zum Neuen Öffentlichen Management*, Nomos, Baden-Baden.

König, K., Benz, A. (1996), 'Staatszentrierte Transformation im vereinten Deutschland', *Der Staat*, pp. 109 ff.

König, K., Heimann, J. (1996), *Aufgaben- und Vermögenstransformation in den neuen Bundesländern*, Nomos, Baden-Baden.

Luhmann, N. (1966), *Theorie der Verwaltungswissenschaft: Bestandsaufnahme und Entwurf*, Grote, Köln.

Luhmann, N. (1975), *Soziologische Aufklärung 2*, Westdeutscher Verlag, Opladen.

Mayer, O. (1924), *Deutsches Verwaltungsrecht*, 3rd ed., Duncker & Humblodt, Berlin.

Mayntz, R. (1985), *Soziologie der öffentlichen Verwaltung*, Müller, Heidelberg.

Naschold, F. et al. (1996), *Leistungstiefe im öffentlichen Sektor*, Edition Sigma, Berlin.
Quaritsch, H. (1970), 'Report at the 48th Deutschen Juristentag', in Ständige Deputation des Deutschen Juristentages (ed.), *Verhandlungen des 48. Deutschen Juristentages*, vol. II, Beck, München, Q 34 ff.
Quaritsch, H. (1992), 'Eigenarten und Rechtsfragen der DDR-Revolution', *Verwaltungsarchiv*, vol. 83, pp. 314 ff.
Ranadé, W. (1995), 'The theory and practice of managed competition in the National Health Sector', *Public Administration*, vol. 73, pp. 243 ff.
Rose, R. (1984), *Understanding Big Government*, Sage, London.
Sachverständigenrat zur Begutachtung der gesamtwirtschaftlichen Entwicklung (1996), *Jahresgutachten 1995/96*, TZ. 314 f.
Scheuner, U. (1960), 'Die neuere Entwicklung des Rechtsstaats in Deutschland', in E. v. Caemmerer, E. Friesenhahn, R. Langen (eds), *Hundert Jahre Deutsches Leben. Festschrift zum hundertjährigen Bestehen des Deutschen Juristentages 1860 - 1960*, vol. II, Karlsruhe, pp. 229 ff.
Schmacke, N. (1996), '"Lean Management" ist ein falsches Rezept. Gesundheit - ein normales Produkt der Warengesellschaft?', *Süddeutsche Zeitung 4.1.1996*, p. 9.
Schulze-Fielitz, H. (1993), 'Der Leviathan auf dem Wege zum nützlichen Haustier?', in R. Voigt (ed.), *Abschied vom Staat - Rückkehr zum Staat?*, Nomos, Baden-Baden, pp. 95 ff.
Scott, G., Gorringe, P. (1989), 'Reform of the Core Public Sector: The New Zealand Experience', *Australian Journal of Public Administration*, vol. 48, pp. 81 ff.
Seibel, W. (1996/97), 'Verwaltungsreformen', in K. König and H. Siedentopf (eds), *Öffentliche Verwaltung in Deutschland*, Nomos, Baden-Baden.
Süle, T. (1988), *Preußische Bürokratietradition. Zur Entwicklung von Verwaltung und Beamtenschaft in Deutschland 1871 - 1918*, Vandenhoeck & Ruprecht, Göttingen, pp. 263 ff.
Thränhard, D. (1978), *Funktionalreform: Zielperspektiven und Probleme einer Verwaltungsreform*, Hain, Meisenheim.
Unruh, G. C. v., Thieme, W., Scheuner, U. (1981), *Die Grundlagen der kommunalen Gebietsreform*, Nomos, Baden-Baden.
Weichmann, H. (1974), 'Einleitung der Fachtagung durch den Präsidenten der Deutschen Sektion des Internationalen Instituts für Verwaltungswissenschaften', in H.-J. v. Oertzen (ed.), *"Demokratisierung" und Funktionsfähigkeit der Verwaltung*, Kohlhammer, Stuttgart et al., pp. 9 ff.
Werner, F. (1959), 'Verwaltungsrecht als konkretisiertes Verfassungsrecht', *Deutsches Verwaltungsblatt*, vol. 74, pp. 527 ff.
Werthebach, E. (1996), 'Die Bundesverwaltung auf dem Weg zum Schlanken Staat', *Zeitschrift für Gesetzgebung*, vol. 11, pp. 270 ff.

Willke, H. (1983), *Entzauberung des Staates. Überlegungen zu einer sozietalen Steuerungstheorie*, Athenaeum Verlag, Königstein/Ts.

Willke, H. (1992), *Ironie des Staates*, Suhrkamp, Frankfurt am Main.

Wollmann, H. (1996), 'Institutionenbildung in Ostdeutschland: Rezeption, Eigenentwicklung oder Innovation?', in A. Eisen, H. Wollmann (eds), *Institutionenbildung in Ostdeutschland*, Leske+Budrich, Opladen, pp. 79-114.

4 Regionalism in the United Kingdom: The Role of Social Federalism

L. J. Sharpe

Introduction

The story of regionalism in the UK is a slightly unusual one[1] since, unlike Belgium, France, Italy and Spain and despite marked cultural heterogeneity – Scotland, Wales and Northern Ireland – no regional government has ever been created until the Northern Ireland Assembly was created in 1998. This regional government was rapidly followed by the creation of the Scottish Parliament and a Welsh Assembly, both in 1999. Historically, the only level of democratic government below the central government has been local government. Unlike much of Western Europe, Britain was totally uninfluenced by the Napoleonic concept of the prefect and his domain. The regional story is therefore one of aspirations and it goes back to the mid-19th century.

It seems likely that the emergence of regional government has been retarded by the existence of what may be called 'social federalism' which has involved the creation and maintenance of special psychic and cultural privileges for the celtic periphery (Scotland, Wales and Northern Ireland) and is one of the most important, but least acknowledged, features of central-subnational relations in the UK until 1999. Another factor which has undermined the emergence of regional government is the existence of the Offices for Scotland and Wales and Northern Ireland which provide additional special arrangements of deconcentrated government for each region without in any sense impeding the unitariness of the British state. It is also possible that the existence of the National Health Service, which is organized on a regional basis, may have further inhibited the emergence of regional government.

This paper is divided into three parts each covering key sectors of the politico-administrative system of the UK which have a clear bearing on the regional issue.

Regional Planning

The first aspect of regional government to be considered is regional planning which in Britain has its origins in postwar regional economic planning. For about two decades from 1964 there was a system of regional planning institutions in the UK comprising nominated representative councils supplemented by boards of civil servants both loosely modelled on the French regional planning system for each of the eight English regions and for Scotland and Wales. The last two were always more powerful institutions than the English regional planning bodies with perhaps a more clear cut mandate reflecting very much deeper sub-national loyalties. As a consequence, and unlike the English regional machinery, they have survived and prospered and now form part of the regional system created in 1998 and 1999.

In the early 1960s, some observers saw these regional bodies as a kind of embryonic regional government on the Italian pattern and their creation stimulated not only a regional consciousness of sorts but also promoted debates, as it did in France and Italy, about regional government being a vehicle for all sorts of fashionable political changes including promoting popular participation, the modernization of the economy and an antidote to over-centralization (Hogwood and Keating, 1982). Following the collapse of the National Plan in 1967, however, these regional institutions slowly atrophied in England and were finally abolished in the early 1980s. They live on partly as standard areas for the collection of official statistics and partly for the purposes of administering land use planning and cognate services. They acquired a new status in 1994 as part of a conscious central decision to revivify its own deconcentrated regional institutions and co-ordinate them. The gradual collapse of local government between 1979 and 1990 and its replacement by other more fragmented forms of local administration may be one reason why central government seemed to be returning to a regional structure for service implementation purposes. The boundaries of the old planning regions were partly re-drawn for the new system (Bradbury and Mawson, 1997).

The 1960s regional planning structure warrants mention now because its creation did lay the foundations for what could have been a fully-fledged regional government. In Wales, and especially Scotland, the regional planning idea had more important consequences since it re-enforced the tendency, already taking shape with the rise of the nationalist parties, to assume both regions to be discrete political and economic entities so that by the 1970s the 'Welsh economy' and the 'Scottish economy' became accepted and unquestioned concepts in political discourse on regionalism. This was despite the fact that both Scotland and Wales lacked any form of common economic structure. In England the 1960s planning regions also live on in an abstract theoretical sense in that they usually form the basis, if not always the precise boundaries, for proposals for regional *government* which is usually called 'devolution', an aspect of regionalism to which we now turn.

In assessing the importance of the regional planning input to the evolution of regional government in the UK it is important to emphasize that although, as we have just noted, the regional planning bodies were invested with some additional roles, including democratization and modernization, there was no severe public disruption that gave these additional roles a special importance and led to the creation of fully-fledged regional governments elsewhere. In short, there was nothing remotely like the French *les evenements* during the late 1960s, the 'hot autumn' in Italy or the need to crown the new democratic order with regional decentralization as in Spain. The regional bodies remain in England stubbornly part of the history of planning and they command only a very limited degree of allegiance among the general population.

Devolution

The second aspect of regionalism in the UK to be discussed is again largely a tale of unfulfilled hopes and forms part of a century-old demand for what is now called devolution but which was formerly known as 'Home Rule' (Bogdanor, 1979). It has usually involved proposals for the creation of elected governments for the celtic periphery. At last they are to be enacted and in Northern Ireland's case have been enacted. Devolution proposals also often include the creation of regional governments for the eight English planning regions. The present government is reluctant to commit itself on this aspect but regional government in England could well follow in the next five years. An attempt at devolution for the celtic periphery was made by the Labour government in the late 1970s but it failed partly because of the very stringent conditions which were set before devolution could not be enacted and partly because the new Conservative government under Mrs Thatcher rescinded the devolution legislation after winning power in 1979 following the Labour government's loss of a vote of confidence in the House of Commons.

This episode requires further comment since it illustrates the unitariness of the British political tradition and its anti-territorial bias, both of which have had a profound effect on the fortunes of the regional concept over the years. It is almost inconceivable under any other Western system that a party like the Labour Party, itself already ineffably the party of the periphery in terms of its support at the polls, would put its position as the governing party at risk over what was, after all, little more than the creation of a glorified county council for Scotland. But such is the dominance of the unitary tradition and the fear of decentralization that the Labour government in 1979 made no attempt to reconcile their erstwhile partners in the Commons, the nationalist parties who alone kept the government in power, by pushing through legislation. More significant still, outside Scottish nationalist circles there have been no critics of the decision by the Labour government not to waive the conditions for enactment of devolution but instead face an extremely risky vote of confidence. Least of all has opposition to the government decision arisen in the Labour Party itself despite the fact that the party remained out of power for fifteen years after losing the 1979 vote of confidence.

It seemed that after 1979 the devolution issue had died as the onset of Thatcherism directed political attention from territorial issues. However, there were very clear indications that in Scotland at least it had become, by the 1990s, a major political issue. In the Spring of 1990 a MORI poll showed that the percentage of Scots favouring some form of constitutional change entailing increased autonomy for Scotland had reached 78 per cent.

It must be emphasized that Scottish devolution (and to some extent the Welsh) is by far the most important decentralization issue in British politics. For Scotland, in reality, is more than a territorial segment of the UK; it is a former state which entered into a voluntary union of the two Crowns in the 17th century and completed the fusion by the Treaty of Union in 1707. Scotland has retained crucial symbols of its distinctiveness ever since, such as its separate legal system, a separate educational system, a separate established Church, a separate local government system (hence the special legislative committees in the Commons), different bank notes and the Scottish Office (which we will come to in a moment). To these must be added Scotland's preferential treatment in the allocation of House of Commons seats at present amounting to 23 per cent more than it would have been if the English ration of votes to seats was followed. This priviliege was abolished as part of the creation of the Scottish Assembly in 1999. Scotland's distinctiveness is also powerfully symbolized by additional extra-constitutional, privileges that may be called 'unobtrusive devolution' (Sharpe, 1985, p.2) or social federalism' which elsewhere are solely the prerogative of nation states, such as acceptance internationally of Scottish sports teams – football, rugby, athletics – which compete with their own 'national flag', regalia and 'national anthem'.

Given such a distinctive status, it is clear that Scotland is not simply another territorial segment of the UK like an English region, but already enjoys a special political status which sometimes goes well beyond that conferred on a constituent state in a federal system, however self-consciously distinctive it may be. Not Bavaria, nor Texas, nor Catalonia, for example, have their own banknotes, nor can they field their own sports teams on the international stage against other nation states. The UK is, in this sense, more socially federal than many federal states. The devolution issue, then, cannot be brushed aside on formal constitutional grounds, and to some extent the 1997 Labour government if it was to retain its dominant position in Scotland and Wales had very little choice other than to follow the path it is following in creating elected bodies with administrative powers for Scotland, Wales and for different reasons Northern Ireland as well.

Confining devolution to Scotland, Wales and Northern Ireland is because there is much less public demand for regional bodies in England although the creation of English regions is still on the Blair Government's agenda. In England there never has been any deeply-rooted political support for English regional government. It cannot be emphasized too strongly that the UK politico-administrative tradition is profoundly unitary, and nowhere is it more unitary than in England (Bogdanor, 1989, ch. 1). The Labour Party's devolutionary proposals attempt to take account of this by specifying an asymmetric process of regionalizing in England whereby the regions will be able to take on powers or not as they feel fit rather in the same way that the non-historic Autonomous Communities have done in Spain.

The combination of the parliamentary sovereignty principle and the popularly accepted role of the central government as the legitimate custodian of both the national interest and individual interests, as against, what are seen as the possibly illegitimate and sectional interests of the localities (Sharpe, 1978), irrespective of the party in power at Westminster powerfully re-enforces this unitary tradition.

Whatever the impact of a governments' policies on sub-national government; whatever the doubts which may arise about central policies which in other democracies could be regarded as constitutional issues, once Parliament has pronounced a favourable verdict on such policies they become law. There is no second bite at the cherry, for the House of Lords dare not thwart the first chamber on a major issue and the Courts always defer to the Executive on such key decisions under the parliamentary sovereignty principle. The war on local government that was systematically and successfully waged by the three Thatcher administrations during the 1980s is merely the most dramatic example of this ascendancy of the centre and the deep thickets of ambiguity that surround the relative autonomy of the sub-national level within the British system. The fact that this centralist tradition is nowhere stronger than in the English trunk of the country is important if only because over 85 per cent of the population live there. England has been a unified kingdom for almost a thousand years, and none of the English regions command anything remotely like the degree of popular allegiance to be found in either Scotland or Wales. Moreover, England has been industrialized for two centuries so that it has a uniformity of culture that probably has no parallel on such a scale anywhere else in Europe. England and its unitary traditions and distinctive culture stands, as it were, as a huge tree overshadowing the celtic periphery.

In Wales, the nationalist movement may be weaker than it was during its peak in the early 1970s, and this was reflected in the very small majority for creating a Welsh Assembly in a referendum that preceded the change. Unlike Scotland, Welsh nationalism is deeply rooted in the language issue despite the fact that only 19 per cent of the population can speak Welsh and a mere 21,000 or so are monoglot Welsh (1981 census). The steady decline in Welsh speakers in the Principality, down from 44 per cent in 1911 (Williams, 1989), provides a critical impetus to the Welsh national movement. Welsh nationalism is very much a rescue of the culture movement. Thus social federalist concessions by the centre in relation to Welsh have probably been very important in moderating the growth of Welsh nationalism. Such concessions include the creation of a Welsh-speaking TV Channel which relays 28 hours of Welsh-only programmes per week; the creation of the Select Committee on Welsh Affairs in the Commons; the enhanced status of Welsh established under the Welsh Language Act of 1967 as an official language both in schools (where children can be educated wholly in Welsh if parents wish it) and in the Courts. Other concessions in relation to the Welsh language were also made in the 1990s. In 1990 a new curriculum was instituted in Welsh schools which requires the learning of Welsh in all schools. Also the Welsh Language Act of 1992 seeks to give Welsh equal status with English, a change backed by a Welsh Language Board whose task is to ensure the use of Welsh in the public sector. The control of higher education in Wales was transferred from central government to a Welsh Funding Council in 1992. Bi-lingual road signs have also been introduced, and state aid has been made available to sustain a Welsh national opera company, a Welsh national symphony orchestra and infrastructural re-development in Cardiff, the Welsh capital, to match its status. The same special privilege of fielding a 'national' sports team complete with flag and anthem that applies for Scotland and Northern Ireland also applies for Wales (Sharpe, 1985).

Another factor which almost certainly enhances the prospects of the two nationalist parties is their somewhat recent enthusiastic embracing of EU regional policies by re-defining their major aim as not being outright separation but, rather, separation from the UK but 'within Europe'. In this way they have been able to outflank the British central governments scepticism towards Brussels and claim that they, the peripheral nationalists, are more internationalist than the centre. This switch has enhanced the nationalist cause in both Scotland and Wales since it has tempered the apprehension of some of their marginal supporters who feared that devolution was the thin end of the separatist wedge. That is to say, it has reassured the more numerous and moderate 'consumption' nationalists in the respective nationalist camps who feared the economic consequences of outright separation for their region (Sharpe, 1989). The pro-EU stance by the nationalists has also attracted the younger voter who found the straight separatist aims of the nationalists old fashioned, if not atavistic.

The Offices

So much for the devolution issue, we now come to another regional feature of the British system and in some ways the most important, the so-called

Offices. The United Kingdom is somewhat unusual for a large Western unitary state in that it has no comprehensive and uniform level of deconcentrated territorial administration between local and central government, not even in a residual form as in Scandinavia. All intermediate administration is therefore either asymmetric, or confined to largely unifunctional service delivery systems. The UK asymmetric administrative intermediate level, or meso, takes the form of the three Offices, which are formally deconcentrated levels of central general government in Scotland, Wales and Northern Ireland and they constitute a feature of the British sub-national system that has loose parallels with a prefectoral system.

The reason for discussing the three Offices is not to claim that they form part of conventional regional government in the accepted sense of the term, but simply because it would be impossible to understand why the evolution of regional government has been so tortuous and unsuccessful if the Offices are ignored. In other words, had the Offices not existed, the pressure for a fully-fledged regional level meso on the French or Italian pattern would probably have been considerably greater, certainly in Scotland and Wales. It would perhaps be an exaggeration to say that the Offices' collective existence actually ruled out the possibility of a uniform regional system for the reasons already given, but their existence certainly made it very much easier to withstand, for example, pressure for such a system during the 1960s and 1970s. Indeed, the Offices have their origin precisely in political pressures for decentralization in the sense that the Scottish Office, the first to be created, was a direct product of the Home Rule movement of the 1880s (Kellas, 1976, p.28). Although the Welsh Office did not begin to achieve fully-fledged status until the 1960s, the growth of Welsh devolutionary pressure later strongly aided the process.

It is also unlikely that Stormont, the quasi-federal system of government in Northern Ireland, could have been abolished so easily in 1972 if there had not been the model of the Office to take its place. The British quasi-regional government to be discussed – the three Offices – are, then, essential to any adequate understanding of why the British regional experience has taken the form that is has. It must be emphasized at the outset that all three Offices are integral parts of British central government. Like all such deconcentrated forms, each Office is under the control of common general superior, a Secretary of State. He is a member of the House of Commons and sits in the Cabinet. Seven features of the Offices need to be noted.

The Special Status of Northern Ireland: The *first* is that the Northern Ireland Office is distinctly different from the other two Offices in a number of respects. In the first place, it is much more a form of direct government from London in which public order, and until the 1994 cease-fire, counter-terrorist policy dominated. The Northern Ireland Secretary is more powerful on his home patch than either of his counterparts and comes closest to being a Prime Minister for his region (Bell, 1987, p.191).

In running the Office and formulating policy the NI Secretary of State, also unlike the Scottish or Welsh counterparts, may or may not be supported by Northern Ireland MPs all of whom belong to parties that are exclusive to the Province (since the national parties until 1990 were banned from operating in the Province) and therefore will never have any particular allegiance to him. He will not sit for a Northern Ireland seat and his role is much more that of being 'a special voice for the territory at the centre of government in London' (Hogwood, 1982, p.3). Moreover, the Northern Ireland Office is the most recent in the sense that up to 1972 Northern Ireland had its own directly elected, bicameral representative institutions (Stormont) and its own government exercising a wide degree of autonomy over internal affairs. Central intervention into Northern Ireland's internal affairs was, until serious civil unrest began in 1968, virtually unknown. This status may decline in the future following the creation of a Scottish Parliament.

In 1972, as a result of the worsening sectarian conflict in the Province, and the unwillingness of the Northern Ireland government to relinquish its control of public order to the centre, Stormont was peremptorily abolished. This action cannot be bettered as exemplifying the extraordinary power of British central government already alluded to and it occurred remarkably swiftly; that is to say, as a result of a simple, albeit well-supported, majority in the Commons. In early 1974 a much weaker 'power sharing' Executive replaced Stormont which was based not on the majority principle, but gave access to power to the minority Catholic parties. For this reason it was very unpopular with the Protestant majority (Protestants outnumber Catholics by almost two to one) which mounted a national strike against it on the grounds that sacrificing such an integral part of the democratic process as the majority principle constituted an unacceptable diminution of their rights. As a result, the power sharing experiment never functioned, collapsing in May 1974. Thereafter, a new Northern Ireland Office took over the reins of power in the Province on a temporary basis, and in 1982 an elected body was revived in the form of the Northern Ireland Assembly. Unlike Stormont, it was merely consultative and deliberative and again, had its Executive been created, it would have followed the power sharing, or non-majority, principle. The aim was to enhance its status and powers over time by means of 'rolling devolution'. It was, however, even less popular in the Province than its predecessor, and the Assembly was dissolved in June 1986.

The Northern Ireland experience is thus the reverse of what has been occurring elsewhere in comparable peripheries Europe since there has been a *decline* in the autonomy of the peripheral ethnically distinctive region, indeed a transformation from government to administration (Rose, 1982). The explanation for this apparent paradox is that the majority in the peripheral region want *closer* ties with the British core in order to protect their peripheral distinctiveness against what they fear may be submergence not by that core, but by an adjacent state, the Irish Republic, whose constitution contains two clauses laying claim to the province. Such Protestant fears are sharpened by the attitudes of the Catholic minority in Northern Ireland a small majority of whom do not recognize the United Kingdom as their country but do recognize the Irish Republic. In a 1990 survey, some 56 per cent of Northern Irish Catholics favoured Northern Ireland joining the Irish Republic (Jowell and Airey, 1990).

The Northern Ireland Office is also different because the province was until 1994 in the grip of an incipient civil war, with strong overtones of irredentism that has led, via the Northern Ireland Agreement with the Irish Republic agreed in the mid 1980s, to the Secretary having direct formal links with a foreign state. Moreover, the Northern Ireland Office is less integrated than its counterparts because its bureaucracy continues to operate outside the direct ambit of the Secretary of State so as to facilitate the transfer to a representative system, should that ever become possible (Bell, 1987).

Functional Variation: The *second* aspect of the Office as a British governmental form to be noted is that no Office embraces all central government functions in their respective areas since some central departments operate a centre-to-periphery implementation hierarchy that is independent of and very much bigger than that of the respective Offices. Essentially, both the Scottish and Welsh Offices perform a representative rather than a functional role in Westminster in the sense that their main task is to defend their area's collective interests and to gain more central resources. Also, the functional range of each Office differs. The largest and the most highly developed is the Scottish Office which is over one hundred years old and unlike the Welsh Office, covers not only the Health Service in

Scotland but law and order, the police and prisons (Keating and Midwinter, 1983, ch. 2).

Distinctive Character of Scottish Office: The *third* aspect of the Offices to be emphasized is that the Scottish Office is by far the biggest and its Secretary is usually more important than his two colleagues. The Scottish Secretary's predominance in London is mainly due to Scotland's separate legal, educational and local government systems already noted, which entails special arrangements in the House of Commons that enhances the role of the Office and the Secretary of State, (he pilots bills through the Commons), and includes the Scottish Grand Committee, two Scottish Standing Committees, and a select committee that together handle most Scottish legislation and debate Scottish affairs.

The Welsh MPs have a Grand Committee and a Select Committee on Welsh Affairs in the Commons (Jones and Wilford, 1986), but neither carries the same weight as their Scottish counterparts since Wales is much more institutionally uniform with England. It must be emphasized, too, that Scotland is by far the largest of the three territorial segments covered by Offices having approximately 5 million population as compared with 2.8 million in Wales and 1.5 million in Northern Ireland. This difference is reflected in the staffing levels of the Scottish and Welsh Offices, the former having about four times the number of staff as the latter (Kellas and Madgwick, 1982, p.9).

The Secretary of State: The *fourth* aspect of the Office to be noted is the unusual nature of the post of Secretary of State who holds a unique position in British politics in the sense that, the Prime Minister apart, he is the only member of the Executive who has a territorial rather than a functional base. In both Scotland and Wales, but particularly in Scotland, the Secretary becomes an important *regional* political figure. This prominence is particularly marked when the Labour Party is in power nationally because it usually holds many more seats than other parties in both regions and has held the majority of Scottish seats for over 30 years. A Labour Secretary is thus able to command a special status within the government and within the parliamentary party. The Conservative Party, by contrast, is particularly weak in both Scotland and Wales. Since 1998 it has held no seats in Scotland or Wales.

The Labour Party is correspondingly strong in the periphery. Except for 1966, it has not won 50 per cent of the English seats since 1957. There has been a more spasmodic decline in the Conservative vote in Wales, but since 1979 the party has had difficulty finding even a Secretary of State for

Wales who sits for a Welsh seat. The Secretary of State for Wales up to the General Election of 1997, for example, was entirely of English origins, sat for an English constituency as did his predecessor, and even refused to respond to letters if they were in Welsh.

As a member of the Cabinet, the Secretary of State is able to give his region what may be a crucial advantage in bargaining with the Treasury over government expenditure, although this advantage is less evident for Northern Ireland and has to some extent been modified since the mid-1960s by rivalry between the Welsh and Scottish Offices and perhaps a more watchful Treasury. But per capita expenditure is appreciably higher in Northern Ireland and Scotland than in England even allowing for needs factors. Figures for 1986/7 demonstrate the advantage for Scotland; 'for every £100 of government spending in England in 1986/87, Scotland received £122. In health the comparative figures were £97 in England and £122 in Scotland' (Dickson, 1988, p.361). In 1987-88 Scotland had 23.8 per cent higher identifiable public expenditure per head than the UK averages and Wales 9.6 per cent (Kellas, 1991, p.96).

Midwinter and Keating state that Scottish expenditure has been consistently higher over the post-war period than the UK average by about 20 per cent overall and very much higher in housing and agriculture. The allocation process, presided over by the Treasury, is both shrouded in secrecy and is very complex, but Midwinter and Keating explain this difference as being attributable in part to the fact that originally the formula (the *Goschen* formula) for allocation was based on Scotland's proportion of the UK population in the 1890s (Keating and Midwinter, 1983, Ch. 10). That proportion has declined and the formula, now the *Barnett* formula, has changed but the *base* budget, derived from Goschen, remains intact and thus so does the skew in Scotland's favour (Heald, 1983). Yet a further example of social federalism.

Direct expenditure is not, however, the only form of governmentally-determined re-distribution and an exhaustive account of its total effect regionally could very well reveal that the direct expenditure advantage enjoyed by Scotland is more than balanced historically by, for example, the massive subsidy entailed in the form of tax relief granted to homeowners repaying mortgages, which in 1990 was estimated to be in excess of £7 *billion* annually (Guardian, 31 December 1990). Only 45 per cent of the Scottish population were at the time homeowners compared with 67 per cent average for the English regions and 68 per cent for the most affluent English region, the South East. Similarly the South East can be said to enjoy another extra 'hidden' governmental subsidy since the percentage of 16 year old children staying on at school for the region was almost 70 whereas for Scotland it was 48.6 per cent.

The Offices and Local Government: The *fifth* aspect of the Offices to be noted is their relationship with local government. In Northern Ireland the local government system is very attenuated, and comprises 26 District Councils which are responsible for minor functions, and most of the services provided by local government in Scotland and England are provided by quangos or by the Northern Ireland Office. These will eventually be subsumed in the Northern Ireland Assembly when it begins operating. The total of Northern Ireland local government annual expenditure in the early 1990s was only about £150 million. This is because normal local government was abolished in the 1970s because of gerrymandering and religious discrimination (in public housing allocation for example) by Protestant majorities within some local authorities. In Scotland and Wales, the respective Offices tend to have a closer relationship with local government and local pressure groups than Whitehall has with English local bodies (Kellas and Madgwick, 1982, p.11). Since the Offices themselves are part of the periphery in relation to London departments, and in particular the Treasury, a sense of identity between local government and the Offices also builds up, so that the Office can intercede on behalf of a locality in conflict with Whitehall (Keating and Carter, 1987). This common front towards London is, perhaps re-enforced by the fact that most of the senior civil servants at the H.Q. of each Office, St Andrews House (Edinburgh) and Cathays Park (Cardiff) tend to be respectively, of Scottish and Welsh birth. In short, senior civil servants of the two Offices develop a dual relationship to their respective territorial areas – reflectors of its interests to the centre as well as instruments of central control – that has its closest parallel to that of a prefect and his staff in what may be called a napoleonic system like France (Machin, 1977).

Ambiguity of Offices' Status: The *sixth* feature of the Offices to be noted is their ambiguous and complex status. For example, they are both a form of deconcentration from the centre *and* a form of decentralization. It is also easy to exaggerate their importance. As we have noted, they form only a small part of the central government apparatus in their respective areas, and the proportion of the total of central civil servants in Scotland and Wales employed by the Offices were in the early 1980s, respectively, 18 per cent and 6 per cent (Parry, 1981). The Offices are a peculiar type of hybrid in the sense that, though formally a form of administrative deconcentration, they have a politician and Cabinet Minister at their head. But he is a relatively junior Cabinet Minister and does not sit on any of the most important Cabinet committees. They are also indubitably part of the national administration and therefore just as subject to Treasury control as any other department within central government (Hood and Dunsire, 1981, ch.11).

The Impact of the Offices: The *seventh* and final aspect to be noted is their impact on policy outcomes, ie. what difference to Government do the three Offices make? In other words, how much real autonomy do they exercise? We have already noted the considerable difference between per capita public expenditure in Scotland and Wales as compared with the UK average. In addition, it must be emphasized that once an Office has received its block grant from the centre the Secretary of State does have considerable freedom to decide priorities within the block (Kellas, 1991, p.96). But in relation to other aspects of policymaking within each Office it is extremely difficult to generalize, simply because of the relative absence of studies of the Welsh and Northern Ireland Offices that confront the question. Keating and Midwinter suggest that, for the Scottish Office, the kind of issue is often crucial in determining the extent of autonomy. If the policy has no cross-border spill-overs with the rest of the UK; that is to say if the policy area is rooted in Scotland's separate legal system, or its local government, high levels of autonomy are permitted. Similarly, where by convention Scotland is recognized as having a special tradition, leeway is again possible. Other lesser factors making for higher autonomy are, first, the greater salience of the issue in Scotland as compared with elsewhere, for example, fisheries policy. Second, when the Labour Party is in power nationally, as we have already noted, the Secretary of State is a more powerful political figure and can use that power if he so wishes to enhance Office autonomy (Keating and Midwinter, 1983, pp.20-3). One final point in relation to the Offices needs emphasis: the very existence of the Offices – each with its Cabinet rank minister at the helm – plus the preferential financial advantage that Wales and Scotland enjoy further enhances the socially federal character of UK government. Peripheral aspirations are met but political power remains firmly unitary.

One final aspect of the Offices demands attention and that is that they will remain after each of the Celtic peripheries has acquired its elected council. It is unclear at this stage (late 1999) how the Secretary of State will liase with the elected council, but it has been agreed that each council will itself have a Chief Minister or Leader. His relationship with the Secretary of State could be crucial in the success of the experiment.

Conclusions

As in so many aspects of its government and politics, regionalism in the UK, despite its cultural heterogeneity, is rather unusual among large Western unitary states, especially those with a comparable degree of cultural heterogeneity. There seem to be a number of reasons for this. The first, which we haven't so far discussed, is that it belongs to the North European, non-napoleonic group of Western states which have coped with the functional need for an enlarged system of local government (because of urbanization and new functions) by enlarging and refurbishing its county level of local government. Napoleonic, Southern European states, by contrast, have not been able to do this because of built-in resistance to local government modernization in their political systems. They have therefore sought to resolve the problems of economies of scale and externalities within their local government systems by the creation of a new regional level of government. Regional nationalist pressures have added strongly to the attraction of this regional solution (Sharpe, 1993, ch.1). The UK, in a sense, straddles both the Northern and Southern European governmental models because it has refurbished its county system of local government yet because of pressure from Scotland and Wales it is about to create regional bodies comparable to those created in Southern Europe.

The British case of regionalism amply demonstrates that the demands of regional nationalists can sometimes be met without changing the distribution of political power that a fully-fledged system of regional government would entail. There can be little doubt, for example, that the reason why the Welsh nationalist movement seemed to be stalled in the 1980s is because a wide range of non-political concessions already noted which were made by the centre to Welsh nationalists, especially in relation to the language issue discussed earlier. At the referendum in Wales on the creation of regional government the 'yes' vote constituted only the very barest of majorities. Similarly the momentum of Scottish nationalism may have been diminished by the retention of a wide range of asymmetrical anomalies not only in the political sphere but also by the re-enforcement of the distinctiveness of Scotland's legal, educational, and local government systems including perhaps the greatest anomaly of all, the Scottish banknote. Above all, we note the crucial concession, in terms of popular attitudes, of allowing Scottish and Welsh and Northern Ireland sports teams with their own colours, flag and anthem, to operate on the world stage as if they were representing sovereign states. In short, the UK has up until now tackled its regional nationalism not by the structural devolution of power, but by what may be called 'unobtrusive devolution' or 'social federalism'. In this way many of the aspirations of the Celtic periphery seem to have been met, but the strongly unitary state and its correlative – parliamentary sovereignty the core principle of British constitutional practice – remained unscathed. This is the essence of the symbiosis: because the British political system is so centralized and unitary it has been forced to accommodate territorial sectionalism outside that political system. Indeed, in a curious way the England core has been 'celtizised' since it, too, has now got its own anthem, flag and colours for its representative sports teams. It must be added that these crucial sports team changes have all occurred without one word of public discussion let alone debate.

The British have in the past also devised another unusual method of avoiding the explicit devolution of power and this is by the very peculiar *Office* mechanism where, again, concessions are made to regional nationalism – their own Minister in the Cabinet, their own mini-Whitehall *en situ*, vigorous economic redevelopment policies, extra resources and so forth – but the key principles of the unitary state operated by a rigid two party system remained inviolate. In sum, in the field of regionalism, the process that has created the new meso level government that is transforming the West European unitary state (Sharpe, 1993), Britain has, as usual, chosen an inimitable path.

Note

1   This paper is drawn from Chapter 9 of Sharpe, L. J. (ed.) (1993), *The Rise of Meso Government in Europe*, Sage, London.

References

Ashford, D. (1982), *British Dogmatism & French Pragmatism*, Allen & Unwin, London.
Bell, P., 'Direct Rule in Northern Ireland', in R. Rose (1987), *Ministers and Ministries*, Clarendon, Oxford.
Bogdanor, V. (1979), *Devolution*, Oxford University Press, Oxford.
Bulpitt, J. (1983), *Territory and Power in the United Kingdom*, Manchester University Press, Manchester.

Chartered Institute of Public Finances and Accountancy (1988), *Local Government Comparative Statistics*, London.
Dawson, A. H. (1981), 'The Idea of the Region: the 1975 Reorganization of Scottish Local Government', *Public Administration*, vol. 59.
Dickson, A. D. R. (1988), 'The Peculiarities of the Scottish', *Political Quarterly*, vol. 59.
Foster, C. D. et al. (1980), *Local Government Finance in an Unitary State*, Allen and Unwin, London.
Greenwood, R. (1982), 'Pressure from Whitehall', in R. Rose and E. Page (eds), *Fiscal Stress in Cities*, Cambridge University Press, London.
Hanham, H. (1969), 'The Development of the Scottish Office', in J. H. Wolfe (ed.), *Government & Nationalism in Scotland*, Edinburgh University Press, Edinburgh.
Heald, D. (1983), *Public Expenditure*, Martin Robertson, Oxford.
Hogwood, B. C. (1982), 'Introduction', in B. C. Hogwood and M. Keating (eds), *Regional Government in England*, Clarendon Press, Oxford.
Hogwood, B. C. and Keating, M. (eds) (1982), *Regional Government in England*, Clarendon Press, Oxford.
Hogwood, B. C. and Lindley, P. D. (1982), 'Variations in Regional Boundaries', in B. C. Hogwood and M. Keating (eds), *Regional Government in England*, Clarendon Press, Oxford.
Hood C. and Dunsire, A. (1981), *Bureaumetrics*, Gower, Farnborough.
Jones, J. B. and Wilford, J. (1986), *Parliament and Territoriality*, University of Wales Press, Cardiff.
Jowell, R. and Airey, C. (eds) (1990), *British Social Attitudes Survey, 7th Report*, Gower, London.
Keating M. and Carter, C. (1987), 'Policymaking and the Scottish Office: the Designation of Cumbernauld New Town', *Public Administration*, vol. 65.
Keating M. and Midwinter, A. (1983), *The Government of Scotland*, Mainsteam, Edinburgh.
Kellas, J. G. (1976), *The Scottish Political System*, Cambridge University Press, Cambridge.
Kellas, J. G. (1991), 'The Scottish and Welsh Offices as Territorial Managers', *Regional Politics and Policy*, vol. 1.
Kellas, J. and Madgwick, P. (1982), 'Territorial Ministries: The Scottish and Welsh Offices', in P Madgwick and R. Rose (eds), *The Territorial Dimension in UK Politics*, Macmillan, London.
Machin, H. (1977), *The Prefect in French Public Administration*, Croom Helm, London.
Madgwick, P. and Rose, R. (eds) (1982), *The Territorial Dimension in UK Politics*, Macmillan, London.
Midwinter, A. (1985), 'Local Government in Strathclyde' in J. Butt and G. Gordon (eds), *Changing Horizons*, Scottish Academic Press, Edinburgh.

Page, E. and Midwinter, A. (1980), 'Remoteness, Efficiency, Cost and the Reorganization of Scottish Local Government', *Public Administration*, vol. 30.

Parry, R. (1981), 'Territory and Public Employment: a General Model and British Evidence', *Journal of Public Policy*, vol. 1.

Parry, R. (1987), 'The Centralization of the Scottish Office', in R. Rose (1987), *Ministers and Ministries*, Clarendon, Oxford.

Reform of Direct Taxation: Report of the Taxation Review Committee (1990), Fabian Society, London.

Rhodes, R. A. W. (1988), *Beyond Westminster and Whitehall*, Unwin-Hyman, London.

Rose, R. (1982), 'Is the United Kingdom a State? Northern Ireland as a Test Case', in P. Madgwick and R. Rose (eds), *The Territorial Dimension in United Kingdom Politics*, Macmillan, London.

Sharpe, L. J. (1982), 'The Labour Party and the Geography of Inequality', in D. Kavanagh (ed.), *The Politics of the Labour Party*, Allen and Unwin, London.

Sharpe, L. J. (1985), 'Devolution and Celtic Nationalism in the UK', *West European Politics*, vol. 8.

Sharpe, L. J. (1989), 'Fragmentation and Territoriality in the European State System', *International Political Science Review*, vol. 10.

Sharpe, L. J. (ed.) (1993), *The Rise of Meso Government in Europe*, Sage, London.

Thomas, I. C. (1987), 'Giving Direction to the Welsh Office', in R. Rose, *Ministers and Ministries*, Clarendon, Oxford.

Williams, C. H. (1989), 'New Domains of the Welsh Language', *Contemporary Wales*, vol 3.

5 The Institutional Framework: Federalism and Decentralisation in Germany

GERHARD LEHMBRUCH

Introduction

As a consequence of a series of regime changes in the 20th century, the political institutions of Germany are often analysed in terms of constitutional engineering. In fact, most German-language textbooks on the political system of (former West) Germany begin by describing the process of constitution-making in 1948/49, the implication being that this is the origin of the present institutional framework. This perspective, however, has two shortcomings. One is the limited time perspective. In principle, the Basic Law was conceived by the constitution-makers as an improved version of the Weimar constitution. Essential elements of the present institutional framework go back, therefore, to 1919 or even further to the constitution of 1867/71. The second shortcoming is that, however important constitutional engineering (including borrowing from foreign models) may have been for fields such as the role of parliament and parliamentary government, there is one important exception, namely that of intergovernmental relations. Germany has a federal system, and the main institutional features of German federalism owe very little to deliberate constitutional design. With the exception of the Nazi dictatorship (which left few vestiges in this field), major successful interventions into the federal structures only took place as the result of wars (as in 1867/71), sometimes in the context of a reorganisation of the international system (1648, 1815), or, in two important instances, with victorious conquerors playing a decisive role (1803-1807, 1946-1949). Even these interventions, however, retained important structural elements, so that we encounter some remarkable institutional continuities.

In a narrow constitutional sense the institutional history of modern German federalism dates back to the establishment by Bismarck in 1867 of the *Norddeutscher Bund* (North German Confederation) which in 1871 became enlarged by the accession of the South German states and since then called the *Deutsche Reich*. This reference to the old 'Holy Roman Empire' which was dissolved in 1806 placed it into a constitutional genealogy of federal systems which had its roots in the medieval history of Germany.[1] Today's *Bundesrat* (Federal Council), for example, is the institutional heir of the *Immerwährender Reichstag* (Permanent Diet) which from 1666 to 1806 had its seat at Regensburg, and of its successors the *Bundestag* of the German Confederation (1815-1866), Bismarck's *Bundesrat* (1867-1918) and the Weimar *Reichsrat* (1919-1933).

The considerable complexities of policy-making in present-day Germany owe much to the federal nature of the German state and federalism is an important constraint on political reform. In the context of reform discussions, it is therefore important to remember that the federal structures of contemporary Germany are essentially not the result of deliberate institutional engineering. Distinctive features of German federalism can perhaps be understood as resulting from important historical compromises, but its basic structures may be best described as the accumulated sediment of path-dependent institutional growth over centuries, and on the actor level as the result of strategic repertories acquired during political socialisation and transmitted from one generation to the next.

Exekutivföderalismus and its Institutional Logic

One of the distinctive features of German federalism which sets Germany apart from other federal systems is the central role of autonomous state administrations in the making and in the implementation of rules. German federalism obeys a specific 'institutional logic' which distinguishes it from other federal systems. Ostensibly, inter-governmental relations (vertical and horizontal) are the crucial mechanism of German federalism. It is therefore not surprising that recent political science research on German federalism focuses largely on their development (Scharpf *et al.*, 1976). This includes, of course, the important and complex problems of fiscal federalism.

This preponderance of bureaucracies in the federalist framework can be traced back to the peculiar German path of state-building. In Germany the emergence of the modern state – defined as the system of differentiated institutions for the exercise of a monopoly of legitimate force within the boundaries of a delimited territory – was not (as in neighbouring France) closely linked to the formation of the nation-state. Attempts at a *Reichsreform* in the 15th and 16th centuries, with autonomous institutions at the level of the Empire, remained unsuccessful. The institutional basis of the Imperial dynasty of the Habsburgs remained confined to their territorial domain of Austria and the last great effort of the Habsburgs to establish their supreme authority failed in the Thirty Years' War (1618-1648). The outcome of this war, agreed in the peace treaty of Westphalia concluded at Münster and Osnabrück, was a historical compromise based on a complex federalist bargain. The first German version of the bureaucratic state developed thereafter at the territorial level in Austria, Prussia, Saxony, Württemberg and Bavaria, to name but the most important. When the French revolutionary armies and Napoleon smashed the *ancien régime* of the old *Reich*, the leading territories responded by introducing profound political, economic and administrative reforms of which the Stein-Hardenberg reforms in Prussia were only the most spectacular example. These reforms further strengthened the pivotal role of bureaucratic state executives in the formation of a modern federal system.

A consequence of this peculiar path of state-building was that the larger German states had an entrenched institutional advantage which Bismarck, when unifying Germany around the Prussian core, could not easily have challenged. One motive for Bismarck's construction of the Empire as a federation of territorial governments was certainly that 'executive federalism', to employ the modern term, provided him the means to thwart liberal and democratic demands for the parliamentary responsibility of the government, but for him this was also a congenial form of governing. As former Prussian plenipotentiary minister to the *Bundestag* (diet) of the German Confederation at Frankfurt he was familiar with the diplomatic bargaining style of traditional German federalism, and this made it relatively easy for him to strike a federalist compromise in which the interests of territorial bureaucracies in organisational survival and the existing networks between these bureaucracies, territorial elites and emerging interest groups were safeguarded. From Bismarck to Helmut Kohl and Gerhard Schröder we find several important examples of German political leaders for whom the familiarity with the federal institutions acquired during their career greatly facilitated the development of the leadership skills required for the management of a complex and polycentric federal system.

The prerogatives of the state bureaucracies thus became one of the distinguishing marks of the German constitutional system that could not easily be challenged. Not only was the execution of the legislation of the *Reich* largely left to the member states. Moreover, the supreme federal organ of the Empire, the *Bundesrat*, remained a congress of the diplomatic representatives of the member states, standing clearly in an institutional continuity linked to the Permanent Diet of the old *Reich* and its successor, the Diet of the German Confederation (1815-1866) mentioned previously. In this respect Bismarck appears to have learned his lesson from the failure of the draft constitution of the National Assembly at Frankfurt in 1848/49, the federal construction of which was strongly inspired by the counter-model of US federalism with the Senate as the elected representation of the states. This attempt to establish a modern second parliamentary chamber failed, among other reasons, because the state bureaucracies strongly resented the loss of power which this would have implied.

This episode prefigured what was to become a dominant feature of German federalism until the present day and which proved – except for the Hitler regime – resistant to all attempts at structural reform. The draft constitution for the Weimar Republic again proposed replacing the *Bundesrat* principle by the model of the US Senate. As happened 70 years earlier at Frankfurt, this attempt was frustrated by the stiff resistance of the state governments (and bureaucracies) which had become political strongholds of regional party leaderships. This story repeated itself during the constitutional deliberations of 1948/49 when Adenauer originally favoured the 'senate principle' but was overridden by a coalition favouring the traditional institutional pattern. This time the initial institutional advantage of the states was clearly greater than in 1919, because in 1945 the central government had been eliminated by the Occupation Powers, and it is therefore not surprising that they re-emerged much stronger than they had been in the Weimar Republic.

Hence German federalism essentially originated from a process of institutional strengthening of inter-governmental relationships. Bismarck successfully blended this institutional heritage with the aspirations of the liberal bourgeoisie for a 'unitary' national state and conceived this 'executive federalism' as a barrier against the development of a parliamentary responsibility of the executive as it had already been in the system of the *Deutsche Bund* (German Confederation) of 1815 (Mommsen 1980). As a logical consequence, the national parliament (*Reichstag*) remained outside the inter-governmental arena. The administration of the *Reich* in Bismarck's federalism first emerged from the Prussian executive. It acquired an autonomous weight as the centre of gravity of policy formation only in the following decades, but inter-governmental relations remained important for policy formation at the level of the *Reich*. Bismarck himself had begun his diplomatic career as the Prussian minister to the confederate *Bundesrat* at Frankfurt and was eager to preserve the characteristic diplomatic style of inter-governmental relations, a legacy of the German Confederation of 1815-1866. He did this with the double aim of easing the integration of the member states into the *Reich* and, at the same time, of keeping the *Reichstag* out of the inter-governmental arena. As a conse-quence, German federalism was always characterised by strong elements of bargaining and quasi-diplomatic accommodation at the executive level. Although Prussia was in a position to exert a hegemonic influence on the *Reich* administration and might always have mustered a majority in the *Bundesrat*, Bismarck and his successors developed a practice of seeking the preliminary agreement of the major states (notably Bavaria) for all major initiatives (Binder, 1971, pp.142ff.; Rauh, 1973; Weber, 1921, p.273f). In this way, a tradition of inter-governmental bargaining developed which has been maintained to the present day. Moreover, the constitution left the responsibility for policy implementation in most fields to the member states. Hence, the central government had to co-operate with the state governments and their bureaucracies, increasingly so with the growth of the welfare state. This resulted in a distinct interdependence of federal and state bureaucracies.

This pattern was of course modified in the Weimar Republic by the parliamentarisation of the central and *Länder* governments after the downfall of the dynasties in 1918, but even later the parliaments of *Reich* and *Länder* were never involved in the inter-governmental relationship. In the Federal Republic after 1949, the executive preponderance in the inter-governmental sub-system was also progressively strengthened. Contributing to this trend was also the increasing complexity of the inter-governmental network, particularly following the institutional reforms of the 'Grand Coalition' government of Christian Democrats and Social Democrats (1966-1969). The autonomous political influence of state parliaments (*Landtage*) declined correspondingly. This preponderance of the state administrations finds its most salient expression in the role of the *Bundesrat* in the legislative process. The Federal Council is not, strictly speaking, a parliamentary 'second chamber' with members enjoying a free mandate, but a body representing the state executives whose members vote on instructions from their cabinets in the state capitals and who are represented in most committee deliberations by civil servants.

It is often asserted that the present strength of the states owes much to the intervention of the Western Allies in the constitutional deliberations of the Parliamentary Council *(Parlamentarischer Rat)* in 1949. These interventions indeed contributed to tipping the balance of power relations in fiscal federalism in their favour. However, the dissolution of Prussia by the Allied Control Council in 1946 probably had more far reaching consequences. It radically altered the power relations between states, and the elimination of the hegemonic state strongly increased the thresholds of consensus-building by inter-state bargaining.[2]

The Paradox of Federalist Unitarisation

This formative period is important because highlights the peculiar German combination of institutional decentralisation and procedural integration. It is certainly correct to characterise Germany as a 'decentralised state' (Katzenstein, 1987, pp.15ff.). Yet it is important to add that the decentralised actors do not dispose of large autonomous ranges of action but are strongly dependent upon each other. Under these conditions, the emergence of a characteristic relationship can be observed between politics and policies, between the institutional framework and the procedural and strategic repertory of political actors. The public prefers the homogenisation and uniformity of policies throughout the federal system. Its expectations are met, and at the same time kept alive, by decentral, but strongly interdependent executive authorities. The institutional autonomy of these actors is limited by their integration into a multilateral bargaining system and the manifest *raison d'être* of this interlocking relationship is the production of homogeneous policies.

Closer inspection reveals two different strategies in the history of modern German federalism, 'centralisation' and 'unitarisation' (Hesse, 1962; Abromeit, 1992). The concept of 'centralisation' must be qualified in this context. It refers to central rule-making but neither excludes participation of the *Länder* in this process nor their continuing importance in rule implementation. Against this strategy of centralisation, the more recent strategy of 'unitarisation' through substantive and procedural harmonisation is based on 'horizontal coordination' between the *Länder* among themselves, or coordination between the *Länder* and the *Bund*. Such 'interlocking politics' (*Politikverflechtung*) link different governmental actors in the process of policy formation but largely safeguard their organisational domain and organisational autonomy.

The centralising strategy meant that much more than in US or Swiss federalism, the states progressively lost their autonomy in large areas of legislation. This was the consequence of the rule that *Reich* legislation superseded the laws of the member states (article 2 of the Constitutions of 1867 and 1871). As already mentioned, in the early 19th century the administrative modernisation of France acted as an important challenge and model for the reform of the larger German states. Yet Germany continued to lag behind its powerful neighbour insofar as the emerging modern economy had to cope with the territorial fragmentation characteristic of traditional German statehood, despite the territorial reorganisation from 1803 to the Congress of Vienna which had very much simplified the map of Germany. The rising German bourgeoisie resented *Kleinstaaterei* with its multiplicity of regional currencies, border controls and laws, and one of its central demands was the achievement of societal and economic unity with instruments similar to those of France, notably by national codifications of civil and penal law. For German liberals, the foundation of the *Deutsches Reich* meant the fulfilment of their aspirations for a 'unitary' national state. Therefore the 'national-liberal' majority of the *Reichstag* in the early 1870s was particularly eager to introduce uniform legislation in order to promote the economic integration of Germany. Bismarck, however, despite his fundamental conservatism, was not immune to the temptation to adopt a centralising strategy if it fitted his political design. The beginnings of the German welfare state are the best illustration. So, the introduction of social security in Germany in the 1880s was explicitly conceived by Bismarck to underline the protective functions of the *Reich*. Finally, however, even this strong leader only gained acceptance for a strongly decentralised version of the original plans.[3]

From its beginnings then, German federalism combined a strong tendency toward uniformity of rules with federally decentralised rule implementation. Nevertheless, the inter-war period saw a progressive centralisation of legislative and administrative responsibilities. After the defeat in the First World War, the resulting crisis of public finance led the Weimar Republic in 1920 to centralise fiscal administration. The National Socialist regime later continued to introduce uniform administrative standards. This centralising trend was reversed after the defeat of 1945. Remarkably, however, the political decentralisation that accompanied the

Allied occupation and their influence on the constitution of 1949 did not lead to an overall resurgence of administrative heterogeneity. Rather, state bureaucracies found it in their interest to further uphold uniform standards through (informal and formal) harmonisation.

In the Federal Republic, therefore, as long as centralisation continued, it increasingly assumed a 'controlled' character. In some important domains the *Länder* were indeed prepared to surrender parts of their original jurisdiction to the *Bund*, but as a rule they insisted by way of compensation that legislation should remain subject to the consent of the *Bundesrat*. This enlargement of the Federal Council's veto power (*zustimmungspflichtige Gesetze*) had the advantage of preserving at least part of the organisational domain of the state bureaucracies.

In a booklet published in 1962, Konrad Hesse (Professor of Public Law and later a member of the Federal Constitutional Court) drew attention to the strong trends toward 'material unitarisation' of policies in German federalism and pointed out that this 'unitary federalism' of the Federal Republic took two different forms, either outright centralisation or co-operative unitarisation (Hesse, 1962). In Hesse's view, such unitarisation was an unavoidable consequence of the growth of the welfare state. However, one can argue that this trend is older than the modern welfare state and that German federalism is distinguished from other federal systems by a remarkably strong aversion to heterogeneity of policies and to differences in public standards and outputs. The Basic Law even introduced the postulate of the 'uniformity of living conditions' (*Einheitlichkeit der Lebensverhältnisse*) within the federal territory as one of the basic principles of fiscal federalism (Art. 106 (3/2)).

Such harmonisation remained paradoxically compatible with the executive autonomy of the German states. In important fields, such as education, harmonisation was not so much furthered by the *Reich* legislator or by centralising the administration, but rather by hegemonic diffusion from Prussia which was able to impose its models on most of the other states. Thus, the remarkable survival of the states coexisted with strong trends toward uniformity, whether by legislative centralisation or by co-operative harmonisation. The dissolution of Prussia by the Allied Control Council in 1946 eliminated an important institutional basis of co-operative harmonisation. In the Bonn Republic, the relationship between the states was characterised by a relative symmetry of power unknown in the past which might have complicated the problems of federal co-ordination. Moreover, the Western Allies insisted on decentralising the fiscal system. However, soon after the restoration of autonomous German political authorities at the state level, these developed alternative mechanisms of policy harmonisation, beginning with informal talks between state bureaucrats (e.g. to safeguard uniform practices of fiscal administration jeopardised by Allied decentralisation efforts), and culminating first in the creation as early as 1948 of the Permanent Conference of Ministers of Education (*Kultusministerkonferenz*), as the functional equivalent of a federal ministry. These developments in the first years after the Second World War signified the discovery of the practice of co-operative federalism, but its adaptation to German institutional tradition also clearly reinforced the immanent bias of co-operative federalism towards the executive level.

These developments interacted with the increasing aversion of large sectors of public opinion to regional disparities and cultural heterogeneity. The massive migration flows in the post-war years due to the expulsion of 13 million Germans from the former provinces in East Germany and from Eastern Europe contributed to the rapid erosion of formerly homogeneous regional cultures. The decline of religion as a factor of cultural identity further reinforced the trend toward a homogeneity which clearly distinguishes present-day Germany from the divisions that still characterised Germany in the first decades of this century. This pervasive trend toward homogenisation was further reinforced by a constitutional and administrative jurisprudence which emphasised the formal equality of citizens' rights and strongly contributed to a defensive strategy of bureaucracies based on procedural formalisation and uniformisation, particularly in sensitive domains such as education. To achieve these aims, instead of outright centralisation, this alternative strategy of 'unitarisation' became characteristic of post-war federalism, i.e. the progressive harmonisation of administrative regulations and standard operating procedures. Conferences of state ministers, of which the Conference of Ministers of Education is the best known example, are the most important instruments for such policy homogenisation. The strategy of 'unitarisation' permitted the further promotion of the overriding imperative of 'homogeneity of living conditions', but as an alternative to outright centralisation it safeguarded the organisational domain and organisational autonomy of the *Länder* administrations.

It is not out of place to mention some exceptions to these generalisations. There are some important fields where the new decentralisation in the Federal Republic led to heterogeneous solutions, most notably in the organisation of local government, the regulation of the media, and the educational system. In local government, different approaches by the Occupation Powers led to a new diversity of institutions. This diversity was long maintained, if only because it was in the obvious political interest of state party organisations to preserve newly established patterns of locally vested interests.[4] Similar trends characterised the regulation of radio and television. In primary and secondary education, on the other hand, party ideology was the driving force behind the re-emergence of contrasting patterns of organisation. Even in these fields, however, harmonisation of standard operating procedures was always strongly valued and encouraged. Here too, contemporary German federalism is thus characterised by a strange combination of decentralisation of autonomous bureaucracies with substantive harmonisation of policies and highly developed procedural uniformity.

Entanglements in Fiscal Federalism

In a parallel development, fiscal federalism has become a strongly integrated revenue sharing system. As a consequence, German fiscal federalism is worlds apart from the model federalism of public choice theories. Its development in recent decades can even be read as an effort to eliminate the principle of 'fiscal equivalence' (Olson, 1969) as far as possible. Instead, the German variant of fiscal federalism has increasingly become characterised by joint decision-making.

The idea of a clear separation of fiscal powers never took root in Germany because of strong vested institutional interests in the entanglement of fiscal responsibilities, which can be traced back for more than a century. When Bismarck's system was first established, customs and indirect taxes were the most important sources of revenue for the *Reich*, and since this was not sufficient in the era of liberal trade policies, the Imperial government depended on additional allocations from the states (*Matrikularbeiträge*) regularly voted by the *Bundesrat*. The introduction of protectionist customs duties after Bismarck's U-turn in economic policy in 1876 might have ended this dependence of the *Reich* on the states. However, the supporters of state rights in the *Reichstag* successfully introduced a clause (*Franckensteinsche Klausel*) capping the *Reich*'s share of duties and giving the rest to the states, with the consequence that for the following decades the *Reich* continued to depend on *Matrikularbeiträge* from the states. What is observed here is the emergence of a policy repertory where the institutionalisation of mutual resource dependency becomes a fundamental guideline of fiscal federalism and which remained important even after the *Reich* had succeeded in establishing its autonomous tax base. As for the Federal Republic it may be sufficient to point out that the system of divided fiscal responsibilities and divided revenues which the Western Allies imposed in 1949 has gradually been replaced by a system of revenue-sharing in which the most important taxes (notably income and value-added taxes) are joint sources of revenue which can only be voted by a federal law with the assent of the *Bundesrat*.

The contrast with the doctrines of 'fiscal equivalence' is particularly striking in the constitutional requirements for the system of revenue-sharing: These requirements include 'achieving a fair adjustment' and 'safeguarding the homogeneity of living conditions on the federal territory' (art.106 (3)). It is therefore not surprising that the *Länder* have virtually no competence to raise their own taxes. Rather, most major taxes are levied on the basis of federal legislation, and their yields are divided in fixed proportions between the federal and the *Länder* governments (*Steuerverbund*).[5] The fiscal resources of the member states are partially equalised through complex formulas for horizontal transfers governed by federal legislation (*Länderfinanzausgleich*).

All this, however, does not signify a hierarchical preponderance of the federal level. The rules for revenue-sharing are subject to approval by the *Bundesrat* and hence must be agreed, always after extremely laborious negotiations, between the *Bund* (the federal level of government) and the *Länder*. The functioning of federal decentralisation is thus strongly dependent on the system of revenue-sharing. On this issue the larger west German *Länder* have a veto position in the *Bundesrat*.

The Emergence of Interlocking Politics (*Politikverflechtung*)

Since the foundation of the Federal Republic, the federal government has increasingly intervened in state policy, notably in economic and social areas, through grants-in-aid to the weaker *Länder*. The resulting *Mischverwaltung* (mixed administration) was often criticised on constitutional and political grounds. In the late 1960s and 1970s, the (hitherto para-constitutional) practice of federal grants-in-aid was therefore transformed into a complex system of jointly administered federal-state programmes (Scharpf *et al.*, 1976). This integration of policies and politics between the different levels of government (*Politikverflechtung*) arose from the typical 1960s' enthusiasm for 'systems politics', in the same way as the design for an integrated system of budgetary planning developed at the same time. However, many of the hopes that were originally placed in these schemes were deceived. The 1980s saw a return toward decentralisation with autonomous action by the *Länder* in areas such as industrial and social policy. (Hucke and Wollmann, 1989; Jürgens and Krumbein, 1991; Hesse, Benz, 1990, pp.158ff.; Schmid, 1990).

In the Adenauer years, co-operative federalism first developed in two directions. One was 'horizontal co-operation', i.e. the evolving practice of inter-state or 'self-coordination' (*Selbstkoordinierung*) including all state governments and based on principles of unanimity conforming with the historical tradition of quasi-diplomatic inter-state relations. The other was 'vertical co-operation', consisting in particular of a growing practice of federal grants-in-aid, especially to states with important depressed regions. A new stage in the evolution of co-operative federalism was initiated by the 'Grand Coalition' of CDU and SPD (1966-1969). This coalition is mostly seen as a mere transitory phase in the development of the German party system and its importance for the institutional development of German federalism is often underrated. One central motive for the formation of this coalition was indeed a re-organisation of the federal system conforming to the postulates of 'systems politics' (Schick, 1969) which were so much *en vogue* at that time when Western governments attempted co-ordinated and long-term policy-making, with budgetary planning, Keynesian management of the macro-economy and of public finance, systematic territorial planning and so on, and when even Walter Ulbricht lectured the SED *Politbüro* on the virtues of cybernetics as the new science of political management. This 'systems approach' to policy formation even survived the Grand Coalition for several years and culminated in the 1972 interim report of a select committee (*Enquete-Kommission*) on constitutional reform which envisaged a complex system of 'integrated joint planning' in which a common 'planning committee' of federal and state representatives should decide on the goals and priorities of joint policy planning, which were to become binding for both federal and state governments.

Following the 1972 elections, the select committee dropped this over-ambitious proposal. Soon afterwards the mood changed, and 'system politics' gave way to a new scepticism toward planning and co-ordination. However, the preceding decade had left a heritage of increased unitarisation, either by outright centralisation, or by joint policy-making in the complex institutional framework of *Politikverflechtung* which had been established in the meantime and which remained a significant feature of German federalism. What calls for explanation is the readiness of state governments to abandon so many fields of autonomous influence without which this new unitarising wave would not have been possible. Essentially it can be explained by a political bargain in which the states exchanged their autonomy against federal funding, and this on the condition that all decisions should be taken in bodies (either in the *Bundesrat* or in federal-state committees) where the state governments had a decisive say and collectively were in a position to veto decisions.

It has often been asserted that state parliaments have lost most of their political influence because of the increased importance of co-operative federalism and *Politikverflechtung*. Indeed, the bargaining role of the executive has been strengthened at the expense of state parliaments. However, it should not be overlooked that state bureaucracies are now closely controlled by the governing parties (Mayntz and Derlien, 1989). Also, since state parties enjoy considerable political autonomy from the federal party organisation, party government at the *Länder* level is an important potential source of political diversity and of political innovation originating from the regional party organisations (Schmid, 1990a/b). Thanks to this autonomy of state parties, it appears justified to speak of a revival of policy diversity at the state level since the late 1970s, in spite of the persistent trend toward inter-administrative unitarisation.

Territorial Boundaries: From Flux to Stability

In current controversies about the complexities of fiscal federalism, probably the most common complaints are about the differences in size and in fiscal strength of the 16 states which allegedly make territorial re-organisation highly desirable. Indeed, such disparities were considerably increased by unification since four of the five east German states are clearly below average size. Such complaints have a long tradition, however. In a longer-term perspective, it is easy to arrive at the conclusion that this reform discussion is politically futile. It is a striking feature of German federalism that, although the number and the boundaries of German states have changed considerably in the course of history, under the impact of democratisation they have become remarkably stable. Napoleon radically redrew the map of Germany in 1803-1807. So did the Congress of Vienna in 1815, Bismarck in 1866 and the Allied Powers in 1946, and this history of territorial re-organisation has apparently created a belief among the German political class that territorial boundaries are still at the disposition of institutional engineering. This assumption, however, is flawed. It is true that the Basic Law included a clause specifying the procedure for re-organising the number and the boundaries of states (art. 29), and in the 1950s and 1960s two expert commissions invested much energy into drawing maps which presumably conformed more closely to considerations of economic and fiscal efficiency and political viability. Similar illusions of power re-emerged in the process of amending the constitution after unification (cf. the new version of art. 29, presumably now rendered more practicable). Although hitherto almost all these efforts were wasted, large sectors of public opinion continue to cultivate this century-old topic, but the main interest of this continuity is that we have here an interesting symptom of the power of traditional rhetorical images such as *Kleinstaaterei* ('small-state-ism') in German federalism. Since 1867, territorial re-organisation not imposed from outside has become a rare exception, the most important cases being the merger of the Thuringian states in 1920 and of Baden-Württemberg in 1952. It can be safely predicted that after the recent failure of an attempted merger of Berlin and Brandenburg the chances of future successful territorial changes in present-day Germany have become extremely remote.

A Polycentric or a Centralised Society?

In his analysis of the (old) Federal Republic of Germany as a 'semi-sovereign state', Katzenstein (1987) argues that 'the dispersion of state power contrasts sharply with the concentration of private power in large social groups' (p.15). This apparent co-existence of a 'decentralised state' and a 'centralised society' is, however, less paradoxical if we take the peculiar institutional logic of German federalism into account. As it emerged after Bismarck, it blended the federal heritage of the *Deutsche Bund* with the unitary aspirations of the liberal bourgeoisie. As has already been pointed out, the German state, although it is decentralised, produces largely uniform policies. As a logical consequence of this 'cooperative unitarisation', social groups affected by these policies co-ordinate their activities through concentrated forms of organisation.

A significant instance of this reactive 'centralisation of society' is the system of industrial relations. Students of cross-national labour relations have often ranked West Germany as a case characterised by (at best) medium-level centralisation (Cameron, 1984, p.165; Thelen, 1991, pp.38ff.). Not only has the German Confederation of Labour Unions (*Deutscher Gewerkschaftsbund*) no authority over collective bargaining. In a majority of the industrial unions collective bargaining formally takes place not on the national but on a regional level. However, this formal organisational distribution of jurisdiction is overestimated in the above-mentioned cross-national rankings. They neglect the pervasive trends toward coordinated settlements. If we take the most important industrial union, the *Industriegewerkschaft Metall* (Metal Workers' Union), a wage agreement reached in one district of the metal industry is typically adopted in a more or less similar form in all other districts. It even often sets the pace for the other industrial unions. There are good reasons to assume that this characteristic 'pattern bargaining', as it is called in the United States, is the result of concertation between the large industrial unions normally considered as 'wage leaders' (the metal workers, public sector, and chemical workers unions) (Seitenzahl, 1976, pp.105ff.). It is still more remarkable that, in spite of repeated calls from segments of the employer community for a greater regional 'spread' of wage rates, the employers' organisations have usually acquiesced to this homogenisation of wage levels. In the public sector there is even a nation-wide collective agreement for white-collar employees (*Bundesangestelltentarif*) with uniform wage levels. It is periodically renegotiated between the public sector unions and a coalition of employers from the federal, state and local governments (*Tarifgemeinschaft des Bundes, der Länder und Gemeinden*) led by the Federal Minister of the Interior.[6] It thus appears that the postulate of 'homogeneity of living conditions' has become a fundamental social norm which is internalised by collective actors in the private as well as in the public sector. Also, it is implemented, just as in inter-governmental relations, through bargaining among formally decentralised organisations.

Another example of this blend of decentralisation and unitary policy outcomes is the organisation of public television. According to the decision of the Federal Constitutional Court, broadcasting belongs to the jurisdiction of the *Länder*. Public radio corporations are therefore mostly state-wide institutions, or they cover two or more states on the basis of inter-state contracts.[7] Television was first organised by these state radio corporations, but they formed also a syndicate (*Arbeitsgemeinschaft der Rundfunkanstalten Deutschlands, ARD*) for tasks such as the joint production of nation-wide news bulletins and the establishment of an international network of correspondents. Later, through an inter-state compact, the *Länder* established a second, nation-wide TV network (*Zweites Deutsches*

Fernsehen, ZDF). Therefore, although broadcasting continues to be formally decentralised, the public has become presented with public nation-wide TV news bulletins which form a distinct contrast to the polycentric organisation of the private print media.

In Germany, therefore, the 'centralisation' of society bears no resemblance to that found in France, for example. So far in the Federal Republic there has been nothing like one 'centre' that might be set in opposition to the 'periphery'. Rather, the strong organisational position of the *Länder* resulted in the maintenance of a plurality of 'centres'. German society, despite its powerful peak associations, thus mirrored the decentralisation of the state by its strongly polycentric organisation. A case in point are the well-entrenched regional policy networks (Lehmbruch, 1989). Again, this institutional regionalisation has strong roots in German history. After 1918, state bureaucracies, now controlled by regional party coalitions, became the focal points of regional inter-organisational networks linking state administrations to the regional society. This polycentrism of regional policy networks linking state and society was again further increased after the Second World War. Under the occupation regime, the central networks of interest articulation and intermediation disappeared with the central government. Instead, new regional policy networks emerged around the West German *Länder*. Important interest associations adopted a decentralised regional organisation. Even after the foundation of the Federal Republic, these regional units remained important because of the salience of the *Länder* for the implementation of federal as well as state policies (Streeck, 1989; Mayntz, 1990).

On top of that, Germany had no capital city as a dominant centre before the foundation of Bismarck's *Reich* in 1867/1871. Even during the eight decades when Berlin was the German capital it did not gain the same overwhelming preponderance which Paris and London had acquired over many centuries.[8] This polycentrism increased when, with the division of Germany after the Second World War, Berlin lost its functions as the German capital. It was not only governmental functions which were displaced from Berlin, however. With the division of Germany, many leading firms and associations moved away from Berlin to the major centres of West Germany. Thus, the big banks were established in Frankfurt/Main, which is now the seat of the Federal Bank. Similarly, the headquarters of the labour unions were dispersed across various west German states. Siemens, the firm that was originally a leader in the drive originating from Prussia, and increasingly from Berlin, towards making Germany a first-rate industrial power, moved to Munich. Here it established close links with the Bavarian government and the governing regional party, the CSU. Bonn, of course, became a central target of lobbyism, and many associations established their federal headquarters in the region. However, apart from its administrative and political importance, Bonn remained a second-rank city compared to the larger west German state capitals. One important aspect of this regionalisation is the organisation of finance. Despite the well-known national finance institutions, such as the three private 'big banks', an important part of the banking system is made up of the public regional institutions (*Landesbanken*) that head the organisations of savings and loan banks.[9] Similarly, the organisation of co-operative banks (for agriculture and small businesses) is strongly decentralised. Even the private regional banks have strong informal links with the respective state governments.

In post-war West Germany, this polycentric organisation of society has had a remarkable impact on the spatial growth patterns of the economy. Whereas 'centralised societies' in a strict sense are often characterised by strong inter-regional economic disparities between the centre and the peripheral regions, the decentralised political organisation of the Federal Republic strengthened the polycentric regional 'policy networks'. These structures served to mitigate tendencies toward a spatial concentration of economic activity. Characteristically, although ordo-liberal indictments of industrial *Strukturpolitik* as being supposedly incompatible with the 'social market economy', found broad public acceptance, this verdict never impaired the legitimacy from which regional economic policy in the Federal Republic benefited. While this policy mix of federal ordo-liberal orthodoxy on the macro level (Lehmbruch, 1992) and *Länder* interventionism had been quite successful for the 'old' Federal Republic, these traditional differences in economic strategies proved fatal when the federal government assumed strategic leadership in the process of unification.

Federalism and the Competitive Party System

It has already been indicated that after 1918 regional parties became autonomous political players at the side of the *Länder* bureaucracies. During the Weimar Republic, however, their political weight was often inferior to that of the party headquarters in Berlin. This predominance of national party organisations did not reappear in the Federal Republic. In particular, the CDU and the FDP emerged as loose federations of regional party organisations, while the regional party leaders (*Landesfürsten* or 'princes') played key roles in the federal party organisation. The SPD was originally characterised by the antagonism of state party leaders and the federal party headquarters under Schumacher and Ollenhauer. But after Willy Brandt, at that time mayor of West Berlin, assumed the party leadership, the influence of regional organisations on the federal party became stronger. In the 1990s, thanks to Social Democratic control of the governments in the majority of German states, this 'regionalisation' of party leadership has reached its highest point.

The symbiosis of federalism and party government has ambiguous consequences. Elsewhere it has been shown how the emergence of a bipolar party system centring around the competition of two big parties, each with a pretension to government leadership, created a structural tension with a federal system based on the co-operation of federal and state executives (Lehmbruch, 1998). In the Weimar Republic, federalism and the party system were structurally compatible because no potential leadership parties existed and the basis of government coalitions at both levels of government was shifting and partially overlapping. This situation changed with the bipolar competition that came to characterise the Federal Republic. At the federal level, it resulted in party conflict impacting strongly on the *Bundesrat*, because an adverse *Bundesrat* majority can greatly complicate the task of a *Bundestag* majority. The anticipation of this interdependence by the first federal chancellor, Konrad Adenauer, opened the way for a tradition of federal coalition politics 'spilling over' on to elections and on to the formation of governmental majorities at the state level. Adenauer systematically endeavoured to destroy broad coalitions that still existed in some states because they might have interfered with his policies, but for the first two decades the government could always be reasonably sure of having its basic policies supported by a sympathetic *Bundesrat* majority. However, it was by no means excluded that the states would close ranks against the federal government if they felt that their interests were being violated.

The election of a Social Democratic-Liberal coalition government in 1969 created a new constellation because until Chancellor Schmidt's defeat in 1982 the CDU retained a majority in the Federal Council (*Bundesrat*). The *Bundestag* majority, therefore, was unable to assume to get its bills passed unamended when the assent of the *Bundesrat* was required. Admittedly, few bills were completely blocked by the CDU state governments. Rather, the Christian Democrats used their veto position to arrive at compromises that were finally worked out in the mediation committee (*Vermittlungsausschuß*) formed of members from *Bundestag* and *Bundesrat*. In the past (see the 1976 ed. of Lehmbruch 1998, p.159) I predicted that the Federal Republic might one day be confronted with a mirror image of this constellation: a CDU-led federal government confronted with a *Bundesrat* dominated by the SPD. This prediction was vindicated in 1989 when the then SPD-*Bundestag* opposition for the first time controlled a majority in the *Bundesrat*. Again the outcome of this constellation was a strong constraint on the capacity of the federal majority to pass its bills without compromises, even if meanwhile the majority had refined legislative tactics to reduce the number of bills subject to the assent of the *Bundesrat*. The victory of the 'Red-Green' coalition in the federal elections of 1998 restored the homogeneity of *Bundestag* and *Bundesrat* majorities for a short time, but with the Christian Democratic victory in the following *Land* elections in Hessen, this coalition too had to enter bargaining processes to manage a legislative majority.[10]

One remarkable consequence of these constellations are changes in the internal structure of political parties. Both big parties developed mechanisms of informal co-ordination between 'their' state governments and, eventually, the federal party level. That does not by itself solve the leadership problem of the opposition, however. After the CDU lost the chancellorship in 1969, it soon discovered that party leadership was best exerted by a holder of power at the state level. This was the basis for the rise of Helmut Kohl, at that time head of the state government of Rhineland-Palatinate. However, given that neither of the *Landesfürsten* of a given party can claim an automatic leadership privilege, situations of rivalry may arise which are sometimes difficult to manage. Until 1982 this was the situation of the CDU, with the rivalry of Kohl and Strauß. Until March 1998, when Gerhard Schröder won comfortably in the state elections in Lower Saxony and was declared the official SPD chancellor candidate, the SPD was confronted with a similar competition for leadership between its state premiers *(Ministerpräsidenten)*, Lafontaine and Schröder. Yet even this can be considered as a nemesis of the tradition of executive federalism which makes opposition parties dependent on their state executives.

Notes

1   Montesquieu counted the old *Reich*, together with Holland and the *ligues suisses*, among the *républiques fédératives* which he defined as *sociétés de*

sociétés, qui en font une nouvelle and to which he ascribed the stability of *républiques éternelles* (Esprit des Lois IX, 1).

2 The most important reform alternative discussed in the Weimar years, a merger of the political structures of the *Reich* and of Prussia, with the smaller states obtaining a status somehow comparable to that of the Prussian provinces with their strong self-administration, would have resulted in the transformation of the federal structures of the *Reich* into that of a 'decentralised unitary state'. This alternative was discredited after some of the elements of these projects were taken up by the Nazi regime, although in the framework of a rather chaotic segmented centralism.

3 Public health insurance funds, for example, are organised on a local basis (*Allgemeine Ortskrankenkassen*) and may set different rates although the benefits are uniform.

4 Recently, however, the institutions of South Germany (notably Baden-Württemberg) with the strong position of the directly elected mayor have become a model for local government reform.

5 This *Verbundsystem* was first established in the beginnings of the Weimar Republic: The turnover tax and the income and corporation taxes were levied by the *Reich* which then transferred a fixed percentage to the Länder.

6 The resulting wage rises are then also adopted, by federal legislation, for the salaries of civil servants of all levels of government.

7 *Südwestrundfunk* (Baden-Württemberg and Rhineland-Palatinate), *Norddeutscher Rundfunk* (Lower Saxony, Bremen, Hamburg, Schleswig-Holstein plus Mecklenburg-Pomerania) and *Mitteldeutscher Rundfunk* (Saxony, Saxony-Anhalt, Thuringia).

8 Even the Hitler regime paid tribute to this tradition. In particular, Munich was named 'capital of the (Nazi) movement' and remained the seat of the party headquarters.

9 These are public institutions under the control of local government.

10 Thus the reform of citizenship laws was achieved by a compromise with the liberal Party which, as the minor coalition partner in Rhineland-Palatinate, were able to deliver the decisive key votes.

References

Abromeit, H. (1992), *Der verkappte Einheitsstaat*, Leske + Budrich, Opladen.
Binder, H. O. (1971), *Reich und Einzelstaaten während der Kanzlerschaft Bismarcks 1871-1890*, Mohr, Siebeck, Tübingen.
Cameron, D. R. (1984), 'Social Democracy, Corporatism, Labour Quiescence, and the Representation of Economic Interest in Advanced Capitalist Society', in J.

H. Goldthorpe (ed.), *Order and Conflict in Contemporary Capitalism*, Clarendon Press, Oxford.
Hesse, J. J. and Benz, A. (1990), *Die Modernisierung der Staatsorganisation*, Nomos Verlag, Baden-Baden.
Hesse, K. (1962), *Der unitarische Bundesstaat*, C.F. Müller, Karlsruhe.
Hucke J. and Wollmann, H. (eds) (1989), *Dezentrale Technologiepolitik?*, Birkhäuser, Basel.
Jürgens, U. and Krumbein, W. (1991) (eds), *Industriepolitische Strategien - Bundesländer im Vergleich*, Edition Sigma, Berlin.
Katzenstein, P. J. (1987), *Policy and Politics in West Germany: The Growth of a Semi-Sovereign State*, Temple University Press, Philadelphia.
Lehmbruch, G. (1989), 'Institutional Linkages and Policy Networks in the Federal System of West Germany, *Publius*, vol. 19, pp. 221-35.
Lehmbruch, G. (1992), 'The Institutional Framework of German Regulation', in K. Dyson (ed.), *The Politics of German Regulation*, Dartmouth Publishers, Aldershot et al., pp. 29-52.
Lehmbruch, G. (1998), *Parteienwettbewerb im Bundesstaat: Regelsysteme und Spannungslagen im Institutionengefüge der Bundesrepublik Deutschland*, 2nd rev. ed., Westdeutscher Verlag, Opladen.
Mayntz, R. (1990), 'Organisierte Interessenvertretung und Föderalismus: Zur Verbändestruktur in der Bundesrepublik Deutschland', in T. Ellwein *et al.* (eds), *Jahrbuch zur Staats- und Verwaltungswissenschaft*, vol. 4, pp. 145-56.
Mayntz, R. and Derlien, H.-U. (1989), 'Party Patronage and Politicization of the West German Administrative Elite 1970-1987 - Toward Hybridization?', *Governance*, vol. 2, pp. 384-404.
Mommsen, H. (1980), 'Gouvernementaler Föderalismus und Repräsentativ-verfassung in Deutschland und Österreich', *Czasopismo Prawno-Historyczne*, vol. 32, pp. 117-54.
Olson, M. (1969), 'The principle of 'Fiscal Eqivalence': The Division of Responsibilities among Different Levels of Government, *American Economic Review*, vol. 59, pp. 479-87.
Rauh, M. (1973), *Föderalismus und Parlamentarismus im Wilhelminischen Reich*, Droste Verlag, Düsseldorf.
Scharpf, F. W. *et al.* (1976), *Politikverflechtung: Theorie und Empirie des kooperativen Föderalismus in der Bundesrepublik*, Scriptor Verlag, Kronberg/Ts.
Schick, A. (1969), 'Systems Politics and Systems Budgeting, *Public Administration Review*, vol. 29, pp. 137-51.
Schmid, J. (1990a), *Die CDU. Organisationsstrukturen, Politiken und Funktionsweisen einer Partei im Föderalismus*, Leske + Budrich, Opladen.
Schmid, J. (1990b), 'Bildungspolitik der CDU. Eine Fallstudie zu innerparteilicher Willensbildung im Föderalismus', *Gegenwartskunde*, vol. 39, pp. 303-13.

Seitenzahl, R. (1976), *Gewerkschaften zwischen Kooperation und Konflikt*, Europäische Verlagsanstalt, Frankfurt a.M.
Streeck, W. (1989), 'The Territorial Organization of Interests and the Logics of Associative Action: The Case of Handwerk Organization in West Germany', in W. D. Coleman and H. J. Jacek (eds), *Regionalism, Business Interests and Public Policy*, Sage Publications, London, pp. 59-94.
Thelen, K. (1991), *Union of Parts: Labor Politics in Postwar Germany*, Cornell University Press, Ithaca N.Y.
Tiebout, C. M. (1961), 'An economic theory of fiscal decentralisation, in National Bureau of Economic Research (ed.), *Public Finances: Needs, Sources, and Utilization*, Princeton University Press, Princeton N.J., pp. 79-96.
Weber, M. (1921), 'Bayern und die Parlamentarisierung im Reich', in M. Weber, *Gesammelte Politische Schriften*, Drei Masken Verlag, München.

6 The Development and Present State of Local Government in England and Germany – a Comparison

HELLMUT WOLLMANN

Introduction

This chapter[1] intends to compare the development and current state of local government in the UK, or more precisely in England,[2] and in (western) Germany. In aiming at identifying developmental patterns of the two countries' local government systems, the chapter necessarily has to take an historical view. As it is primarily interested in institutional development, it tends to follow a predominantly institutionalist focus, looking initially at polity rather than at politics and policy without, of course, ignoring these. The chapter proceeds in two major steps. First, country reports are presented in an attempt to give a developmental analysis. Second, a comparative analysis and summary are given.

In order to pursue the theme of institutional development, the article particularly addresses three dimensions of local government:

- Vertically: the (intergovernmental) status of local government in the national state (e.g. tiers and territorial format, competencies, financial resources etc. of the sub-national levels) which is largely set by central level legislation,
- Horizontally: the provision of the local democratic system as well as of the executive/administrative function of local government, the regulation of which also lies with central level legislation;

- Horizontally: the setting up (and modernisation) of local government, as an administrative system (i.e. organisation, personnel) which is mostly the responsibility of local authorities.

Country Report I: England

The Foundation of Modern Local Self-Government

The development of modern local self-government in England in the course of the 19th century was shaped by somewhat paradoxical constitutional parameters. On the one hand, as a result of England's long development into a parliamentary monarchy, Parliament (*Crown in Parliament*) has risen to hold a politically unchallenged status which has been interpreted as *Parliamentary Sovereignty*. This doctrine is responsible for a number of special features in England's constitutional history. England has no written constitution as a written constitution along with the requirement to have a qualified majority for amendments would bind future Parliaments. Parliament is the master of all other institutions in the country with the power to 'make and break' as it wishes. This is expressed in the *ultra vires* doctrine, according to which all other institutions, including the local authorities, can only exert the powers explicitly assigned to them by an Act of Parliament. When these formal powers are considered, England has the elements of an 'elective dictatorship' with an intrinsically unitary and centralist tendency. On the other hand, England has been ruled by constitutional conventions and practices which have checked such unitary and centralist tendencies and have saved the country throughout its modern history from threats to democracy and civil liberties. This other side of English constitutional history is most strikingly evidenced by the very development of modern English local self-government during the 19th century. English local self-government came to occupy the sub-national level of what has been called a 'dual polity' (Bulpitt, 1983). Despite the formidable *formal* powers of Parliament, the dual polity was characterised by the *practice* of a kind of power-sharing in which the central government level ('Whitehall') and its Oxbridge elite were essentially concerned with 'high politics', such as ruling the Empire and general domestic policy (such as taxation and the general frame-setting for local government). The broad realm of 'low politics' (Ashford, 1982) and policy implementation, however, such as the provision of infrastructure and of social services (in view of the mounting problems raised by industrialisation and urbanisation) were left to the local authorities. Hence, England's central-local government relations were marked by two essential features. First, central government never esta-blished a centralised uniform bureaucracy with a presence at the regional, let alone the local levels (Sharpe, 1993b, p.248; Keating, 1999b, p.3). This contrasts strikingly with Continental Europe where, as a legacy of the former absolutist State tradition, the central State retained a conspicuous institutional presence at the local level as a continuous rival and challenge to local self-government. Second, Parliament chose to restrict itself largely to enabling legislation which put the local authorities in charge without tightly regulating their performance (Jones, 1990, p.171), thus leaving them a wide range of discretion. This again is markedly different from the Continental European legalist system. Against this historical background, 19th century England has been called an unitary, but 'highly decentralised' (Jones, 1990, p.208) country with a 'balanced constitution' (Keating 1999b, p.3). It is under the premise of this 'paradox' (Sharpe, 1993b, p.250) of an almost unlimited potential power of the central government on the one hand, and of the factual 'benign neglect' (Norton, 1994, p.368) of local government by central government on the other, that English local government enjoyed a degree of operational autonomy unparalleled anywhere in contemporary Europe.

In England, the first step towards creating a modern system of local self-government was taken with the Municipal Corporation Act of 1835 which did away with the medieval regime of diverse and haphazardly bestowed rights and privileges of the towns and parishes and placed their powers and functions on a uniform basis (Norton, 1994, p.351). Local responsibilities were assigned to local councils to be elected by general (male) suffrage (Johnson, 1988, p.21). By establishing multi-purpose authorities (along with the continuing existence of many special-purpose authorities, e.g. the Poor Law Boards) and by empowering the localities to levy local taxes (*rates*), the ground rules of modern English local self-government were laid down. In the rural areas, however, the ancient shires remained under the medieval rule of so-called Justices of the Peace appointed by the Crown.

In the 1880s and 1890s, central government entirely reorganised the local government system and created a two-tier local government structure that was to remain until the 1970s. In 1888, by abolishing the medieval regime of the Justices of the Peace but retaining the historic boundaries of the shires, the *counties* (62 in England and Wales) were installed as the upper tier of modern local self-government with a multi-purpose profile.[3] In

1894, in an even more radical move, a completely new local government level was established by creating (535) urban districts, (472) rural districts and (270) boroughs, the elected councils of which were to serve as the lower tier of local government. While the elected councils of the some 10,000 towns and parishes which had been incorporated in 1835 continued to exist, most of their functions were transferred to the district councils.

The fundamental territorial, organisational and political transformation of the sub-national structures in the 1880s and 1890s reveals the very paradox on which English local government has rested and thrived. On the one hand, Parliament was resolved to radically reform the country's sub-national structures. Several reasons for this are apparent. As was already hinted at in the 1835 legislation, central government perceived the need to re-create and modernise local government structures in order to render them capable of coping with the 'low politics' tasks which they were expected to fulfil in the dual polity system, particularly in view of the mounting problems of industrialisation and urbanisation. The plainly rationalist design to create an entirely new level of local government was tinged with utilitarian thinking. The disposition of the national level elite to regard and deal with the sub-national levels in a pronouncedly instrumental way was nourished by an arrogant detachment and even 'culture of disdain' (Greenwood, 1982) with which the central level Oxbridge elite related to the local level and its mundane matters. As a result, local government was seen as an instrument for achieving central government policies rather than as a political entity in its own right rooted in local identity and politically representing its local population. On the other hand, it was the momentous reforms of the 1880s and 1890s that laid the territorial and institutional groundwork for the flowering of the Victorian model of local self-government which was the 'golden age of local self-government' (Norton, 1994, p.352). Elected by general (male) suffrage, the local councils exercised their political and administrative functions through 'government by committee' over a broad range of responsibilities. They enjoyed wide discretion of their own and were subjected to little interference and oversight by central government. As an expression and central feature of their autonomy, the local authorities financed their expenditures almost entirely from a locally levied tax. It is small wonder that liberals and democrats in contemporary Continental Europe admiringly looked at and, to some extent, were also mystified by English local self-government.

The Emergence of the Welfare State

Since the 1920s the Victorian model of local self-government has undergone continuous change as central government, with the emergence of the welfare state, proceeded to 'nationalise' and expand infrastructure and social policy concerns, which had until then been largely left to the local authorities, and to turn the local authorities increasingly into instruments of national welfare state policies. Climaxing in the 1940s and 1970s, this development was promoted by a sequence of central policy measures and legislative acts which significantly changed the profile of local responsibilities, on the one hand, by taking away time-honoured local tasks (gas and electricity were transferred to nationalised bodies in the 1940s, health care was taken over by the National Health Service after 1945) and, on the other, by allocating or strengthening others (particularly education, housing, personal social services). As a result, the local authorities were made the main social service provider and their functional importance was greatly enhanced, bringing their expenditure from 5.1 per cent of GNP in 1900 to 18 per cent in 1975 (Jones, 1991, p.179). At the same time, their financial dependence on central government continuously increased. While until 1920 only 25 per cent of local expenditures came from central government grants, the share of central government money steadily grew after 1940 (Sharpe, 1993, p.250).

Major territorial change took place as a result of the Local Government Act of 1972, when central government recast the Victorian local government structure.[4] The counties were redrawn and their number reduced from 62 to 47 (with an average of 730,000 inhabitants); the number of districts (as well as boroughs) was also drastically cut by means of amalgamation (now averaging 125,000 inhabitants). The level of towns and parishes (with elected councils and minor local functions) was left unchanged. In carrying out this far-reaching territorial reform central government again displayed that instrumental and efficiency-minded resolve which guided it in the great territorial reform at the end of the last century. Compared to the territorial local government reforms which had also been pursued since the 1960s by central governments of other European countries, the territorial changes carried out in England were by far the most radical. Thus, after amalgamation England constitutes an extreme case of what has been called the 'North European type' of local government size (Marcou and Verebelyi, 1993, p.382; Baldersheim *et al.*, 1994, pp.25 ff.).

Administrative Reforms

The steady expansion of local government responsibilities which accompanied the advances of the welfare state have led to a concomitant growth of local government personnel, particularly in the administration of the counties which accounted for 75 per cent of local government expenditure. This development was further driven by the 'principle of self-sufficiency' (Jones, 1991), according to which the social services have been directly delivered by the local authorities rather than by voluntary organisations. The further build-up of local government personnel has been accompanied, particularly since the 1960s, by their progressive professionalisation and departmentalisation (see Schröter and Röber in this volume).

While significantly enhancing the administrative performance of local administration, this progressive professionalisation tends to foster the fragmentation of local politics and administration along sectoral policy, departmental and professional lines (Stewart, 1995, p.7). Furthermore, professionalisation is prone to waken the inherent tensions between the traditional modality of local self-government ('government by committee', i.e. by elected councillors acting on an essentially 'amateur' basis) on the one hand, and the (full-time) professionals on the other hand (Jones, 1990, p.171; Bennett, 1989, pp.5 ff.). During the 1970s, attempts were made to counteract these inherent centrifugal tendencies by promoting 'corporate management' which was intended to bring the functional departments together (Rose, 1982, p.109) and to set up single 'policy and resource committees' designed to co-ordinate the council committees.

Local Government Under Conservative Siege

In 1979 the Conservatives under Mrs. Thatcher returned to power after a landslide victory, opening a period of nearly 20 years of Conservative Party rule. The central government embarked upon a series of policy and legislative measures which have deeply remoulded and significantly reduced the functional and political status of local government. At the outset, the Conservative government was mainly concerned with curbing the financial power and discretion of the local authorities. A series of measures, including particularly the initial attempt at 'capping' the traditional *rate* (property tax) and replacing it by the 'council tax' (a largely flat rate per capita tax), later diluted into a 'community charge', was targeted at curtailing the local discretion on local spending which was at the heart of the traditional local government model. Later the Conservative government, intensifying the neo-liberal battle-cry of a 'minimal state' and proclaiming the tenets of New Public Management, turned to radically cutting back the local government sector. As the local authorities (and their professional staffs) traditionally claimed and exerted a virtual monopoly in the direct delivery of social services, it was these 'municipal empires' (Norton, 1994, p.377) that particularly came under Conservative fire.

In what has been labelled a downright 'war waged by central government' (Sharpe, 1998, p.1) against (largely Labour dominated) local government, Thatcherite policy was pursued on a number of fronts.

- By *privatisation* the local authorities were legally obliged to sell council housing (particularly to sitting tenants),
- By *compulsory competitive tendering (CCT)* local authorities were legally bound to put services and activities out for tender and, hence, to resume an enabling rather than a directly delivering function,
- By *transferring* local government functions and responsibilities from the elected councils to special-purpose agencies and organisations (quasi-non-governmental organisations – *Quangos)*, the boards of which were appointed by central government[5] and financially largely dependent on central government grants. The impact of this 'quangoisation' has been seen by critics as further dismantling the former multi-purpose profile of local government, and adding to the fragmenting tendencies already under way in professional 'departmentalisation', (Stewart, 1995, p.32).
- Under the Local Government Act of 1985 the Greater London Council and the six Metropolitan Councils were abolished, leaving London split up and run by 33 borough councils.

Although far from all of the approximately 100 Conservative Acts of Parliament directed at remoulding local government (Stoker, 1998, p.372) were effectively implemented, while some were explicitly revoked, in their aggregate effect they have reshaped the political and functional status of local government in the British government system more profoundly than any other central government intervention in modern times. They have made the 'central state in Britain now more powerful in relation to the localities than it has ever been in the past' (Sharpe, 1998, p.1). In an international context in which the trend in other European countries has been towards decentralisation, the Thatcherite 'revolution' has turned Britain from an 'unitary, highly decentralised' into a 'unitary, highly centralised country' (Jones, 1991, p. 208) falling 'out of step with the rest of Europe' (Stoker, 1998).

The Swing of the Pendulum?

After Labour's return to power in 1997, it is still unclear at present whether the pendulum will swing back to re-strengthening the autonomy of local government (for the current debate see also Hambleton, 1998). In the recent White Paper 'Modern Local Government in Touch with the People' a series of relevant measures has been proposed and discussed (DETR, 1998). It has been noted, however, that the new 'Labour government seems to have tacitly accepted the diminished role of local government achieved by its predecessor' (Sharpe, 1998, p.19) While declaring that some measures introduced by the Conservative government, such as compulsory competitive tendering (CCT), will be abolished (DETR, 1998, p.15), the Labour government appears to be particularly eager to pursue a project of modernising local government that 'may be interpreted as a further step in the continuing trend of the central regulation and control of local government. Using incentives, inspectorates, regulatory control and reserve powers, the government's plans imply that local authorities work best when closely supervised' (Brooks, 1998, p.26). Thus, it seems likely that Labour will basically continue the high degree of central government control inherited from the Conservative era. This would be a further example of the 'moving consensus' (Rose 1980, Page, 1990) which in British politics has characterised the sequence of government changes.

Yet, prompted by the most recent government changes two new institutional developments have gained momentum. First, the UK has embarked upon regionalising the country. In accordance with its electoral promises, the new Labour government put the establishment of a Scottish Parliament and a Welsh Assembly to regional referendums. The former was approved by an overwhelming majority, the latter only very narrowly (Keating, 1999, p.13). Whether England will also undergo some regionalisation remains to be seen. The second strand of institutional change relates to the regulation of local government as *local democracy*. Alarmed by low local election turn-outs which recently fell below 40 per cent (DETR, 1998, p.14),[6] the new government has proposed measures intended to revive local democracy. First, (consultative) referendums were proposed for a more direct involvement of the local population (DETR, 1998, p.8). This process was first used in London on May 7, 1998 when there was a referendum on whether to have a directly elected (executive) mayor and to establish a 'Greater London Authority' (Schröter, 1998). Similarly, a proposal has been aired to politically and functionally revitalise the parish councils which were referred to recently as 'an essential part of the structure of local democracy in our country' (DETR, 1998, p.19).

Furthermore, a reform drive has gained prominence that is directed at significantly changing a time-honoured assumption underlying traditional local government, namely that political and executive leadership in all local government matters lies solely with the elected council and particularly its committees. It has been increasingly recognised, however, that this collegiate voluntary conduct of the executive leadership has become increasingly incapable of coping with the complex problems of modern city administration and dealing with professional staffs. The result is 'confusion and inefficiency' (DETR, 1998, p.8). In the English reform debate various institutional options have been put forward which all share the idea of a certain separation of power or at least of a 'separation of roles' (DETR, 1998, p.26) moving towards a dualistic distinction between the deliberative competence of the elected council (as a collegiate body) and an executive function (with a monocratic connotation). Most local authorities in England appear, at the moment, to favour a cabinet model with an executive leader elected by the council.

Country Report II: Germany

The Emergence of Strong Local Self-Administration on a Limited Democratic Basis

Dating back to the late feudal times of the Middle Ages and to the emergence of the absolutist State in the 17th century, Germany at the beginning of the 19th century was still divided into a multitude of kingdoms, principalities and small domains with the Holy Roman Empire an ever more fictitious power. After having gained and for centuries defended their status as 'free cities' amid late-feudal rural backwardness and servitude, most cities then lost their independence to absolutist rulers.

After their defeat in the Napoleonic wars, which exposed their political, institutional and economic weaknesses, the late-absolutist German States introduced local self-government as a means, particularly in the eyes of 'enlightened' state bureaucrats (Hesse, 1990, p.354), of modernising the outdated state structure and of invigorating society. In Prussia the liberal reform-minded Freiherr vom Stein masterminded the Prussian Municipal Charter (*Preussische Städteordnung*) of 1808. Programmatically declaring the intention to 'set free and support the civic spirit of the citizens by participation', the Prussian Municipal Charter set out a remarkable local self-government model (Engeli and Haus, 1975, p.100). In a general competence provision the elected municipal council was given 'unrestricted power to decide on all matters of the municipal communality'. In mirroring the historical context of the still authoritarian State, (male) suffrage was, however, restricted and largely linked to property ownership within the municipality. Along with the elected council, an elected board (*Magistrat*) was established by the council, consisting of councillors and other competent citizens and was, in a somewhat 'dualistic' concept, assigned the executive function in local matters. Finally, the provision was made that besides executing local matters, the board, in a double functions modality, could also be put in charge of carrying out tasks delegated by the State. The Charter, however, applied only to municipalities and not to the localities in the wide rural areas still ruled by the feudalistic aristocracy. Similar municipal charters and ordinances followed in the other German States, ushering in the multitude and variety of municipal regulations which have been characteristic of the sub-national legislative history of Germany ever since.

The further fate of local self-government in the course of the 19th century was crucially determined by the largely abortive liberal 1848 Revolution. In the ensuing constitutional compromise, the State and its bureaucracy and military remained firmly in the hands of the semi-authoritarian monarchic rulers with the government appointed by the monarch and not responsible to parliament, while the local level was left to the property-owning and entrepreneurial bourgeoisie as a realm of local self-administration (for a classic treatise of 19th century German local government see Heffter, 1950). The divide between State (remaining in the domain of the authoritarian monarch) and Society (essentially the realm of economic and civic activities separated from, if not in opposition to the State and largely identified with the urban bourgeoisie) became a dominant concept in German 19th century political thinking and was philosophically extolled by Hegel. As both the monarchic rulers and the bourgeoisie were interested in excluding the rapidly growing urban working class from local political influence, local election laws were introduced in the German States after 1848 which, through discriminatory property and income requirements, largely disfranchised urban workers and granted the vote to only between 10 and 20 per cent of the male population. This situation remained until 1919 (Engeli and Haus, 1978, p.375; von Saldern, 1999, p.25). This undemocratic basis of local government was reinforced even more, as in many German States the so-called 'two chamber system' was introduced, meaning that the decisions taken by the elected council (the first chamber) needed to be approved by the board (elected by the council) in order to keep a check on the council itself.

Hence, the development of local self-administration was embedded throughout the 19th century until the First World War in a peculiar kind of 'dual polity'. Central level government and the German States were mainly concerned with foreign and military policies and, following contemporary Manchester liberalism beliefs, largely refrained from directly dealing with the infrastructural and social problems caused by rapid industrialisation and urbanisation. Local government was left the task of dealing with these problems – within the legislative regulations and under the supervision of the central government level. Increasingly giving their support to the monarchic State, conservative liberals came to welcome the idea of local self-government being but a decentralised modality state administration to be carried out by local worthies on a voluntary basis. Supported by the contemporary legal doctrine, the concept of local government constituting an essentially unpolitical form of local self-administration, and even as a form of 'indirect State administration' (*mittelbare Staatsverwaltung*) has influenced the juridical thinking and terminology on local self-government to the present day (Wollmann 1999b).

It was on this model of local self-administration and its plutocratic political basis that the German municipalities embarked upon an increasing range of local government activities. Between 1850 and 1913, expenditure on personnel and other items in the German municipalities increased more than twenty-fold, whereas that of the States grew only by six times (Hoffmann 1965, pp.717f). The municipalities assumed an (all-purpose) range of tasks which, encompassing city planning, water, sewage, sanitation, transport, cultural facilities etc. (see Gröttrup, 1973; von Saldern, 1999, p.30) and also 'delegated' State tasks, came to be more comprehensive than probably anywhere in contemporary Europe, including England. Despite their plutocratic political basis, the municipalities, by continuing the poor law tradition of medieval cities, moved towards early welfare state policies which contemporary liberals attacked as 'municipal socialism'. Particularly in the big cities, the establishment of professional administrations proceeded swiftly.[7] They financed their expenditure largely from their own revenues (particularly from a locally levied property and trade tax (*Gewerbesteuer*) and, since 1893, from a locally levied surtax on State income tax).[8] This indicates the remarkable degree of financial independence which the municipalities possessed until the First World War.

Throughout the 19th century, in view of the power retained in rural areas by the landed aristocracy, the introduction of local self-administration in the rural localities and counties (*Kreise*) took a largely separate course. In Prussia, for instance, it was only with the Prussian County Charter of 1872 that the late-medieval counties were finally turned into the upper level of a modern two-tier local self-administration structure (Schmitz, 1991). On the one hand, somewhat linking up with the feudalistic self-government by the landed gentry, the elected councils of the counties were given the power to decide on the county's own matters. On the other hand, reflecting their incorporation into the State and its administrative structure, the *Landrat* as head of the county administration was appointed by the State government and was charged with carrying out delegated state functions as an agent of the State. While, regarding local self-administration matters, the supervision by the State was restricted to a control of legality *(Rechtsaufsicht)*, its control over the execution of State functions was much tighter *(Fachaufsicht)*. This double function model, which was first invented by the French municipal legislation of 1789, came to full institutional and administrative fruition in the German county administration (see Marcou, 1996b, p.371; Wollmann, 1999b, p.200) and eventually became an essential feature of the Germany local administrative tradition.

Local Self-Government in the Turbulence of the Inter-War Years

After the 1918 Revolution and Germany's political transition from the still semi-authoritarian *Reich* of the *Kaiser* to the democratic Weimar Republic, the institutional ground rules of local government were significantly changed in a number of ways.

- The Weimar Constitution of August 11, 1919 guaranteed the communes and counties the right to 'self-administration within the limits of the law' (art. 127) and established the principle of general (male and female) suffrage for local elections. With the enactment of these electoral laws in all the German *Länder*, full local democracy was finally introduced. With the introduction of elective democracy and political party competition at all political levels (*Reich*, *Länder* and local), the integration of decentralised local self-government into the State was completed (Hesse, 1990, p.357) with the 19th century divide between State and Society losing its political and conceptual significance.

- When, in the face of the massive social and economic problems of the post-war period, the new *Reich* government led by the Social Democrats proceeded to make welfare policies a prime national concern, local government was increasingly drawn into the expansion and operation of the welfare state policies (e.g. social housing) now mainly promoted by the *Reich*, but also by the *Länder* governments.
- A fundamental reform of the revenue system in 1920 led to a significant centralisation of the entire tax system, depriving local government of the previously locally levied surtax on income tax, but still leaving them the property and trade tax. As a result, the municipalities became increasingly dependent on *Reich* and *Länder* government grants (von Saldern, 1999, p.33). As a consequence of the worsening economic and social troubles of the late 1920s and early 1930s, the municipalities were thrown into an unprecedented financial crisis and into conflicts with the *Reich* and *Länder* governments to which the latter responded by installing state inspectors (Hesse, 1990, p.358). After the National Socialist seizure of power, the municipalities were muted on their submission to the uniformity (*Gleichschaltung*) of the dictatorial *Führer* principle.

Local Government in the Federal Republic of Germany

After the unconditional surrender of Nazi Germany in 1945, in pursuit of the Western Allies' concept to re-install in their zones of occupation democratic and decentralised structures starting from the bottom, democratic local authorities were the first to be re-installed, before the new *Länder* and finally, in 1949, the Federal Republic of Germany were established. In fact, the local institutions, which were the only administrative units still intact, resumed their activities immediately after the end of hostilities and played a crucial role in coping with the unprecedented destruction and misery caused by the war (Hesse, 1990, p.359).[9]

In the Federal Constitution (*Grundgesetz*) of 1949 it was laid down in the traditional general competence clause that the communes *(Gemeinden)* and, to a slightly lesser degree, the counties *(Kreise)* have the right 'to regulate all matters of the local community within their own responsibility in the framework of the law' (art. 28). Given the two-tier federal system, the local government level is, legally speaking, a constituent part of the *Länder*.

Following their formation, the (West) German *Länder* enacted municipal (and county) charters which exhibited considerable variance in the regulation of the local constitution, depending on different regional traditions and also on the zone of occupation. Some of the *Länder*, typically located in the British Zone, such as North Rhine-Westphalia, enacted council/city manager charters obviously influenced by the (monistic) model of English local self-government. Others, situated in the American Zone, such as Baden-Württemberg and Bavaria, legislated for council/(strong) mayor charters with a mayor directly elected by popular vote (drawing on American local government experience), while *Länder* belonging to the French Zone of Occupation, such as Rhineland-Palatinate, introduced council/mayor charters with the mayor elected by the council (drawing on earlier local charters in the French *maire* tradition). In both variants of the council/mayor charters the executive function was, in a dualistic manner, assigned to the mayor (see Schefold and Neumann, 1996; Knemeyer, 1999).

Accompanied by the growing influence of the federal level in what might be described as a creeping re-centralisation when compared to the early decentralist design of the Federal Republic, the gradual emergence of the welfare state in the 1950s and particularly in the 1960s and 1970s had a number of important repercussions on local government. First, between 1968 and 1977 far-reaching territorial reforms were carried out by the *Länder*. Matching the territorial reforms in progress in other European countries, these were intended to improve the planning and administrative capacities of the some 24,000 communes and 240 counties which existed in 1968 with boundaries often dating from the 19th century and even earlier (Laux, 1999, p.175). Confronted with a conflict of goals between increasing administrative efficiency and retaining the small scale of local democracy, the *Länder* chose different strategies, depending in part on the regional political culture and the intensity of local opposition. In North Rhine-Westphalia, which followed a course of large-scale amalgamation, the municipalities now average 43,000 inhabitants, which puts them among the 'North European type' of territorial reform. By contrast, other *Länder*, particularly in southern Germany, pursued a more restrained policy of amalgamation by allowing many small localities to retain their legal entity and their own elected council and mayor; yet obliging them to give up their own (tiny) administrations and to have their administrative tasks performed, together with other small localities, by a joint administrative unit organised in different modalities (*Ämter, Verwaltungsgemeinschaften* etc.). Thus, while the total number of some 24,000 communes was reduced to about 8,400, less than half of these have their own administration. The number of counties was cut from 425 to 237 (Laux, 1999, p.175). Since a new level of joint administrative units (*Ämter* etc.) was created, institutionally located between the counties and the communes, another (fifth!) institutional level has been added to the already overcrowded set-up of the *Länder*, which already consisted of the *Land* government, the administrative district (*Regierungspräsidium*), county and commune levels.

Furthermore, the status and the functions of local government in the political and administrative system of the Federal Republic have been significantly affected by the expansion of federal as well as *Länder* legislation and policy programmes with the development of the welfare state. This is particularly true for the 1960s and early 1970s when, especially promoted by the Social Democrat-led federal government which took office in 1969, a broad range of reformist policies was embarked upon, such as infrastructural policies (urban renewal, urban mass transport) as well as social and environmental policies, which were not only of immediate local concern but were to be implemented mainly by the local government level (Bönker and Wollmann, 1996, p.447).

Administrative Reforms

In the face of the new policy tasks which the local government level was expected to carry out, and in response to the planning creed and administrative reform discussions of the 1960s and 1970s, many municipalities and counties endeavoured in this period to modernise their organisational and personnel structures. One crucial area of establishing new staffs and procedures was seen in city planning, which was regarded as a key to future city development. Other reform efforts were directed at making the administration more accessible to the citizen (*bürgernahe Verwaltung*) (Wollmann, 1997c, pp.85 ff). The wave of administrative modernisation which seized the German municipalities in the 1970s was probably more intensive and consequential than in most other European countries.

Since the early 1990s, the German municipalities and counties have embarked upon a new wave of administrative reform as a response to their mounting budgetary difficulties and have finally joined the *New Public Management* (NPM) debate which has raged internationally since the early 1980s and had an early impact in the UK. There seem to be several reasons why the German municipalities were such latecomers to the debate. First, while NPM, in one of its central criticisms, attacks the monopoly of local government in service delivery (as is the case in the UK), it should be remembered that according to the so-called traditional subsidiarity principle in German local government, social services have been delivered by non-public non-profit-making (welfare) organisations rather than by the local authorities and their personnel. Furthermore, dating back to the establishment of a professional administration in the late 19th century, German local administration has had the reputation, not least among foreign observers, of being efficient and correct. Meanwhile, the NPM discussion and modernisation projects are in full swing (Reichard, 1994; Reichard and Wollmann, 1996; Grunow and Wollmann, 1998; more generally on public sector modernisation in Germany: Wollmann, 1997c; Schröter and Wollmann, 1997; Derlien, 1996; Benz and Goetz, 1996). So far, however, under the acute financial pressure, the local authorities have employed NPM concepts, such as new budgeting procedures, mostly for cost-cutting purposes (for [critical] accounts, see Kissler *et al.*, 1997, Wollmann, 1999c).

Towards More Direct Democracy?

In a further recent development, local government and the relevant *Länder* legislation have been seized by a surprisingly strong current strengthening its direct democratic potential. As in the other European countries, with the noted exception of Switzerland, (West) *Germany's* local democracy since 1945 was until recently dominated by the principle of *representative democracy*. An exception to this rule was the South German *Land* of Baden-Württemberg where, since the mid-1950s, a (binding) local referendum procedure was in force. Since the early 1990s, this situation has changed almost dramatically. Obviously inspired by the historical experience that the East Germany communist regime was toppled largely by East German basic democratic movements, the (democratically elected) Parliament of the (still existing) German Democratic Republic also inserted provisions for (binding) local referendums in its municipal charter of May 1990.[10] Since 1990, with a surprising demonstration of harmony, legislation on the introduction of (binding) local referendums has been passed by all the east German as well as west German *Länder*. While the referendum procedures (in their two typical stages, i.e. the initiative and the referendum proper) may address all 'local matters', they must not, as an important exception, concern local budgetary and financial matters (for details, see Wollmann 1999a, p.40).

In another conspicuously parallel institutional development, since the early 1990s the direct election of the mayors (and in most *Länder* also of the *Landräte*, i.e. the heads of administration of the counties) has been introduced in all *Länder*. The east German *Länder* parliaments, in opting for the directly elected mayor and *Landrat*, were obviously again motivated by the basic democratic experience of the political turn-around (*Wende*) and the wish to give the population a further elective lever. By contrast, in the west German *Länder*, for instance in North Rhine Westphalia, adopting the elected strong mayor (with its dualistic implication) model was largely motivated by managerialist considerations directed at enhancing the governability of the cities and counties, thus finally giving up the monistic model introduced after 1945 (guided somewhat by the English local government model). In their recent legislation, some (particularly east German) *Länder* even provided for the recall of mayors and *Landräte* by local referendum.[11]

Comparative Conclusions

Comparative Scheme

In order to place the observations on decentralisation put forward in this article in a comparative perspective,[12] different typologies can be drawn which should be complementary rather than mutually exclusive. Particularly three such typologies are employed in the following.

A typology suggested by Page (1991) and followed up by Andrew and Goldsmith (1998, pp.108f.) is based on the distinction between legal and political localism. The former term addresses the local levels in terms of being (constitutionally/legally) endowed with powers and functions. By contrast, the latter term is to see the local level as a locus of political representation, local identity and community. The distinction made by Hesse and Sharpe (1990, pp.603ff) between the functional and the political roles of the local government levels is premised on a similar understanding.

In another typology which draws on earlier work by Leemans (1970) and on its further elaboration by Bennett (1993b), the analytical emphasis is placed on the institutional architecture and the vertical distribution of political and administrative powers and functions between the national and the sub-national levels. The types of institutional arrangement following from such an analytical perspective include a vertical separation of functions (dual system), a horizontal separation of functions (parallel system) as well as an arrangement in which different functions are (horizontally) fused; the latter may be also seen as a double functions model.

Thirdly, in order to conceive local government as a local political (democratic) system, typological distinctions may be useful regarding the political role of the citizen in the local political process (e.g. representative versus direct democracy), the relations between the elected council and the head of local administration (such as monistic versus dualistic distribution of powers) as well as the modality of installing the head of administration (direct election versus election/appointment by the council).

The periodisation which underlies the following comparative interpretation roughly distinguishes (see Bennett, 1993a, p.12): the historical *take-off* period of modern local self-government in the 19th century; the emergence of the modern welfare state (roughly beginning after the First World War and climaxing in the 1960s and early 1970s); the crisis of the welfare state (since the mid-1970s and well into the 1990s); and finally, the current period.

Comparative Interpretation

In the following, the three typological schemes will be applied in order to briefly interpret the observations, omitting as much detail as possible.

First, the functional/political typology: English 19th century (Victorian) local government can be seen as an exceptional case of both functional (multi-purpose) and political strength in view of the conditions of the dual polity (Bulpitt 1983) in which it was embedded and which provide the setting for what has been labelled the Anglo type (Hesse and Sharpe, 1990, p.606). Reflecting the policy of central government with the emergence of the welfare state to turn local government into an instrument of central government welfare state policies, the functional dimension of local government, as manifested by steep expenditure growth, was conspicuously enhanced, while its political role of local government was weakened (among other reasons, probably because of the 'anonymisation' of large-scale units). In the course of policy reforms under Thatcher, local government was shattered particularly functionally by the severe cutting back of its operational basis (for instance, by the quangoisation of its functions). Historically starting from an exceptional strong Victorian form of local self-government far ahead of local government abroad, English local government is now exceptional in the degree of its enfeeblement. Under the Labour government some re-strengthening of the political function appears likely, while with regard to its post-Thatcherite functional status Labour may adopt it in a 'moving consensus' (Rose, 1982).

In the late 19th century until the First World War, local government in the German States achieved functional importance through a (multi-purpose) scope of activities probably unparalleled in contemporary Europe, while its political function remained truncated because of the highly restrictive suffrage. Since 1945, after the turbulence of the inter-war years and its elimination under the National Socialists, local government, in conjunction with the advances of the welfare state, developed significant political as well as functional strength. In the most recent development, because of the introduction of direct democratic procedures, the political function is likely to further strengthen the combination and balance of political and functional salience which is seen as typical of the North and Central European type (Hesse and Sharpe, 1990, p.607), conducive to effective and viable decentralisation. In some respects, it may be analytically more appropriate to speak of a Central European, perhaps even of a Germanic type.

Second, the institutional architecture scheme: 19th century England was the classic case of a 'dual system' in which the two layers of government had distinct functions with little interference. With the emergence of the welfare state, local government was turned into a '(moderately) centrally integrated system', thus normalising and modernising the exceptionalism of the 19th century dual polity. The Thatcherite attacks then turned local government into a 'centrally penetrated system'.

In Germany, local government has been traditionally characterised by the parallel structures of (multi-purpose) local government structures on the one hand, and a State administration with comparatively few areas of activity on the other. State functions are delegated to local government to be carried out in its double function, thus making for a '(local administration-related) administratively integrated model' (Baldersheim *et al.*, 1996, p.41).

This double function model has continued with almost path-dependent persistence. It has the effect of locally integrating state functions and, at the same time, keeping the state administration outside local government to a minimum. It thus seems conducive to the strengthening of effective decentralisation, given the trend. Towards delegation of state functions, in particular the trend in Germany for state functions to be 'communalised' by transferring these functions to the local authorities as local self-administration matters (Wollmann, 1997c).

Third, the local democracy scheme: In both countries local democracy has been dominated by the principle of representative democracy with significant differences in duration. In England general (male) suffrage was first introduced in 1835 (town councils) and 1888/94 (county and district councils), but in Germany, after highly restrictive suffrage in the 19th century, only in 1919. Since the early 1990s, in a strong movement towards direct democracy procedures, local referendums and the direct election and possible recall of mayors have been introduced in most German *Länder*. Together with Switzerland with its traditional direct democracy, Germany is now a European pacesetter in what looks like an almost ironical reversal of the historical development to which Germany was a notorious late-comer.

In the constitutional arrangement of local government England has traditionally followed a monistic concept of local government in having the elected council fulfil both deliberative and executive functions by acting in a collegiate and voluntary manner. Most recently, in the face of the increasing complexity and professionalisation of local administration, there are moves to have some dualistic form of administrative leadership. Throughout Germany's institutional history the states or *Länder* have displayed an abundance of institutional options, ranging from monistic municipal constitutions to dualistic versions, with the mayor elected by the council or with the mayor elected by the local population. Most recently, practically all *Länder* have introduced directly elected (strong) mayor charters, while some have also installed recall procedures as a counterweight to the power of the mayors. Particularly the latter may be seen as a case in point in Germany's recent moves to strengthen local democracy.

Notes

1 The chapter draws in part on an earlier paper covering England, France, and Germany (see Wollmann, 1999d).

The Development and Present State of Local Government 127

2   The chapter will focus on *England* and omit Scotland, Wales and Northern Ireland as the other 'nations' of the United Kingdom with independent and significantly different local government systems (Rose, 1982, p.121).
3   Constituting the upper level of local government, the 62 counties (in England and Wales), because of their territorial and demographic size, can be somewhat compared to the (about 80) *départements* in France rather than to the counties (*Kreise*) in Germany.
4   The 1972 reform was prepared by a Royal Commission established in 1966 (under the chairmanship of Lord Redcliffe-Maude).
5   Meanwhile, appointments to such Quango boards number 60,000 (Stewart, 1995, p.31).
6   Compared to 72 per cent in Germany and 68 per cent in France (see DETR, 1998, p.14).
7   In Mannheim, for instance, the number of municipal employees rose from 48 in 1870 to 1,127 in 1906, see von Saldern, 1999, p.26.
8   Prior to the First World War, local revenues were made up of 45 per cent from the locally levied extra tax on income tax, 35 per cent from the locally levied tax on real assets, including Gewerbesteuer, 20 per cent from local loans (von Saldern, 1999, p.33).
9   The extraordinary importance which the municipalities and counties had in the immediate post-war period is illustrated by the fact that in 1950 local government employees made up 40 per cent of the entire public sector work force while a few years later the figure had returned to some 30 per cent (see Lorenz and Wollmann, 1999, p.498).
10 The historic process of rebuilding democratic local government in east Germany in the wake of German unification will not be treated here for lack of space. In an unprecedented 'transfer of institutions', (Lehmbruch, 1993) it largely followed, at least in its foundation period, the blueprint of West German local political and administrative structures (see Wollmann, 1996; Wollmann, 1997b).
11 It is worth mentioning that in the East German *Land* of Brandenburg, since the end of 1993, when the new legislation came into force, about 10% (!) of the full-time mayors have lost office as a result of local *recall* referendums (Wollmann, 1999a, p.48).
12 For a concluding summary which tries to comparatively synthesise and interpret the findings on local government and on social services (Hill; Bönker and Wollmann in this volume) see also the final section of the author's introductory chapter.

References

Andrew, C. and Goldsmith, M. (1998), 'From Local Governmnent to Local Governance', *International Political Science Review*, vol. 19, pp. 101-18.

Ashford, D. E. (1982), *British Dogmatism and French Pragmatism. Central-Local Policy Making in the Welfare State*, Allen and Unwin, London.

Baldersheim, H. (ed.) (1996), *Local Democracy and the Processes of Transformation in East-Central Europe*, Westview Press, Boulder.

Bennett, R. J. (1989), 'European Economy and Administration', in Bennett, R. J. (ed.), *Territory and Administration in Europe*, Pinter, London, New York.

Bennett, R. J. (1993a), 'Local government in Europe: common directions of change', in Bennett, R. J. (ed.), *Local Government in the New Europe*, Belhaven Press, London and New York, pp. 1-27.

Bennett R. J. (1993b), 'European local government systems', in Bennett, R. J. (ed.), *Local Government in the New Europe*, Belhaven Press, London and New York, pp. 28-50.

Benz, A. and Goetz, K. H. (1996), 'The German Public Sector: National Priorities and the International Reform Agenda', in A. Benz and K. H. Goetz (eds), *A New German Public Sector?*, Dartmouth, Aldershot, pp. 1-16.

Brooks, J. (1998), *Labour's Modernisation of Local Government: A Critical Approach*, unpubl. ms.

Bulpitt, J. (1983), *Territory and Power in the United Kingdom*, Manchester University Press, Manchester.

Derlien, H.-U. (1996), 'Patterns of Postwar Administrative Development in Germany', in A. Benz and K. H. Goetz (eds), *A New German Public Sector?*, Dartmouth, Aldershot, pp. 146-79.

DETR – Department of the Environment, Transport and the Regions (1998), White Paper, *Modern Local Government in Touch with the People*, London.

Engeli, C. and Haus, W. (1975), *Quellen zum modernen Gemeindeverfassungsrecht in Deutschland*, Kohlhammer, Stuttgart et al.

Gröttrup, H. (1973), *Die kommunale Leistungsverwaltung*, Kohlhammer, Stuttgart et al.

Hambleton, R. (1998), 'Strengthening Political Leadership in U.K. Local Government', *Public Money & Management*, vol. 18, pp. 41-51.

Heffter, H. (1950), *Die deutsche Selbstverwaltung im 19. Jahrhundert*, Kohlhammer, Stuttgart et al.

Hesse, J. J. (ed.) (1990), *Local Government and Urban Affairs in International Perspective*, Nomos, Baden-Baden.

Hesse, J. J. (1990), 'Local Government in a Federal State: The Case of West Germany', in J. J. Hesse (ed.), *Local Government and Urban Affairs in International Perspective*, Nomos, Baden-Baden, pp. 353ff.

Hesse, J. J and Sharpe, L. J. (1990), 'Local Government in International Perspective: Some Comparative Observations', in J. J. Hesse (ed.) (1990),

Local Government and Urban Affairs in International Perspective, Nomos, Baden-Baden, pp. 603 ff.
Hoffmann, W. G. (1965), *Das Wachstum der deutschen Wirtschaft seit der Mitte des 19. Jahrhunderts*, Kohlhammer, Berlin et al.
Hogwood, B. W. (1996), 'Devolution: The English Dimension', *Public Money & Management*, vol. 16, pp. 29-34.
Johnson, N. (1988), 'Die kommunale Selbstverwaltung in England', in H.-U. Erichsen (ed.), *Kommunalverfassungen in Europa*, Stuttgart, pp. 19 ff.
Jones, G. W. (1991), 'Local Government in Great Britain', in J. J. Hesse (ed.), *Local Government and Urban Affairs in International Perspective*, Nomos, Baden-Baden.
Keating, M. (1996), 'Regional Devolution: The West European Experience', *Public Money & Management*, vol. 16, pp. 35-42.
Keating, M. (1999), 'Reforging the Union. Devolution and Constitutional Change in the United Kingdom', unpubl. ms.
Knemeyer, F.-L. (1999), Gemeindeverfassungen, in H. Wollmann and R. Roth (eds.), *Kommunalpolitik*, Leske + Budrich, Opladen, pp. 104-22.
Laux, E. (1999), 'Erfahrungen und Perspektiven der kommunalen Gebiets- und Funktionalreform', in H. Wollmann and R. Roth (eds.), *Kommunalpolitik*, Leske + Budrich, Opladen, pp. 168–85.
Leemans, A. R. (1970), *Changing Patterns of Local Government*, International Union of Local Authorities, The Hague.
Lehmbruch, G. (1993), 'Institutionentransfer. Zur politischen Logik der Verwaltungsintegration in Deutschland', in W. Seibel, A. Benz and H. Mäding (eds), *Verwaltungsreform und Verwaltungspolitik im Prozeß der deutschen Einigung*, Nomos, Baden-Baden, pp. 42-66.
Lorenz, S. and Wollmann, H. (1999), 'Kommunales Dienstrecht und Personal', in H. Wollmann and R. Roth (eds), *Kommunalpolitik*, new edition, Leske + Budrich, Opladen, pp. 490-511.
Norton, A. (1994), *International Handbook of Local and Regional Government*, Edward Elgar, Aldershot.
Page, E. C. (1990), 'Die "do parties make a difference"-Diskussion in Großbritannien', in B. Blanke and H. Wollmann (eds), *Die alte Bundesrepublik*, Westdeutscher Verlag, Opladen, pp. 239-52.
Page, E. C. (1991), *Localism and Centralism*, Oxford University Press, Oxford.
Page, E. C. and Goldsmith, M. J. (eds) (1987), *Central and Local Relations: A Comparative Analysis of West European Unitary States*, Sage, London.
Reichard, C. (1994), *Umdenken im Rathaus. Neue Steuerungsmodelle in der deutschen Kommunalverwaltung*, Edition Sigma, Berlin.
Rose, R. (1980), *Do Parties make a Difference?*, Macmillan, London.
Rose, R. (1982), *Understanding the United Kingdom*, Longman, London.

Saldern, A. von (1999), 'Rückblicke. Zur Geschichte der kommunalen Selbstverwaltung in Deutschland', in H. Wollmann and R. Roth (eds), *Kommunalpolitik*, 2nd rev. ed., Leske + Budrich, Opladen, pp. 23-36.

Schefold, D. and Neumann, M. (1996), *Entwicklungstendenzen der Kommunalverfassungen in Deutschland: Demokratisierung und Dezentralisierung?*, Birkhäuser, Basel et al.

Schmitz, M. (1991), *Der Landrat. Mittler zwischen Staatsverwaltung und kommunaler Selbstverwaltung*, Nomos, Baden-Baden.

Schröter, E. (1998), 'Ein Bürgermeister für London: Neue Pläne und alte Probleme der Metropolenverwaltung', *Verwaltungs-Archiv*, vol. 89, pp. 505-25.

Schröter, E. and Wollmann, H. (1997), 'Public Sector Reforms in Germany: Whence and Where? A Case of Ambivalence', *Administrative Studies/Hallinnon Tutkimus*, vol. 16, pp. 184-200.

Sharpe, L. J. (1993), 'The United Kingdom: The Disjointed Meso', in L. J. Sharpe (ed.), *The Rise of Meso Government in Europe*, Sage, London.

Sharpe, L. J. (1998), *British Centralism Re-visited*, Paper presented at the Anglo-German Workshop 'Public Sector Modernisation', Humboldt University at Berlin.

Stewart, J. (1995), *The Role of Local Government in the United Kingdom*, INLOGOV, Birmingham.

Stoker, G. (1998), 'British Local Government. Under New Management?', in D. Grunow and H. Wollmann (eds.), *Lokale Verwaltungsmodernisierung in Aktion*, Birkhäuser, Basel et al., pp. 372-85.

Wollmann, H. (1996), 'The Transformation of Local Government in East Germany: Between Imposed and Innovative Institutionalization', in A. Benz and K. H. Goetz (eds), *A New German Public Sector?*, Dartmouth Publishing Co., Aldershot et al., pp. 137-63.

Wollmann, H. (1997a), 'Institution Building and Decentralization in Formerly Socialist Countries: the Cases of Poland, Hungary and East Germany', *Government and Policy*, vol. 15, pp. 463-480.

Wollmann, H. (1997b), 'Between Institutional Transfer and Legacies: Local Administrative Transformation in Eastern Germany', in G. Grabher, Gernot and D. Stark (eds), *Restructuring Networks in Post-Socialism*, Oxford University Press, Oxford.

Wollmann, Hellmut (1997c), 'Modernization of the Public Sector and Public Administration in the Federal Republic of Germany. (Mostly) A Story of Fragmented Incrementalism', in M. Muramatsu and F. Naschold (eds), *State and Administration in Japan and Germany. A Comparative Perspective on Continuity and Change*, deGruyter, Berlin and New York, pp. 80-103.

Wollmann, H. (1997d), '"Echte Kommunalisierung" der Verwaltungsaufgaben: Innovatives Leitbild für umfassende Funktionalreform?', *Landes- und Kommunalverwaltung*, vol. 7, pp. 105-9.

Wollmann, H. (1999a), 'Kommunalpolitik – zu neuen (direkt-)demokratischen Ufern', in H. Wollmann and R. Roth (eds) (1999), *Kommunalpolitik*, 2nd rev. ed., Leske + Budrich, Opladen, pp. 37-49.

Wollmann, H. (1999b), 'Entwicklungslinien lokaler Demokratie und kommunaler Selbstverwaltung im internationalen Vergleich', in H. Wollmann and R. Roth (eds), *Kommunalpolitik*, 2nd re. ed., Leske + Budrich, Opladen, pp. 186-205.

Wollmann, H. (1999c), 'Modernisierung der Kommunalverwaltung in den neuen Bundesländern. Zwischen Worten und Taten', *Landes- und Kommunalverwaltung*, vol. 9, supplement 1/1999, pp.7-13.

Wollmann, H. (1999d), 'Local government systems: From historic divergence towards convergence? England, France, and Germany as cases in point', *Government and Policy*, vol. 17 (forthcoming).

7 The Public Service in Britain: From Administrative to Managerial Culture

FREDERICK F. RIDLEY

Introduction

This chapter looks at the public service, that is to say public officials (civil servants and local government officers), the way they work and the way they see themselves – values, attitudes and behaviour: culture in short. It considers the distinctive features of British administration and administrative culture in relation to the 'reinvention of government', the model of public administration developed by the Conservative governments of Margaret Thatcher and John Major, not reversed by Labour's victory. It considers the factors that explain changes in administrative culture and whether, as a result, formerly 'bureaucratic' public services have in Britain themselves become agents of change. In the past, as the experience of many countries shows, bureaucracies have resisted change that affects themselves, notably their interests as determined in civil service laws or conditions of employment. In other respects, at least at the top, bureaucracies have sometimes encouraged public administration reform; they have nearly always drawn the line at reforming themselves.

In Britain, reform of the civil service hit the agenda with the Fulton Report of 1968. Little came of it. Mandarin power protected mandarin culture. In different ways, trade union power protected established interests at other levels. The last two decades saw a dramatic transformation of the public service in all its branches. Its role in this process also changed, moving from reforms imposed externally (the Thatcher/Major project) to situations in which it is a partner in the drive for reform: officialdom is changing itself through an internal dynamic.

In this discussion we are concerned partly with the higher civil service, those involved in policy-making at the top, Whitehall for short. We are also concerned with those responsible for the delivery of services to the public, the middle managers in Executive Agencies and other national government offices outside London or in local government, together with the counter-level staff ('street officials' in American) who actually deal with ordinary people – in other words the real interface between administration and public. Service delivery, after all, has become the focus of administrative reform in Britain and service delivery, rather than policy, is what government is about for most people most of the time.

There is a problem here. Most of what is written about the British civil service refers to its highest levels, and much of that is about their relationship to ministers and politics. One sees this in looking through recent books entitled in some variation of words The Changing Civil Service. Of course they deal with organisational reforms and changes in terms of employment that affect all civil servants, but they say little about the way the non-elite 95 per cent behave or what they think. The explanation is probably that the study of public administration is still largely located in the political science departments of British universities. For local government there are now rather different books focused on public sector management, more vocational, but there too it is hard to find much sociological study of staff culture. One's comments on changing culture thus tend to be somewhat impressionistic. That is nothing new however. Our views of past officialdom depend a good deal on novels and then films, plus biographies for the mandarin elite. Leaving aside some good studies of the old Administrative Class, that was still the case as regards ordinary officials in the post-1945 decades.

Anglo-German Comparisons

This is a volume comparing Britain and Germany, and it is obvious that there are still considerable differences in administrative culture between the two countries despite all the 'modernisation' pressures sweeping the world. Much of any public service is historically shaped, reflecting political, administrative and legal history. However, administrative cultures also reflect current organisational frameworks, administrative procedures and civil service rules – differently reformed in different countries. All this leads to differences in self-perception, in work styles and in relations with the public. The comparison of administrative cultures is a complex matter. Here we shall pick themes that help to explain what makes Britain different from Germany, using some key words as pegs to hang comparison on.

The first word is the state. In Germany civil servants are officials of the state (*Staatsbeamte*) and exercise state power (*Staatshoheitsträger*: literally, carriers of state sovereignty). That relationship defines their status; that authority distinguishes them from other public sector personnel. English law does not recognise the state as a legal entity: the civil servants of national government are servants of the Crown. The term state, indeed, is barely to be found in law textbooks, and there, as in 'security of the state', means the same as country. Of course the word is often used in other contexts, but generally as a shorthand for government or, for political sociologists, as a shorthand for power structures. Civil servants do not really see the state as an institutions in its own right, above government and politics, to which they can relate, nor does service of the state give them a social cachet, an invisible uniform, as it may elsewhere. Top civil servants, the mandarins, no doubt saw themselves – perhaps some still see themselves – as engaged in what used to be called statecraft, but that only meant high politics or, preferable to them, non-political politics.

One can draw various conclusions from this. One here is simply that it is easier to transform officials into managers if they do not start with a picture of the state as an institution which is not only different from other institutions but above others, a state of which they are guardians. Instead, civil servants at all levels were told that as servants of the Crown they must serve its constitutional representatives, the ministers of the day – and this was given a democratic spin: ministers are responsible to parliament which is elected by the people; parliament and voters alone can determine the national interest. Civil servants are not told, as in Germany, that they have a personal responsibility for the 'common interest'.

This is reinforced by another set of words. German, like French, makes a distinction between the political leadership (*die Regierung*) and the administration (*die Verwaltung*). In English, these words overlap. In the past one talked of a government as e.g. the Gladstone administration, and some, perhaps rather formal, still refer to the Thatcher, Major or Blair administrations. Now, however, we talk of their governments, but government also means the ministries, the administration, as in central government. This running together must have an effect on civil service culture. Civil servants are the non-political, permanent branch of government, but they cannot think of themselves as an autonomous branch in the way that German civil service law seems to mean, nor is it easy to make the Weberian distinction between politics/policymaking and administration.

It is true that the Next Steps programme, with the establishment of Executive Agencies, was based on that distinction – policymaking on the one hand, implementation, called service delivery, on the other . But that is recent; it is not part of a long German tradition of administration as the quasi-independent activity of a legal-rational bureaucracy. And what is has brought instead is managerialism.

That brings us to the role of administrative law. Britain does not really have administrative law in the way that other countries of Europe do. True, there are rules developed by the judiciary that can be used in appeals against decisions by public authorities, broad principles (to simplify) of 'natural justice' in decision-making. Textbooks entitled Administrative Law deal mainly with 'judicial review' and are intended for lawyers bringing cases against public authorities: they are not compendiums of laws (e.g. on building, welfare or taxation) applied by public authorities in their work. Although the scope of judicial review and the number of cases have increased over recent years, the number remains very small compared to the workload of German administrative courts and few officials are likely to be involved with such cases even once in their career.

Moreover, the courts concern themselves with the output of decision-making, the actual decisions. There is no law (code) of administrative procedure. Officials are relatively free in their procedures preparing decisions. The some applies to the organisation of offices and e.g. (to simplify again) the handling of public money. Of course there are likely to be internal rules but these are not 'law'. In other words, the situation is not very different from other large ('bureaucratised') private sector organisations where staff must also be aware that a decision may land their company in a lawsuit. The routine work of public administration is not dominated by formalised decision-making (the *Verwaltungsakt* in Germany). Few civil servants thus need much legal training; perhaps rather more local government officers do; but in both cases it is not very different from the familiarity with relevant branches of the same law required of private sector managers. British officials do not require special qualifications in law, making them members of a specialised professionism, nor do they see their main function as the application of rules to cases in the quasi-judicial legal-rational manner of Weber's classic bureaucracy. Managerialisation is much easier in that context. Administration in central government has traditionally been seen as an 'art' not a 'science', with 'generalists' recruited at all levels (meaning educational qualifications unrelated to work, traditionally history, classics, literature for the higher levels). Local government favoured a more professional background, but with specialisms largely shared with other sectors of employment (e.g. accountancy, engineering). While those employed in the public service were socialised into a public service ethic, and at higher levels acquired certain 'political' skills, they never had professional qualifications in the old Administrative or Executive Classes of the civil service and few public service specific qualifications in local government. This now facilitates movement in or out and helps explain the decline in Britain of the sort of career distinctiveness associated with traditional bureaucracies.

Of course, all large organisations, especially those involving much office work, may become bureaucracies in a generalised sense of the word – hierarchy, division, of labour, work to rules. Tales were endlessly told in Britain of red tape or the petty tyranny of the keepers of the rules in a public office, but this differed little from the reception an ordinary person might receive in an insurance office, for example. It is clear that this is not really Weber's classical bureaucracy as mentioned above. Moreover, such bureaucratisation has been the main focus of the reforms of the last decades. We return to debureaucratisation later, especially in relation to local government at the interface with its customers. The point here is simply that much of British administration, not just the actual building of roads but the work of building permits department for example, can be managerialised more easily than in a system where work must follow legally prescribed procedures.

A further effect, perhaps, is that senior and middle level staff without professional training may be more open than their counterparts abroad to acquiring a modern profession of their own – management. A 'generalist' background, even a mandarin generalist, may be less saleable today for the career hopper than a couple of decades ago. Management training has been widely embraced, not just as a result of pressure from above but as a career-beneficial (and portable) skill. In Germany, of course, lawyers have long been promoted to senior management posts in private enterprise – but that is in a culture where law has traditionally been the University subject of intending businessmen, while in Britain it has been seen as a vocational training for practising lawyers.

We come now to the term public service, which has several meanings, often differently translated in other languages. We talk of public services, as in the now current phrase 'delivery of services' (*Dienstleistungen*), e.g. health services; but in this meaning it may also refer to the institution delivering the service, as in the Health Service. We talk of a service as an organisation of personnel – the civil service, the armed services, the police and fire services, or the local government service. We talk of the public service ethic as a set of values supposedly shared by those employed in the public service. And we talk of public service in a quite different way, as good work for the community, unpaid, by private citizens.

What we mean by public services in the first sense above is hard to pin down in the absence of a concept of the state or administrative laws. Market testing in central government and compulsory competitive tendering in local government have led to the contracting out of services which in other countries might be considered specific to public administration. The computerised handling of taxation and welfare benefits might just pass as non-specific, though it raises issues about confidentiality and, more important, that such data relates to enforceable tax liabilities or benefit entitlement. What about privatised prisons? Debate about privatised prisons has focused on their efficiency or on the morality of profit-making in such business: no legal question seems to arise about the private employees of private companies, not wearing a uniform of the state, detaining citizens by force – so long as legislation permits. The point is simply this: there is no concept in law of acts which must – or should – be performed by an official of the state exercising state power. This greatly facilitates the dismantling of public administration in Britain and the manageralisation of what remains.

If is not clear either what we mean by the public service as a body of personnel. In the singular (unlike *der öffentliche Dienst*) it reflects no reality in law. The civil service is increasingly disjointed; its conditions of employment, recruitment, grading, pay, are diversified, though service of the Crown remains a unifying factor of sorts. The local government service consists of labour law contractual employees of some five hundred local authorities, many appointed to specific jobs rather than to a service. The advertisements for those jobs are exactly like advertisements for the private sector. How many now see themselves as part of an all-embracing public service, different moreover from private sector employment, is questionable. Some, of course, like teachers, the largest bloc of local government employees, never regarded themselves as officials and would be puzzled at inclusion in such a class. Recent reforms make it increasingly hard to distinguish public and private employment; this was made easier by the fact that there never was in Britain a public service covering central and local government, distinguishable in some sense of identity as well as law, from private sector employment.

Finally and another meaning altogether: the culture-related question of civil servants' sense of responsibility, a central part of their ethic. Who or what do they believe they serve, or, more generally, what values do they apply in their work? One tends to talk about the elite and their relation to ministers. For middle managers or street level bureaucrats in the civil service that is a pretty meaningless question. It is pretty meaningless too for local government staff, much more likely to talk in terms of their authorities' mission statements and their own responsibilities to citizen-customers.

Civil servants around Europe may consider a whole range of responsibilities, some conflicting – to the state, to the law, to the democratically chosen government, to the national interest and so on. If asked why they joined the civil service in Britain, they were unlikely ever to have answered 'to serve the state' and certainly not 'to serve the democratically chosen government'. The Oxbridge-educated Administrative Class might well have answered that they saw it as a form of public service, meaning a worthy job, serving their country in some way, with status and pay of course. That is where public service comes in again. The term is used in a private person's CV to describe unpaid activities like being a Justice of the Peace, a school governor or, higher up the ladder, a trustee of the National Gallery. It is used in the Queen's Birthday and New Year Honours Lists to explain many of the awards listed there – involvement with good causes.

Society changes and this sort of public service ethos changes with it. It is certainly stronger now in the voluntary sector than in the civil service or the local government service. Nevertheless, it is relevant to our country comparisons. Perhaps we can make another comparison here. Priests in the Church of Rome have a vocation, the service of God, but they do this through the Church, an institution to which they are committed, with a hierarchy and a head. Anglican ministers, even in earlier days when hierarchy still involved social respect, did not have that sort of institutional focus – they serve God by serving their parishioners, doing good in their community. If ordinary civil servants and local government staff have a public service ethic (and some are simply doing a job for its pay), then it is rather like that – they hope to do something worthwhile while earning a living. Of course that is true in other countries also. But it fits well into English traditions, involves little state focus, and makes public service staff very like staff in other non-profit organisations. It is an important element in the mission-oriented customer-oriented approach to staff motivation pursued by our best local authorities.

For the rest, what does the public service ethic consist of? Having hived off the majority of civil servants into managerially-directed Executive Agencies, described in training courses as 'our businesses', the Conservative government was nevertheless anxious to reassure the public that a mangerialist service would retain traditional civil service values. These are described as integrity, fairness and so on – little more than any good employer would expect of staff, certainly in such sectors as banking and insurance (even if, at top level, international market speculators are different). Again, the point is that on such a definition of ethics (even if one includes rules about corruption, conflict of interest, confidentiality, etc.), there is now little differences in the value systems of staff in public and private sectors – a universal trend, I suspect, but one that has perhaps developed more easily in Britain for reasons already listed.

I will turn now to change and the factors involved. Again, an obvious question is: are these factors special to Britain – either to facilitate adoption of a more or less universal reformist trend or to give that trend characteristics specifically British (or at least non-continental)?

There is a tendency to assume that New Public Management is a universal trend, reflecting on the one hand a change in economic climate (end of growth, taxpayer resistance, fiscal austerity and so on), managerialism as getting Value for Money; and on the other hand a change in social climate (more demanding citizens expecting friendly as well as efficient service), customer orientation in other words. Since ideas have a life of their own once launched, the managerial movement has become a force with its own momentum, effectively managed by international consultants as well as converted officials in key places. The role of New Right political leaders is usually cited as well, though, Thatcherism apart, few European Conservative parties have subscribed to the full ideology.

What is remarkable in Britain, I think, is the speed of change. The phrase 'reinventing government' can be applied to recent developments, with new models of the state (using that term in its generalised sense) or new models of public administration in both central and local government. The Thatcher and Major governments, spurred on by New Right think tanks, thought more radically than most other European governments – but that is not a sufficient explanation. The question remains: how were they able to push through radical administrative reforms so easily?

As noted above, these are some cultural factors that made it easier than in Germany: the absence of a state focus for civil servants for example, or the absence of a code of administrative procedure to regulate work. Other factors can be listed briefly. There is no written constitution to limit parliamentary legislation (leaving aside the EU aspect as irrelevant here) – no provision, for example, that the civil service must be organised on traditional lines. In parliament a single party has a disciplined majority and is not checked by coalition partners or a federal system. In fact, civil service reform did not even require legislation as the organisation of government is Crown (i.e. Executive) prerogative. Important reforms like Market Testing and the Executive Agencies did not even get serious parliamentary debate. Local government reform, Compulsory Competitive Tendering for example, was imposed by legislation – with considerable effects on the culture of local government staff. On the other hand, the internal organisation, work procedures and staffing conditions are not generally regulated by law (but left to the authorities themselves), so that internal reform was relatively easy in those authorities where there was a will to reform. In fact, there are considerable differences between authorities, which can be largely explained in terms of their leadership – and that is the case in personal rather than party-political terms. Leadership is of course a factor at central government level also. Margaret Thatcher's commitment to debureaucratisation is well known. John Major, for his part, made administrative reform, including the Citizen's Charter, an important part of his programme. This is unlike most other European countries where reforms, whether efficiency or citizens oriented, play a less prominent programmatic role. The weakened place of unions was another British factor. This is simply to say that a host of diverse factors, some historical, some contemporary, combined to create a British situation rather different from the German situation.

Of course, there has been talk of civil service reform for a long time, with the Fulton Report of 1968 a high point, but nothing dramatic happened until Margaret Thatcher became Prime Minister. She brought political will as well as political power to her project. One needs to stress that radical reform, the reinvention of government was a project, not a matter of adjusting technicalities. Unlike some predecessors, she was not much interested in details of the machinery of government or new procedures. Efficiency (Value for Money) was the aim. If one looks at the administrative reforms that followed, underlying all was a drive for cultural change in the public service, more managerial ways of thinking and behaving. Institutional and procedural reforms can be seen as instruments to this end, part of an unarticulated grand design.

Here we can just list some main thrusts. The first, the Efficiency Scrutinies, were intended not only to save money in particular fields but to encourage new ways of thinking about managerial efficiency everywhere. The Next Steps programme, with its separation of policymaking and implementation, was intended to managerialise (de-mandarinise) Executive Agency leadership – echoed in the purchaser/provider split and Direct Service Organisations of local government. The Competition for Quality programme introduced elements of competition into civil service administration through Market Testing, echoed by Compulsory Competitive Tendering (CCT) in local government, forcing staff in both to reconsider their work methods in relation to private enterprise and think in efficiency terms. The Benchmarking that has now replaced CCT is less privatisation oriented but serves a similar purpose. The introduction of quasi-contractual rather than bureaucratic relationships, Service Level Agreements in local government, also stressed managerial approaches. Managers' freedom to manage, e.g. within the Framework Agreements of Executive Agencies, meant devolved financial responsibility within bloc funding. Important too is the Citizen's Charter programme, customer orientation, supported by sector charters and local authority Mission Statements, and the linked stimuli to competition, Performance Indicators with comparative league tables. Devolved management also involved flexibilised personnel management: grades, pay, numbers, recruitment and promotion to meet 'business needs'. The opening of top grade civil service posts, with national advertisements, increased mobility between civil service and private sector and forced career officials to compete against others for promotion; with this came the contractualisation of Senior Civil Service appointments; most local government posts are advertised – all changing culture by dismantling walls between public and private careers. Performance incentives, Performance Related Pay for individuals or collective reputation through the league tables mentioned above, deserve mention. Finally, management training as in the modernised Civil Service College.

How Change Was Driven

How does cultural change actually happen – how were behaviour and attitudes modified in the civil service and in local government? One can look at this under a number of headings. External and internal factors are a starting point. The former involves society as a whole. The young people who enter the public service are very different from earlier generations. Of course, once in the service, socialisation takes place – though this, much written about, was always more effective in the higher civil service in London than in lower ranks or in local government. However, at all levels the public service is less closed as a way of life with an ethos of its own than in the past. Staff share a lifestyle with circles of friends outside and reflect the changing values (job expectations, work commitment, morality in general) of social networks unrelated to public administration – so that the process of externally-shaped change continues throughout the career.

Then there are internal changes. Some can be related to the selection of different types of people than in the past through altered criteria in recruitment systems and, more important, through promotion systems which emphasise personal characteristics such as leadership and enterprise. This is perhaps the Darwinian model of evolution through selection of the fittest (most managerial). Alternatively, there is the attempt to 'reculture' all staff. One set of techniques is education (training courses and so on), exhortation (preaching, if you like) as through mission statements, or setting a good example from above (socialisation). Another set of techniques involves institutional arrangements and work procedures which shape (or reshape) behaviour. Putting staff into competitive situations is part of this; rewards and punishments (performance related pay, for example) can be added. The techniques are many and varied. The point however, is that most of the public administration reforms adopted in Britain over recent years are not only intended to increase efficiency and customer service directly but are meant to encourage ongoing reform further by changing the culture of staff.

Generational change in society is a very important factor. Both the civil service and the local government are less closed careers than in the past. Much has been written about the Whitehall Village, a system in which higher civil servants spent most of their time; even when they met businessmen, or representatives of other interests, the contact was fleeting and peer group mandarins remained their point of reference. From studies of that group only a few decades ago, one got the impression of a relatively closed way of life, little time for outside activities (gardening, a solitary occupation, frequent hobby). True, many still have a middle-class Oxbridge background, from which in the past they could pick up manners and dress as well as a moral code, reinforced in their Village – but neither family nor Oxbridge now bring much uniformity. More important, senior civil servant, except the oldest, now spend non-work time in circles that include journalists, actors, bankers, academics, drinking and talking with friends far removed from government service or public service ethos. They are probably attached to their jobs because these are interesting and influential (the reason most favoured by respondents to an earlier survey of higher civil service entrants), but that response is no different from what their friends in other occupations might say and fits as well into managerial ethos as into some career-distinctive public service code.

Much the same could be aid of senior staff in local government, though much less is written about them. In the past they enjoyed a different sort of club life from the Whitehall Village, mixing with prosperous city merchants for example, but that has now gone. Nor does the sort of status now attach to middle-ranking local government officials that 'working in the Town Hall' gave in the past.

For most staff, whether in the civil service or in local government, their position bestows little in the way of status and, in that respect, little sense of identity: their job is just a job. It maybe more relaxing for some than the rough and tumble of private enterprise, more satisfying than the simple pursuit of profit, but the job-holder does not wear on invisible yet generally recognised uniform of the state, nor does he have an identifying title of rank by which (as in some German circles) he may be introduced. This is not the place to study comparative social stratification – the point is that change in a public service is much easier when there is little distinctive identity or culture.

This is reinforced if one also asks why young people enter the public service. In the past, status was an element, especially at lower levels, a way to rise from the working class (becoming a school teacher did much the same); so was relatively good pay and above all security of employment. Status has gone, good pay has gone, and security of tenure has gone. Some join the public service because the work is interesting, some because they do not feel suited to competitive business or because they hope to 'contribute to society' as part of their work – but this could lead them as easily to employment in non-profit organisations (voluntary sector, professional associations, etc.) or even in less competitive sectors of work in private enterprise. In the main, however, it is now the labour market that determines: young people apply for jobs across all sectors in the hope of landing one as unemployment threatens. That, of course, could be countered by career-distinctive socialisation after recruitment, and efforts along these lines are made by local authorities which emphasise their 'customer service' mission, but even that is rarely enough to inculcate a distinctive public service identity.

One reason for this failure is the growing mobility of staff. At lower levels, local government officials or officials in local offices of central government, will readily change jobs if a better offer comes along or, for example, if they have to move to another town because a spouse is posted elsewhere: pension rights are probably the most serious restraining force. Higher level civil servants, if they see that promotion to highest levels is unlikely, may also move out mid-career. Local government, of course, is based on a job rather than career system anyway, with vacant posts publicly advertised, open to anyone with relevant qualifications (and that means professional skills, work experience, personality – not a diploma in public administration). 'Career hopping' is not unusual. Again, that affects self-identification – it is better to be a manager, for example, because that is a transferable skill, than to be an administrator. Significantly, there are no longer textbooks on public administration (except for students of political science) – they are called Introduction to Public Sector Management; and the demands are for Masters in Business Administration rather than Masters in Public Administration, even in schemes sponsored by the Civil Service College.

We return now to some of the public administration reforms that are relevant to changing attitudes and behaviour, though here only touching relevant structural changes without attempting to describe them further.

Reference was made earlier to recruitment. Top posts in the civil service must now be publicly advertised; outsiders may be appointed, bringing in business experience for example (though few are, and salaries remain far behind what a captain of industry receives). Local government posts are all advertised, open to outsiders, and the language used is indistinguishable from private sector advertisements. As regards internal promotion, appointment to top posts, Margaret Thatcher's interventions are well known: she chose civil servants she believed would make managerial leaders, not traditional mandarins skilled in writing policy advice but vigorous 'hands on' chief executives who did not respond to her policy proposals by trying to 'educate' her but said 'can do, will do'. Her interventions underline the fact that she had less faith in structural reforms than in the changing bureaucratic culture through example from above and because ambitious younger staff will adapt to the new style to get promoted.

The civil service itself underwent structural changes. The great majority no longer serve in ministries but in Executive Agencies which have taken over delivery of services. Responsibility for personnel management was left to the Agencies, with considerable powers as regards recruitment, pay and conditions of employment generally. The idea of a unified service, the traditional cross-ministry Administrative, Executive and Clerical Classes, replaced some time ago by a common Administration Group covering all three, gave way to something more like ministry or Agency-specific employment (staff identification). That is found another countries; but as conditions of employment also began to diverge, many critics suggested that it would destroy any sense of belonging to a common service at all, reinforcing again the growing perception mentioned earlier that this was employment little different from other employment.

Conditions of employment have been further adjusted to those of the private sector. The security of tenure of Crown servants (always assumed as a fact of life even if not of law) is no longer pretended. Civil servants may be made redundant (i.e. dismissed on the grounds that their work is no longer required) just like private sector employees, or they may be transferred to private sector employers if their work is contracted out. Pay rates are to take account of the labour market, what is needed to attract and retain adequate staff in different skills and in different parts of the country. Flexible and overlapping pay bands allowing management greater discretion than before. Individual pay reviews relate to individual performance (an element of performance related pay in all cases and no automatic annual increments). The Senior Civil Service (the top five grades) are on individual contracts, some open-ended but with provision for termination; some may be fixed-term or 'rolling' contracts (the latter needing regular renewal). This is not a Weberian-model bureaucracy.

Competition has been introduced into central and local government, bringing with it further cultural changes as people have to think in new ways, comparing their units with private enterprise in relation to staffing levels, work methods and costs generally. Of course the Conservative government responsible for the reforms in question has been replaced by a Labour government which pursues gentler lines (e.g. benchmarking), but the culture shock has had its effect. In central government this was the Market Testing programme and in local government Compulsory Competitive Tendering, requiring virtually all services to compete against outside bidders for their work. While the majority of bids have been won 'in-house', staff have been forced to think of themselves as in a business that needs to survive against competition rather than as career officials carrying on administration according to pre-set rules (administrative law) and pre-set expenditure (budget) in privileged services of the state. Internal trading between departments of a local authority has also introduced new quasi-contractual relationships between departmental heads, acting very much like branch managers in a conglomerate enterprise.

The Citizen's Charter programme reinforced competition, though of a different sort, by the requirement imposed on local authorities to publish Performance Indicators. It is important in another respect in relation to cultural change, namely customer orientation. Here it must be said that much of the driving force came from progressive local authorities. Mission statements make pledges of good service, supported by service-specific local charters, and where leadership is effective these have changed the behaviour of counter staff. Cultural change of this sort has been promoted in all branches of the public service, but it probably works best in local government (a German experience also) where relations with citizens may be closer and where institutional reforms that facilitate such contacts (one stop shops for example) are more often found.

Finally, from a different angle, there are moves to dismantle Weberian bureaucracy (hierarchy, division of labour, rules of procedure, depersonalised decisions) as a way of organising office work. This, of course, reflects similar moves elsewhere: empowerment of staff, 'ownership' of a service or unit, responsibility delegated down as far as possible – a way of heightening staff motivation as well as achieving more flexible, thus more efficient, management. Cutting across service divisions by teamwork is another example of anti-bureaucratic trends, designed to focus on problems (or problem groups) at the cost of functionally specialised hierarchies. 'Staff ownership' of a service could sit uncomfortably with customer-orientation but experience often shows that part of the pride in work it engenders is a desire to serve citizens better. However, this must not be exaggerated and for many their job remains a job, poorly rewarded, with little social recognition attached, little different from other jobs one might get to earn one's living.

A New Culture?

Of course the reforms are more complex, and there are more of them than have been mentioned here. Broadly, they add up to managerialism, competition, customer orientation and an end to employment distinctions in the public sector. The effect of these reforms on public service culture must be considerable, but it is impossible to disentangle the effect of wider societal change (new lifestyles all round), the leadership influence of recently selected top staff, motivation through staff empowerment, the sticks and carrots of market testing or performance related pay, the success of training courses, and so on.

Among other things, this makes it hard to be certain what the lessons are. There are too many variables. While this may be a disadvantage if one wants to pick effective reforms for consultants to sell abroad (always assuming their clients want to move in broadly the same direction), the mixture seems to have some good results, even if one cannot be entirely sure how and why.

Whether the reforms are desirable does of course depend on where one wants to go. They were introduced as part of a project, not always clearly articulated but underlying the policies of the Thatcher/Major governments 1979 to 1997. The New Right think-tank intellectuals popularised phrases like 'Enabling State' and 'Contracting State'. The model of a 'Skeleton State', or a 'Skeleton Administration,' is as compatible with a welfare state as with a capitalist market economy. The fact remains, however, that the recent reinvention of government has been associated with Conservatism. Most academic writing on the subject is critical. This may reflect understandable hostility to Thatcherism or simply a tendency of academics to see themselves as critics rather than consultants (possibly another cultural difference between Britain and other European countries). Unfortunately, too many of the critics have run together failures due to teething problems as new systems are run in, unacceptable politicisation (e.g. Health Service management boards), and weaknesses inherent in the new models (e.g. erosion of public service ethos, democratic deficit).

Let us return, however, to the question: has public service culture changed? Managerialism first. Everyone now claims to be a manager, from Permanent Secretaries at the top to small office supervisors at the bottom. The Civil Service College's directory of courses uses the word management whenever it can, and almost all its course titles are in 'management speak', identical to what Business Schools will offer. It defines mangers as top managers, with policy and chief executive responsibilities; middle managers; and line managers, the bottom grade but two in the Administration Group, effectively anyone supervising anyone. Though associated by some with Thatcherite privatisation, the use of 'managers' is really intended to stress that work involves the running of organisations rather than work on case files, as the *Verwaltungsbeamte* does.

Increasingly, too, training publications talk of 'your business' and managers of 'our business'. In English, that is a new word for public service organisations and also rings oddly because of its private enterprise connotations. However, it does not mean that public services are run as commercial concerns selling their services to customers at market determined rates. (In German, *Geschäft* may have a more neutral meaning – non-commercial organisations have a *Geschäftsführer*).

Similarly, the word customer is now common usage in publications, e.g. leaflets for the public. One might think it merely a public relations exercise: even the tax office has its customers. But the word is increasingly used by officials, not just leaders trying to set the tone in a local government service, for example, but by others also. It is a significant word. It does not mean, in the public service context, that a market economy relationship exists – customers do not 'buy' the services they receive. What it does mean is that citizens should be treated with the respect due to customers, not regarded as persons to be administered (the notorious French *l'administration et les administrés*), nor (fashionable continental European substitute for that) as users of a service which officials can then still regard as theirs. It relates, perhaps, to client as in client-oriented social work, distinguishing at the same time individual members of the public from citizens who play a collective role in policy.

One may ask whether officials mean all this. Almost certainly, the new language of managerialism has been widely internalised by now and comes naturally to the tongue. To a large, though lesser, extent, the same is time of customer orientation. That does not necessarily mean that behaviour will match language. There is long experience of churchgoing Christians repeating phrases, some not even believing, some believing but not living in accordance. Nevertheless, language has an effect: it is an important cultural force in itself.

Managerialisms is easier to practise than customer-orientation, indeed work situations now require it and, as we have noted earlier, there may be fewer barriers in Britain than in Germany to it. Even then, older-style bureaucrats survive. Some higher civil servants, with no responsibility for running anything, engaged in scrutinising the work of other units (non-governmental public bodies for example), may retain the negative paperwork approach that Margaret Thatcher so disliked.

Customer orientation requires rather more in terms of ethics and personal commitment. Despite all charters and mission statements, staff live in a materialist and sell-interested society and those engaged in boring office work may have little interest in its outcome. Dedication was also hard to maintain for those employed in the local offices of Executive Agencies forced to implement 'Thatcherite' policies that caused widespread upset among 'customers' – with abuse, even physical threats (e.g. offices dealing with unemployment and social welfare benefits). For many local government staff, however, a helpful, friendly approach to the citizens they deal with, and genuine attempts to solve their problems in non-bureaucratic fashion, are the experience of everyday life.

In criticising the erosion of traditional public administration and civil service organisation, it is easy to forget what the public service culture of the past too often meant: bureaucrats in lifetime careers distinct from ordinary people, with security of tenure, titles of rank, social status and identification with higher causes whose guardians and interpreters they were (national interest, common good), exercising state power, applying rules of law, authoritarian attitudes, red tape procedures, depersonalised administration. Why did anyone ever think Weber's classical bureaucracy was a good thing?

In the past, changes in public service organisation have generally depended on external forces, the bureaucracy, like other professions, trying to protect its established ways and established interests. The new model introduced in the Thatcher/Major years and broadly continued under Blair (continuity and change, the first year slogan) may add an internal dynamic: internal competition and managerial culture should be a driving force to better quality service delivery as well as greater efficiency in delivery. Perhaps that is over-optimistic and external pressures need to be maintained. Perhaps, indeed, the managerial dynamic will drive public services in socially undesirable directions. Whatever the case, we all live in a world of change but in Britain public administration change has come quicker and gone further than elsewhere in Europe.

8 Actor Constellation, Opportunity Structure and Concept Feasibility in German and British Public Sector Reforms

HANS-ULRICH DERLIEN

Introduction

Low blood pressure is not treated medically in Britain; the *crise de foie* is a typically French phenomenon while neurosis is not found in the diagnostic repertory of German medical doctors; bathing cures are prescribed solely in Europe, while Americans rely on laboratory based medicines (and psychoanalysis). Similarly, perceived public sector reform needs and remedies deemed feasible vary from country to country, notwithstanding some international consensus about the instrumental value of certain concepts. Political and administrative cultures might have a certain bearing on the propensity to adopt concepts for administrative reform. Further, reform protagonists or actor constellations can vary between countries and over time, and resulting reform patterns are further influenced by structural possibilities and constraints (opportunity structures) imbedded in a national polity.

In a previous essay (Derlien, 1996) I pointed out that by 1992 there had been, in retrospect to the 1960s, two reform waves in Germany, the first peaking in 1970 and the second brought about by unification in 1990 and taking place in the eastern part of the country. Nevertheless, sectoral, functional or level-bound reforms occurred continuously – owing to the federal structure of the FRG – in an *incremental and piecemeal* way; they produced a patchwork of innovations limited to just one level of government, confined to one functional aspect of the machinery of government, or concerned with one specific policy area (see the synopsis in Derlien 1998, pp.55-61). Incrementalism in a national reform history implies path-dependency as outcomes of previous reforms provide premises and constraints for ensuing reforms. Secondly, the fact that bureaucracy in the past pragmatically adapted to perceived contingencies through self-generated reforms and mutual adjustment (in Lindblom's sense) rather than being pushed (and bashed) by politicians and reformers called in from outside justified the notion of the *intelligence of bureaucracy*. Bureaucracy as a reform subject drew on its expertise and a professional consensus among administrative scientists about which improvements were rational and consistent with the inherited bureaucratic structure. Indeed, this leading role can be traced back to the 1806/1812 Prussian Stein and Hardenberg reforms, for, in contrast to Britain and the United States, bureaucracy in Germany is the product of the absolutist state. Bureaucracy – the sitting and the standing armies (Rosenberg, 1958) – preceded democracy and the emergence of a class of genuine, parliamentary politicians, a fundamental fact partly responsible for Germany's 'special path' in 20th century history.

Contrary to the German case, public sector reforms in the United Kingdom and other Commonwealth states since the 1980s have been pushed by politicians and appear to be secular and comprehensive and based on a coherent reform philosophy. Even during the first major reform wave in Germany (1964-75) there was not such a common reform philosophy or a comprehensive reform program extending to all levels, functional areas and sectors of governance. The transfer of the basic western model to the eastern part of the country in 1990, was, of course, comprehensive but based on western traditional rules of appropriateness (March and Olsen, 1989) and not on a new rationale. Since then, undoubtedly, a change of guiding ideas has been taking place in Germany; today the bureaucratic structure is being disputed and no longer retains the self-legitimisation arising from its alleged superior effectiveness and efficiency (Weber). At the local government level New Public Management, albeit in a reduced version, is gaining ground (Reichard and Wollmann, 1996). Politicians have taken over and are driving for public sector reforms under the banners of 'administrative modernisation' and 'lean state'.

Once we have gone through the mist and clouds of reform rhetoric, the question has to be asked how large the differences between UK and German reforms really are and what can be explained by national public sector cultures and concepts, constitutional features and configurations of reform protagonists.

I shall advance my argument in three steps: First, I shall discuss the recent change in the reform climate in Germany and point out specifics of the competing bearer strata of the new ideas. Second, I shall take stock of the similarities, for there are such, and differences of administrative reforms in the UK and Germany during the last decades. Fundamental differences of regime type will be indicated that condition the opportunity structure for putting reform concepts into practice. Third, I shall point to some inherent problems of key modernisation concepts that not only make them partly incompatible with traditional German public sector thinking but have also led to disputes in the Anglo-Saxon reform discussion. It is argued that these theoretical problems concern the instrumental value of modernisation concepts regardless of national context and might also explain the resistance of administrative scientists in both countries to these ideas.

In my conclusion, I return to the concept of strategic choice as elaborated by John Child (1997); within Child's framework, the implementation of reform concepts is assumed to be guided by actor configurations according to their more or less subjective notions of feasibility within given structural constraint.

From 'Intelligence of Bureaucracy' to Politicians and Management Consultants

In 1990, contrary to the movement in the Anglo-Saxon world, managerialism was not visible in Germany, nor was there any bureaucrat bashing by politicians or the public (Derlien, 1991). Rather, the status of the civil service and its principles of training, recruitment and performance had not basically changed in West Germany since its rebirth in 1949. German bureaucracy, despite 30 years of constant adjustment, had remained Weberian. The concept of a legal-rational polity with a bureaucratic staff was dominant: professional training, relatively closed career service, promotion as the only incentive and according to objective criteria (including age), hierarchy both within and between offices, special jurisdictions, clear distinction between public and private means of production, neutral, impersonal and rule-bound execution of public tasks oriented towards service in the name of the public.

Continuous rationalisation of bureaucracy had not altered its basic organisational features. Problems facing the integration of the East German state functionaries after national unification were attributed to the GDR's deviation from this *historical legacy*. Thus, one could assume that there was a basic configuration or macro-structure of a 'classical continental bureaucracy' (König, 1992) into which the eastern part of the country had to be fitted, notwithstanding variations of this underlying melody. Furthermore, government and opposition politicians in Bonn repeatedly praised the professional performance of the ministerial bureaucracy in drafting the complex unification treaty with East Germany and thousands of public servants engaged in reconstructing public administration in the eastern part of the country. Nevertheless, under the surface of civil service principles some erosion was visible: party politicisation, mixed careers and an increasing proportion of non-jurists in the administrative elite.

The Traditional Reform Community

In most of the pre-1990 reforms, intensive interaction between reform minded bureaucrats and scientists took place (Derlien, 1996). Reforms were usually well prepared in a long feed-forward process involving commissions, academic research and publications. Most of the reforms were elaborated by mixed commissions of administrators and administrative scientists from the universities. Private policy institutes, party research foundations and management consultants played almost no role in administrative reforms.

Reform commissions are usually technically attached to the Ministry of the Interior when general administrative matters or civil service affairs are at stake. At the federal level, even the interdepartmental task force for government reform (1969-1975) resided with the Ministry of the Interior, although it reported to a cabinet committee. Furthermore, the ministry was in charge of the *Ernst* commission for redrawing *Länder* boundaries (1970-1973), of the civil service reform commission (1969-1973) and, of course, in the early 1980s, the de-bureaucratisation hearing (1980) and the subsequent (Waffenschmidt) commission to cut down on rules and regulations. In 1990, the ministry was responsible for drafting the unification treaty and for its implementation as far as the structure and personnel of public administration were concerned (Derlien, 1993).

Until 1990, the network of reformers and advisers was structured around the Ministry of the Interior, the graduate school of administrative sciences in Speyer, a number of professors from other universities, and the federal civil service academy. This network was imbedded in the German Section of the International Institute of Administrative Sciences. Furthermore, there was a high degree of personnel continuity for 25 years between reform commissions, the ministry, the German Section and the Speyer academy. A similar network exists for local governments. Their associations maintain a consultancy centre in Cologne (KGSt), whose former spokesman, like commission president Bulling (Baden-Württemberg 1985), was awarded an honorary professorship in Speyer. Local governments, in addition, maintain a research centre in Berlin.

This network provided the venue for normal learning for administrative reforms. Here, performance of the administrative system was subjected to social tests (Thompson, 1967), and it is here where reform needs, reform concepts and reform consequences were defined and the paradigmatic interpretation of reality became almost monopolised. Not surprisingly, in the 1960s and early 70s, there was a relative resistance against fashionable ideas to reform the public sector; neither was PPBS with its derivatives adopted – the Germans settled for middle range fiscal planning – nor were management concepts readily imported and nor did the senior civil service experience a shake-up as in the USA with the introduction in 1978 of the SES concept.

Different Horses for Different Courses

Ultimately though, administrative reforms in Germany too could seldom be accomplished without politicians. The function of politicians used to be to legitimise reform concepts developed by the bureaucracy, in particular reforms involving legislation, e.g. territorial and constitutional local government reforms. This support was a requirement for privatising rail and mail, and would become necessary if the traditional civil service principles (Article 33, Section 5 *Grundgesetz*) were to be abolished. Internal government reforms and house-cleaning exercises (de-bureaucratisation), however, depend solely on the consent of executive politicians. All other reforms were brought about without broad public discussion. This might be the reason why politicians, at least at the national level, did not associate themselves with specific reform models. They neither drove reforms, nor did they claim their merits. Also, public sector matters were rarely issues in party platforms or electoral campaigns as, e.g., of US presidents. Exceptions to this rule are reforms aimed at strengthening citizens' rights (data protection officers; equal opportunity commissioners; ombudsman in the *Länder*). Politicians in Germany tend to propose substantive policy improvements rather than structural (formal) innovations. Of course, politicians could block reforms, as happened with the civil service reform in 1973. They are also needed for building consensus for particular reform concepts like the plans to move government departments to Berlin. Ultimately though, politicians need and would rarely reject reform concepts originating from the bureaucracy, for in Germany, in particular, executive politicians are often jurists themselves and tend to rely on the intelligence of bureaucracy.

This traditional reform network has gradually changed since Chancellor Schmidt complained about the incomprehensibility of his private water bill in 1978 and initiated de-bureaucratisation attempts. Later on, privatisation and deregulation became topics of interest to Chancellor Kohl's first government. Kohl's 'Falkland war', German unification, stalled further reforms, not least because the traditional administrative structure and public service model proved to be a reliable tool for transforming eastern Germany. Politicians' initiatives since 1991, however, and public sector reform topics on party platforms are clear indications that the 'bearer strata' is changing. In his government declaration of January 1995, Chancellor Kohl borrowed the metaphor 'lean state' from management consultants and appointed a 'Lean State' reform commission in July 1995. Also in 1995, the parliamentary (*Bundestag*) group of the Green/Alliance 90 party organised a hearing under the headline 'Father State takes retirement. Public Administration under pressure for change'.

Notably local governments and their associations, squeezed for years by the costs of implementing federal programmes, are facing the consequences of the federal government's cutbacks in unemployment benefits and the simultaneous decline in or lack of (eastern German) revenues. Orders to cut budgets had already appeared during the decade 1975 to 1985. Since then, local governments have been more innovative in responding to scarcity. Therefore, it is no wonder that it was at first the municipalities that were attracted to new managerialist models, stressing the service function of local government in rhetoric and reinforcing cost accounting and the controller concept in practice (Banner, 1991).

Considerably later, the Premiers of various *Länder* took positions: Simonis (Social Democrat, Schleswig-Holstein), Biedenkopf (Christian Democrat, Saxony), Stoiber (Christian Social Union, Bavaria) – to name just a few. In January 1995, Simonis started bringing to public consciousness what had been recognised by scientists as early as 1988 (Färber, 1988): the mounting fiscal burden that will be felt heavily when large cohorts of civil servants retire after the year 2000. Soon the *Länder* started pleading for measures to cut personnel costs by reducing the size of the public service, abandoning public tasks, having civil servants work after the previous retirement age, limiting early retirement, making civil servants contribute to their pensions and, last but not least, substituting public employees on private contracts for civil servants. In particular, the Social Democrats summarised these initiatives under the term 'modernisation'.

The Federal Ministry of the Interior, traditionally in charge of public service affairs and principles of federal government organisation, reacted by putting together a shopping list of civil service reform items that became effective in July 1997. Among other things, performance related pay by giving bonuses (although intending to keep total personnel expenditure constant) is emphasised and performance appraisals are to be encouraged. Promotions to leading positions are to be for a probationary period. Automatic pay increases every two years, a loyalty premium until now, are to accelerate at the beginning and to slow down at the end of a career to make the public service more attractive, particularly for policemen. When the Minister of the Interior, in finally presenting his concept to the public, spoke of the 'broadest approach to public service reform for decades', the weekly paper *Die Zeit* (21 April 1995, p.33) qualified the plans as 'adaptive amendments'.

Concomitantly, idea givers and advisers now tend to be professors of business administration and, increasingly, management consultants. Previously, only in exceptional circumstances were commercial consultants brought in, such as McKinsey in the Agricultural ministry's PPBS-attempt (1973). The general experience with management consultants in Germany up to the 1980s was that they had little understanding for the particular circumstances under which public administration operates. The private Bertelsmann Foundation, which has sponsored research and experimentation in public management since 1987, initially had no access to the centres of power, although the former foreign policy adviser to the chancellor, Horst Teltschick, administered the foundation for a while. Only when certain professors from the Speyer academy, in alliance with one of their honorary professors from the KGSt, started co-operation with Bertelsmann, did the traditional 'Speyer front' crumble and NPM ideas spread in local government circles. Besides honouring local governments in a world-wide competition for excellent performance (according to NPM standards), publications increasingly became less analytical, rather attempting to convince and to create a 'new reform spirit' (Hill, 1993). Most dazzling to traditional observers, the Bavarian government, usually known as a guardian of traditional values, the monopoly of jurists and a clean public service, recently published the draft of a public service *Leitbild* in order to create a 'corporate identity' for the '*Unternehmen Freistaat Bayern*', following the example of *Siemens* and advised by a management consultant.

At the present time, certain journals are dominated by articles from a new training college generation propagating the *Neue Steuerungsmodell* of the KGSt. Most significantly, though, the federal government, too, has increasingly relied on management consultants such as Roland Berger and McKinsey. In 1996 consulting the public sector was a 1.4 billion DM business (*Frankfurter Allgemeine Zeitung* 3 June 1997, p.8). Indicative of the change of protagonists is the composition of the federal government's reform commission, 'Lean State', that was inaugurated in 1995 and which staged a conference and a fair (sic) in 1997. Seven of its 18 members are *Länder* and Federal politicians, three are from the business sector including consultant R. Berger, three are professors (including Hill and Scholz, who are also politicians), three represent the important public sector unions, and only two are from the area of public administration, a mayor and a former political civil servant. Obviously, business administrators as a class are successfully fighting for new 'life chances' (Weber), selling their concepts to politicians and thereby creating positions in particular for accountants and controllers.

The traditional reform community is viewing this tendency with some scepticism. In their view, much of what is claimed, proposed and discussed nowadays, takes on the rhetoric of the international NPM movement. In this respect, the divide in German academic circles on recent administrative modernisation (Wollmann, 1996) has a parallel in the UK and the US where the scientific community is far from unanimous in advocating NPM or 'reinventing government'. This tends to be overlooked by reform protagonists (Gresham's law of reform: Pros drive out Cons). Of course, Miles's law (where you stand depends on where you sit) does not *per se* invalidate the arguments of either side. The instrumental value of some reform suggestions is discussed later.

Similarities and Differences Between the UK and Germany

On closer inspection, there are not merely differences between the British reform movement and the German reform discussion. In fact, my argument is that the cases are rather asymmetric than contrary in nature.

On the one hand, the UK in the 1980s had to cope with a severe modernisation lag and produced changes that, for various reasons, already constituted reality in Germany. On the other hand, the German polity and the institutional heritage of this country are adversarial toward sweeping changes, thus allowing only for limited and gradual adaptations according to the decision pattern of disjointed incrementalism. These adaptations, hesitant as they are, are nevertheless often in accordance with general reform movements in OECD countries, last but not least with what was exemplified in the UK.

To start with, the change of the *reform protagonists* observed in the case of Germany has a forerunner in the UK. Major advisers to Prime Minister Thatcher were recruited from the business sector (Rayner and his efficiency unit), and in the process of implementing public sector reforms the accountants also took over in many fields (such as the NHS). In the 1960s, UK reforms had been initiated by the largely self-controlled civil service. Civil service reforms were elaborated in the UK (Fulton report 1968) before Bonn – on the request of *Bundestag* – followed suit with explicit reference to the British endeavour. Equally the federal civil service academy (1970) was an imitation of the Civil Service College. Territorial local government amalgamations swept over western Europe, probably most dramatically in the UK and West Germany (1964-1978). Metropolitan developmental planning was a mutual reform topic, too, as were reforms in the functional areas of policy planning (Johnson, 1972) and evaluation (Gray, Jenkins and Segsworth, 1993).

While these reforms took place during the social-democrat/Labour era in both countries, the conservative age was to bring about privatisation and deregulation in both countries, albeit to a different extent. Screening public tasks started on the local level in about 1974, and a debate about privatisation began considerably before the Kohl conservative government came to power in 1982. De-bureaucratisation in the broadest sense, including what later came to be called deregulation and privatisation as in the UK and the US, was taken up at the federal level in 1980 after the *Länder* had set up commissions to 'simplify administration and administrative regulations' as early as 1978 (Ellwein, 1989). Deregulation of the economy took place most significantly in the telecom-sector and was basically a response to EU policy. Railways and Postal Affairs (including Telecom and the Postbank), in a reversal of their 19th century establishment, were transformed into private law corporations in both countries by 1995. Finally, privatisation of the state economy occurred on an unprecedented scale in eastern Germany. In general, however, many tasks that were privatised in other EU countries had either never been public but private in Germany (e.g. safety inspections) or were left to the 'third sector' (Seibel, 1992), had always been decentralised on public self-governing bodies (e.g. pension funds), or are a matter of the *Länder* (e.g. prisons) and local governments (e.g. water and electricity supply). On the other hand, the German education and university sector had been operated by the state from the early 19th century onwards.

The extent of British privatisation was broader (Wright, 1994, p.110) because the number of nationalised industries was far larger than in Germany, where Volkswagen and VEBA had already been privatised in 1960, and Lufthansa was a private law company from its inception. Also, many local water and electricity supply or traffic enterprises no longer had public law status (*Regiebetriebe*) in Germany when the UK central government started its privatisation 'bandwagon'. Last but not least, there was nothing comparable to the UK National Health Service in Germany. Therefore, the Financial Management Initiative appeared to be much more dramatic than the further 'selling of the family silver' in Germany. Although compulsory competitive tendering (involving public offices as bidders) is not known in Germany, functional privatisation (cleaning office buildings, construction plans, hospital laundry etc.) dates back at least to the 1970s.

Looking at the similarities from the point of view of 1997, in both countries attempts at a second civil service reform in the early 1990s are recognisable. The reform attempts mentioned above and promoted by German politicians have an equivalent in kind in the White Paper 'Continuity and Change' (the Treasury and Civil Service Select Committee's Report on the Civil Service) and the Government's Command Paper 'Taking forward Continuity and Change'. Furthermore, the managerialist re-introduction of a politics-administration dichotomy (or the separation of policy and operations) is at the heart of the '*Neue Steuerungsmodell*' proposed for local government. Common to both countries, however, are also doubts about the compatibility of the new internal control system with the principle of ministerial accountability, and, more generally: disputes about the potentially de-politicising effects of this policy-operations separation (Gray and Jenkins, 1995; Ridley, 1995).

Nevertheless, there are differences between both countries which should remind German discussants that the concept of NPM is broader than the *Neues Steuerungsmodell.* An essential part of NPM is the idea of decentralising the administrative macro-system. However, this is a device typical for a unitary state. Be it the UK discussion about devolution of Scotland and Wales, which resurfaced from the 1970s, be it the Next Steps Programme, both do not apply to a federal state like Germany where the federal government has few responsibilities for the implementation of federal laws and programmes. For instance, in Germany, operation and oversight of prisons falls under the authority of the *Länder.* Furthermore, federal ministries are surrounded by roughly 100 more or less independent agencies ranging from the federal statistical office to the *Bundesverwaltungsamt* (general administration under purview of the ministry of interior). Therefore, it could be argued that the UK government, in its attempt at decentralisation, is trying to close a modernisation gap that has, partly for constitutional reasons, never occurred in the German system. Thus, differences in type of reforms (National Health Service, decentralisation) and in their scope (privatisation in general) derive from special British conditions.

Explanations of the remaining differences between the countries might be found in the fact that the UK faced *economic and fiscal problems* a decade before Germany. More important is the difference in regime type. In a *unitary state*, central government reform programmes are more encompassing than in a federation where reforms are likely to follow the pattern of disjointed incrementalism because of the many *veto points* built into the system. In addition, the UK is not only a unitary state but, most importantly, enjoys also a *single party majority government.* Therefore the statement that the UK has or had a comprehensive reform philosophy almost amounts to a tautology.

In any case, Christopher Hood (1996) pointed out that some of the British reform measures had precedents reaching partly as far back as the Fulton report; furthermore there are indications of cumulative learning throughout the 1980s, i.e. although the reform elements are fairly consistent and largely derive from a belief in the superiority of market mechanisms over administrative allocations, they were not laid down in a master plan in 1979.

Disputed Key Concepts

Nevertheless, this rather formal inspection of public sector reforms in both countries conceals important differences in the substance, aims and justification, and impediments to specific devices. It is here, where there is room for institutional legacies.

'Slimming Down the State' vs. the 'Skeleton State'

In particular, substantive national differences in public service reforms originate from divergent concepts of the public service. Curbing public tasks, be it in extent or by categorically terminating them altogether is behind the slogans of 'lean state' and 'restructuring the welfare state'. These are repetitions and extensions of the privatisation and deregulation attempts of the 1980s. In Germany, since 1990, more emphasis was placed on cutting back social transfer programmes, and the financing system of the self-regulating health care and pension systems is being trimmed. The constitutional, programmatic notion of *'Sozialstaat'*, though, as well as corresponding political convictions in both major political parties in Germany and the tradition of consensus in these matters does not allow for sweeping changes. Contrary to Britain, where the notion of 'hollowing out the state' (Rhodes, 1994) or its reduction to a "skeleton state" (Ridley, 1995) may feasibly be applied because there are no constitutional safeguards, I would argue that in Germany the public sector is losing some weight because of a shortage of food (revenues) and is undergoing plastic surgery rather than amputations.

Peculiar Public Service Fragmentation in Germany

Curbing public tasks is one way of cutting personnel costs in the public service, another is reducing personnel size in persisting task areas, thus lowering the quality of services for instance in schools (class size) or reducing public opening hours in libraries or recreation parks. Of course, having the public servants work longer (per week or in an entire professional life) will also reduce personnel costs. Add periodic recruitment stops and lowering of entry grades and then this resembles the traditional mixture of public service expenditure controls.

A new element, though, is the determination of some *Länder* to reshuffle the public service from the allegedly more expensive civil service to public employee status. The protagonists have obviously overlooked what has been going on in eastern Germany since October 1990. Abolishing the traditional separation of the three public service status groups, though, is hardly a new idea: creating a uniform public service was a plan harboured by Social Democrats and unions since 1918; the civil service reform commission had produced models to that effect in 1973. Conflicts between unions representing the three status groups and political parties aligned with them prevented the necessary change of the federal constitution – a constellation obviously repeated today. On the other hand, public employees as a status group are enjoying some of the alleged privileges of civil servants (including *de facto* tenure after 15 years of service), thanks to union bargaining in the past.

It is superfluous to say that the UK, too, knows a differentiation of civil servants (basically in Whitehall) and the rest of the public service. What matters here is that public service affairs are regulated in a different way: they are Crown prerogative and can be regulated by Her Majesty's Government. Thus, institutions both in the weak sense of the concept (public service ideology) and in the strong sense (constitutionally enshrined in Art. 33, Section 5) are relevant here. However, Art. 33, sections 4 and 5, can, in principle, be altered – presupposing there is a sufficient majority. Furthermore, there is some room for interpretation that allows for adjustment. For instance, it is far from clear what the expression '*hoheitliche Befugnisse*' (authoritative acts) ultimately implies and it is increasingly doubted whether teachers and professors are necessarily covered by this term. Also, this functional reservation for civil servants is a rule allowing for exceptions; in fact, often employees and civil servants are doing the same job.

The 1997 reform of the civil service code led to a re-interpretation of the principle of full devotion to one's office that traditionally meant full-time employment. Applicants to the civil service are now permitted to enter on part-time jobs; formerly, part-time employment was granted civil servants only as a measure of social policy later in professional life.

Finally, this debate shows that there is nothing like a homogeneous public service in Germany (nor in the UK). Ellwein and Zoll (1973) have already questioned this notion. The normative and social differentiation of the service and its functional specialisation according to *Länder*, branches and levels of government make it highly unlikely that there is something like a unifying role understanding.

Civil Service Performance Measurement and Pay

Not only were certain elements of the German Fulton Commission's 1973 report widely discussed, for example, the suggestion to appoint top administrators only for a fixed number of years; some of those devices that did not require constitutional change were even applied after 1973, such as improved performance appraisal and re-assessment of the fit between salary grades and job requirements. Yet, the reform expired about 1978. Thus, the 1997 reform (strengthening the merit principle and appointments on probation) brought about a renaissance of old ideas – and a re-emphasis of a traditional civil service principle.

As long as there is no consensus on how to measure individual performance, in particular on jobs with qualitative requirements, performance appraisals will have little validity. If quantitative criteria are applied this is likely to result in goal displacements. Under these conditions, as foreign experience shows, bonus systems will soon become inflationary and be regarded as a substitute for lagging general pay increases. Furthermore, if bonuses are limited in number due to budget constraints, withholding them will create dissatisfaction, and suspicions of nepotism will spread (Ingraham, 1993). The introduction of a performance related pay scheme in the UK (1982, 1988) failed, *inter alia*, because the beneficiaries of the scheme, the higher civil servants, showed scruples in taking extra payments while lower ranks had to carry the burden of restrictive pay policy (Keraudren, 1994). Another innovation in the UK was the decentralisation of civil service recruitment from the civil service commission to ministries and agencies (Johnson 1994, p.198). Again, this is long-standing practice in Germany. Thus, there are serious doubts about the instrumental value of performance related pay.

In principle, efforts to define performance indicators for agencies are facing the same problem of selectively measuring outputs. This point is relevant for another reform element: Performance contracts with agency heads will suffer from the same instrumental weakness. One of the consequences could be a tendency to de-couple senior executive pay from general public service pay. In Germany, this was the case in top positions of the *Bundesbank*, Railways, Telecom etc. even before they were privatised and the separation from the public salary scheme became possible. Top salaries are justified with the need to recruit managers from private industry; yet in recent years top positions in privatised agencies and enterprises were often staffed with top civil servants and merited politicians in both countries

(Gray and Jenkins, 1996, p.239). In general, though, public sector pay in Germany remains status-related as it used to be in the UK until 1982; promotion, traditionally, is the only reward for good performance in both countries. Besides, there is ample evidence that executive pay in the cherished private sector is hardly coupled with company performance.

The performance principle is no German particularity. There may be, however, national differences as to the extent to which the principle is violated (e.g. by patronage) and the sincerity of developing performance measurement techniques. The methodical problems of this undertaking, once again, are universal and of a purely technical nature. These problems could, in the long run, nevertheless impair public service qualifications, morale and attractiveness, in particular if appointments on probation or terminated contracts are used for party politicisation or disciplinary purposes. With respect to civil service independence as a prerequisite to giving neutral advice to executive politicians, fears in the UK resemble German criticisms.

Separation of Policy-making from Management

The Next Steps programme, *inter alia*, contained the above mentioned setting up of agencies outside the ministries. As stated above, there was hardly a principal need to do so in Bonn. The measure entails the notion that policy can be separated from operations without impairing parliamentary accountability of executive politicians. This underlying idea can be found in the *Neue Steuerungsmodell en vogue* with local government in Germany. While the local council is to concentrate on goal setting and controlling results (including those of local enterprises with private law status), the executive under the leadership of an often directly elected mayor is to manage the implementation process. Concomitant delegation of budgetary responsibility is to allow for reallocations in departmental budgets and to improve productivity in terms of stated goals. This implies goal specification of all activities (well known from 'management by objectives' of the 1970s) and performance indicators (a premise of management by results). As concomitant formal privatisation could reduce local councils to controlling goal achievement, 'liberation from the rigidity' of parliamentary budget right and civil service law and pay scheme, as well as managerialist role understanding among civil servants, will re-introduce an artificial politics-administration dichotomy. It is feared that this will lead to executive leadership and reverse the enlarged citizen participation of the 1970s, thus inducing a de-politicisation of local self-government (Derlien, 1996a; Wollmann, 1996).

It could be argued that such a reform is more appropriate in the UK due to the notion of strict civil service neutrality than it is in Germany; it might also, as a normative concept, apply better in the U.S. owing to W. Wilson's legacy and the particular view of separation of powers in the U.S. presidential system. The alleged impartiality of the German (senior) civil service and its seemingly apolitical role understanding, however, did not stand the test of the Weimar Republic. Not only would it be undesirable to have senior civil servants conceal their functionally politicised role once again (Mayntz and Derlien, 1989), it is also hardly imaginable how to turn them into apolitical managers. Possibly, the formal neutralisation of civil servants in the UK and the absence of the safety valve of temporary retirement as in Germany could be reasons for an easy adoption of a managerialist role understanding in the UK. There are some indications, however, that the loss of (apparently) neutral policy advice, including the ethics of remonstration, is viewed by some civil servants as a qualitative loss.

Furthermore, the concepts of agencification and contract management have obviously not yet solved the problems involved for parliamentary ministerial accountability of administrative operations (Foster, 1996). A hierarchy of offices and positions ultimately deriving from parliament is obviously needed for politically legitimating public administration. Hierarchy as the most prominent trait of bureaucracy tends to be less visible these days, for orders are culturally no longer accepted as a suitable style of communication. In the last resort, though, orders can be issued. Equally, contracts between ministers and managers, senators and university presidents (in Berlin) conceal the basically asymmetrical relationship between the two sides and the possibility to cancel contracts unilaterally. Frequent interference of ministers with agency operations reported from the UK (Gray and Jenkins, 1996, p.235), annoying as they may be for the manager concerned, can be understood as expressing the continuing information and control need implied in ministerial accountability.

Conclusion

A number of parallels, both in the reform process and its substance and problems, were observed in the UK and Germany.

NPM gained ground in the UK more than a decade before it was introduced in Germany, predominantly at local government level. In fact, the UK must be regarded as a forerunner of this movement. In the 1960s, both countries kept pace with each other and there are instances where Germany benefited from cross-fertilisation (Fulton report). In addition, the change from the high priests of administrative reform in the bureaucracy to political prophets of reforms occurred in the UK first, whereas it is a recent, post-unification phenomenon in Germany. In both cases, fiscal pressures have triggered reforms, again with Britain facing these problems already at the end of the 1970s.

No wonder that today economists are believed to control the reform dogma (and to have the on 'salvation' options). Administrative scientists in both countries who emphasise the peculiarities of the (national) public sector have lost centre stage. This change of bearer strata goes hand in hand with the spread of seemingly universally applicable reform models. In Germany, slogans and metaphors borrowed from the international wave of managerialist thinking gained ground at local government level ('the citizen as customer' and 'the commune as a service enterprise'). These products of semantic management are met with suspicion by those who prefer a more sober approach to taking seriously the traditional imperative of economy and effectiveness (*Wirtschaftlichkeit und Sparsamkeit*). Criticism is backed by academic observations from the very field of business administration that point at the myth-creating function of management models (Kieser, 1996), and an insider from the consultant industry recently revealed the consultants' strategy of 'concept recycling' from private enterprises to the public sector (Staute, 1996). Compared to public sector reforms in Great Britain that are ideologically rooted in the belief of the superiority of the market, recent German modernisation attempts once again are not comprehensive, neither in their logic nor in their abandonment of established public sector principles; but they are comprehensive in being dominated by a new style post-modernist eclecticism (Derlien, 1995; 1996b; König 1996). On second thoughts, this is, however, in line with customary piecemeal engineering.

Uncertainty divides the reform community in both countries (and elsewhere) about whether the reforms offer the high road to administrative modernisation or the slippery slope to paralysis of national administrative cultures, possibly a sort of retrograde progress. In trying to economise, modernisers seem not to be aware of the danger of spilling the baby with the bathwater. This is expressed in increasing concerns, not dealt with in this paper, about the erosion of public sector ethics that the neo-Taylorist emphasis on monetary incentives and the economising of transactions in the service and in interactions with the public could engender. Functional privatisation and competitive tendering could well create additional leverage points for corruption. As long as no serious evaluations of reforms are undertaken, the notion of the potentially regressive character of certain reform measures cannot be dismissed easily.

It was shown that in copying British reform elements, the regime type of the UK as a unitary state with initially little internal de-concentration, a large sector of nationalised industries and a national health service should be taken into account. Similarly, a Citizen Charter may be urgently needed in a country without a system of administrative courts (Ridley, 1995).

Sweeping reforms are facilitated in a unitary state with a single party majority government, in particular when matters of bureaucratic structure and the public service can be regulated by executive order. Germany's reform pattern of disjointed incrementalism, on the contrary, is due to its character as a federal state with a high degree of local government autonomy and to the predominance of coalition governments. This fragmented system provides too many veto points for encompassing reforms. In addition, basic civil service reforms can only be initiated following changes of the federal constitution.

Nevertheless, certain NPM reform elements have been introduced in Germany, too. These tend to be of a universalistic, policy-neutral, instrumental character and do not contradict constitutional norms: performance measurement and pay, more delegation and, in particular, a broader gap between policy and operations, and privatisation. However, these measures occasionally conflict with existing legal norms (strict performance pay vs. the alimentation principle), have to be enacted within a narrow room for manoeuvre (programme curtailment and the '*Sozialstaatsprinzip*') or are meeting resistance for reasons of political culture (managerialist role understanding of top civil servants, de-politicisation of local government).

Consequently, in a survey of modernisation policies in OECD countries, Naschold (1995, pp.68-72) concluded that Germany was going a much more selective developmental path compared to the UK and other unitary states. Peters argued that reform models are selectively absorbed according to different state philosophies (Peters, 1994), and Hood (1991) pointed at different value sets NPM is more or less compatible with. Taking into account the undoubted importance of regime type, situational factors and the international *Zeitgeist* – how much of the remaining variance between the two countries is left for an institutionalist explanation emphasising bureaucracy and the notion of public service? Maybe, I do not see the forest for the trees, but my answer would be: not much. To a certain extent the reason is that features like political neutrality of the senior civil service (vs. party politicisation) or the British notion of ministerial accountability are part of the respective regime type and the broader configuration and can therefore only analytically be singled out. In methodological terms, my argument therefore is that judgements of the performance of an administrative system and resulting reform attempts can best be conceived of as strategic choices (Child, 1997): objective situational constraints, power-dependency relations including their normative underpinning, and cognitive maps, such as the notions of bureaucracy and public service, have to be taken into account simultaneously when explaining public sector changes in a country and differences between countries. Each of these aspects might be a necessary but not sufficient factor of explanation.

References

Banner, G. (1991), 'Von der Behörde zum Dienstleistungsunternehmen', *Verwaltungsführung, Organisation, Personal*, vol. 13, pp. 6-11.
Child, J. (1997), 'Strategic Choice in the Analysis of Action, Structure, Organizations and Environment: Retrospect and Prospect', *Organization Studies*, vol. 18, pp. 43-76.
Derlien, H.-U. (1991), 'Historical Legacy and Recent Developments of the German Higher Civil Service', *International Review of Administrative Sciences*, vol. 57, pp. 385-401.
Derlien, H.-U. (1993), 'German Unification and Bureaucratic Transformation', *International Political Science Review*, vol. 14, pp. 319-34.
Derlien, H.-U. (1995), 'La modernisation administrative en Allemagne – "du vieux vin dans de nouvelles bouteilles"', *Revue francaise d'administration publique*, vol. 75, pp. 413-22.
Derlien, H.-U. (1996a), 'Germany: The Intelligence of Bureaucracy in a Decentralized Polity', in J. P. Olsen and B. G. Peters (eds.), *Lessons from Experience. Experiential Learning in Administrative Reforms in Eight Democracies*, Scandinavian University Press, Oslo, pp. 146-79.
Derlien, H.-U. (1996b), 'Verwaltungsmodernisierung: modern, modernistisch, postmodern?', in G. Färber (ed.), *Schlanker Staat. Zwischen Paradigmen und Pragmatismus*, GfP-Werkstattbericht 18, München, pp. 103-21.
Derlien, H.-U. (1998), *From Administrative Reform to Administrative Modernization*, Verwaltungswissenschaftliche Beiträge 33, Bamberg.

Ellwein, T. (1989), *Verwaltung und Verwaltungsvorschriften. Notwendigkeit und Chance der Vorschriftenvereinfachung*, Westdeutscher Verlag, Opladen.
Ellwein, T. and Zoll, R. (1973), *Berufsbeamtentum - Anspruch und Wirklichkeit. Zur Entwicklung und Problematik des öffentlichen Dienstes*, Westdeutscher Verlag, Düsseldorf.
Färber, G. (1988), *Revision der Personalausgabenprojektion der Gebietskörperschaften bis 2030*, Speyerer Forschungsberichte 110, (3rd ed. 1995).
Foster, C. (1996), 'Reflections on the True Significance of the Scott Report for Government Accountability', *Public Administration*, vol. 74, pp. 567-92.
Gray, A. and Jenkins, B. (1995), 'Public Administration and Government 1993-94', *Parliamentary Affairs*, vol. 48, pp. 1-23.
Gray, A. and Jenkins, B. (1996), 'Public Administration and Government 1994-95', *Parliamentary Affairs*, vol. 49, pp. 235-55.
Gray, A., Jenkins, B. and Segsworth, R. (eds) (1993), *Budgeting, Auditing and Evaluation*, Transaction Publishers, New Brunswick/London.
Hill, H. (1993), 'Strategische Erfolgsfaktoren in der öffentlichen Verwaltung', *Die Verwaltung*, vol. 26, pp. 167-81.
Hood, C. (1991), 'A Public Management for All Seasons?', *Public Administration*, vol. 69, pp. 3-19.
Hood, C. (1996), 'United Kingdom: From Second Chance to Near-Miss Learning', in J.P. Olsen and P.G. Peters (eds) (1996), *Lessons from Experience. Experiential Learning in Administrative Reforms in Eight Democracies*, Scandinavian University Press, Oslo, pp. 36-70.
Ingraham, P. W. (1993), 'Of Pigs in Pokes and Policy Diffusion: Another Look at Pay-for-Performance', *Public Administration Review*, vol. 53, pp. 348-56.
Johnson, N. (1972), 'Reorganisation in Central Administration: Developments 1970-72', in *Projektgruppe Regierungs- und Verwaltungsreform*, Anlagenband, Bonn (unpublished).
Johnson, N. (1994), 'Der Civil Service in Großbritannien: Tradition und Modernisierung', *Die öffentliche Verwaltung*, vol. 47, pp. 196-200.
Keraudren, Ph. (1994), 'The Introduction of Performance Related Pay in the British Civil Service (1982-88): a Cultural Perspective', *International Review of Administrative Sciences*, vol. 60, pp. 23-36.
Kieser, A. (1996), 'Moden & Mythen des Organisierens', *Der Betriebswirt*, vol. 56, pp. 21-39.
König, K. (1992), 'The Transformation of a "Real-Socialist" Administrative System into a Conventional Western European System', *International Review of Administrative Sciences*, vol. 58, pp. 147-61.
König, K. (1996), 'On the Critique of New Public Management', *Speyer Forschungsbericht 155*, Speyer.
March, J.D. and Olsen, J.P. (1989), *Rediscovering Institutions. The Organizational Basis of Politics*, Free Press, New York.

Mayntz, R. and Derlien, H.U. (1989), 'Party Patronage and Politicization of the West German Administrative Elite 1970-1987 - Towards Hybridization?' *Governance*, vol. 2, pp. 384-404.

Naschold, F. (1995), *Ergebnissteuerung, Wettbewerb, Qualitätspolitik. Entwicklungspfade des öffentlichen Sektors in Europa*, Edition Sigma, Berlin.

Olsen, J.P. and Peters, B.G. (eds) (1996), *Lessons from Experience. Experiential Learning in Administrative Reforms in Eight Democracies*, Scandinavian University Press, Oslo.

Peters, G. B. (1994), unpublished IPSA paper, Berlin.

Reichard, C. and Wollmann, H. (eds) (1996), *Kommunalverwaltung im Modernisierungsschub*, Birkhäuser, Basel.

Rhodes, R.A.W. (1994), 'The Hollowing out of the State: the Changing Nature of the Public Service in Britain', *Political Quarterly*, vol. 65, pp. 138-51.

Ridley, F.F.(1995), 'Re-inventing British Government', *Parliamentary Affairs*, vol. 48, pp. 387-400.

Rosenberg, H. (1958), *Bureaucracy, Aristocracy and Autocracy. The Prussian Experience 1660-1815*, Harvard Univ. Press, Cambridge, Mass.

Seibel, W. (1992), *Task Reform: Privatization, Deregulation, Debureaucratization, Third Sector Development*, Konstanz, unpublished research report.

Staute, J. (1996), *Der Consulting-Report. Vom Versagen der Manager zum Reibach der Berater*, Campus, Frankfurt/New York.

Thompson, J. D. (1967), *Organizations in Action*, New York, McGraw-Hill.

Wollmann, H. (1996), 'Verwaltungsmodernisierung: Ausbildungsbedingungen, Reformanläufe und aktuelle Modernisierungsdiskurse', in C. Reichard and H. Wollmann (eds), *Kommunalverwaltung im Modernisierungsschub*, Birkhäuser, Basel, pp. 1-49.

Wright, V. (1994), 'Reshaping the State. The Implications for Public Administration', *West European Politics*, vol. 17, pp. 102-37.

9 Local Government Services in the United Kingdom and Germany

ECKHARD SCHRÖTER AND MANFRED RÖBER

Introduction

No analysis of the British and German public sectors can be made without an extensive discussion of local government as a core element of the national administrative system (see also Hellmut Wollmann's contribution on local government in this volume). In fact, the popular cliché that local authorities 'look after you from the cradle to the grave' describes relatively accurately the wide-ranging responsibilities of local administrations in both countries. Despite the differing constitutional status and structural set-up of the two national local government systems (Barlow and Röber, 1996), our investigation into the characteristics of employment and human resource management in British and German local authorities starts from a broad area of common ground: In both countries, local self-government has traditionally been an important feature of political and administrative life, and people in Germany and Britain rely heavily on public services provided or 'enabled' by their local councils. It is not surprising, therefore, that British and German local authorities are, by any standards, major employers and account for a considerable part of total public employment. Given the highly labour-intensive nature of their services, the major share of local authorities' expenditure falls on staff costs, and thus the performance of local government is heavily dependent on the quality of its workforce. Consequently, human resource management deserves closer attention as a critical variable for the effectiveness and efficiency of local government services and has rightly become a prime target for reform critics and protagonists alike.

In neither country is there a single legal or sociological entity called *the* 'local government service'. Rather, local government employment appears to be a particularly intractable subject in view of the multiplicity of separate employing authorities and the hundreds of occupations needed to deliver the whole range of local services. In addition, the ongoing reforms in public sector management, designed to reduce bureaucratic uniformity and to break up monolithic organisational structures in order to permit greater flexibility in human resource management, have probably made it more questionable than ever before in this century to speak indiscriminately of a single, unified 'local government service'. Nevertheless, it still holds true for both countries that employment in local authorities has certain common characteristics and is generally guided by an agreed set of nationwide standards. Thus, in this paper the term 'local government service' is used interchangeably with 'local government workforce' or 'employment'.

Against this background, this chapter seeks to explore both the common traits and distinctive features of employment patterns and developments in human resource management in British and German local authorities. The first step in this analysis puts the current state of modern local government and its workforce into its historical perspective in order to reveal long-term trends which may have an impact on present-day administrative developments. Secondly, the size and composition of the local government service, which are closely tied to internal and external structural arrangements of the national local government systems, are considered. Thirdly, we shall turn to essential components of human resource management, paying particular attention to aspects of education and training as well as to the recruitment and career development of local government employees. The final section attempts to draw the threads of the discussion together by raising the question of 'convergence' or 'divergence' of the two national systems.

The Historical Development of Local Government

Given a simplified view of the roots and origins of the modern local government service, it would seem that the similarities between the two countries still continue – at least as long as this development is discussed in broad categories (for historical accounts see Stoker, 1991; Laffin and Young, 1990; Poole, 1978; Wunder, 1986; Saldern, 1999). In both cases, forceful socio-economic and political factors such as the advent of industrialisation and urbanisation in the 19th century or the expansion of public services and the establishment of a fully-fledged welfare state in the wake of the Second World War have conditioned the development of local government and its workforce. In the 19th century, for example, pressure came from industrialists to improve local infrastructure and from social reformers to fight the mounting problems of disease and poverty arising from urbanisation. In addition, local politicians came to value public utilities such as gas and electricity as an important source of local government income. As a result, local authorities in both countries took on a wide spectrum of new tasks ranging, among others, from road building and maintenance, the provision of low-cost housing, street lighting, poor relief, water supply and sewerage, refuse collection, public works projects, elementary education, local hospitals and asylums to town and land-use planning. In Britain, this growth of powers and responsibilities in the hands of local councils was accompanied by an organisational development which laid the foundation for modern local authorities. The plethora of rural parishes and municipal corporations alongside a great number of single-purpose boards and other ad hoc bodies was increasingly replaced by elected multi-purpose local authorities. As a corollary of this organisational change, the forebears of today's local government workforce found their role, first, as contractors to local boards and corporations and later as employees of the council and holders of traditional offices such as those of town clerk, surveyor of highways or sanitary engineer. The gradually emerging contours of the 'local government service' were also clearly reflected by the new associations of local government employees, e.g. the Municipal Engineers (1873), the Institute of Municipal Treasurers and Accountants (1885), and, most importantly, the National Association of Local Government Officers (1905) as well as the Institute of Town Planning (1919), which must be seen as early signs of the steady rise of both professionalism and unionisation in British local government (Poole, 1978; Laffin and Young, 1990). These parallel processes helped to prepare the ground for the creation of a national local government labour market by the middle of this century. The protagonists of Whitleyism, who favoured national negotiations on conditions of service, worked, however, unwillingly hand in hand with political interests at the centre to argue in favour of a greater say by central government in local staffing matters as expressed by the 1929 Commission on Local Government, which gave wide currency to the term 'local government service'. Eventually, a national system of employment standards, qualifications and training schemes was established in 1946.

The historical development of local government in the German *Länder* broadly followed a similar pattern to that in Britain, although some notable deviations suggest systematic differences. In general, there was less need for organisational 'streamlining', since the substantial proliferation of ad hoc bodies and the complex network of British local government agencies (frequently with overlapping jurisdictions) was largely unknown in 19th century Germany. Nonetheless, local authorities in the German states and their small and poorly trained staff were completely ill-equipped for the test of the Industrial Revolution. For example, Prussian legislation of 1808 only made provision for at least one jurist, a city treasurer and a municipal building inspector to be included in paid staff positions (Wunder, 1986, p.86). In contrast to the British situation, however, the inevitable change from a lay administration to a qualified local government workforce in Germany was far less influenced by the various academic professions (such as engineers, architects, medical doctors etc.), but was modelled on the civil service which was already deeply rooted at state level. By the turn of the century, every second member of the workforce in German city administrations enjoyed the job guarantees and legal status of a civil servant, while the other half were classified either as salaried public employees or as workers whose conditions of service were governed by private law contracts. In line with the established tenets of the German civil service, the well-known 'monopoly of lawyers' was starting to invade the local government level. In addition, most local authorities adopted a grading structure similar to that of the civil service and even local training institutions for professional administrators were set up in order to make the local government service more compatible with the civil service. Similarly, the emerging associations and unions of public employees were not so much organised along professional lines, but reflected the division of the German public sector workforce into three status groups, namely that of civil servants (*Beamte*), salaried employees (*Angestellte*) and workers (*Arbeiter*) (for details see Röber, 1996).

The post-war period witnessed a further expansion of state activities, and local government authorities became key agents of what has come to be known as the welfare state. Although British local councils lost major responsibilities in the area of public health to the newly established National Health Service and many public utilities became part of the nationalised industries, the scope of local activity in fields such as town planning, transport, housing provision, social services and education broadened immensely. In many instances, post-war legislation was also used as a vehicle to foster professionalism in the local government service and to increase the control of central government over local staffing decisions in order to set and maintain common standards. For example, provision was made for the appointment of senior health and education officers or directors of social services until most obligations to fill statutory posts were abolished by the 1972 Local Government Act. As for the expansion and specialisation of local services, the German case shows, if at all, only slight signs of deviation from this general pattern of development. Indeed, commitment to the paternalistic welfare state was also a cornerstone of the West German republic and the role of local government in reconstruction and easing social hardship in the aftermath of the Second World War can hardly be overestimated. The heyday of expanding state and local government activity, however, also sowed the seeds of future discord. Eventually, the growing strain on resources to fund government programmes and the increasingly critical stance towards paternalistic state intervention provided the fertile ground for these seeds to develop fully. In Britain, this changed context and ideological climate was brought about by the economic recession and budget crisis of the mid-1970s which triggered far-reaching reform programmes. In Germany, the general perception did not change before the early 1990s, when the comparatively comfortable economic situation gave way to increasing financial stress and soaring public debt.

Currently, local authorities in both countries find themselves in a period of radical change which calls into question the traditional role of elected local government as a monopolistic service provider as well as the long-established modes of internal management and steering. In this respect, policy-makers and reform-oriented practitioners in Britain and Germany are following an international trend of administrative modernisation in the shape of the 'New Public Management' (NPM) which highlights the beneficial effects of introducing market-type incentive structures and private sector management styles into the public sector. Rather than sharing the high hopes of 'social engineers' in the problem-solving capacities of government intervention and emphasising the effectiveness of public policy programmes, the efficiency of public management and service provision has now moved into the foreground.

Despite this common trend in local government modernisation, however, reform programmes in Britain and Germany do not seem to follow a single masterplan (see for the German case also Schröter and Wollmann, 1997). Most conspicuously, the vigorously pursued strategy of marketisation of British local government services differs significantly from the comparatively cautious and hesitant approach in Germany. Whereas British reform protagonists have been leading the international reform movement since the late seventies, most policy-makers in Germany only reluctantly joined the bandwagon of NPM-inspired public sector modernisation in the early 1990s. In stark contrast to the German experience, in the UK the prime moving force behind the shift from the traditional model of public administration towards that of the new public management process has been central government. By contrast, the German federal government and many Länder authorities have kept a relatively low profile, while the strongest reform impetus has come from local practitioners (Klages and Löffler, 1995) who are acquainted with the deficiencies of public service delivery from first-hand experience and for whom the financial constraints have been most tangible. Although international calls for NPM-driven public sector reform were originally greeted in Germany with little enthusiasm, a wide variety of management-oriented reform experiments can now be observed at the local level (Reichard, 1994a, 1996; Grömig and Thielen, 1996; Grömig and Gruner, 1998). The core elements of this emerging reform profile are mainly concerned with internal rationalisation and streamlining (e.g. new budgeting and cost accounting systems or decentralised organisational structures), while market-type incentives have so far played only a minor role. In many cases, several aspects of personnel management also rank high on the reform agenda, although the scope of action is severely restricted by tight civil service regulations which apply in a more or less standardised way to all three administrative levels in Germany. It is to these general frameworks of local government employment that we now turn.

The Characteristics of British and German Local Government Services

The Organisational Context: Internal and External Structures of Local Government

Local authorities in Britain and in Germany are multifunctional, providing a wide variety of services to the local community in a restricted geographical area, although in Germany it is a much wider variety than in Britain (see for example Naschold, 1997). They depend on local election and enjoy some autonomy including the power of taxation (see Sharpe 1970, p.154). Although local government in both countries seems to be designed according to a similar political *raison d'etre* their constitutional status is quite different. In the unitarian British system local authorities have no powers except those conferred upon them by Act of Parliament, and thus depend to a large extent on the goodwill of central government (see for example Johnson, 1983). Especially under the Thatcher governments the position of local authorities was drastically weakened (see Butcher *et al.*, 1990). By contrast, German local self-government is based on and safeguarded by the Basic Law which stipulates that 'local authorities must be guaranteed the right to regulate on their own responsibility all the affairs of the local government within the limits set by law' (Wagener, 1990, p.59).

On looking at the external organisational structure of the two national local government systems, another important difference can be identified. Most strikingly, the lower tier of government in the UK stands out from other European examples by reason of the large size of local authorities, both in terms of territory covered and population. Thus, the British local level is organised in 34 English county councils, 32 London boroughs, the Corporation of London, 36 English metropolitan districts, 238 English shire districts, 46 English shire unitary councils plus 22 Welsh unitary councils and 32 Scottish unitary councils (Wilson and Game, 1998, p.58-63). Local government in Germany, which is generally carried out within a two-tier system, consists of 324 counties, 112 county-free cities (which combine county as well as city functions) and about 14,800 towns and municipalities (of which most have formed local authority associations in order to increase their administrative capacities and to employ full-time officials). This, by British standards, huge number of local authorities includes no less than 7,000 cities and villages in the eastern *Länder* where the organisational structures inherited from the old regime are still the subject of ongoing projects of territorial reform. This major discrepancy between the size of local authorities in Britain and Germany has relevant implications for human resource management to which we will return later.

Similarly, the structural features of internal organisation as well as the dominant patterns of decision-making processes within local authorities have had a decisive impact on public personnel management. At first sight, the long-established Weberian model of bureaucracy seems to have served as a guiding organisational principle for local authorities in both countries. A closer look behind this common trait, however, reveals interesting variations. Thus, the British case deviates notably from organisational practice in German local government by its even higher degree of specialisation and departmentalism. This remarkable internal fragmentation appears to be attributable to traditional political and administrative patterns as well as to recent modernisation strategies which have apparently worked in similar directions (see also Alexander, 1991). On the one hand, today's organisational pattern still reflects the origins of modern local authorities which were preceded by a collection of ad hoc bodies. This historical development has also given rise to the still prevailing committee system. More often than not, this peculiar mechanism of political steering has brought about the danger of insularity and activism, hence the creation of a political microcosm for each individual service (Byrne, 1992). On the other hand, the NPM-inspired process of decentralising responsibilities and splitting up large organisations has led to an even more fragmented system with severe effects on the corporate identity of each local authority. As Stoker puts it, '[c]ompetition between service providers and the introduction of quasi-market mechanisms have encouraged a fragmentation and differentiation within the system' (Stoker, 1996, p.18 with reference to Leach, Stewart and Walsh, 1994).

Although far from immune to these organisational ills, the monocratic style of political leadership in German local authorities has helped to moderate disintegrating tendencies. It would go far beyond the scope of this paper to discuss in detail the various local government charters which have been enacted by the *Länder* parliaments. It may suffice here to amplify the prevailing pattern of political control. With the notable exception of those *Länder* which formed the British occupation zone, the administrative power at the top of the organisational hierarchy in local authorities has traditionally been either in the hands of a mayor (or *Landrat* in the case of county authorities) or a small collegiate body (*Magistrat*). During the last decade most local charters in Germany have shifted towards a 'strong' mayor model. As a result, the position of mayors as political leaders and top administrators has been greatly reinforced by a direct mandate from the citizenry (for further details, see Hellmut Wollmann's chapter in this volume).

Size and Composition of the Local Government Workforce

The growth of local activities is, not surprisingly, well reflected in the increasing numbers of local government personnel. While British local authorities employed about 1.4 million staff in 1952, this figure had risen by 1962 to 1.8 million and soared to 2.5 million in 1972 (Poole, 1978, p. 39).

The expansion of the local government service was slowly halted by the mid-1970s, when total staff numbers approached 3 million (Hogwood, 1997). Interestingly, this continuous increase occured under Labour as well as Conservative governments, giving further evidence of the broad welfare consensus and the force of socio-economic factors. This non-partisan interpretation also appears appropriate for the period 1979 to 1988 when local government employment remained relatively stable at a high level and showed no sign of an immediate 'Thatcher effect' (Hogwood, 1997). During the last decade, however, local authorities in Britain have experienced a sizeable reduction in their workforce. This drop in staff numbers has been partly due to the steady reduction of manual workers as a consequence of increased private sector competition and the contracting-out of services. In addition, this trend can be attributed to functional transfers – most significantly, the reclassification of polytechnics and the removal of other institutions of further and higher education from local government control, and most recently, the setting up of combined police authorities. As a result, in 1996 local councils in Britain employed some 2.5 million full- and part-time staff, which amounted to half of all public employment or 10 per cent of the total workforce in the UK (Wilson and Game, 1998, p. 239).

Employment trends in German local government generally follow a similar pattern (for statistical data on the local government workforce and German public sector employment in general see Derlien, Heinemann and Lock, 1998 and Derlien, 1999). Thus, in West Germany the local government workforce expanded continuously from around 550,000 staff in 1950 to 750,000 in 1960, while the 1960s saw a further increase to almost one million employees in 1970. Parallel to the British case, this rapid upward trend was interrupted by the economic recession of the 1970s. Thus, the personnel statistics for the period 1970 to 1990 show a comparatively static picture for the local government service with, if at all, only marginal rates of increase. Of course, German unification brought a boost for local government employment figures. Staff numbers jumped from 1.3 million in 1990 to 2.0 million in 1991 due to the inclusion of east German local officials. This massive increase also points clearly to the problem of over-staffing in most east German local authorities, which in the initial aftermath of unification employed more than 30 per cent of the total German local government workforce, but served little more than 20 per cent of the total population. In the meantime, this disparity has been significantly reduced by means of internal rationalisation, major redundancy programmes and transferring public tasks to private or third sector parties, although local government employment in the east German *Länder* still exceeds west German standards by up to 50 per cent (see also Wollmann 1996, p.132). The downsizing of the local government workforce in the eastern *Länder* eventually resulted in a reduction to 1.7 million in 1996, representing 36 per cent of overall public employment or about 5 per cent of all full- and part-time jobs in the Federal Republic.

A consideration of general 'headcount' labour statistics alone, however, conceals two major employment trends which have changed the composition of the British and, to a lesser extent, the German local government service: the growing importance of part-time employment and the rising share of female employees in local government. Particularly in Britain, the workforce of today's local authorities is characterised by its high proportion of female employees, who account for 70 per cent of total employment and occupy most of the part-time jobs (see Wilson and Game, 1998 and Hogwood, 1997). In Germany, too, the share of part-time and female employment is highest at the local government level, though the numerical predominance of female employees, who fill 58 per cent of local government job positions (as compared to 51 per cent in the public sector), is less than in the British case. In addition, German local authorities offer markedly fewer opportunities for part-time jobs (25 per cent) than their British counterparts (45 per cent).

Since overall employment figures only present aggregates of a multiplicity of policy programmes, we need also to examine more closely the various local government functions in order to arrive at an adequate picture of the local workforce in each country (for the German case see Derlien, Heinemann and Lock, 1998, pp. 27-43). Breaking down the British employment statistics into functional categories (see Audit Commission, 1995 and 1997, Wilson and Game, 1998, p. 240, Farnham, 1998), it soon becomes plain that education has traditionally been the largest single employment sector in local government. About half of all local government jobs fall into this category (including administrators etc.), with teachers alone accounting for one quarter of total employment. In view of central government policies which have removed many educational institutions from local control, however, the size of this staff group has already decreased (e.g. the number of teachers has fallen by 14 per cent since 1987) and is likely to decline further. This finding stands in stark contrast to the German case where school and university teachers are on the pay-roll of the *Länder* administrations, while local authorities are only responsible for adult education centres and maintain parts of the administrative and supporting staff of the general school system. Nevertheless, this employment group together with library and museum staff amounts to approximately one fifth of the local government service in Germany. The second largest proportion of British local government staff work in the social service sector, which employs almost one fifth (i.e. 354,000 full- and part-time workers) of the total workforce. Again, the situation in German local authorities, particularly in the western *Länder*, differs remarkably: Although social policies generally rank high on the local agenda, fewer than 10 per cent (i.e. 142,000 staff) of all employees can properly be grouped into the 'social service' category. These figures also throw an instructive sidelight on the crucial role of welfare associations in the German model of social welfare provision. Whereas jobs in the social service sector play only a minor role as compared to the British case, German local government employment is distinct because of its substantial share of health service staff, which numbers about 425,000. Since in the UK this functional responsibility lies with the NHS, this staff group is virtually non-existent in British local government. Until recently, the third major heading in British local labour statistics was traditionally the police force and its civilian support staff (totalling 194,000 full-time equivalents in 1990) before 'law and order' was transferred from direct local council control. In Germany, local authorities have never been entrusted with the area of law enforcement, which falls solely under the jurisdiction of the *Länder*.

Cross-national comparisons in public employment are admittedly fraught with a number of problems, since service responsibilities are differently allocated and directly comparable statistical data are often lacking. Thus, in summarising this section we confine ourselves to a rough guide to local manpower figures. Allowing for the varying local responsibilities as far as education and health services are concerned, British local government staff still outnumber local employment in Germany, despite the draconian cuts in the number of manual workers resulting mainly from Thatcherite management reforms. Relating the employment figures to the size of population, this gap between British and German figures widens even further. Thus, it is relatively safe to assume that British levels of local government employment well exceed German standards.

Professionalism vs. Civil Service Orientation

While the diversity of occupational groups employed by local authorities and the specialisation of job profiles are common characterictics of the German and British local government workforces, the underlying notions of a 'local government service' are quite distinct. The relative weight accorded to professional expertise or generalist knowledge will serve as an example to illustrate this difference. In fact, the dominance of professionalism has been a long-established feature of British local government staff. In this respect, the 'local government service' presents an opposite case to the Whitehall Civil Service which has a reputation for being a 'generalist elite', thus restricting access of specialists to higher management and policy-making posts. Contrary to the British case, however, employment standards and staff development in German local authorities have traditionally favoured the generalist administrator modelled upon the example of the archetypal civil servant. It is, therefore, appropriate to set the British emphasis on professionalism against a greater 'civil service' orientation in Germany.

Similar to the rise of 'departmentalism', the primacy of the established professions took root very early in the history of local government, which 'justifies its existence as a provider of services' (Poole, 1978). In the late 19th century, strengthening the professional corps of officials was seen as a remedy for the amateurish style of the boards and commissions of the time as well as a strategy to fight corruption and nepotism in local government (Laffin and Young, 1990). After 1945, the expansion of local services eventually laid the foundation for modern-style professionalism. In this context, the widespread influence of professional groupings was also conducive to implementing nationwide and uniform service standards. Most importantly, however, professional organisations gained increasing influence over training programmes, examinations and entry requirements of the local government service and, of course, lobbied effectively for their members in staffing decisions (Laffin and Young, 1990, p.19).

Undeniably, the reliance on local government officers holding professional or technical qualifications has been to some extent a necessary response to the challenges of a complex and demanding social environment and has been advantageous in improving the quality of services. For some time, however, the drawbacks of professionalism have also been recognised. Generally speaking, critics have attacked two aspects: the lack of accountability and the problems of internal co-ordination. Regarding the former, they argue that professionalism appears to be typified by a paternalistic 'I know best' attitude and to be unresponsive to the political direction of the authority or the citizens' needs. As for the latter, commentators have turned a critical eye on the lack of concern for the management of the authority as a whole (Barlow 1993, p. 6). Especially in view of the existence of large departments each supervised by a committee, the segregation of professionals has been seen as a serious obstacle to effective co-ordination and planning (Byrne, 1992; Poole, 1978; Laffin and Young, 1990; Morphet 1992, pp. 93-4). In particular, this strand of criticism was brought to the forefront by the 1972 Bains Report, which gave wide currency to the so-called 'corporate management' approach before the reorganisation of local government encouraged further moves in this direction. According to the recommendations of this inquiry into the local government service, most local authorities – also encouraged by the reorganisation of local government in 1974 – have appointed chief executive officers as 'heads of the paid service' who have been given responsibility for securing co-ordination of advice on the forward planning of objectives and services and for ensuring efficient resource allocation across departmental boundaries. At the same time, the concern for corporate management also enhanced the role of central administrative services and accorded higher value to general managerial qualifications. 'However, it has been only during the 1980s that key aspects of corporate reforms have been implemented and professional departmentalism been seriously curtailed' (Laffin and Young, 1990, p.23).

Undoubtedly, the development of local government services in Germany also owes much to the expertise of officers who are members of individual professions, and yet professionalism has never become the dominant occupational paradigm of local government employment. Rather, technical and professional experts lack an independent status and are frequently subordinated to administrators. In fact, local authorities in Germany have sought to establish the 'general administrative class' as a profession in its own right. In organisational terms this has been reinforced by the strong position of central administrative services under direct control of the political and administrative leader of the authority. In addition, the whole system of education and training has been geared to produce the prototype of an administrative generalist characterised by his or her abiding 'by the letter of the law' and the ability to carry out duties in various departments.

While the structure of the local government service in Germany largely rests upon the traditional principles of the civil service, only a minority of the local government workforce enjoys the legal status of civil servants

(*Beamte*). In fact, no more than 10 per cent of total employment fall into this category, while the bulk of the staff (about 60 per cent) are salaried employees and the rest public workers (about 30 per cent). This finding is easily reconcilable with our earlier propositions when two additional aspects are taken into consideration: First, we should not lose sight of the 'status-group-biased' hierarchy which favours the career advancement of civil servants who, as a consequence, fill the top posts of the local government service. Second, the tenets of civil service law have also proved pervasive in collective bargaining processes for public employees, so that in practice the conditions of service for civil servants on the one hand and for public employees and workers on the other hand have become more and more similiar (Siedentopf 1990, p.237, Röber and Löffler, 1999).

Managing Local Staff

The Legal Framework

Before turning to some individual components of personnel management, however, we need to look at the general framework set by civil service law or the nationwide negotiating machinery which to a large extent have shaped distinct national approaches towards public personnel management.

Given the legalistic style of German policy-making it is not surprising that important guidelines for public personnel management are decided by federal or *Land* legislation. Again, it is civil service law which sets the tone and works effectively towards the integration of local government staff into the 'public service' as a whole. Although the regulation of civil service affairs is largely left to the *Länder*, the right is reserved at federal level to determine the legal status of all public servants as part of general or framework legislation (*Rahmengesetzgebung des Bundes*) and to decide on civil service pay and pensions by act of parliament (*konkurrierende Gesetzgebung*). This, however, must secure the approval of the *Länder* representatives in the second chamber, the *Bundesrat*. The decisive influence of national actors in the political bargaining process is also reflected by the fact that the federal government, which, in quantitative terms, plays only a minor role in public employment, leads the employers' side in negotiations on national salary scales and conditions of service for public employees and workers (see also White and Löffler 1997, p.7). The staff side is mainly drawn from representatives of public sector unions (most notably the *ÖTV* (*Gewerkschaft Öffentliche Dienste, Transport und Verkehr*) and its rival unions *DAG* (*Deutsche Angestelltengewerkschaft*) and *DBB* (*Deutscher Beamtenbund*) which all enjoy a relatively strong position among local government staff. The binding agreement reached by the two sides lays down in minute detail most aspects of employment, ranging from salary and grade scales to rules of discipline, terms of advancement in the service and pension arrangements for public employees and workers, thus leaving local authorities only very limited room for manoeuvre. Notwithstanding these difficulties for innovative strategies in human resource development, the readiness to depart from the well-trodden paths of public personnel management is greatest at the local level of government. In part, this trend towards greater flexibility can be explained by pointing at the peculiar mix of public service status groups in city and county administrations. As mentioned above, the vast majority of local government staff is employed on the basis of contracts of service governed by private law and negotiated agreements, while civil servants only account for one tenth of the workforce. This constellation seems to have given an increasing number of local authorities the opportunity to experiment with new methods of personnel management, provided that the management and employees' sides agree (see also Röber and Löffler, 1999).

Complaints about unduly rigid and nationally determined provisions for staff and pay management are certainly not unknown in British local government. While the formal legal position remains that each local authority is free to pay reasonable remuneration and establish conditions of service as they see fit, in practice salaries and conditions of service have become substantially standardised throughout the country (see Byrne, 1992, p.183; Elcock, 1994, p.221). Most significantly, the framework for the national local government labour market is provided by the National Joint Council for the Administrative, Professional, Technical and Clerical (APT & C) staffs or, separately for the upper brackets of the workforce, by the Local Authorities Services and the Joint Negotiating Committee for Chief Executives and Chief Officers which are made up of representatives of the local authorities' associations and the trade unions. The establishment of a national negotiating machinery in the 1940s was supported by the creation of the Local Authorities Conditions of Service Advisory Board (LACSAB), the functions of which have now been absorbed by the Local Government Management Board (LGMB) (see Elcock, 1994, p.221; Byrne, 1992, pp.185, 189, 201). The national conditions of local government employment as published in the APT & C Scheme (or 'purple book' as it is sometimes referred to), however, which were originally established to overcome the injustices and inconsistencies of piecemeal local bargaining, are now increasingly perceived by local managers as constraints on the ability to introduce change or to respond adequately to local labour and pay markets. As a consequence, some authorities have withdrawn from national agreements and many others remain only formally within the negotiating system while applying only selected provisions of the national schemes.

This discernible trend towards greater local flexibility finds its equivalent in organisational developments within British authorities aiming at an increasingly decentralised system of personnel management (see Gyford, Leach and Game, 1989, p.119 and for more details Fowler, 1988). In this respect, the pendulum is swinging back after a period in which the personnel role had been more and more detached from line managers and service departments and transferred instead to central departments vested with fully-fledged personnel responsibilities. In the main, this centralising movement was triggered in the early 1970s by local government reorganisation and the growing complexity of staff matters when the Bains Committee fervently presented the case in favour of an integrated system of personnel management. In line with the recommendations of the Bains Report, uniform and formalised procedures were widely introduced and specialist personnel officers appointed in order to ensure standardised staff policies. 'The result of these various centralising pressures was a system that was slow and seen by officials in service departments as unresponsive and control-oriented' (Leach, Stewart and Walsh, 1994; p.188; see also Farnham, 1998, p.3).

Undoubtedly, this critical comment sounds all too familiar to German students of local government. Here, personnel has traditionally been truly ruled 'by the book', while personnel management in the sense of human resource management has only recently emerged as a new issue in the context of administrative modernisation. Meanwhile, personnel management is seen as one of the important elements in administrative reform because '... the new divisions of roles and increased managerial autonomy demand highly motivated and qualified employees' (Klages and Löffler, 1998, p.49). Nevertheless, this new concern among German local authorities has brought about less visible results than in Britain.

Recruitment and Career Development

Staff members in both countries are recruited by individual local authorities according to their own employment requirements. In Britain, recruitment is for a specific job vacancy and not for a career. Traditionally, the point of entry has been after leaving school, while professsional qualifications were obtained by part-time training on and off the job. 'Promotion depended on the acquisition of these professional qualifications as well as on the ability to perform in the job. [But] over the past twenty years graduate recruitment into local government has increased considerably as professional qualifications have become readily available at universities' (Barlow, 1993, p.11). A large expansion of graduates entering local government has taken place especially in the field of technical professions such as architecture, engineering, town planning, environmental science, but also in social welfare professions. In Germany, the dominant patterns of recruitment vary considerably between status groups. Whereas civil servants are recruited for a particular career path, i.e. 'administrative class', 'executive class', 'clerical class' or 'sub-clerical class' (see for details Röber, 1996), members of the other status groups are employed to fill a specific post. In keeping with the basic principles of a merit-based career service, entrance to the civil service classes is strictly linked to certain qualification requirements, with positions in the top category being reserved for university graduates. Similar rules, however, apply for salaried employees, which indicates once again that despite the continued dual employment structure, the boundaries between the two categories of service law have in practice become increasingly blurred.

'The need for new skills and changed patterns of work has led to some emphasis on the importance of developing staff, ... improving the ability of individuals (and changing) organisational culture' towards greater flexibility (Leach, Stewart and Walsh, 1994, p.189). Where far-reaching models of market competition (compulsory competitive tendering, see for example Boyne, 1998) have been forced upon British local authorities by central government the necessity of introducing organisational flexibilities was immediately understandable: On the one hand, local authorities had to reduce staff in order to win contracts; on the other hand, they had to cope with the problem of redundancies when they lost contracts. For these reasons many local authorities have tried 'to introduce greater flexibility into their employment patterns. In 1996, for example, a fifth of chief executives were on fixed-term contracts and the LGMB's evidence showed that this was an increasing trend. In local government as a whole, the number of staff on fixed-term arrangements is more than double that for the whole economy' (8.5 per cent vs. 3.6 per cent; see Wilson and Game, 1998, p.255). In addition, since the mid-80s many large local authorities have been developing 'policies for redeployment, premature retirement and temporary contracts' (Leach, Stewart and Walsh, 1994, p.189). Under these circumstances, getting rid of local government employees is not any longer an empty threat (see for example Byrne 1992, p.190). It cannot be surprising that many managers '... who obtain their sense of personal identity and related ideas of personal success or failure through ... an orderly career progression, feel threatened by actual or potential reductions in promotion and job security. This is especially the case for those managers 'anchored' to their careers through a desire for career stability and security or through 'vertical' career growth by climbing the corporate ladder to more senior positions' (Keen and Scase, 1996, p.170). This tendency has been reinforced by the process of decentralisation which 'tended to disrupt traditional career patterns, which were based on the concepts of hierarchy and centralised control' (Leach, Stewart and Walsh, 1994, p.192).

In the German public sector personnel development and human resource flexibility are still relatively underdeveloped. There is, however, some indication of change (see the surveys by the German Cities Association (*Deutscher Städtetag*), Grömig and Thielen, 1996 and Grömig and Gruner, 1998). Many municipalities have in the meantime been giving a much higher priority to personnel management and human resources flexibilities in the administrative reform process in order to reduce costs, to enhance the skills of staff and to meet changing and increasing requirements of service delivery. Obviously, however, the pressure in terms of a politically initiated competitive environment has been much weaker compared to the British case (see Röber, 1999). Therefore, steps towards more flexibility in the public service have been relatively small and cautious. The Civil Service Reform Law of 1997 can be regarded as one of the first small steps in this direction, although it falls far behind what scholars and practitioners have considered necessary for a modern public personnel management (see for example Oechsler and Vaanholt, 1997). It provides local authorities some scope at least in terms of employment contracts, performance-oriented pay and career mobility.

As far as contracts are concerned, civil servants and public employees will be given the opportunity to work part-time without any preconditions. It also provides better opportunities for delegation (*Abordnung*) and transfer

(*Versetzung*) of staff and larger scope for flexible working hours, job sharing and sabbaticals. The main aim is to increase the internal flexibility of local authorities because according to public service regulations the 'external option' of making local government staff redundant is practically impossible. The new civil service reform law opens up the opportunity to introduce moderate financial incentives for those staff members who perform better than others (see for details Röber and Löffler, 1999). An integral part of the new system is a new arrangement of the salary scale, one-off bonuses for exceptional results *(Leistungsprämien als Einmalzahlung)*, and extra pay for a limited period of one year *(Leistungszulagen)*. Finally, the new law contains options for an extended probation period for leading positions (*Verlängerung der Probezeit*) and for temporary executive duties (*Führungsfunktionen auf Zeit*).

In general, the traditional ethos in local government service has been similar in both countries for a long time. But the different philosophies and strategies of administrative modernisation that have predominated in Britain and in Germany over the last 20 years have obviously influenced local government service in both countries. On the one hand, due to the much stronger market pressures in Britain, the whole system of public service at the local level has become more flexible and fragmented. On the other hand, changes in the system of local government service in Germany have not been so radical, due to less external market pressure and to the fact that the integrating feature of the traditional German civil service has continued to have an effect on the whole system. According to these findings, it seems reasonable to assume that there is a fit between external interactions (such as the type and extent of competition) and internal features of public institutions (such as organisation structure, management systems, personnel management etc.). This also hints at the discussion of converging or diverging trends in public management to which we will return in our conclusion.

Education and Training

In many respects appropriate training policies and schemes can be aptly described as a prime prerequisite for efficient and effective local government services and ought to be a criterion of any major organisational reform (e.g. Clarke, 1998; Maguire, 1997). Regrettably, however, local authorities in both countries have often ignored the issue of training. Thus, the neglect of systematic and comprehensive training programmes by many British local councils has frequently been criticised (Leach, Stewart and Walsh, 1994, p.188; Elcock, 1994, p.225; Kerley, 1994, p.90). Similarly, German commentators lament the frequently insufficient investment in human resource training, especially when compared to training capacities in the private sector (Klages and Löffler, 1998, p.49). While training has traditionally received little attention, problems in both British and German authorities have even been compounded by the fiscal stress of recent years. This critical view, however, should not overlook the fact that in some cases the commitment to training has even been increased in order to meet the challenges arising from New Public Management (or, in Germany, the so-called New Steering Model). Although this general description applies to both German and British local government, the differences still persist as far as the national systems of administrative education and training are concerned.

Not unexpectedly, the pre-eminence of professionalism in British local government has also fashioned the general patterns of pre-entry education and in-house training. Consequently, 'training for professional qualifications is the main training in local government and has been supported by most authorities for decades' (Fowler 1988, p.50). This approach has been advantageous for employees who can improve their long-term career prospects in and outside the public sector by professional training. At the same time, local authorities have benefited from up-to-date professional expertise in their ranks without having to establish training facilities of their own. The pitfalls of this strategy are, however, easily discernible. Thus, 'qualification syllabuses meet the examination requirements of professional institutes, not the service needs of individual authorities.(...) Obviously, this type of training cannot explain and promote an authority's own policies and procedures' (Fowler 1988, p.51). The Bains Committee (1972) sought to counter these tendencies by advocating a more proactive role for local authorities in developing a greater awareness among staff of the range of the local authority's activities and in encouraging general administrative staff to improve their qualifications (Elcock 1994, p.219) in addition to the strong tradition of 'training on the job' and 'learning by doing'. Most of these training courses are offered by universities and colleges, or are organised as correspondence courses, on a day-release or block-release basis leading to Certificates and Diplomas in Management Studies or similar qualifications. Furthermore, specialist management institutes established at universities such as the Institute of Local Government in Birmingham (INLOGOV) offer training courses for more senior staff members (Elcock, 1994, p.224-5). Other training opportunities are provided by the Institute of Chartered Secretaries and Administrators (ICSA) or the Civil Service College which offers a wide range of shorter training courses, also for staff in local government (Greenwood and Robins, 1989, p.114).

The education and training of local government officers was given substantial impetus by the establishment of the Local Government Training Board in 1967 which was merged with other national local government bodies (LACSAB, LAMSAC) to form the Local Government Management Board in 1991. Rather than directly providing training capacities, its role is more of an advisory and coordinating kind. Thus, its original functions included spreading the cost of training among local authorities and promoting a 'training awareness' at the local government level. In addition, the Board is responsible 'for identifying and meeting the skills and training needs of the various local government employment sectors. It provides examinations and awards, promotes careers in local government, provides information on good employment practice, and represents local government's training and education interests to government' (Wilson and Game, 1998, p.136-7). This national local government institution has recently been joined by the National Training Organization for Local Government (LGNTO) whose 'task is primarily one of co-ordinating standards developed elsewhere. The aim is improve vocational qualifications and training materials of interest to local authority service departments' (Farnham, 1998, p.8).

In Germany, state and local governments have always had a tight grip on administrative education and training. Rather than confining themselves to a coordinating or 'purchasing' role, the provision of (pre-entry as well as in-service) training courses for service posts in public bureaucracies has generally been considered a public task. The provision of in-service training courses for public servants and employees of all four grades follows the familiar pattern. They are normally supplied by Academies of Public Administration (*Verwaltungsakademie*). It must be stated, however, that until recently their training schemes were much less responsive to new requirements of public service delivery and actual problems of local government management than in the British case (see for Great Britain, Keen and Scase, 1996).

As far as pre-entry training is concerned, administrative training for the lower ranks of the hierarchy (sub-clerical and clerical classes) is typically conducted in a dual system combining vocational 'training on the job' with classroom teaching in state-run administrative schools. The most senior local government posts of the administrative class are usually filled by university graduates (mainly from the legal profession) and therefore the direct influence of administrative training institutions on this group is less pronounced compared to the other three classes. However, successful candidates have to complete two years of preparatory service which includes practical training in various public bureaucracies (even outside local government) and complementary courses in public administration and management. Undoubtedly, this initial phase greatly assists young members of the high-ranking administrative class to integrate into the service and emphasises, together with their typical educational background in law, their role as generalists rather than as specialists (see also Humes IV, 1991, p.64).

The 'backbone' of the service, however, is formed by the executive class (*gehobener Dienst*), the middle management level of local authorities. It is here that the tight grip of administrative education and training can be best exemplified. (The following observations are focused on civil servants, but similar education and training programmes for public employees have also been set up). Applicants for the executive class have to complete a three-year course of study at an internal College of Public Administration (*Fachhochschule für Verwaltung*). These colleges are now also called 'Universities of Applied Sciences for Public Administration and Legal Affairs'. The concept of college education for middle-level managers in the public service was an innovation of the early 1970s when, similar to the British situation, concern about improving skills and qualifications of local (and state) government officers was growing. Since then candidates for the general non-technical cadre and for certain other services (like tax officers or police) study at these colleges, which have been established by each *Land* as well as at the federal level, for a Diploma in Public Administration. Formally, this diploma only provides a qualification for administrative work in the public sector. For technical or social services, four years of study at an external College of Applied Sciences for Engineering or Social Work (*Fachhochschule für Technik* or *Fachhochschule für Sozialarbeit*) and normally two years of preparatory service in public administration are required.

Selection of candidates is the responsibility of the administration. The number of students in these colleges of public administration is related to the personnel requirements of public employers. The decision on recruitment is taken at an early stage of a person's career (e.g. just after the *Abitur* examination for executive class entries), thus allowing for an early adjustment to the traditional principles of the civil service. On recruitment to the college, the students become civil servants with a status subject to revocation, while for the duration of their training they receive a salary from government. In nearly all colleges of public administration great emphasis is put on producing legal skills and qualifications (about 60 per cent of the curriculum), while economics, business administration and social sciences only play a minor part in the curriculum. As with the administrative class, the aim of traditional education and training of middle managers in local authorities is to 'produce' a highly qualified administrative generalist able to work in a system based in many of its procedures and decision-making processes on the principle of the rule of law.

Recent administrative reforms at the local level have already had effects on debates about public administration curriculum development in general and on training requirements at the local level in particular. This discussion is mainly centred on the executive class (and with less emphasis on the administrative class) because of complaints by local politicians and chief executives that traditional training programmes for the middle- and upper management levels no longer meet the new requirements of a changing environment for local authorities (the statement of the *Deutscher Städtetag* dated 11.8.1992 cited in Reichard, 1994b). For this reason, some local authorities have already changed their recruitment policy. They now increasingly seek to attract candidates with a more professional managerial background, though there is still a lack of qualified management experts. This need is especially felt in those cities and counties which have embarked on reform projects aimed at bringing their administrative structures and procedures into line with the so-called 'New Steering Model'. In these local authorities various training programmes have been set up to furnish local employees with the skills necessary to put the 'New Steering Model' into practice. In addition, new courses of study for public management have been established at various – internal as well as external - *Fachhochschulen.* The major subject of these courses is business administration with special reference to the public sector (see for example the Public Management-course 'PUMA' in Berlin; for details see Reichard, 1998) which is meant to include not only local and state authorities, but also public enterprises and non-profit organisations. This development may well have the medium-term effect that at the local government level the legally trained generalist will be superseded by a different type of generalist who may be called the 'new public manager' (Farnham *et al.*, 1996).

Concluding Thoughts

Undoubtedly, country-specific historical developments have left visible marks on today's local government services in Britain and Germany. In view of these peculiar national traits and characteristics, in each country a common wisdom has evolved as to what typifies the national model and what the particular strengths and weaknesses of this model seem to be. Interestingly enough, the two countries in question can be presented as complementary cases with the relative strength of one model being a problematic feature of the other. The emphasis on civil service orientation in German local government *vis-à-vis* the (private) business-like flexibility in human resource management which ranges high in the British context may serve as examples to illustrate this point. On the one hand, the concept of a more or less unified local government service has effectively worked against outright fragmentation of local authorities and has helped to mitigate the clashes between various and competing professions – a most palpable problem for British local government and its workforce. On the other hand, the law-based culture of the German public service and the bureaucratic rigidities in human resource management make local politicians and chief executives look with great envy at their British neighbours.

Looking at recent changes in both countries, however, there seem to be indications of a convergent trend which appears to be mainly driven by various effective socio-economic factors, commonly labelled with the catchword 'globalisation'. In view of similar contingencies, such as, for example, international competition, budgetary strains and value changes favouring individualistic attitudes, a move towards similar organisational patterns and modes of steering is hardly surprising. In fact, local authorities in Britain and Germany have come under increased pressure in recent years to rethink their established paradigms. Although the drive to unleash market forces and to follow the managerial creed has been particularly pronounced in the British case, German local authorities have also sought to introduce more business-like management techniques. Putting this current trend towards administrative modernisation into historical perspective, it becomes obvious that this 'new convergence' is merely a return to earlier positions on the 'divergence-convergence' spectrum. In fact, one should not lose sight of the far-reaching similarities of the German and British local government services before the Thatcher governments abruptly departed from the traditional paradigm of public *administration*, both being shaped and conditioned by the mould of the modern welfare state, instrumental in the delivery of wide-ranging public services, and governed in a more or less bureaucratic mode of external and internal management. Seen from this angle, the latest quest for change nourished by globalising tendencies appears to fulfil a function similar to the secular trends of industrialisation and urbanisation about the end of the 19th century and the welfare state consensus in the post-war era. Thus, it may well be the case that both national systems – after a period of apparent divergence – are again back on parallel tracks of administrative development.

References

Alexander, A. (1991), 'Managing Fragmentation – Democracy, Accountability and the Future of Local Government', *Local Government Studies*, vol. 17, pp. 63-76.
Audit Commission (1995), *Paying the Piper: People and Pay Management in Local Government*, HMSO, London.
Audit Commission (1997), *The Melody Lingers On: People and Pay Management in Local Government*, HMSO, London.
Barlow, J. (1993), *Public Managers in the UK: Local Government*, Paper for Personnel Study Group (EGPA), Strasbourg, Sept. 1993.
Barlow, J. and Röber, M. (1996), 'Steering not Rowing. Co-ordination and Control in the Management of Public Services in Britain and Germany', *The International Journal of Public Sector Management*, vol. 1, pp. 73-89.
Boyne, G. A. (1998), 'Competitive Tendering in Local Government: A Review of Theory and Evidence', *Public Administration*, vol. 76, pp. 695-712.
Butcher, H., Law, J. G., Leach, R. and Mullard, M. (1990), *Local Government and Thatcherism*, Routledge, London and New York.
Byrne, T. (1992), *Local Government in Britain*, Penguin, London.
Clarke, M. (1997), 'An Agenda for Re-inventing Local Government', *Public Money and Management*, vol. 17, pp. 17-20.
Clarke, M. (1998), 'The challenges facing public service training institutions', *International Review of Administrative Sciences*, vol. 64, pp. 399-407.
Derlien, H.-U., Heinemann, S. S. Lock, S. (1998), *The German Public Service – Structure and Statistics*, Verwaltungswissenschaftliche Beiträge No. 34, Universität Bamberg, Bamberg.
Derlien, H.-U. (1999), 'Unorthodox Employment in the German Public Service', *International Review of Administrative Sciences*, vol. 65, pp. 13-23.
Elcock, H.(1994), *Local Government*, Routledge, London.

Farnham, D., Horton, S., Barlow, J. and Hondeghem, A. (eds) (1996), *New Public Managers in Europe. Public Servants in Transition*, Macmillan Press, Basingstoke.

Farnham, D. (1998), *Human Resources Management for Local Government Employees in the UK: Current Issues and New Developments*, Paper presented to British-German Workshop: Public Sector Modernisation in the United Kingdom and Germany: Towards Mutual Learning from Experience?, Humboldt University Berlin.

Fowler, A. (1988), *Human Resource Management in Local Government*, Longman, Harlow.

Greenwood, J. and Robins, L. (1998), 'Public Administration Curriculum Development in Britain: Outsider or Insider Influence?', *International Review of Administrative Sciences*, vol. 64, pp. 409-21.

Grömig, E. and Gruner, K. (1998), 'Reform in den Rathäusern. Neueste Umfrage des Deutschen Städtetages zum Thema Verwaltungsmodernisierung', *Der Städtetag*, vol. 51, pp. 581-87.

Grömig, E. and Thielen, H. (1996), 'Städte auf dem Reformweg. Zum Stand der Verwaltungsmodernisierung', *Der Städtetag*, vol. 49, pp. 596-600.

Hogwood, B. (1997), 'Towards a New Structure of Public Employment in Britain?', *Policy and Potitics*, vol. 26, pp. 321-40.

Humes IV, S. (1991), *Local Governance and National Power. A Worldwide Comparison of Tradition and Change and Local Government*, Harvester Wheatsheaf, New York.

Johnson, N. (1983), 'Die kommunale Selbstverwaltung in England', *Deutsches Verwaltungsblatt*, vol. 98, pp. 250-57.

Keen, L. and Scase, R. (1996), 'Middle Managers and the New Managerialism', *Local Government Studies*, vol. 22, pp. 167-86.

Kerley, R. (1994), *Managing in Local Government*, Macmillan Press, Basingstoke.

Klages, H. and Löffler, E. (1995), 'Administrative Modernization in Germany - a Big Qualitative Jump in Small Steps', *International Review of Administrative Sciences*, vol. 61, pp. 373-83.

Klages, H. and Löffler, E. (1998), 'New Public Management in Germany: The Implementation Process of the New Steering Model', *International Review of Administrative Sciences*, vol. 64, pp. 41-54.

Leach, S., Stewart, J. and Walsh, K. (1994), 'The Changing Organisation and Management of Local Government', Macmillan Press, Basingstoke.

Maguire, C. (1997), *Training Strategies for Developing Human Resources in Local and Regional Authorities. Implications for Local Government*, Paper presented to the 10th ENTO Seminar, Vienna, Austria.

Naschold, F. (1997), *The Dialectics of Modernising Local Government - An Assessment for the Mid-90s and an Agenda for the 21st Century (Agenda 21)*, WZB-paper FS II 97-205, Berlin.

Poole, K. P. (1978), *The Local Government Service in England and Wales*, George Allen & Unwin, London.

Reichard, C. (1994a), *Umdenken im Rathaus*, Edition sigma, Berlin.

Reichard, C. (1994b), 'Public Management – ein neues Ausbildungskonzept für die deutsche Verwaltung', *VOP (Verwaltungsführung/Organisation/Personal)*, vol. 16, pp. 178-84.

Reichard, C. (1998), 'Education and Training for New Public Management', *International Public Management Journal*, vol. 1, pp. 177-94.

Röber, M. (1996), 'Country Report: Germany', in D. Farnham *et al.* (eds), *New Public Managers in Europe. Public Servants in Transition*, pp. 169-93.

Röber, M. (1999), *Competition – How Far Can You Go?*, Paper presented at the Third Internatinal Research Symposium on Public Management, Aston Business School, 25-26 March 1999, Birmingham.

Röber, M. and Löffler, E. (1999), 'Country Report: Germany', in: Farnham, D. and Horton, S. (eds.), *Human Resources Flexibilities: International Perspectives*, Macmillan Press, Basingstoke (forthcoming).

Saldern, A. v. (1999), 'Rückblicke. Zur Geschichte der kommunalen Selbstverwaltung in Deutschland', in H. Wollmann, R. Roth (eds), *Kommunalpolitik*, Leske + Budrich, Opladen, pp. 23-36.

Schröter, E., Wollmann, H. (1997), 'Public Sector Reforms in Germany: Whence and Where? A Case of Ambivalence', *Hallinnon Tutkimus/Administrative Studies*, vol. 16, pp. 184-200.

Sharpe, J. (1970), 'Theories and values of local government', *Political Studies*, vol. 18, pp. 153-74.

Siedentopf, H. (1990), 'The Public Service', in K. König, H. J.von Oertzen and F. Wagener (eds), *Public Administration in the Federal Republic of Germany*, Kluwer, Amsterdam, pp. 235-46.

Stewart, J. and Stoker, G. (eds) (1989), *The Future of Local Government*, Macmillan, Basingstoke.

Stoker, G. (1991), *The Politics of Local Government*, Macmillan, Basingstoke.

Stoker, G. (1996), 'The Struggle to Reform Local Government: 1970-95', *Public Money and Management*, vol. 16, pp. 17-22.

Wagener, F. (1990), 'The External Structure of Administration in the Federal Republic of Germany', in K. König, H. J. von Oertzen and F. Wagener (eds), *Public Administration in the Federal Republic of Germany*, Kluwer, Amsterdam, pp. 49-64.

Wilson, D. and C. Game (1998), *Local Government in the United Kingdom*, Macmillan Press, Basingstoke.

Wollmann, H. (1996), 'Institutionenbildung in Ostdeutschland: Neubau, Umbau und "schöpferische Zerstörung"', in M. Kaase *et al.* (eds), *Politisches System*, Leske + Budrich, Opladen, pp. 47-154.

Wunder, B. (1986), *Geschichte der Bürokratie in Deutschland*, Suhrkamp, Frankfurt/Main.

10 Culture's Consequences? In Search of Cultural Explanations of British and German Public Sector Reform

ECKHARD SCHRÖTER

Introduction

This paper tries to shed some light on cultural patterns in both the British and German societies, which may help to explain the conspicuous differences in the national policy programmes for public sector reform. Few commentators seem to dispute that despite the official rhetoric of the 'lean state' recent public sector reform programmes in Germany have been of only modest range if compared to the overall British approach which stands out for its vigorously pursued market-orientation and the emphasis on the explicitly 'managerial' side of the new public management ('freedom to manage').

How are these obviously contrasting developments linked to the respective national political or managerial cultures? Does a greater civic assertiveness, and a stronger libertarian tradition in Britain account for the quest for public sector efficiency and the rise of market-driven reform steps in the 1980s? Does a political culture in Germany that is still state-centred help to shield the public sector from pressures for fundamental changes? The established distinction between Germany's state-centred political culture and Britain as the 'stateless society *par excellence*' (Nettl, 1968, p.562) – which is also intimately linked to the alleged 'individualist-collectivist' divide – appears to be the starting point best suited for our purpose. In line with this thinking, Dyson employs the various notions of 'state-society' relations to distinguish between British ('non-etatist' society) and German ('etatist' society) cultural traits (Dyson, 1980). Rohe's typology of political cultures also highlights this distinction (Rohe, 1982, 1984). From a philosophical point of view, German philosophy – if compared to the liberal and utilitarian strand of thought well-entrenched in British philosophical tradition – is commonly seen as a reflection for metaphysical certainty and belonging. This assumed strive for collectivism stands in marked contrast to the alleged individualist virtues of the English: 'The majority of people in England from at least the 13th century were rampant individualists, highly mobile both geographically and socially, economically rational, market-oriented and acquisitive, and ego-centred in kinship and social life' (Macfarlane, 1978, p.163). Not surprisingly, the reference to this supposedly 'quintessentially British outlook' was also used as both an explanation and ex-post justification of Thatcherite policies. For the understanding that holds the key to Thatcherism, so it is claimed, is very old: 'It is a distinctive but unidentified British morality' (Letwin, 1992, p. 336). Consequently, seen from this vantage point of British individualism, 'human activity cannot be arranged in a hierarchy' (Letwin, 1992, p.343). In part, this interpretation echoes Sartori's distinction of 'pragmatic' and 'deductive or rationalist' cultures which also dwells on the divide between common law and Roman law traditions. According to this reasoning, abstract and rigid rules or hierarchical, unpersonal organisational settings find far less acceptance in the Anglo-Saxon 'pragmatic' culture than in Germany's highly developed 'rationalist' culture (Sartori, 1969, p.402).

This conventional wisdom, however, seems to present a rather one-dimensional account of cultural characteristics which may cast doubt on the accurateness of the simple picture presented so far.[1] Moreover, some commentators do not appear to have taken much trouble to distinguish between 'objective' (e.g. institutional developments or policy changes) and 'subjective' (e.g. value and attitudinal patterns), i.e. cultural, factors. In addition, most typologies and characterisations cited above do not allow for much cultural change. As a consequence, they seem to run the risk of arriving at static depictions of 'national character'. Against this background, we thus employ – in line with the traditional strand of comparative political culture research, and in accordance with the dominant current in the organisational culture literature – an attitudinal concept of culture in order to assess more systematically the facets of contemporary cultural patterns. We also try to blend into the argument advanced below the findings of both organisational and political culture studies.

The structure of this chapter is as follows. First, we turn to cross-national comparisons of managerial cultures, before the second section looks at various dimensions of political culture, such as the degrees of system trust, political efficacy and citizen involvement. The third and major part of this chapter focuses more specifically on public attitudes towards the range and scope of government activities. By and large, the argument is restricted to the comparison between British and West German samples, with only occasional references to cultural patterns in eastern Germany (for a broad overview of cultural changes after unification, see Gabriel, 1997).

National Modes of Management: Entrepreneurial vs. Bureaucratic Culture?

Turning to the 'internal dimension' or 'micro-level' of public management, we start from the premise that national cultures will have a notable impact on the dominant styles of management within a given society. From this perspective both private and public organisations are 'culture-bound'; they are imbedded in societal cultural patterns which in turn influence the ways the organisation deals with salient managerial problems such as authority, uncertainty or participation. These emerging managerial styles, so it is maintained by an established strand of organisational research, carry an important national component which the organisation can modify but not entirely change (see also Hickson, 1993, Tayeb, 1988, Randlesome, 1990, Joynt and Warner, 1985, and Egan, 1997). It flows from this assumption that national 'business' or 'management cultures' will transcend the public-private divide, thus also making a difference to national public management styles.

A brief overview of cross-national work in organisational cultures and private sector management reveals some interesting tendencies, which in many respects echo the salient elements of the cultures stereotypes discussed above. This resemblance is most visible in Bendix's distinction between 'entrepreneurial' and 'bureaucratic' cultures, with Britain representing the former case and Germany the latter (Bendix, 1956, p.211-244). This early distinction still seems to be intellectually thriving. For example, Hickson alludes to Britain 'as a culturally very individualistic nation' (cf. also Tayeb, 1993) and points, not without ironic exaggeration, to the 'law of the jungle' situation, 'where company management and (...) financiers are ever on the lookout for bargains.(...) A shifting capitalist battleground frowned upon in Germany, The Netherlands and Scandinavia' (Hickson, 1993, p.253). However, there is also mention of the English as being more deferential towards authority, for instance, when compared to their Scandinavian peers. As for the German case, the 'efficient forms of bureaucracy' and 'its orderly and controlled organisations' are highlighted (Hickson, 1993, p.256). In fact, specialists are believed to play a much larger role in German management than in other western European societies, and even private sector management in Germany seems to be more product-oriented rather than market-oriented (Warner and Campbell, 1993). Without labouring this point too much, there is some indication that the observed variations in national management approaches also seem to cover some distinct elements of public management reforms in the relevant countries: the market-driven concept in Britain, emphasising the rights and competencies of managers, and the striving for internal, bureaucratic fine-tuning in Germany.

When looking for a systematic and comprehensive treatment of these issues, one must still largely rely on the conceptual framework and the empirical evidence generated by Hofstede's path-breaking work on 'culture's consequences' (Hofstede, 1980; cf. also 1991 and 1993). In this massive study of cultural dimensions across 40 countries, including Britain and West Germany, Hofstede succeeded in identifying four major cultural dimensions which were linked to the differences between the dominant values in the national organisations. These four main dimensions in which country cultures differ were revealed by theoretical reasoning and statistical analysis, and were labelled Power Distance, Uncertainty Avoidance, Individualism and Masculinity. In the following, we set out to decipher these indices which were used as a yardstick to measure work-related values.

Power Distance Index (PDI): This index was designed to tap values related to human inequality and the distribution of power within organisations. In short, 'power distance represents the extent to which the less powerful in a culture accept and expect that power is distributed unequally' (Hofstede, 1993, p.2). The PDI was compiled from responses to questions which dealt with perceptions of the superior's style of decision-making, and of colleagues' fear to disagree with superiors, and with the type of decision-making which subordinates prefer in their boss (Hofstede, 1980, p. 92). According to this concept of power distance, in countries scoring low on this index authority is less concentrated. As far as organisational behaviour is concerned, in low PDI countries ideal-typical managers are more satisfied with participative superiors, subordinates evaluate close supervision negatively and show a preference for manager's decision-making style clearly centred on a consultative, give-and-take style (Hofstede 1980, p.119). As shown in Hofstede's study these cultural characteristics also correlate positively with pluralistic societal and political structures, where competition between groups and leaders is encouraged and democratic politics are fostered (Hofstede, 1980, p.135).

Uncertainty Avoidance Index (UAI): This cultural dimension is related to anxiety, need for security and dependence upon others – in short: the level of (in-)tolerance of ambiguity (Hofstede, 1980, p.154). The three indicators, which together produce the UAI, are rule orientation, employment stability, and work-related stress. In fact, Hofstede presents an interesting list of connotations which are normally associated with a low UAI and which also appear to be of particular relevance for students of public management, too. In terms of organisational behaviour, in countries ranking low on the uncertainty avoidance dimension there can be found a stronger ambition for individual advancement (paired with a stronger achievement motivation), a greater acceptance for individual and authoritative decisions (which, however, at the same time goes hand in hand with a greater readiness to delegate responsibilities to subordinates) and more optimistic attitudes about people's amount of initiative, ambition and leadership skills. In a similar vein, low scores on this index are associated with the strongly endorsed views that managers should be selected on other criteria than seniority, that managers need not to be experts in the fields they manage, and that hierarchical organisational structures can be by-passed for pragmatic reasons. In broader societal and political terms, lower UAI scores were found to be positively correlated with a greater public assertiveness as measured by stronger feelings of citizen competence, more tolerance for citizen protest and more acceptance of dissent. Eventually, the effects attributed to the UAI also spill over into the realm of public policy making and public administration, since both the societal norm that 'public authorities are there to serve the citizen', and a by far less legalistic approach to public policy appeared to be typical for low UAI countries in the original study (Hofstede, pp. 178, 184).

Index of Individualism: Hofstede's third dimension was designed to describe the type of relationship between the individual and the collectivity which prevails in a given society (Hofstede, 1980, p.222-39). At the organisational level, individualist values would result in a greater emphasis on individual initiative and achievement, a stronger belief in individual decisions and a larger emotional independence of members from organisations or institutions. In the opposite case, managers are inclined to aspire to conformity and orderliness, to rate security in their position higher than having autonomy, and to choose duty, expertness and prestige as important work goals.

Masculinity vs. Femininity: According to this conceptual design 'masculine' cultures stand for greater assertiveness, and members of those cultures are expected to be more ambitious, concerned with money and 'to admire whatever is big and strong' (Hofstede, 1980, p. 279-97). These dispositions would translate into behavioural patterns in which individual earnings and advancement are the prime work goals and extrinsic motives are particularly important. In contrast, the label of 'femininity' was taken to stand for a much less competitive approach: modesty, concern with personal relationships and desirable working conditions, as well as a greater sympathy for co-operation are typical connotations attributed to this cultural dimension.

As shown in table 10.1, British and German cultural characteristics have much in common as far as the 'power distance' and 'masculinity-femininity' dimensions are concerned. Most importantly, however, the data reveal significant differences in the ability to cope with uncertainty. Here, the variance between both nations is most visible. Combined with the apparent, though less pronounced, discrepancy on the individualist-collectivist dimension, this cultural trait seems to have a noteworthy impact on the practices and policies of organisational management. Thus, it has been suggested that the peculiar German cultural cluster of 'low power distance-high uncertainty avoidance' would lead in comparative perspective – other factors such as task and size of the organisation being equal – to organisational structures of the 'workflow bureaucracy' type in which work processes are rigidly prescribed (preferably by formal rules and laws) (Hofstede, 1980, pp. 319, 382-5). So, it may not come as a surprise that a number of important features of the 'New Public Management' wisdom seem to fall on more fertile ground in 'low' rather than in 'high uncertainty avoidance' countries.

	Britain	W. Germany
PDI	35 (Low)	35 (Low)
UAI	35 (Low)	65 (Medium)
Individualism	89 (High)	67 (High)
Masculinity	66 (High)	66 (High)

Table 10.1 Managerial culture on four dimensions: index scores and relative positions
Source: Hofstede, 1980 and Hofstede, 1993

On balance, however, the overall pattern revealed by Hofstede's inquiries does not easily fit into the framework of Bendix's categorisation which placed the British and German cases at the polar extremes of a continuum. Rather, the cultural dispositions seem to be in most aspects more or less homogeneous as the grouping of the countries in a lower, middle, and upper third of all countries studied worldwide suggests (cf. Hofstede, 1993). Here one also has to add a note of caution here as regards the shifting – and possible convergence – of cultural dispositions which may have occurred since the data were gathered in 1968 and 1972 – a period marked by specific historic events which brought in their wake significant value changes as shown by political culture research.

National Patterns of Political Attitudes: Civic vs. Subject Culture?

When it comes to questions about civic assertiveness, trust in the political process and support for democratic rights, the stereo-typical images of national cultures seem to return to us in the guise of the classical accounts of political culture research which have become part of the conventional wisdom of comparative public policy. In their seminal study on political culture in five nations, Almond and Verba describe the British case as a close approximate to their normative model of the civic culture (Almond and Verba, 1963). In other words, the predominant British cultural patterns were praised for blending active and passive roles in the democratic process, thus providing the prerequisites for relatively stable and successful democracy. The 'civic culture' is founded not only on a positive identification of the political system and a wholehearted acceptance of democratic values (including tolerance of dissenting opinions), but also on a comparatively high degree of political competence among the citizenry ('nation of joiners').

Thus, Almond and Verba found a strong bias in favour of citizen involvement in the British case, whereas in Germany they could trace various elements of a 'subject culture' (see also Verba, 1965). Despite the remarkable degree of satisfaction with democratic politics, which, however, appeared to be more of a by-product of successful government and economic performance, the data for the German case also showed a considerable amount of political detachment. 'This package of values is readily recognizable as a hierarchical culture in which individuals identify with the system but believe their participation should be limited to its proper sphere' (Thompson, Ellis and Wildavsky, 1990, p.251). Moreover, these cultural traits also reflect, so it can be argued, the British and German traditions regarding the historical development of parliamentary rule on the one hand, and a fully-fledged state bureaucracy on the other: Whereas in the late 1950s the British respondents held the democratic institutions in particularly high regard, the German sample showed – in line with a deeply rooted 'Rechtsstaat' tradition – higher esteem for the judicial-administrative institutions. Based on these findings there does not seem to be too much common ground. Indeed, Ralf Dahrendorf described Germany and Britain as opposite cases when it comes to the discussion of crucial political values (Dahrendorf, 1980).

However, the streamlined profiles of the British 'civic culture' and the German 'subject culture' seem to be less than complete. Furthermore, these images, based on data generated in the late 1950s, can no longer serve as accurate descriptions of contemporary British and German political cultures (cf. Almond and Verba, 1980). As a case in point, the British preference for strong political leadership has often been unsufficiently appreciated, particularly within the general German perception of British government and the British political tradition (see also Döring, 1990, 1994). This facet, which added a slightly authoritarian note to British cultural traits, had already been identified in Almond and Verba's classical study. The authors nevertheless ignored this cultural trait in their original analysis. In a similar vein, Almond and Verba did, however, make mention of the alleged 'deferential' component of political life in Britain (see also Rose, 1965), which has eventually become the object of heated debates in political culture studies (see Kavanagh, 1971, cf. also Heath and Topf, 1987). Although it could be shown that the essential sense of a truly deferential society is missing in Britain, certain pro-establishment tendencies have been widely accepted among political scientists: 'Governments of any party can rely on a generally rather compliant electorate when it comes to implementing unpopular policies' (Jowell and Topf, 1988, p.120).

In the case of Germany, there seems to be every indication that the political detachment diagnosed decades ago has given way to much more participatory attitudes which are well documented in a new body of literature on the 'new politics' and the 'new political culture' in Germany (see for example Baker, Dalton and Hildebrandt, 1981, cf. also Barnes and Kaase, 1979 and Jennings et al., 1989). This fundamental change was also recognised by Conradt (1980) who concluded from his data base that the 'participatory revolution' had left its marked traces on German cultural patterns which also showed a significant increase of system trust and commitment to pluralist politics. It corresponds with the argument advanced so far that the types of 'detached' or 'alienated subjects' as described in Almond and Verba's work only have very limited descriptive or even explanatory power for contemporary Germany. Research undertaken by Derlien and Löwenhaupt to explore the relationships between German public authorities and their clients seems to be best suited to illustrate this point. In fact, the largest proportion of the sample members appear to be well-versed and prepared to seek redress for maladministration, if necessary, and usually do not feel intimidated by public authorities (Derlien and Löwenhaupt, 1997, p.433).

Trends of this kind are also reflected in the general value shift from 'materialist' to 'post-materialist' values. Here, the distribution of 'materialist' and 'post-materialist' values in Germany and Britain follow identical patterns (Inglehart, 1977, 1990; Gabriel, 1994). This notable convergence, which anything but conforms with the conventional distinction between German and British political and societal norms, also extends to another value item which has received particularly wide currency since it seems to be best suited to tap the underlying 'individualist'-'egalitarian' dimension: Do people rank freedom over equality or vice versa if asked to choose between two alternatives? Indeed, in the early 1980s Germany stood out among the western European countries for being the only nation where equality exceeded freedom in popularity (39 per cent supported the 'equality' option; 37 per cent opted for 'freedom'). The British case was located at the opposite end of the spectrum, with 68 per cent of the respondents voting for the 'freedom' option. In 1990, however, a replication of the survey yielded rather different results, with Germany (59 per cent support for 'freedom') ranking only second to Britain (61 per cent) in international comparison and showing the least support for the 'equality option' among all countries studied (see Harding and Philips, 1986, p.86-7; Brettschneider et al., 1994, p.553, cf. also Ashford and Timms, 1992).[2]

Whereas German political culture apparently shifted towards the 'civic culture' model during the 1970s and 1980s, citizens' attitudes in Britain moved in the opposite direction. As a case in point, the British sample ranged among the least politically interested as compared to other established democracies, thus showing clear signs of political estrangement (cf. Johnston, 1993). In 1990, 34 per cent said they were 'not at all' or 'not very' interested in politics, while only 21 per cent of the German sample member did so (Brettschneider et al., 1994, p.564). Following this route of interpretation, we can observe other signs of considerable political alienation in Britain which have given rise to controversial debates over the 'decline of civic culture' since the mid-1970s (see for discussion e.g. Kavanagh, 1980; Heath and Topf, 1987; Döring, 1994). Thus, it has been reported that levels of system efficacy – the belief that the system can and will respond to popular demands for change – like levels of political trust, have reached an unprecedented low in Britain (Curtice and Jowell, 1995). A similar trend has been observed with regard to personal efficacy, i.e. the confidence in one's own ability to articulate a demand for change and to affect the political process. Traditionally, the British political culture was praised for its high level of 'citizen competence'. Recent surveys, however, have consolidated earlier trend reports, showing that a growing proportion of respondents think that they had no say in government or that government and politics were too complicated to understand (Curtice and Jowell, 1995).

Returning to the comparative perspective, the German and British political cultures seem to have moved on some important dimensions (i.e. commitment to and involvement in the democratic process) from their original positions as described in Almond and Verba's Civic Culture study, thus shifting towards the centre ground. As mentioned above, the level of political distrust tends to be particularly high in Britain (Borre, 1995, p.348), with 49 per cent of the respondents in 1985 expressing distrust as opposed to 23 per cent of the German survey participants. On the issue of general support for unconventional political protest, the figures for the German sample jumped from 21 per cent in 1985 to 46 per cent in 1990, which even surpassed the traditionally high British score (33 per cent in 1990; 29 per cent in 1985; see Borre, 1995, p.348). Also, the British and German respondents seem to be, by and large, equally committed to values of liberal democracy as measured by their support for civil rights. When asked, however, whether they had actually protested, thus using their civil rights in any (conventional or unconventional) way, the answers from the British sample show a slightly higher level of political involvement (Brettschneider et al., 1995). This tendency holds especially true when we look at the frequency of citizen contacts with their representatives in parliament. Nonetheless, the contours of the German political culture profile no longer seem to have any resemblance to the type of 'subject culture' which was established back in the late 1950s.

Could it have been possible, as a rather conventional argument would suggest, that a strong popular backing of traditional public, and in particular administrative, institutions in Germany has prevented 'new public management' from taking root in the German public sector? Indeed, in international comparison the German respondents – in keeping with the longstanding legalist tradition in the country – hold the judiciary in particular awe (Gabriel and Brettschneider, 1994, p.562; although, one should be quick to point out that the variance between Great Britain and Germany is only marginal.) With regard to public bureaucracies, however, the findings generated by comparative survey studies certainly call for a re-assessment of commonly held views on the acceptance of and trust in public administration in Germany. In Britain and Germany, the civil service scores rather low in public trust, with no more than 44 per cent of the British respondents saying that they trust the civil service very much, and even fewer than 38 per cent of the German sample members saying so. (Brettschneider et al., 1994, p.562. Percentages are given for 1990. The figures for 1981-1983 are 32 per cent for Germany and 45 per cent for Britain.) Most strikingly, however, the civil service in Britain ranks even higher in public trust than parliament, which seems to be at odds with the powerful standing of parliament in British history, and at the same time stands in marked contrast to the German situation where trust in parliament is only exceeded by trust in the legal system and the police.

Looking at public personnel policies in Britain and Germany, the cross-national differences in approaching public sector reforms become only too obvious. Thus, the professional civil service in Germany (*Berufsbeamtentum*) still appears to be one of the strongholds of traditional public sector management. Can this reluctance towards any major changes in this respect be linked to prevailing cultural patterns in the German public? Rather than supporting this hypothesis, recently gathered data on this issue signal that the popular basis for legitimising the constitutionally guaranteed status of *Beamte* is increasingly crumbling (Noelle-Neumann, 1997). Asked whether they would maintain or abandon the traditional principles guiding the '*Beamtentum*', the vast majority of the interviewees voted in favour of doing away with most of the fundamental civil service norms. Most importantly, more than two thirds of the sample members (69 per cent) voiced serious concern about the guaranteed job security of civil servants, and opted for changing the law in this respect. In unexpected unison, the overwhelming majority of respondents would also like to see civil servants stripped of other privileges (e.g. superannuation acts, special health insurance schemes). In addition, the introduction of performance-related pay systems was particular popular with most respondents (81 per cent supporting this reform measure). To sum up, only 14 per cent of the sample members endorsed the view that the '*Beamtentum*' is 'in', whereas 57 per cent claimed that this institution is 'out'. Consequently, there seems to be no evidence for the assumption that supportive public attitudes have shielded off any hostile reforming attacks on the German civil service.

National Cultures and 'Big Government': Liberal-Leaning Britain vs. State-Centred Germany?

Having paved the way by reviewing the lessons from organisational and general political culture research, this section now aims at the heart of the matter of 'rolling back the frontiers of the state'. It therefore sets out to probe more specifically and systematically the prevailing public beliefs about the range and degree of government activity. In doing so, this section also examines the bearing of the established 'etatist' and 'non-etatist' distinction on the comparative analysis of public sector reform. Again, the expectations, based on the classical categorisation of welfare state regimes, seem to be clear-cut: whereas sample members from liberal-leaning Britain are expected to resent state intervention, respondents socialised in corporatist Germany would give a higher priority to government services (Taylor-Gooby, 1998, Mau, 1998). As a first step, our investigation looks at attitudes towards the range of government responsibilites, focusing on core services of the established welfare state. On this issue, relevant data have been gathered in the (first) Political Action study (the data are from 1974; see also Barnes and Kaase, 1979) and three surveys (1985, 1990 and 1996) of the International Social Survey Programme (ISSP) which also allow for comparisons over time. The Political Action study, which covered seven countries, identified twelve policy areas, ranging from traditional welfare concerns to economic and law-and-order policies, and probed citizens' attitudes towards the role of government in those selected issues. In a slightly different manner, the ISSP questionnaire, which was first used in a six-country study in 1985, specified seven policy items, asking all respondents whether they thought it was or was not the government's responsibility to: (1) provide a job for everyone who wants one, (2) keep prices under control, (3) provide health care for the sick, (4) provide a decent standard of living for the old, (5) provide industry with the help it needs to grow, (6) provide a decent standard of living for the unemployed, (7) reduce income differences between the rich and the poor (Kaase and Newton, 1998, p.43). One should be quick to mention that the data gathered by the 1974 and 1985 studies are not comparable in a strict sense due to the differing batteries of questions about government responsibility. However, the figures may still provide us with a rough picture of the dynamics of attitudinal change between the mid-70s and the mid-80s.

Looking at the data generated by both surveys, we find widespread support for government activity in the selected policy areas. In fact, there appears to be a well-founded consensus in favour of 'big government' among the countries under study, with the variance between nations being remarkably low (Huseby, 1995, p.95-6). Most notably in Britain and Germany, however, the figures also indicate some significant changes from 1974 to 1985. Interestingly, attitudes in Britain and Germany had apparently been shifting in opposite directions: In Germany, attitudes were more supportive of a wide range of government responsibilities in the early 1970s and much less favourable in 1985 and 1990, whereas the British data reveal that attitudes have moved significantly towards a more 'expansionist' view of government's role in society. For example, the mean percentage of German respondents who thought it was 'essential' or 'important' that government should take responsibility in the twelve policy areas included in the 1974 survey was 88 per cent (British respondents: 78 per cent), while the mean percentage who thought government should 'definitely' or 'probably' be responsible for the seven policy fields of the 1985 study dropped to 80 per cent in the German case, but raised to 88 per cent in the British case (Huseby 1995, pp.95-6). Moreover, Britain and Germany switched places in the international 'league table': in 1974, Germany was among those countries which showed the highest level of support for government assuming a large range of responsibilities, while Britain had the lowest mean score. In contrast, in both 1985 and 1990 German respondents were the most hesitant in their support for improved mass welfare services, whereas the British sample scored on or even above the cross-national average (Huseby, 1995, p.96; for the 1990 ISSP survey see also Taylor-Gooby, 1993).

In the following, we confine our review of empirical findings to the series of the ISSP surveys in order to allow for valid comparisons over time. For the same reason, the analysis of the 1985, 1990 and 1996 surveys mainly focuses on responses from western Germany. Drawing on the work of Kaase and Newton (1998, p.45), the tables below show the percentages of respondents who felt that it should definitely or probably be government's responsibility to provide any of the seven services specified above. This 'index of state intervention in general' can serve as a single, broad-brush measure of the preferred breadth of government activities.

	1985	1990	1996
0-4	20%	29%	26%
Five	18%	20%	19%
Six	30%	24%	25%
Seven	33%	27%	30%
Average	5.41	4.91	5.07

Table 10.2 **Index of state intervention for W. Germany**
Note: The index runs from 0 (not in favour of government responsibility in any area) to 7 (in favour of state responsibility in all seven areas).
Source: *Kaase and Newton, 1998, p.45*

	1985	1990	1996
0-4	11%	15%	15%
Five	12%	15%	15%
Six	19%	24%	25%
Seven	58%	47%	45%
Average	6.02	5.78	5.76

Table 10.3 Index of state intervention for Britain
Note: The index runs from 0 (not in favour of government responsibility in any area) to 7 (in favour of state responsibility in all seven areas).
Source: *Kaase and Newton, 1998, p.45*

As the figures indicate, in both countries only a minority of respondents are hesitant to assume a government responsibility in most of the specified policy areas. According to the latest survey, roughly two in three British sample members (70 per cent) and every second German interviewee (55 per cent) are in favour of an active role of government in at least six of the seven areas of state activity they were asked about. Also, the index shows consistent attitudinal patterns inasmuch as answers from the British samples are generally more supportive of social and economic state interventions than responses from western Germany – a pattern which has apparently been rather robust during the 1980s and 1990s.

Rather than exploring citizens' attitudes towards the scope of government intervention in general terms, we now turn to a more detailed discussion of individual questionnaire items. Also, we seek to dissect the general index by disaggregating the response categories, which will reveal even larger cross-national differences. To this end, the findings for three traditional welfare concerns are laid out in the tables below. Considering only those respondents who think that government is 'definitely responsible' for providing the services in question, the results shows that British sample members – compared to their German peers – prove much more enthusiastic in their support for established mass welfare services, which holds particularly true for the provision of health services (cf. also Döhler's, 1990, account of the National Health Service, which considers the NHS part of the 'collectivist' element in British political culture; in a similar vein also Mau,

1998). The data also reveal a slight decline in public commitment to these services of mass need, but this change does not appear large enough to conclude that attitudes were becoming explicitly 'contractionist'. More to the point of our two-country comparison, this trend seems to be at work in both Britain and Germany to the effect that cross-national differences are relatively persistent.

A similar pattern of attitudes emerges if one also takes the 'degree' dimension of governmental activity into consideration, too. For this purpose, we again rely on the data generated by the ISSP surveys which also included a number of questions asking about the extent to which people wanted more state spending on a range of services. Using factor analysis, three broadly defined groups of government activities could be identified (Huseby, 1995, p.101-2, Kaase and Newton, 1998, p.49-51). The first factor, which deserves particular attention here, includes typical welfare concerns such as old age pensions, health, and unemployment benefits. The second factor ('law and order policies') unites attitudes towards spending on law enforcement and defence policies, while environmental and cultural policies were added to form the third factor. Apart from public spending on environmental issues, which the vast majority of German interviewees – in contrast to their British counterparts – felt very strongly about, calls for more government spending have been much more frequently voiced by British sample members. Focusing on the 'welfare group', it appears that – apart from smaller fluctuations – no major movement of attitudes has occurred. Thus, the overall picture fits into the mosaic of empirical evidence laid out above. Most notably, at all three time points the proportion of 'welfare seekers' was considerably lower in Germany than in Britain. (In 1996, one quarter of the German sample members advocate more or much more social spending, whereas well above one half of the British respondents do so.)[3] These cross-national differences were most clearly brought into the open when the sample members were asked to choose between the options of reducing taxes or spending more on social services. In the latest survey, 71 per cent of the Britons opted for higher welfare spending, while 68 per cent of the west Germans voted in favour of lower taxes (Mau, 1999, p.31).[4]

	1985	1990	1996
W.Germany	54	57	51
Britain	85	85	82

Table 10.4   Percentages of respondents definitely approving government responsibility to provide health care for the sick
Source: Taylor-Gooby, 1998, p.63

	1985	1990	1996
W. Germany	56	54	48
Britain	78	79	73

Table 10.5   Percentages of respondents definitely approving government responsibility to provide a decent standard of living for the old
Source: Taylor-Gooby, 1998, p.63

	1985	1990	1996
W. Germany	24	19	17
Britain	44	32	29

Table 10.6   Percentages of respondents definitely approving government responsibility to provide a decent standard of living for the unemployed
Source: Taylor-Gooby, 1998, p.63

Admittedly, these findings partly reflect the relatively high standards of social welfare in Germany as well as the relatively high German tax burden on the one hand, and the draconian cuts in British welfare benefits on the other hand, but they nevertheless also throw some light on a more 'collectivist' and 'interventionist' component of British political culture.

Since the questionnaire items of the 'government responsibility' battery discussed so far have focused on the traditional service-oriented welfare statism, it remains to be seen whether there is similar support for more interventionist and consciously redistributive policies (cf. Roller, 1995). While examining popular support for these areas of government activity, we at the same time take issue with the well-established proposition that in an Anglo-Saxon cultural setting the government's major task is rather to guarantee 'life, liberty and property', rather than to achieve social equality (cf. also Döring, 1993).

	1985	1990	1996
W. Germany	36	30	28
Britain	38	24	29

Table 10.7 Percentages of respondents definitely approving government responsibility to provide a job for everyone who wants one
Source: Taylor-Gooby, 1998, p.64

	1985	1990	1996
W. Germany	28	22	25
Britain	48	42	36

Table 10.8 Percentages of respondents definitely approving government responsibility to reduce income differences between rich and poor
Source: Taylor-Gooby, 1998, p.64

Not unexpectedly, policies of a more interventionist kind apparently appeal much less to the electorate than the services tested before which are mainly concerned with the issue of 'social security' (particularly retirement pensions and health services) rather than 'social equality'. By and large, however, the overall trend of the analysis remains relatively stable. While people in the former West Germany are more suspicious of the role of government, support in Britain for 'interventionist' policies – with the notable exception of the responsibility for providing jobs – in Britain exceeds by far the West German level.[5]

	1985	1990	1996
W.Germany	42	42	39
Britain	45	37	48

Table 10.9   Percentages of respondents in favour or strongly in favour of controlling prices and wages by law
Source: Kaase and Newton, 1998, p.46

	1985	1990	1996
W. Germany	67	73	77
Britain	73	75	83

Table 10.10   Percentages of respondents in favour or strongly in favour of job creation and protection by government
Source: Kaase and Newton, 1998, p.46

	1985	1990	1996
W. Gerrmany	67	67	82
Britain	49	48	53

Table 10.11   Percentages of respondents in favour or strongly in favour of 'less government regulation of business' and 'less government spending'
Source: Kaase and Newton, 1998, p.47

State management of the economy has been one of the dominant areas of policy debate over the last two decades which have witnessed a revival of economic neo-liberalism as marked, for example, by the Thatcher governments in Britain. It follows from this that public sentiments in favour or against certain government intervention in the economy also deserve our closer attention. In their analysis of the ISSP data, Kaase and Newton devised three measures in order to touch upon these attitudinal patterns (Kaase and Newton, 1998, p.45-7).

As shown by the indices, there does not seem to be any consistent 'expansionist' or 'contractionist' ideology underlying the preferences of the citizens towards state interventions in the economy. On the one hand, we find widespread consensus in both countries when it comes to evaluating government action in creating jobs or to subsidising ailing industries – the overwhelming majority of the British and German samples (1996: 77 per cent and 83 per cent respectively) would like to see a helping hand from the state in these cases. On the other hand, there are clear signs that people – particularly in Germany – have become increasingly disinclined towards government regulation of business and too much government spending (1996: 53 per cent in Britain and 82 per cent in Germany). The issue of wage and price control appears to stir up more controversy among the samples, especially in the German case where – according to the 1996 survey – the group which favours both measures surpasses the group of opponents only by 6 percentage points (in the British sample the margin is 23 percentage points). All in all, however, the contours of the emerging picture follow the lines of the by now all-familiar pattern: the British seem to be consistently more sympathetic to state intervention than the west Germans.

The 1985 and 1990 ISSP surveys offer another route of inquiry since they also tapped citizens' attitudes towards state ownership of economic enterprises (see Taylor-Gooby, 1993, p.87, Borre and Viegas, 1995, p.253). According to the survey results, the overall level support for state ownership was rather modest, but the discernible patterns of support for 'welfare statism' revealed in earlier analyses of attitudes to state responsibilities became visible again. As a rule, positive attitudes towards nationalisation seemed to be more widespread in Britain than in the former West Germany. In 1990, for example, no fewer than 30 per cent of the British respondents (26 per cent in 1985) thought that the electricity sector should be in the hands of the public sector, thus reaching the level of support for state ownership of public utilities in eastern Germany. However, only 16 per cent of the interviewees from the 'old' Federal Republic (1985: 19 per cent) did so. Interestingly, attitudes in Britain appear to have shifted slightly in favour of nationalisation from 1985 to 1990. It has been convincingly argued that this movement of attitudes can be understood as a reaction to Thatcherite policies. Thus, the rapid progress of a neo-liberal programme, which involved the privatisation of monopolies providing essential services, together with fears that this policy would generate more social inequality, might explain the change in attitudes towards during the later 1980s (see Taylor-Gooby, 1993; Borre and Viegas, 1995).

Conclusion

According to findings from survey research the bearing of well-established distinctions between 'state-centred' vs. 'stateless' societies or between 'individualist' vs. 'collectivist' traditions on the current British and German cultural profiles should not be overestimated. In important instances the general message that these classical images convey may even be misleading. In fact, in many relevant areas of 'political culture'-research a convergence or even cross-over of the prevailing attitudinal patterns can be observed. So there is only little chance, if any, of tracing in (western) Germany any noteworthy relicts of a state-centred 'subject culture' which could be set against the model of the British 'civic culture'. Rather, there has been a convergent trend as regards the patterns of general political values and the strength and vitality of civil society.

A slightly different perspective opens up if one turns to organisational cultures which also seem to carry a distinct national component. At first glance, the observed 'culture clusters' at the work-related level seem to accord better with both the popular images of British and German national cultures (with regard to the 'individualist' and 'uncertainty avoidance' dimensions) and, more importantly, with the common classification of 'New Public Management' approaches in Europe. Indeed, this finding may help to account for the low standing of 'managerialism' on the German reform agenda. However, the explanatory power of this factor is somewhat limited, since the empirical data base for this research field is still underdeveloped, to say the least. Also, the emerging cross-national variations are not of a fundamental nature; rather, the differences are a matter of degree.

The reform of the welfare state has been at centre stage of public sector change. In this regard, the demands in Germany and Britain for traditional welfare state services or interventionist and redistributional government activities appear to differ only gradually and, above all, not in the anticipated way. As for the British case, the surveys suggest that public mood was at its most Thatcherite and 'right-wing' in the second half of the 1970s, when the resistance to the idea of (too) big government increasingly gained strength (Crewe and Searing, 1988; Kavanagh, 1990). Following the experience of major reform measures designed to replace most of the post-war welfare consensus, however, attitudes have again become more supportive of government responsibilities (Jowell and Topf, 1988). In Germany, public support for 'big government' appears to have declined since the 'social-democratic' 1970s, though showing no clear evidence of any widespread wish to significantly redraw the boundaries of the state. In sum, there is 'a close family resemblance of attitudes and values, with the British a little more supportive of state involvement than the Germans' (Kaase and Newton, 1998, p.52).

Notes

1 Thus, many observers appear to have lost sight of the well-founded collectivist tradition in British political culture. It may suffice here to point to W. H. Greenleaf's work on 'The Rise of Collectivism' and a 'Much Governed Nation' (1983, 1987). The tensions in ideology and governmental practice between collectivist and libertarian values is also captured in Pugh (1994). Similarly, Rose's early analysis (1965) reminds us of the positive value placed in Britain upon government as beneficent in general and on the collective provision of welfare in particular.
2 It still remains to be seen, however, whether this drastic swing is a mere reflection of the 'peaceful revolution' in East Germany and Eastern Europe at large. In fact, national surveys indicate a slightly decreasing support for the 'freedom'-option in the western part of the country. In the 'new' German *Länder*, the results have been reversed, with more than 60 per cent of the respondents giving priority to the 'equality-option' (Noelle-Neumann, 1999).
3 Cf. also the figures presented by Huseby, 1995, Mau, 1998, and Taylor-Gooby (1998) who report higher percentages of 'welfare seekers' in both countries. Nevertheless, the observed cross-national variations are the same and the number of British 'welfare seekers' exceeds the size of the equivalent German group by a wide margin of up to thirty percentage points.
4 Here, the clashes between west and east German cultural dispositions are most pronounced, with the attitudinal patterns in the new *Länder* taking the shape of the British distribution of responses (Mau, 1998, p.31; cf. also Taylor-Gooby, 1993, p.85).
5 It is not surprising that support for an active role of government in evening out socio-economic differences is strongest in eastern Germany. The number of east German respondents advocating the reduction of income differences, for example, surpasses their west German peers by 25 percentage points (Taylor-Gooby, 1993, p.85; Mau, 1998, p.30).

References

Almond, G. A. and Verba, S. (1963), *The Civic Culture: Political Attitudes and Democracy in Five Nations*, Princeton University Press, Princeton.
Almond, G. A. and Verba, S. (eds) (1980), *The Civic Culture Revisited*, Little Brown, Boston.
Ashford, S. and Timms, N. (1992), *What Europe Thinks: A Study of Western European Values*, Ashgate, Aldershot.
Baker, K. L., Dalton, R. J. and Hildebrandt, K. (1981), *Germany Transformed: Political Culture and the New Politics*, Harvard University Press, Cambridge, Mass.
Barnes, S. H. and Kaase, M. *et al.* (1979), *Political Action: Mass Participation in Five Western Democracies*, Sage, Beverly Hills.
Bendix, R. (1956), *Work and Authority in Industry*, John Wiley & Sons, New York.
Berger, M. and Watts, P. (1994), 'Management Development in Europe', in C. Mabey and P. Iles (eds), *Managing Learning*, Routledge, London, pp. 248-59.
Borre, O. (1995), 'Scope of Government Beliefs and Political Support', in O. Borre and E. Scarborough (eds), *The Scope of Governmen*, Oxford University Press, Oxford, pp. 343-66.
Borre, O. and Viegas, J. M. (1995), 'Government Intervention in the Economy', in O. Borre and E. Scarborough (eds), *The Scope of Government*, Oxford University Press, Oxford, pp. 234-80.
Brettschneider, F. *et al.* (1994), 'Daten zu Gesellschaft, Wirtschaft und Politik in den EG-Mitgliedstaaten', in O. W. Gabriel and F. Brettschneider (eds), *Die EU-Staaten im Vergleich*, Leske + Budrich, Opladen, pp. 460-626.
Conradt, D. (1980), 'Changing German Political Culture', in G. Almond and S. Verba (eds), *Civic Culture Revisited*, Little Brown, Boston, pp. 212-72.
Crewe, I. and Searing, D. D. (1988), 'Ideological Change in the British Conservative Party', *American Political Science Review*, vol. 82, pp. 361-84.
Curtice, J. and Jowell, D. (1995), 'The Sceptical Electorate', *British Social Attitudes*, 12th Report, Ashgate, Aldershot, pp. 141-71.
Dahrendorf, R. (1980), 'Unsere Einstellungen zu zentralen Werten müssen wir wahrscheinlich ändern', *Materialien zur politischen Bildung*, pp. 29-44 (34).
Derlien, H.-U. and Löwenhaupt, S. (1997), 'Verwaltungskontakte und Institutionenvertrauen', in H. Wollmann *et al.* (eds.), *Transformation der politisch-administrativen Strukturen in Ostdeutschland*, Leske + Budrich, Opladen, pp. 417-72.
Döhler, M. (1990), 'Der National Health Service in der Ära Thatcher', in R. Sturm (ed.), *Thatcherismus – Eine Bilanz nach 10 Jahren*, Brockmeyer, Bochum, pp. 199-222.

Döring, H. (1990), 'Autoritärer Populismus', in R. Sturm, R. (ed.), *Thatcherismus - eine Bilanz nach 10 Jahren*, Brockmeyer, Bochum, pp. 257-93.
Döring, H. (1993), *Großbritannien: Regierung, Gesellschaft und politische Kultur*, Leske + Budrich, Opladen.
Döring, H. (1994), 'Bürger und Politik - die Civic Culture im Wandel', in H. Kastendiek,, K. Rohe and A. Volle (eds), *Großbritannien*, Campus, Frankfurt, M./New York, pp. 155-69.
Dyson, K. (1980a) *The State Tradition in Western Europe. A Study of an Idea and Institution*, Oxford University Press, Oxford.
Egan, M. (1997), 'Modes of Business Governance: European Management Styles and Corporate Cultures', *West European Politics*, vol. 20, pp. 1-21.
Gabriel, O. W. (1994), 'Politische Einstellungen und politische Kultur', in O. W. Gabriel and F. Brettschneider (eds), *Die EU-Staaten im Vergleich*, Leske + Budrich, Opladen, pp. 96-137.
Gabriel, O. W. (ed.) (1997), *Politische Orientierungen und Verhaltensweisen im vereinigten Deutschland*, Leske + Budrich, Opladen.
Greenleaf, W. H. (1983), *The British Political Tradition*, vol. 1: *The Rise of Collectivism*, Methuen, London.
Greenleaf, W. H. (1987), *The British Political Tradition*, vol. 3: *A Much Governed Nation*, Methuen, London.
Harding, S. and Philips, D. (1986), *Contrasting Values in Western Europe*, Macmillan, London.
Heath, A. and Topf, R. (1987), 'Political Culture', *British Social Attitudes. The 1987 Report*, pp. 51-69.
Hickson, D. J. (1993), 'Many More Ways Than One', in D. J. Hickson (ed.), *Management in Western Europe: Society, Culture and Organization in Twelve Nations*, Walter DeGruyter, Berlin, pp. 249-62.
Hofstede, G. (1980), *Culture's Consequences: International Differences in Work-Related Attitudes*, Sage, Beverly Hills.
Hofstede, G. (1991), *Cultures and Organisations: Software of the Mind*, McGraw-Hill, New York.
Huseby, B. M. (1995), 'Attitudes Towards the Size of Government', in O. Borre and E. Scarborough (eds), *The Scope of Government*, Oxford University Press, Oxford, pp. 87-118.
Inglehart, R. (1977), *The Silent Revolution. Changing Values and Policy Styles among Western Publics*, Princeton University Press, Princeton.
Inglehart, R. (1990), *Culture Shift in Advanced Industrial Society*, Princeton University Press, Princeton.
Jennings, M. K., et al. (1989), *Continuities in Political Action: A Longitudinal Study of Political Orientations in Three Western Democracies*, Walter DeGruyter, Berlin.
Johnston, M. (1993), 'Disengaging from Democracy', in *International Social Attitudes*, The 10th Report, Ashgate, Aldershot, pp. 1-22.

Jowell, R. and Topf, R. (1988), 'Trust in the Establishment', in *British Social Attitudes*, The 5th Report, Ashgate, Aldershot, pp. 109-26.
Joynt, P. and Warner, M. (eds) (1985), *Managing in Different Cultures*, Universitetsforlaget, Oslo.
Kaase, M. and Newton, K. (1998), 'What People Expect from the State: Plus Ca Change', in *British and European Social Attitudes. How Britain Differs. The 15th Report*, Ashgate, Aldershot, pp. 39-56.
Kavanagh, D. (1971), 'The Deferential English: A Comparative Critique', *Government and Opposition*, vol. 6, pp. 333-60.
Kavanagh, D. (1980), 'Political Culture in Britain: The Decline of the Civic Culture', in G. Almond and S. Verba (eds), *The Civic Culture Revisited*, Little Brown, Boston, pp. 124-76.
Kavanagh, D. (1990), *Thatcherism and British Politics: The End of Consensus?*, Oxford University Press, Oxford.
Keraudren, P. (1996), 'In Search for Culture: Lessons from the Past to Find a Role for the Study of Administrative Culture', *Governance*, vol. 9, pp. 71-98.
Letwin, S. R. (1992), *The Anatomy of Thatcherism*, Fontana, London.
Macfarlane, A. (1978), *The Origins of English Individualism*, Basil Blackwell, Oxford.
Mau, S. (1998), 'Zwischen Moralität und Eigeninteresse – Einstellungen zum Wohlfahrtsstaat in internationaler Perspektive', *Aus Politik und Zeitgeschichte*, no. 34-35/98, pp. 27-37.
Nettl, J. P. (1968), 'The State as a Conceptual Variable', *World Politics*, vol. 20, pp. 559-92.
Noelle-Neumann, E. (1997), 'Des Staates treue Diener: Zur Krise des Berufsbeamtentums', *Frankfurter Allgemeine Zeitung*, 12 February 1997, p. 5.
Noelle-Neumann, E. (1999), Der Zauber der Freiheit, *Frankfurter Allgemeine Zeitung*, 24 June 1999, p. 12.
Pugh, M. (1994), State and Society. *British Political and Social History 1870-1992*, Arnold, London.
Randlesome, C. (ed.) (1990), *Business Cultures in Europe*, Heinemann, Oxford.
Rohe, K. (1982), 'Zur Typologie politischer Kulturen in westlichen Demokratien', in H. Dollinger et al. (eds), Weltpolitik, Europagedanke, Regionalismus, Aschendorff, Münster, p. 581-96.
Rohe, K. (1984), 'Großbritannien: Krise einer Zivilkultur?' in P. Reichel (ed.), *Politische Kultur in Westeuropa*, Campus,Frankfurt/M, New York, pp. 167-93.
Roller, E. (1995), 'The Welfare State: The Equality Dimension', in O. Borre and E. Scarborough. (eds), *The Scope of Government*, Oxford University Press, Oxford, pp. 165-97.
Rose, R. (1965), 'England: a Traditionally Modern Political Culture', in L. Pye and S. Verba (eds), *Political Culture and Political Development*, Princeton University Press, Princeton, pp. 83-129.

Sartori, G. (1969), 'Politics, Ideology and Belief Systems', *American Political Science Review*, vol. 63, pp. 398-411.

Tayeb, M. (1988), *Organisations and National Culture: A Comparative Analysis*, Sage, London.

Tayeb, M. (1993), 'English Culture and Business Organisation', in D. Hickson (ed.), *Management in Western Europe*, Walter DeGruyter, Berlin, pp. 47-64.

Taylor-Gooby, P. (1993), 'What Citizens Want from the State', *International Social Attitudes. The 10th Report*, Ashgate, Aldershot, pp. 81-102.

Taylor-Gooby, P. (1998), 'Commitment to the Welfare State', *British and European Social Attitudes. How Britain Differs. The 15th Report*, Ashgate, Aldershot, pp. 57-76.

Thompson, M., Ellis, R. and Wildavsky, A. (1990), *Cultural Theory*, Westview Press, Boulder.

Verba, S. (1965), 'Germany: The Remaking of Political Culture', in L. Pye and S. Verba (eds), *Political Culture and Political Development*, Princeton University Press, Princeton, pp. 120-70.

Warner, M. and Campbell, A. (1993), 'German Management', in D. Hickson (ed.), *Management in Western Europe*, Walter DeGruyter, Berlin, pp. 89-108.

11 Regressive Modernisation? The Changing Patterns of Social Services Delivery in the United Kingdom

JOHN CLARKE AND PAUL HOGGETT

Introduction

This paper addresses changes in the organisation of two forms of social services in the United Kingdom: the provision of social security (cash benefits) and the provision of social care (personal services). The two systems are structurally distinct but both underwent substantial processes of reform during the period of Conservative government (1979–1997). Unlike in the Federal Republic of Germany where both services are delivered through local level organisations, in Britain the social security service has always been the responsibility of central government. In contrast, provision for social care has become largely the responsibility of local authority social services departments. In this chapter we seek to trace the distinctive patterns of reform in the provision of these two services and examine the differences and similarities in the processes of restructuring. We focus on the period of intense public service reform in the 1980s and 1990s. Readers seeking a longer historical analysis should look at the chapter by Michael Hill in this volume.

The Social Security Service

Before the Second World War the precursor of social assistance, the 'outdoor relief' dispensed under the old Poor Law system, was the responsibility of local Poor Law Boards of Guardians whose membership overlapped with elected representatives on local authorities. In the inter-war period heightened social tensions led to the politicisation of a number of Boards of Guardians and the government, alarmed at the fiscal and political consequences of this decentralised approach, embarked upon a gradual but consistent process of centralisation which culminated in the National Assistance Act of 1948 which replaced the Poor Law (Hill, 1990). Thus, in marked contrast to Germany, where social assistance is funded and delivered by local authorities, in Britain both social insurance and social assistance type benefits have been funded and delivered by central government agencies since the inception of the post-war welfare state. Equally, the management of social insurance has not involved any sort of corporate arrangement with the 'social partners'. That system has been very much under central control to the extent that even the fiction of 'funding' was undermined early in its history, and eventually totally abandoned. These features of the British system have led to a blurring of the distinction between social insurance and social assistance. However it was not until 1966 that a unified ministry was created for both types of benefit. Almost immediately the Ministry of Social Security was amalgamated with the Ministry of Health and the resulting Department of Health and Social Security survived until 1988 when the health and social security functions were separated again.

Again, almost immediately, the Department of Social Security was subject to a radical process of restructuring in line with the Conservative government's 'Next Steps' reforms – ie. the 'agencification' of central government. The administration of most social insurance and social assistance type benefits was devolved to the Benefits Agency, the largest of all the agencies created under the Next Steps programme. Since the creation of the Benefits Agency in 1991 the delivery of social security services has been subject to a series of sweeping reforms exemplifying nearly all of the main features of the New Public Management. What is particularly interesting however is that although the overall outline of the reform process has been set by government the menu of changes introduced and the style of their implementation has been noticeably influenced by the senior executives placed in charge of operations in the post-1991 period. The arrival of the new Labour government in 1997 has perhaps moderated the pace of change slightly but does not seem to have affected its general course. To understand the nature and impact of the many changes to have been introduced since 1991 it is useful to consider developments during three time periods – the pre-1991 period; the 'Bichard era', 1991-5 (Michael Bichard was the first Chief Executive of the new Benefits Agency); the 'Mathison era', 1995-present (Ian Mathison is the second Chief Executive).

The Pre-1991 Period

As we noted earlier, since 1966 the social security service assumed the form of an integral, centralised bureaucracy that coordinated policy making, policy review and policy implementation and delivered transfer payments through a network of local offices throughout the country. As such social security was a function of the unified civil service staffed primarily by low-grade civil servants performing largely routine clerical and administrative functions. The culture of the service was strongly hierarchical and status conscious exhibiting many of the classic elements of the Weberian bureaucracy: tight role specification, functional specialisation, a complex system of job grades, reliance on rules and procedures, etc. The different benefits – sickness, pensions, disability, social assistance – were administered by different specialised groups of clerical officers using different information systems. By the late 1970s the administrative costs of handling, transferring and storing the vast amounts of data, compounded by the incompatibility of the different information systems which had evolved, led to a growing crisis within the service (Bellamy, 1996). In the early 1980s a massive programme of computerisation of client information systems was commenced which at least one commentator likened to 'the largest civil computing project ever undertaken in the world' (Margetts, 1991). Implementation of the programme ran into a number of difficulties and was never fully completed: nevertheless, considerable savings in human resources were achieved particularly at the clerical officer level. Despite the introduction of decentralised forms of financial management, the basic organisational form of the service remained intact until 1991.

By the late 1980s the social security service was managed through seven regional centres which in turn supervised the running of over 800 local social security offices in England, Scotland and Wales. The processing of claims occurred at two different sites. Long-term benefits, such as the majority of national insurance type benefits, were processed at three national offices on centralised mainframe systems. Short-term, national assistance type benefits, were processed at the local offices. The other main function of the local offices was to deal with enquiries regarding longer-term benefits and to act as a general reception and advice service. Hill (1990) notes that from the inception of the post-war British welfare state national insurance benefits were set at such a low level that the need for social assistance, far from fading away as the authors of the 1948 Act had anticipated, steadily grew. By the early 1960s it had become an important focus for the emerging anti-poverty lobby who attacked both the means-testing, stigmatising, 'Poor Law' character of this benefit and what was felt to be the abuse of discretion by local benefits processing officers. From the point of view of service users it is probably not an exaggeration to say that the dominant orientation towards service users was a punitive one. Social security offices were typically dreadful places and staff were often notorious for their lack of civility. In most urban centres 'claimants' (the term used for service users) could be subject to waiting periods of several hours, they could be sent from one reception point to another, waiting areas were minimally furnished and chairs were normally screwed to the floor (ostensibly to prevent them being used in attacks on staff).

The social security service was therefore an isolated and stigmatised service. There were few, if any, links between local social security and personal social service personnel. In contrast to the latter, the former were untouched by processes of professionalisation. However, the 'factory' conditions of many offices and the politicisation of younger staff who could see how, particularly in poor urban areas, local offices constituted a sponge for the anger of the socially excluded led to high levels of trade union militancy in the 1970s and 1980s.

1991-1995: The Formation of the Benefits Agency

The creation of the Benefits Agency was a significant element in the Conservative government's 'Next Steps' (HMSO, 1988) programme of reform. The 'executive agency' model exemplifies elements of the New Public Management, particularly in terms of the separation of policy from implementation/operations. Policy making remained centralised within a much reduced Department of Social Security, operations being decentralised to the new agency which operated within a 'framework agreement'. This attempt to separate policy from operations has not been unproblematic. In the case of the Benefits Agency there have been a number of occasions, the implementation of controversial changes to the Disability Allowance being the most notable, where Central Government was strongly attacked for shielding itself from responsibility by attempting to define as 'operational' matters which were seen by opponents as important policy issues (Cooper, 1995). Established during a period of escalating unemployment and at the time when the Major government was developing its own approach to the quality of public services through the Citizens Charter initiative (HMSO 1991a) the first Chief Executive of the Benefits Agency was Mike Bichard. For many this was a surprise appointment. Bichard had been a local authority Chief Executive (in the left-wing London Borough of Brent, and subsequently in the county of Gloucestershire) and had a reputation as a progressive, consumer-oriented leader. Cultural change within the agency was symbolised by the adoption of four core values: customer service, care for staff, value for money and bias for action.

The new Agency was organised in a quite different way to the department which preceded it. Power was both centralised and decentralised. On the one hand local offices lost their administrative identity and were grouped together within a district structure under a single manager. There was a genuine devolution of powers within the agency to the 159 newly created districts (Fairbrother, 1994). Each district essentially became a self-contained business unit with control over capital, maintenance and revenue budgets and most industrial relations matters including the hiring and firing of staff up to 'executive officer' grade (which accounted for over 90 per cent of agency staff). A typical district would contain up to 400 staff and would serve a population area of about 300,000 people but the district boundaries bore virtually no relationship to the administrative boundaries of surrounding local authorities. The districts were supported by 24 area offices with coordinating rather than executive powers. The new district managers were recruited from the ranks of the local office managers of the old department. Although they were now responsible for staff in several offices there was no upgrading of this position. This was the first of what was to become a regular 'cull' of managers as more and more non-operational posts were stripped out of the new agency.

The entire restructuring of the organisation was achieved with virtually no new recruitment. Whilst good for morale and for keeping expenditure low, the task of accomplishing cultural change was clearly made more difficult by the lack of an infusion of 'new blood'. The emphasis on training, particularly for the new management cadres, was therefore considerable. This, combined with a strong push for change from the new Chief Executive and his management team and the 'liberation' of the districts from hierarchical control was sufficient to inaugurate a period of radical change focusing on traditional working patterns and organisational systems. A new ten year information systems strategy was adopted which took up many of the more radical Whole Person dimensions which were part of the original 'informatization' agenda of the early 1980s (Bellamy, 1996). Each district acquired its own Customer Service Manager responsible for training, complaints investigation and a range of customer care initiatives. Included within the latter were district-based customer surveys, consultative bodies for communities (Community Benefits Councils), regular forums with local voluntary sector organisations, benefits surgeries run in sites such as hospitals and housing offices, mobile 'benefits buses', etc. A comprehensive programme for upgrading of reception offices was introduced. This provided integrated service points staffed by multi-skilled reception teams, well appointed waiting areas, publicised minimum standards for waiting times for different kinds of enquiries, etc. (Hoggett, 1994).

Behind the reception point the traditional forms of specialisation which characterised the benefits processing task were replaced by the introduction of new working methods and the introduction of the generic benefits specialist in some districts or multi-specialist teams in others. Thus the distinction between the delivery of social insurance and social assistance type benefits was dramatically undermined in some districts as a single team or in some cases a single officer was deployed in the processing and delivery of both. This shift towards multi-skilling in particular aroused a considerable amount of staff resistance (Foster and Hoggett, 1999). Many felt that the existing benefits were so complex and the supporting IT systems so incompatible that the idea of 'one-stop' was largely rhetorical. Although there was considerable cynicism from many staff towards these changes the culture of the service did undoubtedly change in many ways. There was a flowering of bottom-up initiatives in many of the devolved districts with few top-down attempts to standardise developments. Instead the centre sought to steer developments through cultural means and by providing incentives for the adoption of desired practices. The new service counters were widely acclaimed by users, staff and trade unionists in many districts and the movement away from role specialisation was welcomed by many, if not by all, staff. Perhaps most noticeable to staff was the abandonment of much of the formality and status consciousness that was part of the old civil service culture, as a consequence office culture became much more open and relaxed and team-based philosophies much more prevalent.

The Bichard era is fascinating for the many contradictions it sought to manage. For instance, there was a serious attempt to move away from the

Weberian bureaucracy towards more 'organic' forms of organisation on the back of a reconceptualisation of service users from 'claimants' to 'customers' and yet agency staff were acutely aware that these were customers with no choice. Moreover despite the movement towards more organic organisational forms, team working and multi-skilling the fact remained that the vast bulk of the work was, by its nature, of a routinised, low discretion character (Foster and Hoggett, 1999). Nor did the brief flowering of concern for quality during John Major's first full administration diminish the Conservative commitment to markets and competition. The same year as the Citizens Charter was introduced a separate initiative, *Competing for Quality* (HMSO, 1991b), was designed to bring market-type reforms to the newly created executive agencies. A range of non-core activities such as catering, security and cleaning were quickly subject to 'market testing' within the Benefits Agency. About 70 per cent of the contracts have been won in-house. By 1993 the rapid growth in unemployment combined with accumulating anxieties about the sustainability of the welfare safety net given an ageing population led to a growing 'moral panic' about the size of the social security budget and calls for tough government action particularly in the area of sickness and invalidity benefits (*Economist*, 28th May, 1993). Research conducted at the time revealed that staff were acutely aware of contradictory political messages which spoke of service quality for valued customers on the one hand and introduced regressive legislation for some of the most vulnerable claimants on the other (Hoggett, 1994). The return of more punitive attitudes towards benefits claimants was confirmed when Peter Lilley, the Social Security Secretary, replaced the traditional unemployment benefit by the Job Seekers Allowance in 1996. This linked benefit entitlement to a claimant's proven willingness to work, a harking back to the days of the old Poor Law.

1995 - Present: The Mathison Era

The implementation of the Job Seekers Allowance was the last major change introduced by Mike Bichard before he left to become Permanent Secretary at the Department of Education and Employment. His successor, Ian Mathison, was an accountant by background, whose first task was to gear the agency up for dramatic cuts in its administrative budget. Mathison introduced 'the Change Programme' in early 1996 with the objective of achieving a 25 per cent reduction in the agency's administrative costs by

1999. Many of the innovations of the Bichard period were immediately put into reverse. Most services (e.g. surgeries, benefits buses, etc) that encouraged people to claim unclaimed benefits were removed at a stroke (*The Guardian*, March 1st 1996) and Community Benefits Councils were allowed to die away. Increased resources were put into fraud detection and a public 'Shop a Cheat' phoneline campaign was begun. Whilst there was a real sense in which, between 1991 and 1994, the ethos of the service was to reach citizens who were entitled to claim benefits, by 1996 the focus of the service had shifted rapidly away from those who were entitled but not claiming towards those who were claiming but not entitled. The Change Programme combined elements of internal restructuring with an extension of market principles. The agency was reorganised so that many districts were merged to save management overheads. Power was removed from the districts and placed in the hands of revamped 'areas' which were now given executive rather than coordinating responsibilities. Internal market models were introduced by the areas who established a purchaser/provider relationship with the local district units. This also tended to throw into reverse the progress made towards multi-skilling as new business units were formed upon disciplinary lines. Three areas took the market approach still further by forming Private Sector Partnerships. This was a one year programme in which private contractors partnered the BA in delivering the service, followed by an option for renewal and/or invitations to existing contractors to bid for further work which would not necessarily be subject to open tendering.

In addition, some centrally located specialist units, such as the Child Benefits Section, were put out to tender as free standing business units. Finally a modified form of privatisation was also launched via the Private Finance Initiative in which agency assets (specifically physical assets such as the buildings which housed the local offices) were sold off and then leased back. The bid was won by Trilion, a consortium led by the merchant bank Goldman Sachs. A final group of change initiatives launched under the Change Programme are potentially the most far reaching. With developments in information technology it has become possible to spatially disperse functions which had been previously performed within the district offices. For several years benefits processing work in the London region had been outplaced to Glasgow where labour costs were much lower. The introduction of the purchaser/provider split provides the possibility for this option to be pursued by other regions, a possibility which civil service trade unions were already acutely conscious of. Linked to this has been a growing interest in the adoption of the Direct Line model of delivering financial services. Direct Line was a comparatively new and highly successful insurance company which dealt with customers almost entirely via the phone and other forms of telecommunications. Estimates vary but the Benefits Agency considered that approximately 80 per cent of its business was already transacted by phone and letter. In 1996 the agency announced its Blue Print for Change in Wales which recommended closing virtually all of the service's public reception points in the region to replace them by three Telephone Call Centres and a handful of benefits processing offices. Public and trade union protest led to the intervention of MPs from Plaid Cymru who insisted on a proper period of consultation – another example of an 'operational issue' whose the policy implications were only made apparent after political intervention by opposition parties.

What has been the impact of the new Labour government upon the Change Programme? Some initiatives such as the Private Finance Initiative were allowed to continue largely unaltered (interestingly enough, one of the leading lights of Goldman Sachs is Gavin Williams who is a close adviser to Gordon Brown the new Chancellor of the Exchequer). On the other hand the outsourcing of the Child Benefits Section was abandoned. The Blue Print for Wales failed to get beyond the consultation phase but the 'Direct Line' model has resurfaced within another agency within the Department of Social Security, namely the Child Support Agency. Otherwise most of the elements of the Change Programme have remained in place. Market testing has continued. When Trilion took over the estate management function they took over responsibility for cleaning, security and catering services which have been contracted out to two private security firms, Midi and Group 4. A range of other non-core activities were consolidated into 8 contracts, 3 of which stayed in-house the rest being won by private contractors. Finally, the Benefits Agency's IT strategy for the 1990s is entering its third phase, one where the integration of the different benefits systems becomes a real possibility. Thus the further delocalisation of benefits processing work seems highly probable in a routinised service which largely consists in handling various kinds of information. Who knows, but the day may not be far off when the sickness benefit of a man in Birmingham may be processed by an office in Bombay.

Providing Social Care

The provision of social care has differed in significant ways from the provision of Social Security. Social care refers to the variety of domiciliary, residential and other support services provided to people defined as 'in need' of care and protection (e.g. elderly, disabled or mentally ill people). 'Care' and 'cash' are formally divided, with social care being the responsibility of local government. Local authority Social Services Department (SSDs) were established in the 1970s to bring together a range of 'personal social services' previously provided by diverse agencies (Langan, 1993a and b). These departments centred on a professionalized role (the 'generic social worker'), although many services were in practice delivered by unqualified care workers.

The role and work of Social Services Departments (SSDs) have been profoundly reshaped by two major pieces of legislation. The 1989 Children Act redefined the basis for social work with families and children but will not be a focus of attention here. The 1990 National Health Service and Community Care Act (whose implementation was delayed until March 1993) brought 'marketising' and 'managerialising' reforms to both the National Health Service (NHS) and the organisation of Community Care. The Act introduced 'marketising' reforms to the NHS, creating distinctions between purchasers (Health Authorities and some General Practitioners) and providers (hospitals and other services). Contract thus became the primary mechanism for coordinating health care, although it was interwoven with continuing centralized control systems and requirements for both consultants and cooperation (see Flynn and Williams, eds, 1997). The Act gave SSDs the central role in the process of *organising* social care for mentally ill, disabled and older people. SSDs were to perform the tasks of assessing needs, identifying how they might best be met and then purchasing 'packages' of care services from a diverse range of providers. The Act placed a premium on the development and use of services to be purchased from the private (for-profit) and voluntary (not-for-profit) sectors as well as emphasizing the importance of the support and care that could be provided by family, friends and other networks of 'informal' care within the community. The transfer of resources to local authorities to support this new role was accompanied by a requirement that 85 per cent of the new money must be spent purchasing services from the voluntary and private sectors. Organisationally, SSDs were expected to separate their own functions of 'purchasing' and 'providing', such that their own services came to be purchased alongside and possibly in competition with those from voluntary and private sector organisations (for an overview, see Wistow *et al.*, 1994). The Act's reforms have created the category 'social care' as an effect of distinguishing what is provided through SSDs from the care provided by the health service (health care). This distinction has become a significant one for the assessment of needs, the provision of services and the attribution of costs to the budgets of different services. The Act has made *contracting for care* a central process.

The 1990 Act aimed to promote several changes in social care: towards care in the community rather than residential or institutional care; towards greater choice for those in need of support; towards an internal differentiation between purchasers and providers within social services departments and towards a greater role for the private, voluntary and informal sectors at the expense of local authority direct services. The Act aimed primarily to change the balance of sectors within mixed economies of care and to subject their working to more marketised forms of relationship in which a priority would be placed on processes of competition and contracting (Le Grand and Bartlett, eds, 1993; Mackintosh, 1995; Walsh, 1995). Harden's idea of the 'contracting state' (1992) conveys the move towards contractual modes of relationship as a central feature of the organisation of service provision alongside the reduction of direct service provision by public institutions. The development of community care policy (and that of NHS reform) identified the user of public services as a consumer and the introduction of marketising reforms has been legitimated by reference to improving the services available to such consumers, see also (Clarke, 1997 and 1998). For example, the White Paper *Caring for People* stressed the move to contracting as a process of innovation:

> Stimulating the development of non-statutory service providers will result in a range of benefits for the consumer... a wider range of choice of services; which meet individual needs in a more flexible and innovative way ... competition between providers resulting in better value for money and a more cost-effective service. (Secretaries of State, 1989, para. 3.4.3.)

The reforms were represented as marking a shift from 'resource led' services that were dominated and directed by 'provider interests' to a new focus on user/consumer interests in a 'needs led' service that would be more attentive to individual circumstances and would deliver services more closely 'tailored' to individual needs. Although this objective commanded widespread support (social work as a profession has always celebrated the uniqueness of individual clients as part of its ethical statements), the practice resulting from the reforms has been rather murkier (e.g. Barnes, 1997). Resource limits have meant that the determination of levels of need and levels of service have constrained what services can be and are offered to individuals. More significantly, two recent test cases (involving Gloucestershire and Sefton councils) have determined that local authorities have no overriding legal obligation to meet identified need and may take financial judgements into consideration when determining levels of service. In practice, the distinction between 'needs led' and 'resource led' approaches to service provision had been fundamentally blurred by the way in which the assessment function was organised in the 'care manager' role. Care management is the central process of social care, combining assessment and (more or less real) purchasing of packages of care. Langan and Clarke have argued that:

> Despite the 'user-led' language of community care, the pre-eminent tests of managerial efficiency are likely to remain resource centred and there is a clear danger that user pressure towards diversity of needs will not fit easily with cost-effective management concerns. These issues expose the ambiguities of the 'user-led/customer-oriented' discourse of community care. Although such conceptions have been deliberately directed at undermining bureau-professional paternalism in the name of empowering the customer, it is difficult to identify exactly what power has been transferred. Little attention has been given to the involvement of users in service planning or service review, as opposed to the more generalised and ambiguous commitment to consultation. Equally, it is hard to tell what effective power the individual user can exercise in relation to a personalised care package – other than 'expressing preferences'. This is a rather attenuated version of consumer sovereignty and rests on the (charitable) assumption that managerial discretion is intrinsically more user friendly than professional discretion. (1994, pp. 86-7)

In the case of social care, the attractions of 'marketised' relationships – the process of contracting for care – have been muddied by a recognition in the legislation and subsequent guidance that 'social care is different' (Wistow *et al.*, 1994, chapter 6). This difference is made visible in the attention paid to the variety of non-contractual relationships within which patterns of social care are to be developed: consultation, collaboration, forms of joint working (planning, commissioning, purchasing etc.). For example, the Department of Health's guidance on joint commissioning (the collaboration of multiple agencies in planning how to obtain – usually purchase – service provision to meet needs that are of common concern) stressed the importance of 'transcending organisational boundaries':

> Joint commissioning is both an overarching strategic activity, and at the same time a problem solving tool. It transcends organisational boundaries, making an impact at the level of individual assessment and care packages, and at the level of strategic commissioning... A joint commissioning approach also integrates the strategic needs assessment process. This gives a more holistic picture of need, unfettered by organisational boundaries, and provides a sound basis for joint discussions about purchasing activity. It also allows agencies to coordinate their efforts in developing care markets. (Department of Health, 1995, p.3)

This praise for joint commissioning occurs in a context where the creation of markets and devolved systems of budgetary responsibility have given rise to significant disputes about how to distinguish between needs for social care and needs for health care. In the quasi-markets of social and health care, needs do not represent untapped customer demand (and the customer's spending power) but a cost to be set against a finite budget. The perverse incentives contained in these market forms have led to the pursuit of what the Department of Health calls 'cost shunt', but others have termed 'boundary disputes' in which organisations aim to transfer 'needs' and their implied costs by reclassifying them and making them 'not our business' (Vickridge, 1995).

Underlying these changes is a commitment to reducing the level of direct provision of services through public agencies. In social policy analysis, this has been conventionally described as a movement towards 'welfare pluralism' or a *mixed economy of welfare*', identifying the more expanded roles to be played by non-public sector organisations. The idea of a 'mixed economy' is useful for identifying the shifting pattern of provision, although it needs to be tempered by a recognition that most fields of welfare services in Britain were already 'mixed economies' rather than having public services as sole providers (Wistow *et al.*, 1994). The concept of a mixed economy of care needs to be treated as involving particular *local* configurations, with specific patterns of local provision articulated around SSDs (Charlesworth, Cochrane and Clarke, 1995). These are not just what are often termed 'local variations'. There is no *national* mixed economy of care against which such variations may be assessed. Although it is important to be careful about not adopting the neo-conservative view of the past as one dominated by public welfare 'monopolies' (and recognising that there have always been mixed economies of welfare) what is clear is that there has been a sustained attempt to shift the balance of provision towards the independent sector of private and voluntary providers (Langan and Clarke, 1994). In the process, direct provision through what we used to refer to as the welfare state has been decentred and dislocated to a substantial extent. These processes have had the effect of blurring the boundaries between state and non-state welfare provision, since they may be seen as contracting *out* activities previously performed by state agencies but may also be seen as bringing independent agencies *into* new relationships of partnership with, regulation by, and even dependence on the state (Charlesworth, Clarke and Cochrane, 1996).

The reform of social care has also been marked by the intensified transfer of responsibilities from *formal to informal provision*: a shift towards 'care *by* the community'. Although this is most explicit in the field of social care, this is only part of a wider privatisation of welfare responsibilities, including aspects of health, education, income maintenance for adolescents and parental responsibilities for criminal behaviour. The processes of familialisation have been extensively discussed in social policy and their specifically gendered character have received much attention (e.g. Brown and Smith, 1993; Finch and Mason, 1993; Graham, 1984; Langan, 1992). The boundaries between public and private are being blurred as the state both transfers tasks and responsibilities to the familial realm while simultaneously extending the scope of surveillance and regulation of that realm. For example, the expansion of forms of voluntary and informal care, sometimes linked to 'payment for caring' (Ungerson, 1993), opens up new issues about how such caring work is to be organised and supervised.

Finally, we want to draw attention to processes of *managerialisation*. Neither markets nor mixed economies run themselves: they require *agents* to make them work. In the contemporary public sector the preferred form of that agency is 'management'. More particularly, it is management as opposed to administrative bureaucracy or professionalism. This opposition has been especially significant in relation to social work where there has been considerable New Right hostility to the perceived 'liberalism' and 'softness' of social workers (see Clarke, 1996; and Jones, 1998). The transformations of welfare involving markets and mixed economies seem to naturally require 'managers as the embodiment of the types of skills, knowledges and capacities needed to make such processes work efficiently (these arguments are developed more fully in Clarke, Cochrane and McLaughlin, 1994; Clarke and Newman, 1997).

Some of the tendencies of the reforms in social care have been given extra impetus by the changing relationships between central and local government. In the most general terms, the dynamics of these relationships have involved a shifting balance of power (particularly in relation to both policy and finance) to the centre. Local government has also been displaced by the shift of resources, power and functions to non-elected agencies. In the context of social care, this relates primarily to the voluntary and private sector provider agencies but also involves the complex relations with NHS trusts and other agencies in the commissioning of health care. Finally, what has remained within the hands of the local state has been subjected to a growing range of control or disciplinary mechanisms. These range from the evaluation of functional and financial performance. There have been significant developments in the surveillance of service providers through forms of audit, inspection and evaluation that have addressed both financial performance and service performance. In social care, both the Social Services Inspectorate and the Audit Commission have played significant roles and are currently undertaking an extensive joint survey of Social Services Departments. The recent Labour government has announced its intention to strengthen the evaluation and regulation of social care by establishing regional commissions responsible for scrutinizing core standards (Secretary of State for Health, 1998). Such agencies have delivered isomorphic pressures about the best or most appropriate organisational forms and regimes. Central to these are the expectations of 'business-like' behaviour, both in the creation of relatively autonomous business or trading units and in the development of new forms of managerial authority. At this level, then, it is possible to see some points of similarity or convergence between the reform programmes in the two institutional settings under discussion.

Modernising Social Services?

Although there have been a range of structural and organizational reforms of public services in the UK, the central role allocated to 'new and better management' has been a linking thread (Clarke and Newman, 1997). Managerialism has led the challenge to both the 'old style' bureaucratic administration which pre-existed the creation of the Benefits Agency and forms of professional autonomy in welfare services such as social care. Managerialism has been presented as the organisational 'glue' that will make radical changes work effectively and efficiently. The rationalism of managerialism provides an apparently non-partisan (and de-politicised) framework within which choices can be made. While different professional or occupational groups may pursue their parochial interests within the organisation, management represents itself as the bearer of the organisation's best interests (for example, see Green and Armstrong's discussion of 'bed management' in the NHS, 1995). The calculative technologies of managerialism thus provide a foundation for enacting the new logics of rationing, targeting and priority setting. Its quantitative and evaluative technologies form the basis for the new roles of contracting, audit and regulation. The scientific knowledges which they deploy position managers as neutral and impersonal.

The New Public Management can be seen as a manifestation of a more global process of managerialisation. This new global discourse exemplifies a form of unreflexive modernization which construes change as a 'good' in itself. It is preoccupied with the 'how' of things rather than the 'why' and thus exhibits a shallowness in its use of values (Hoggett, 1992, 1997). As such it embodies an instrumental rather than substantive rationality (Habermas, 1987) and public managerialism therefore can be seen as the encroachment of this 'scientific' and calculative means-ends rationality into the public sphere. The rational/technical character of managerial knowledge offers the promise of resolving two different forms of 'chaos'. The first is the chaos of the old regime – the irrationality of unmanaged systems in which the decision making of 'street level bureaucrats' cannot be effectively controlled, and in which bureaucratic control mechanisms proliferate seemingly stupid and irrational systems of rules which get in the way of effectiveness (Peters, 1987). Managerialism represents a way of imposing an illusory rationalised order on this chaos. The second promise of managerialism is that of coping with the complexities and uncertainties of the modern world – the 'chaos of the new' – through the quasi-scientific techniques of strategic management (Greer and Hoggett, 1999) and the delivery of fast paced change and innovation. Where bureaucracies adapt slowly and in a rather ramshackle fashion, creating new rules and functions to cope with new situations within a framework of getting by and making do, managerialism promises to organise the irrational within a rational framework.

Within the public sector the combination of new organisational systems based on 'regulated autonomy' (Hoggett, 1996) and managerialised coordination in a new state form has established the basis for a potential political consensus about social welfare and the role of the state (Clarke and Newman, 1997). In the UK the social security service reveals both the contradictory elements of specific managerial regimes and the way in which managerial and policy regimes may move in and out of alignment. In social care the elementary forms of mixed economies, markets, mothers and managers have been installed as a paradigm of 'delivering welfare' within which political manoeuvring can take place. The creation of a 'welfare pluralism' involving multiple sectors, primarily linked by contracting mechanisms, forms the basis for this new consensus (Rao, 1996). The importance of 'well managed organisations' in making this new order work is taken for granted. The basic forms of this political-economic settlement have led Hay to conclude that we are seeing the revival of what used to be called 'managerial politics': the competition between parties about who can best manage British capitalism (1996, chapter 8). We would want to suggest that what is emerging is better described as a *managerialised politics*. This indicates the changed relationships between government, the state and welfare in the 1990s and the distinctive role being played by managerialism within those new relationships. The emergent consensus includes the widespread commitment that government needs to draw on the new managerial techniques and technologies. Nevertheless, except for a brief period within the social security service in the early 1990s, the programme of economic and institutional reform has been accompanied by policies based on social traditionalism and authoritarianism in a contradictory mixture that Stuart Hall identified in describing the New Right project as one of 'regressive modernisation' (1988, p.164). We think this is a valuable concept to deploy in the evaluation of public service reform, particularly in a period when almost every reform proposal is self-identified as 'modernising'. The imagery of 'modernization' has formed a central thread in 'New Labour' approaches to public service reform (Clarke and Newman, 1998).

Are the new organisational forms and regimes that we have outlined the outcome of a particular model of neo-liberal restructuring whose impact may be diminished or altered by a change in government? Or are these reforms better conceived of as forming part of a new 'organisational settlement' structuring the relationship between welfare, society and the state? Our hunch is that the arrival of a new Labour government is unlikely to undo this new organisational settlement which fragments and depoliticises the organisation and delivery of welfare services. Indeed we may anticipate the intensification of some of its elements as a pragmatic 'what works best' comes to characterise political choices: efficacy becomes everything (Benjamin, 1978).

References

Barnes, M. (1997), *Care, Communities and Citizens*, Longman, London.
Bellamy, C. (1996), 'Transforming Social Security Benefits Administration for the Twenty-First Century: Towards One-Stop Services and the Client Group Principle?', *Public Administration*, vol. 74, pp. 159-79.
Bellamy, C. and Taylor, J. (1994), 'Exploiting IT in Public Administration: Towards the Information Polity?', *Public Administration*, vol. 72, pp. 1-12.
Benjamin, J. (1978), 'Authority and the Family Revisited: Or, a World Without Fathers?', *New German Critique*, vol. 13, pp. 35-57.
Brown, H. and Smith, H. (1993), 'Women Caring for People: The Mismatch Between Rhetoric and Women's Reality', *Policy and Politics*, vol. 21, pp. 185-93.
Burrows, R. and Loader, B. (eds) (1994), *Towards a Post-Fordist Welfare State*, Routledge, London.
Charlesworth, J., Clarke, J. and Cochrane, A. (1995), 'The Politics of Local Mixed Economies of Care', *Environment and Planning 'A'*, vol. 27, pp. 1419-35.
Charlesworth, J., Clarke, J. and Cochrane, A. (1996), 'Tangled Webs? Managing Local Mixed Economies of Care', *Public Administration*, vol. 74, pp.67-88.
Clarke, J. (ed.) (1993), *A Crisis in Care?*, Sage, London.
Clarke, J. (1996), 'After Social Work?', in N. Parton (ed.), *Social Theory, Social Change and Social Work*, Routledge, London.
Clarke, J. (1997), 'Capturing the Customer: Consumerism and Social Welfare', *Self, Agency and Society*, vol. 1, pp. 55-73.
Clarke, J. (1998), 'Consumerism', in G. Hughes (ed.), *Imagining Welfare Futures*, Routledge, London.
Clarke, J. and Newman, J. (1993), 'The Right to Manage: a Second Managerial Revolution?', *Cultural Studies*, vol. 7, pp. 427-41.
Clarke, J. and Newman, J. (1997), *The Managerial State: Power, Politics and Ideology in the remaking of Social Welfare*, Sage, London.
Clarke, J. and Newman, J. (1998), *A Modern British People? New Labour and Welfare Reform*, Working Paper No.32, Department of Intercultural Communication, Copenhagen Business School.
Clarke, J., Cochrane, A. and McLaughlin, E. (eds) (1994), *Managing Social Policy*, Sage, London.
Cooper, P. (1995), 'Separating Policy from Operations in the Prison Service', *Public Policy and Administration*, vol. 10, pp. 4-19.

Fairbrother, P. (1994), *Politics and the State as Employer*, Mansell, London.
Finch, J. and Mason, J. (1993), *Negotiating Family Responsibilities*, Routledge, London.
Flynn, R. and Williams, G. (eds) (1997), *Contracting for Health: Quasi-Markets and the National Health Service*, Oxford University Press, Oxford.
Foster, D. and Hoggett, P. (1999, forthcoming), 'Change in the Benefits Agency: Empowering the Exhausted Worker?', *Work, Employment & Society*, vol. 13, 1, March.
Graham, H.(1984), *Women, Health and the Family*, Wheatsheaf Books, Brighton.
Green, J. and Armstrong, D. (1995), 'Achieving Rational Management: Bed Management and the Crisis in Emergency Admissions', *Sociological Review*, vol. 43, pp. 743-64.
Greer, A. and Hoggett, P. (1999, forthcoming), 'Public Policies, Private Strategies and Local Public Spending Bodies', *Public Administration*, vol. 77, 2, Summer.
Habermas, J. (1987), *The Theory of Communicative Action, Vol. 2: Lifeworld & System*, Polity Press, Cambridge.
Hall, S. (1988), *The Hard Road to Renewal*, Verso, London.
Hay, A.C. (1996), *Re-stating Social and Political Change*, Open University Press, Buckingham.
Hill, M. (1990), *Social Security Policy in Britain*, Edward Elgar, Aldershot.
HMSO (1988), *Improving Management in Government: The Next Steps*, HMSO, London.
HMSO (1991a), *The Citizen's Charter*, HMSO, London, Cm 1599.
HMSO (1991b), *Competing for Quality*, HMSO, London, Cm 1730.
Hoggett, P. (1992), *Partisans in an Uncertain World: The Psychoanalysis of Engagement*, Free Association Books, London.
Hoggett, P. (1996), 'New Modes of Control in the Public Service', *Public Administration*, vol. 74, pp. 9-32.
Hoggett, P. (1997), 'Human Responses to Destructive Regimes', in E. Smith (ed.), *Mental Health in the Market Place*, Routledge, London.
Hoggett, P. and Martin, L. (1994), *Consumer-Oriented Action in the Public Services: National Report for the United Kingdom*, European Foundation for the Improvement of Living and Working Conditions, Dublin.
Jones, C. (1998), 'Social Work: Regulation and Managerialism', in M. Exworthy and S. Halford (eds), *Professionals and the New Managerialism in the Public Sector*, Open University Press, Buckingham.
Langan, M. (1992), 'Who Cares? Women in the Mixed Economy of Welfare', in M. Langan and L. Day (eds), *Women, Oppression and Social Work*, Routledge, London.
Langan, M. (1993a), 'The Rise and Fall of Social Work', in J. Clarke (ed.), *A Crisis in Care?*, Sage, London.

Langan, M. (1993b), 'New Directions in Social Work', in J. Clarke (ed.), *A Crisis in Care?*, Sage, London.
Langan, M. and Clarke, J. (1994), 'Managing in the Mixed Economy of Care', in J. Clarke, A. Cochrane, E. McLaughlin (eds), *Managing Social Policy*, Sage, London.
Le Grand, J. and Bartlett, W. (eds) (1993), *Quasi-Markets and Social Policy*, Macmillan, Basingstoke.
Mackintosh, M. (1995), 'Competition and Contracting in Selective Social Provision', *European Journal of Development Research*, vol. 7.
Margetts, H. (1991), 'The Computerisation of Social Security: The Way Forwards or a Step Backwards?', *Public Administration*, vol. 69, pp. 325-43.
Peters, T. (1987), *Thriving on Chaos: Handbook for a Management Revolution*, Pan, London.
Pollitt, C. (1993), *Managerialism and the Public Services*, (2nd ed.), Basil Blackwell, Oxford.
Rao, N. (1996), *Towards Welfare Pluralism*, Dartmouth Publishing Company, Aldershot.
Secretary of State for Health (1998), *Modernising Social Services*, HMSO, London.
Taylor-Gooby, P. and Lawson, R. (eds) (1993), *Markets and Managers: New Issues in the Delivery of Welfare*, Open University Press, Buckingham.
Ungerson, C. (1993), 'Payment for Caring - Mapping a Territory', in N. Deakin and R. Page (eds), *Paying For Welfare*, Avebury, Aldershot.
Vickridge, R. (1995), 'NHS Reforms and Community Care - Means Tested Health Care Masquerading as Consumer Choice?', *Critical Social Policy*, vol. 43, pp. 76-80.
Wistow, G. *et al.* (1994), *Social Care in a Mixed Economy*, Open University Press, Buckingham.

12 Social Administration in Germany: Basic Structures and Reform History

DIETER GRUNOW

Historical Influences on the Construction of the German Social Security System[1]

Before social affairs and social welfare became a state activity in Germany in 1881, they had been exercised by various kinds of societal institutions. Responsibility for the sick and poor who received no support from their families lay with church-related organisations and local government, at first according to the *Heimatprinzip*, and later according to the so-called *Unterstützungswohnsitzprinzip* (*Armenfürsorge*). The latter was more strictly legally defined within the *Reichsfürsorgepflichtverordnung* (1924). This line of development established the decentralised component of the German welfare system. This component was re-emphasised after the Second World War, when the local church-based welfare associations, the *Caritas* and *Diakonie*, and local administrations were the first to react to the urgent problems and needs of the German population, especially of the homeless and the refugees from the former provinces in the East. This aspect of welfare state provisions has also been reinforced by its proven functionality during the process of German unification.

These early achievements led to the basic legal codification of these welfare programmes in the federal social welfare law, the *Bundessozialhilfegesetz (BSHG)* of 1963. The preceding controversies regarding legal competencies (national or state level) and the role of various implementing actors (public agencies or voluntary associations) were 'resolved' by this law. It established a model which still operates today: national policy; state and local responsibility for implementation, where the preference given to voluntary associations as producers of social services should be observed.

As a result of the industrial revolution (especially in the 19th century) social and health risks and problems for workers reached new dimensions. Unions and other related associations developed their own instruments and institutions offering relief (the so-called *Konsumvereine, Bildungsvereine, Hilfskassen*). In part, this also facilitated trends towards an alignment of workers in the sense of class conflicts.

The beginning of the involvement of national government in social affairs was connected with a specific function: the prevention of an empowerment of the unions and the political parties (with which it co-operated) at the end of the 19th century. Therefore, Bismarck's *Kaiserliche Botschaft* (1881) was formulated only three years after the prohibition of all Social Democratic interest organisations. In other words, political tactics marked the beginning of the social security system in Germany. This issue has been termed die *Arbeiterfrage*. This was a quite different approach to social welfare and social insurance when compared to the idea of equality (as in the Scandinavian countries) or to the battle against poverty (as in the United Kingdom) or to the idea of strengthening family support (as in France).

The strategy of societal conflict resolution by developing social security measures was combined with the definition of a common interest of the population (i.e. workers). Although the early transfer payments only reached about 10 per cent of the population, the idea that they might assist conflict resolution allowed for an emphasis on common interest development. This was also fostered by the idea of a well-organised and healthy work (and military) force. To fulfil this function, the central government would have to play an important role. The multiple goals which were linked to social security as tasks at the national level still prevail in recent descriptions of the system (Brück, 1981, pp.40-49): protective function, distributive function, productivity function, socio–political function, redistributive function. The priorities during the early stages of development can be deduced from the sequence of legal codifications: *Krankenversicherung* (health insurance) 1883; *Unfallversicherung* (accident insurance) 1884; *Rentenversicherung* (pension scheme) 1889; *Arbeitslosenversicherung* (unemployment insurance) 1927; *Pflegeversicherung* (nursing care insurance) 1994. The institutional principles of Bismarck's national project are basically still the same today:

- the principle of compulsory insurance (reciprocal system with elements of solidarity);
- the reference to the labour force (workers; later, employees in general) as a contribution-paying and service-receiving collective, also including the involvement of employers;
- the combination of national policies and multiple institutions under the principle of *Selbstverwaltung* (self-organisation or self-government) as implementation structure;
- the establishment of an extremely complex institutional system, which combines aspects of federalism as well as a differentiation along differences in the labour force, especially for the health insurance scheme (with over 500 independent institutions);
- the policy field is included in a complex system of jurisdiction (*Sozialgerichtsbarkeit*).

Targeting political (workers') opposition meant at the same time that state activities were not in direct competition or conflict with those traditional societal institutions which had previously offered social services and developed social infrastructures. This can still be seen in recent statistics about the producers of services in Germany (about two-thirds being delivered by non-public agencies). Of course, when *Sozialhilfe* (social welfare) was developed towards a nationally codified welfare programme, the relationship between the dominant (self-organised) insurance system and the social welfare scheme had to be clarified. For this, an extended version of the principle of subsidiarity was used. Originally only used to prioritise between self-management/self-help and assistance from other organisational forms, including local administration and the nation state, this principle now in addition defined a series of social security schemes. In the first instance the insurance systems should be called upon. If they are inapplicable or unsuccessful, the *Sozialhilfe* scheme should come into force. An important step towards an integration of the diverse programmes of the social security system was the formulation of the *Sozialgesetzbuch* (social law book) in 1975, beginning with its general section.

In the following, I shall concentrate on developments after the Second World War. In addition to the establishment of a democratic political system in West Germany, the insistence of the Western Allies on a strictly federal construction of the German politico-administrative system has had a major influence on the polity and on the politics during the last fifty years. With regard to social policies these decades have also been influenced by West

Germany's geographical position as 'front-line state' in the East-West conflict. As unification of the divided Germany was always part of the political goals (at least in West Germany), the (mutual) observation of the 'two Germanys' had a special impact on the development of the *Soziale Marktwirtschaft*, a socially tamed form of capitalism. Although often only implicitly formulated, there was always some form of competition between both systems with regard to social welfare and social insurance measures. This was mainly related to those areas of East German 'achievements' in which West German performance was rather poor (such as social services for very young children, occupational training for all, job security, access of women to the labour market, and the like).

These issues have also played a part in the discussions about the unification process, in particular the construction of a *Sozialunion* (Eichener *et al.*, 1992). Although most of the ideas and propositions of East German discussants were ruled out by the West German planners of unification, demands from the East German population were included in the necessary re-formulation of state or communal constitutions (e.g. in Brandenburg). With regard to the social sector, this refers to the specification of material goals of the welfare state (especially the right to work). With regard to the general politico-administrative system, the emphasis laid by the unification process is on extended citizen participation and direct democracy, which appeals primarily to local politics.

Furthermore, similarity and continuity within the population can be shown with survey data of the last ten years. They show an overall high level of support for social security and welfare in Germany, whereby the population of east Germany shows an even higher rate of support for all these measures than the statistical average (Statistisches Bundesamt, 1997).

In the following, two basic segments of the social security system in Germany will be described in more detail: *Rentenversicherung* (retirement pension system) and *Sozialhilfe* (social welfare payments). As already indicated, they represent two different traditions and institutional settings.

Principles of the Architecture of the German Social Insurance and Welfare System

It is not surprising that these and other historical trends during the last 100 years of the development of social policy at the national government level have had an impact on the general design of the system. Altogether, it can be described as a combination of a partly centralised and partly decentralised system of compulsory social insurance, fragmented according to the principle of subsidiarity. The fragmented structure stems from the various historical origins together with the emphasis on the federal constitutional imperative, which allocated the federal states (and thus, in addition, the communal level) responsibility for the organisational structures and processes of implementation. The appearance of the system is stable over time and yet at the same time flexible, offering decentralised alternatives. Institutional changes are primarily a bottom-up phenomenon, whereas national policies are much more concerned with financing and the definition of entitlements. This all makes it quite different from the nation-state centred (and top-down implemented) system in the UK.

The Retirement Pension Scheme

The retirement pension scheme (Kolb, 1983; Nullmeier and Rüb, 1993) is part of the compulsory insurance system and, therefore, similar to the organisation of the health, nursing, unemployment, accident and other insurance systems. The pension scheme provides a major source of income for the elderly. It accounts for 10 per cent of GNP in Germany today. The overall development of this scheme since its establishment has been expansion: a) regarding the (labour) groups included, b) regarding the number of persons included (more elderly persons; earlier retirement; extension of payments to the bereaved), c) regarding the average payment per person from 'additional' contributions aimed at maintaining pre-retirement living standards. Groups which are excluded from compulsory participation (such as the liberal professions) may become voluntary members. Thus, the coverage of the general population is very high (about 85 per cent). Contributions to the pension scheme are made by the members (employees) in work and their employers. Together they contribute about 20 per cent of the gross income of the employees. This basic arrangement is called the *Generationen-Vertrag* (contract between generations), because the working population pays for the retired population.[2]

The design of the retirement pension system still follows the early principles. It is a fragmented system, differentiated into regional and labour-force aspects, as there are 23 separate institutions for workers (*Landesversicherungsanstalten*) and one for salaried staff (*Bundesver-sicherungsanstalt für Angestellte*). In addition, there are special institutions for employees of the national railways, of the coalmining companies (*Bundesknappschaft*) and for seamen (*Seekasse*). What is noteworthy is the persistence of this differentiated structure, because the policy components with regard to these labour-force groups have been harmonised since 1992. In addition, all these institutions rely on self-organisation (*Selbstverwaltungskörperschaften*). The councils made up of representatives and the executive committee consist of 50 per cent employees' representatives (elected by *Sozialwahlen* for 6 years) and of 50 per cent employers' representatives (Standfest, 1978). The performance of these quasi-legislative and quasi-executive structures are under criticism, because there is only limited discretion in terms of payments and services. Too many obligations are legally prescribed, too little spare resources are available. This is also the reason why the federal audit office (*Bundesrechnungshof*) in 1998 proposed changes in the overall architecture of this system, suggesting a reduction in the number of agencies.

Such a reform project might undermine one of the few changes which the architecture of the pension system has undergone during recent decades, namely the decentralisation of counselling and advice units (30 *Auskunfts- und Beratungsstellen*). These were developed in the late seventies during campaigns for a 'responsive administration'. In addition, about 1800 *Versicherungsälteste* (voluntary advisors) provide assistance to members – especially when they are applying for payments under the scheme – or when they are informed (this takes place automatically) about their entitlements. Finally, all public social service institutions are obliged to accept benefit applications from members of these schemes and to forward documents to the relevant institution. This reform strategy towards more citizen orientation was urgently needed, not only because of the location of the *Bundesversicherungsanstalt für Angestellte* in Berlin. It was also necessary because of the increasing complexity of the pension system as a whole, being much more than a 'virtual purse' which reimburses exactly according to the contributions paid earlier. As the working biography of the population becomes more complex and contingent, ever more heterogeneous elements are included in the decisions about contributions and benefits in the form of pension payments. One important element is the definition of periods for which contributions are waived (e.g. parental leave, vocational training, military service, etc.), but which are nevertheless recognised in calculating the final pension award. Finally, the system also consists of additional components (such as health services and rehabilitation measures), which could possibly help to prevent early retirement.[3]

Except for this development towards openness vis-à-vis its clients, which was induced by reform initiatives at the local level, there was almost no substantive reform of the institutional organisation of the retirement pension system. Even the inclusion of the East German states was not used as an opportunity to change the structure. This observation stands in sharp contrast to the numerous marginal changes that have been continuously enacted in recent decades, for example with regard to the criteria of entitlement and enforcement and with regard to the contributions and the amount of benefits.

This is not to say that there was no criticism of this expensive structure. Criticism was targeted at too complicated regulations and centralised and bureaucratised structures and procedures. In the health insurance system the dominance of the producers of services (doctors) and the exaggerated professionalism were attacked. However, these criticisms normally addressed different corporate actors or institutions at different levels with more or less organisational autonomy. These only reacted in part and, sometimes, even quite differently. This observation also leads us to a specific hypothesis: the insurance scheme shows a stable institutional structure over time, because the necessary responsiveness and flexibility is implemented through the locally based welfare scheme. By this, *Sozialhilfe* plays the role of a 'stopgap'.

Sozialhilfe (Social Welfare) and Local Social Administration

The dominant structures of compulsory social insurance, including health, unemployment, retirement, accidents and nursing care, promote the idea of reciprocity and capacity – perhaps even of equivalence – of input into the system (by payment of the necessary contributions) and output (through payments for income maintenance and services). A very large proportion of the output of this social security sector implies transfer payments which leave choices on how and where to spend this.

In the context of this overall system, welfare payments, which, especially in the case of social welfare (*Sozialhilfe*), are financed by tax revenues, traditionally play a minor role. Typically, they are seen as the last resort in the 'social net' or have even been defined as 'minority programmes' which eventually might find little acceptance among the general population (BMJFFG, 1985). It is necessary to mention important additional welfare schemes, which have a separate legal basis and most often also have their specific organisational arrangement at the local level: *Wohngeld* (housing benefits), *Jugendhilfe* (youth welfare), *Bafög* (grants for school and university students).

Qualitative and Quantitative Development of Sozialhilfe

The *Bundessozialhilfegesetz* (federal social welfare law: BSHG) was passed in 1962 and since then has undergone more than 30 revisions (Birk and Brühl, 1991). The law integrated earlier regulations and changed the general terminology from *Fürsorge* (assistance) to *Sozialhilfe* (social welfare), implying a shift in perspective. Taking the place of *Fürsorge* as a benefit defined by the government, *Sozialhilfe* has been declared as the individual right to live under clearly defined humane economic and social conditions (*menschenwürdiges Leben führen*, BSHG, §1). As a result, the individual situation has to be taken into account. Therefore, allowances can be granted because of low income or pension benefits, or they can result from special additional needs (illness, handicaps, old-age deficiencies). In each case, the individual need has to be proved and other sources of help must be exhausted first, be it family support, voluntary help or benefits from the insurance system. The concept implies two additional expectations: *Sozialhilfe* should 'normally' be used only for a short period of time and the transfer payments and services should be designed as a means of help for self-help.

There are basically two forms of Sozialhilfe: a) *Hilfe zum Lebensunterhalt*, a supplement if cash income is inadequate (poorly paid jobs; large family size; low pension); b) *Hilfe in besonderen Lebenslagen* (covering special needs such as sickness, child care, impairment). With the latter, assistance is not just a question of cash payments but also of the provision of adequate services. Therefore, the assistance can be provided as personal service (*persönliche Hilfe*) or material/technical and monetary support (*Geld- und Sachleistungen*). Such a 'compensating' system is a good indicator of deficiencies in the insurance systems that also reflects shifts in social problem developments. In the 1960s and 1970s there were many elderly people without sufficient pension-based income among the recipients of *Sozialhilfe*. Today, the deficiencies of an insurance system which is based on a traditional model of work-biography have become even more evident. Increasing numbers of unemployed persons and single parent families are among *Sozialhilfe* recipients. The most expensive part of social welfare payments, however, is devoted to nursing services (*Krankenpflege*) in an ageing society.

The discussion of *Sozialhilfe* reveals that the function of this part of welfare state provision has changed. More and more people are inadequately covered by their own self-help resources or by the provisions of social insurance systems. The steep increase in social welfare payments by local governments (in 1997: about 45 billion DM for 2.8 million people) is a major cause of the fiscal crisis of local government and administration. It also contributes to severe problems and reform pressures within the whole social sector.

The Institutional Structure of the *Sozialhilfe*

The welfare system differs substantially from the rather centralised – even though deconcentrated – social insurance systems. It is decentralised, heterogeneous in its arrangements and open to the social environment (i.e. the needs and demands of the population). However, it is also seen as a model of closer inspection (and control) over the population groups 'at the edge' of society ('regulating the poor'). The law (BSHG) defines the counties and the communes as the responsible institutional actors. Although the federal states have some options to add to the BSHG-legislation (i.e. by defining operational aspects), the implementation of the law is included in the general principles of the *Selbstverwaltungsgarantie* (guarantee of self–government) for German communes (art. 28 of the Basic Law).[4]

The BSHG does not define what kind of social administration should be set up. However, the establishment of a *Sozialamt* (social welfare office) as the basic institution has been a uniform organisational response (Kühn, 1985, 1994). Beyond this, many local variations have emerged and disappeared over time. Even in cross-sectional reviews, different organisational 'models' are used at the same time; only the core task of providing income substitutes seems to be a generally included element. The variations stem from differences in organisational size, with staff sizes ranging from slightly over ten to several hundreds. Differences also relate to the number of tasks included in the activities of the *Sozialamt*, especially the inclusion of tasks beyond those defined by the BSHG (i.e. from other legislation such as *Wohngeld*, *Jugendhilfe*, and the like). Finally, the division of labour between county and communes may lead to varying solutions. All this is a local affair and not an issue of national policy making.

Even within the tasks defined by the BSHG a profession-related 'dividing line' between the 'cash-payers' (*wirtschaftliche Sozialhilfe*) and the 'personal service providers' (social workers) has always played a major role in the design of social administration. This has developed into a cleavage, because the vocational training for the two staff groups, i.e. the training of public servants (organised for different qualification levels) and the training of social workers (Kulbach and Wohlfahrt, 1994), is different. This cleavage has often increased in practice, because it also implies the division between indoor and outdoor work. Traditionally, the outdoor service was performed by social workers. As this function included 'inspections' of the living conditions of clients, this led to conflicts with the counselling or 'therapeutic' role of the social workers (Flösser, 1994). Nowadays, this difference might also include the establishment of a 'welfare police' with staff from the *Sozialamt* pursue cheating welfare recipients. In such cases, the 'outdoor action' is delegated to members of the administrative staff.

Over time, there have been a large number of organisational models in order to allocate both tasks and personnel. One major effort was devoted to the organisational integration of social work as a separate department (*Amt für soziale Dienste*) as part of one or all public agencies related to social welfare functions. This development has been accompanied by varying service philosophies: specialisation/professionalisation vs. whole person approach; treatment (compensation) vs. help for self-help (emancipation), case-orientation vs. streetwork or community-orientation; and the so-called *Komm- vs. Gehstruktur* (Olk, 1986). Only little of this has been put into practice effectively. No permanent, not to say uniform, solution to the question of differentiation and integration has been found or implemented.[5]

The complexity and variety of the institutional arrangements also stem from a further element in the BSHG: the obligation to guarantee the necessary local service infrastructure and the inclusion of existing welfare associations or self-help initiatives. The first aspect is quite evident, because otherwise a continuous service provision would be impossible. This issue had been formulated most explicitly in the SGB (§17) of 1975: 'The service providers are obliged to assure 1) that every entitled person receives adequate services within an acceptable time, in a complete form and according to recent standards; 2) that the service infrastructure is sufficient and available within an acceptable time; 3) that access is facilitated by the use of intelligible application forms.'

Included in the set of service producers were mainly the traditional welfare associations (i.e. their local sub-structures) and self-help initiatives. This was specified as an aspect of subsidiarity, i.e. the provision by organisations of the third sector should be given priority (§ 93 BSHG). This was a major breakthrough for the traditional legally established role of welfare associations in Germany.

The creation of the required organisational and personal infrastructure installs another set of inter-organisational relationships. Besides the local actors, the regional actors come into play (*überörtlicher Träger*). This can be an institution at the federal state level (*Landessozialamt*) or at an intermediate level (such as the *Landschaftsverband* in North-Rhine Westphalia). They were set up to contribute to investment costs (on the local level) and to organise parts of the infrastructure at the regional level. Although it was the federal parliament that passed the BSHG, the federal states and the communes have to bear most of the costs of the basic infrastructure and of everyday operations. The state and local governments are not reimbursed by earmarked taxes but by general revenues (which are shared between the levels of the politico-administrative system). This situation often leads to intensive distributional conflicts.

The complex infrastructure for ambulatory services and for institutionalised care requires local (social) planning procedures (Stadt Bielefeld, 1994), in which all relevant local and regional actors are included, such as *Altenhilfeplanung* (planning services for the elderly), which began in the mid-1960s. In this context, the division of labour is defined and the types of contracts between different parties are specified. In the early implementation phases of local services, local government either paid all the costs of the institutions and the person-related services (*Kostendeckung*), or it covered the deficits of the units after all other resources had been utilised and calculated (*Defizitausgleich*). Nowadays limited budgets and tight contracts have become more prominent.

Although the necessary co-ordination of this heterogeneous sphere of service producers was already mentioned in the original version of the BSHG, there have always been new attempts to meet this demand. Nowadays, the pressure comes from the scarcity of local resources (Merchel and Schrapper, 1996). This has led, in some cases, to new forms of exchange and agreements, such as *runde Tische* (round-table meetings), *Pflegekonferenzen* (conferences regarding nursing arrangements) or new organisational units in the sense of *Plan- und Leitstellen* (Berlin) or moderators of *ortsnaher Koordinierung sozialer und gesundheitsbezogener*

Dienste (North-Rhine Westfalia). All this adds to the traditional role of local committees, which prepare the decisions of the council.

Summing up, the social sector in Germany can be described as a highly fragmented system, and a complex welfare mix. It includes several principles of the design of social insurance and assistance measures: compulsory social insurance with the idea of reciprocity and equivalence; transfer payments on the basis of tax revenues; social assistance on the basis of a proven problem and need situation; transfer payments, material support and personal services. This also includes a large number of actors at different levels of government and society: national government as well as state and local government; employers' associations and employees' associations (unions); various types of voluntary associations, self-help organisations or groups and private profit-making providers. Also the way of securing the necessary (financial) resources adopts different modes: contributions by employers and employees, by different family members in terms of charges or taxes, collected and redistributed by the federal, the state or the local government. A division of labour between financing, provision and producing of services exists. Whereas the national policy has continuously formulated changes concerning benefits, entitlements and contributions, only few initiatives have been taken to modernise the institutional structure of the system. Looking ahead at the forces and trends of reforming the social sector in Germany, it is quite clear that there is almost no possibility of moving the whole system in a controlled way and into one direction.

Forces and Trends Toward Reforms in the Social Sector

Changes Within the Options of the System Arrangements

This issue can only be dealt with if there is a common understanding of the different terms to be used: change, reform, fundamental system transformation. The social sector in Germany has continuously undergone changes in the application of different insurance and welfare principles: in the scope of transfers and services provided; in the admission of participating and producing actors and the like. There is no doubt that the last 100 years can be described mainly in terms of an expansion of services and transfer-payments: from the *Arbeiterfrage* to the compulsory insurance of the *Arbeitnehmer* and their families; from minimal income to the preservation of living standards; avoiding and/or compensating for inequality. Underlying this path of change is the more or less continuously existing 'grand coalition' of social policy-makers. It is also a consequence of the continuous support for the ideas of the welfare state (expansion) within the population, who at the same time as members of insurance schemes (which collect compulsory contributions), as taxpayers and as consumers pay the largest part of the bill.

The change of policies is tied to the economic development in general and to the employment/unemployment rates in particular. With the deterioration of these context conditions (at least) temporary counter-trends can be observed (mainly in the 1980s and 1990s), namely restrictions in entitlements and the reduction of the amount of transfer payments per client. With regard to *Sozialhilfe* there has been a new basis for calculating the 'objective' demands of the recipients has been established (now based on the development of national income and no longer on a goods basket): exclusion of certain types of service, such as nursing care and types of recipients, such as asylum-seekers (*Asylbewerber-Leistungsgesetz* 1993); in service emphasis (*Arbeit statt Sozialhilfe*) and closer inspections to avoid malpractice.

Reform Initiatives

Looking for reforms of the system means looking for some more general shifts in the guiding principles for the design of the system, the inclusion of completely new types of services of entitlements (Schmid and Niketta, 1998). The shift of responsibilities between ministries has never played an important role in reform initiatives.[6] One of the is related to the complexity of the system itself. If the path of expanding the social sector is followed beyond a certain point of complexity, the effects can be counterproductive. Therefore, one of the first challenges to the path-dependent development of the social sector in Germany was the 'emergence' of so-called secondary problems within the system. Perceived to suffer from over-bureaucratisation, over-regulation and over-economisation, the whole system seemed to have become unmanageable. This led to a strategy of clarification and delineation by compiling a book of social law (*Sozialgesetzbuch*, SGB of 1976), in which a general section was included. This general part of the SGB describes basic features of the insurance and welfare system in Germany and tries to harmonise different subsets of the system.

The SGB also indicates a slight shift from the predominant insurance system to the provision of social infrastructure and personal social services.

The idea of a responsive local social environment emerged (Grunow, 1988), to which the resources of the welfare state were to contribute. This development towards a 'strategy of personal services' as a governmental concern in the social sector was not just a reaction to secondary (system) deficiencies but also related to the experience of diminishing contributions by other sectors of society (especially of the church-related organisations and institutions).

The development of the personal service strategy as an additional systematic part of the German social sector also marked an innovation within the system design, which can be described as a reform process: the increase in bottom-up initiatives. Because social infrastructure and social services were provided mainly at the local level or at least in deconcentrated, often decentralised units of state government as well as by voluntary associations and private initiatives, a stronger impact from below could now be exerted on the development of social policy.

One of the important new features of the bottom-up strategies in the late 1970s was the development of the self-help movement in social and especially in health affairs (Grunow, 1998). It became a relatively important reform issue because it was first of all a criticism against professionalisation within the newly developed services and social infrastructure. As this coincided with the first fiscal crisis (combined with the oil-price shock), it led to a growing emphasis on cut-back strategies in *Sozialhilfe* expenditures. Thus, before it was substantially developed and integrated, the self-help movement was used to relieve costly professional services and infrastructure. This development is still going on. It even includes an attempt to use the self-help activities for an 'attack' on the dominant role of the voluntary associations in the social sector. It is clear that the veto-power of the large, politically institutionalised voluntary associations is much stronger than the veto-power of the rather fragmented self-help movements and organisations. This also means that pressures from public providers of services can be applied much more easily on self-help organisations than on the voluntary associations.

One of the more recent reforms has been the introduction of an insurance system for nursing care (*Pflegeversicherungsgesetz* 1994), which had been in preparation for 20 years. It can be defined as a reform because it tries to solve the enduring problems of the increasing number of persons in need of nursing care and who are without the resources to pay for it, especially if institutionalisation is necessary. Previously this service had to be paid out of the *Sozialhilfe* budget of the communes. It was seen to be necessary to establish a new basis for financing services in the form of an insurance system. The details of financing, however, mark an important change in the system construction. For the first time, employers were exempted from paying their share of the contributions.

Another important change in this new insurance system (SGB, vol. XI) are new guidelines for the provision of services. They abolish the preference which had been defined in favour of the voluntary associations. The reform dimension stems from the decision that the inclusion of private profit-making producers of services should also be applied in the context of other social services and social infrastructure (e.g. applied in the context of health insurance agencies). Consequently, in the future the range of service producers will include a quantitatively more important segment of private profit-making actors.

During recent years the fiscal crisis has dominated the debate about the social sector and its reform. This development has contributed to closer inspections of each service programme and an intensified debate about so-called *versicherungsfremde Leistungen*; meaning the different sections of the social sector pay for services and transfers which are believed to be unrelated to the general concept and design of the particular system programme. Here again, the subsequent changes are more or less an issue within the system and not a general reform of the system.

Effects of Local Modernisation on Social Administration

Policy changes with regard to the insurance systems have increasingly shifted financial burdens towards the local level. This has contributed to the fiscal crisis of the communes. As they have only limited influence on law-making procedures concerning the 'grand coalition' of social policy makers, the local actors have had to react to the situation by setting up a 'modernisation project', namely the reform of local government in general. In other words, the *Sozialamt*, together with other local welfare institutions, is taken into the 'draught' of local reform projects, whether these are relevant to this specific policy or not. This situation is not at all new, but perhaps more severe and more enduring than during other phases of social welfare development. Again, these changes do not take place 'nationwide' and are not a national policy issue (as they are in the UK). Some of the important changes have been:

- the territorial reform in the late 1960s (in east Germany in the mid 1990s), which led to an increase in the size of cities and counties in order to enlarge administrative capacities;
- the movement towards a responsive administration (which mainly affected social service production) in the 1970s;
- the introduction of computers into local offices (e.g. ProSoz software programmes in the social welfare offices) in the mid 1980s;
- the repeated enforcement of cutback measures to cope with fiscal problems, especially in the early 1980s and the mid 1990s.

The latest developments (since 1994) include three directions of change:

- the renewal of local constitutions, which have basically enlarged the forms of direct democracy;
- modernisation measures, which have largely followed concepts of 'new public management';
- sometimes severe cutback measures.

It is difficult to say where these three simultaneous reform trends support or block each other. A relatively new feature following this 'triple trend' might be seen in the widespread application of multiple modernisation strategies in the communes, which is supported by (nationwide) best practice competitions and benchmarking. Paradoxically, especially the costs of social welfare payments can be reduced only to a minor extent, although they are a major cause of the fiscal crisis. The regulations and provisions are not at the disposal of communal administrations. In addition, many of the proposed reform elements (the so-called *neues Steuerungsmodell*: KGSt, 1993) are not 'new' but have a long tradition in the *Sozialhilfe* sector. Especially the idea of 'contracting out' or decentralisation of service production and the responsiveness towards clients demands (now being discussed under the heading of customer orientation) is a traditional aspect of welfare service implementation at the local level.

In the process of local modernisation, other services were put much more under pressure than the problematic *Sozialhilfe*. Especially the voluntarily established social infrastructure and personal services (*freiwillige Aufgaben*) were reduced or abolished. Consequent effects have been witnessed by the local service producers 'under contract'. As the modes of the contracts have changed towards more detailed prescription and strict cost control, the effects of local administrative changes have been more or less transferred to the contract partners (i.e. service producers). Here, in addition to the traditionally active voluntary associations the private profit-making alternatives, have been increased – eventually producing something like a competitive situation (Öhlschläger and Brüll, 1996).

As complexity and heterogeneity are important features of the decentralised structure of social welfare, it is quite unlikely that the modernisation strategies will lead to common change. The starting point for each local social administration is different in almost every organisational or inter-organisational aspects. The goals of reform are also much more defined in general crosscutting lines than in social policy related terms. Therefore, one can observe different adaptations to external demands (Bassarak, 1997): to be more cost-oriented and economical, to administer more cases per staff member, to define 'products' instead of tasks, to define recipients of *Sozialhilfe* as 'customers' and to abolish positions at the middle management level (*Amtsleiter*). At present, there is no clear policy-related trend except for budget and staff reductions. The pressures demand action and perhaps reflection about the structure and process of the delivery and service organisation of *Sozialhilfe*. Most probably the changes will not fix the boundaries of the options that have been discussed, realised, evaluated, criticised and reorganised again and again since the very beginning (Wohlfahrt, 1998) and involves debates concerning: integration vs. specialisation; professionalisation vs. lay competence; concentration of organisational units vs. deconcentration; centralisation vs. decentralisation of decision making and budgetary competences; whole person vs. segmented person as client model; contracting out or privatisation and the like.

Some recent (general) reform debates, which, if realised, could be described as a truly fundamental transformation of the system, centre around the model of a 'basic income' for all citizens (*Bürgergeld*; *soziale Grundsicherung*), whereby the transfer payments would be counted against income-tax (so-called negative income tax). *Sozialhilfe* and other transfer payments on a tax basis would be integrated into such a scheme. Recently, this model was rejected by an expert commission of the Ministry of Finance (in Bonn), because it was not expected to achieve the main aim, namely the reduction of the transfer costs. This goal still dominates the debate and will also motivate major policy changes in the foreseeable future. So far, however, every attempt at a fundamental system transformation has been blurred by the complexity of the institutional setting, in which the recipients as well as many producers of services and the deliverers of transfer payments exert strong veto powers.

Conclusion

If the modernisation theme is seen in the context of a relevant policy field as complex as the social sector in Germany, it is predicable and understandable that a reform concept of a rather diffuse origin (such as NPM as well as its German variations) has only limited relevance and impact on the changes and reform issues that this (path-driven) sector has to address or is concerned with.

Structural arrangements (polity; constitution) and policy-related path-dependence explain most of the differences found between Germany and the UK. Consequently, the principle of self-organisation in the compulsory insurance systems, the Bismarck model, was used for the newly established provisions of nursing care. The division of labour between national policy making and local implementation accounts for the continuity within the principles of *Sozialhilfe* and also for the dynamics of professional and organisational changes in the local social administration.

Another issue of path-dependency concerns the question of linear or circular development. Looking at the changes in the German social sector there seems to be a combination of both processes. Whereas in the development of the basic principles of design we can observe a rather linear development of a broadening, continuous application of principles, with regard to the implementation structures in detail (organisation, procedure, staff arrangements) it is much more a cyclic phenomenon. This is the consequence of the inherent ambivalence of all decentralised design components. In search of an optimum the direction of change is frequently shifting. Thus, as has been shown above, the direction chosen in one municipality might just have been established/rejected by another. It is questionable whether borrowing or imitating successful models can be (generally speaking) 'helpful' in another context, i.e. within another long-term path and another change cycle. However, it can be suspected that a number of issues are to be seen as meso- or micro-elements of the overall system which might function somewhat independently of the general system context. This 'micro-convergence' can be best shown with regard to technical tools such as photo-copiers, which might become a 'small island of increased efficiency' in many sections of the social sector, whereas other 'micro-tools' such as complaint management might become a 'small island of increased responsiveness'. This is also often a functioning basis for the transfer of instruments between different sectors of society and between different countries.

Notes

1. The following analysis covers an extensive field of norms and research. References will be kept at a minimum to save room for argumentation. For a major source for the description of the respective norms see BMA (1998); for a review of the history of the social sector see Blüm and Zacher (1989); a well-known textbook is Lampert (1991).
2. However, this arrangement pays only for about 80 per cent of the costs of the pension system. The rest of the resources needed are paid out of the tax revenues of the state (national level).
3. Typically the overall system includes numerous 'cutting lines' which either have led to a harmonisation of similar components (such as in the case of rehabilitation), or they have led to a debate about priority setting rules along the themes of: *Reha vor Rente* or *Ambulant vor Stationär*.
4. This means that communes have autonomy in staff, organisational and budget-related affairs (naturally within the limits of existing laws).
5. In contrast to centralised arrangements (as in the UK), in which any 'new' solution must be 'sold' as *the* solution, there have always been quite opposite arrangements in the communes at the same time. Even today models are 'created', e.g. in the sense of decentralised, integrated, client group-related services, which had already been established elsewhere (e.g. in Bremen and Berlin) in the 1970s (Kühn, 1994).
6. Welfare policy was prepared by the Ministry of the Interior from 1949-1969, by the Ministry of Youth, Family and Health until 1982, by the Ministry of Labour and Social Affairs until 1989 and by the Ministry of Health up to the present.

References

Bassarak, H. (ed) (1997), *Modernisierung kommunaler Sozialverwaltungen und der sozialen Dienste*, Hans-Böckler-Stiftung, Düsseldorf.

Birk, P. and Brühl, A. (1991), *BSHG. Lehr- und Praxiskommentar*, Nomos Verlag, Baden-Baden.

Blüm, N. and Zacher, H.F. (eds) (1989), *40 Jahre Sozialstaat Bundesrepublik Deutschland*, Nomos Verlag, Baden-Baden.

BMA (ed.) (1998), *Überblick über das Sozialrecht*, Bonn.

BMJFFG (ed.) (1985), *Bürgernähe der Sozialhilfeverwaltung*, Kohlhammer Verlag, Stuttgart.

Brück, G.W. (1981), *Allgemeine Sozialpolitik*, Bund Verlag, Köln.

Eichener, V., et al. (eds) (1992), *Organisierte Interessen in Ostdeutschland*, Metropolis Verlag, Marburg.

Flösser, G. (1994), *Soziale Arbeit jenseits der Bürokratie*, Luchterhand Verlag, Neuwied.
Grunow, D. (1988), *Bürgernahe Verwaltung*, Campus Verlag, Frankfurt a.M.
Grunow, D. (1998), 'Selbsthilfe', in K. Hurrelmann, U. Laaser (eds), *Handbuch Gesundheitswissenschaften*, Juventa Verlag, Weinheim, pp.683-706.
KGSt (1993), *Das neue Steuerungsmodell*, Köln.
Kolb, R. (1983), 'GRV', in *Sachverständigenkommission Alterssicherungssysteme*, Berichtsband 2, Bonn.
Kühn, D. (1985), *Kommunale Sozialverwaltung*, Kleine Verlag, Bielefeld.
Kühn, D. (1994), *Jugendamt - Sozialamt - Gesundheitsamt*, Luchterhand Verlag, Neuwied.
Kulbach, R. and Wohlfahrt, N. (1994), *Öffentliche Verwaltung und soziale Arbeit*, Lambertus Verlag, Freiburg i.B.
Lampert, H. (1991), *Lehrbuch der Sozialpolitik*, de Gruyter, Berlin.
Merchel, J. and Schrapper, C. (eds) (1996), *Neue Steuerung. Tendenzen der Organisationsentwicklung in der Sozialverwaltung*, Votum Verlag, Münster.
Nullmeier, F., Rüb and F.W. (1993), *Die Transformation der Sozialpolitik*, Campus Verlag, Frankfurt a.M.
Öhlschläger, R. and Brüll, H.M. (eds) (1996), *Unternehmen Barmherzigkeit*, Nomos Verlag, Baden-Baden.
Olk, T. (1986), *Abschied vom Experten. Sozialarbeit auf dem Weg zu einer alternativen Professionalität*, Juventa Verlag, Weinheim.
Schmid, J. and Niketta, R. (eds) (1998), *Wohlfahrtsstaat: Krise und Reform im Vergleich*, Metropolis Verlag, Marburg.
Stadt Bielefeld (ed.) (1994), *Organisation der kommunalen Sozialplanung*, Böllert Verlag, Bielefeld.
Standfest, E. (1978), *Sozialpolitik und Selbstverwaltung*, Bund Verlag, Köln.
Statistisches Bundesamt (ed.) (1997), *Datenreport 7*, Bonn.
Wohlfahrt, N. (1998), 'Sozialverwaltungsreform in der BRD: eine Zwischenbilanz', *Theorie und Praxis der sozialen Arbeit*, vol. 49, pp. 363-68.

13 Privatisation of Social Services in the United Kingdom

BRIAN MUNDAY

Introduction

This chapter discusses the introduction of new public management (NPM) principles and methods into social services in the UK, within the broader context of a policy of privatisation of public services. Privatisation in social services is considerably more advanced in the UK than elsewhere in Europe, with NPM principles and methods highly prominent in this development. However, the appropriateness of privatisation with the associated NPM implementation methods remains a matter of considerable debate and controversy in the UK.

'Social services' are difficult to define precisely, with alternative meanings and manifestations in different countries. In one country a particular service may be part of social services, while in another it may be within the health services. For example, in Germany youth services are integral to social services but not so in the UK. For the purposes of the discussion in this chapter the following meaning of social services in the UK will suffice:

> These services are mainly for specified user groups such as elderly people, children and families, and are provided in different locations such as the home, day centres and residential establishments. The services are staffed by personnel such as social workers, home helps and occupational therapists. (Munday and Ely, 1996, p.6)

It should be added that these services may be provided by state agencies, mainly local government social services departments; not-for-profit/ voluntary agencies; and commercial, for-profit organisations. It is important to emphasise that, unlike the situation in many other countries, in the UK social services do not include cash benefit payments, the latter being a responsibility of a different national service known as the Benefits Agency.

The term 'social care' is increasingly preferred in the international literature because of the inclusion of informal sources of care provided by family, friends etc. in substantial addition to formal services provided by state and non-state agencies. The two terms will be employed in this chapter.

Social services are a particularly interesting subject of study in relation to the theme of this book because of the controversy surrounding the introduction of privatisation and NPM methods in social services. A landmark in the privatisation of social services in the UK was the publication in 1989 of the government's White Paper 'Caring for People'. This proposed a change in role for local authorities from that of service providers to enablers, alongside the introduction of markets or quasi-markets into social services. Subsequent legislation has brought about nothing less than a cultural change in the world of UK social services, as will be discussed in this chapter.

New public management methods are now very evident in the daily operation of these services. In an oft-quoted article Hood (1991) constructs a table (pp.4-5) containing the seven most referred to aspects of the NPM doctrine, together with their meaning and rationale. Most of these aspects are prominent in government policy initiatives and requirements for UK social services, and increasingly visible in the operation of local authority social services departments. These include

- Explicit standards and measures of performance: with definition of goals, targets, performance indicators;
- Greater emphasis on output controls: stressing results rather than procedures, allocating resources according to measured performance rather than bureaucratic traditions;
- Shift to greater competition in the public sector: use of tendering and contracts, with rivalry seen as the key to lower costs and better standards;
- Stress on private-sector styles of management practice: greater flexibility in hiring and rewards, use of PR and marketing in management and promotion of public services.

In their discussion of the new (NPM) forms of local government in the UK, Keen and Scase (1998) refer (p.7) to the new public sector model as comprising, amongst other aspects, the enabling authority, the competitive council, management by contract and influence, and customer orientation, quality and choice. All these aspects of NPM are visible in the new culture of UK social services.

An updated lexicon of regularly used terms in UK social services would now include previously unheard of terms such as benchmarking, cost-effectiveness, contracting, value-for-money and best value, budget centres, performance indicators, cost centres, and evidence based practice. Sometimes the verbalising of such terms suggests a somewhat superficial 'political correctness', along with the outward trappings of the dark suits, leather brief cases and expensive cars associated with management in the private sector. Nevertheless, to varying degrees change towards private sector style and methods of management has become increasingly imbedded in UK social services since 1990, and will continue.

Privatisation

Privatisation may be an unwise term to use in relation to the field of social services, given – in the UK – its association with the right-wing Thatcher governments' selling of public utilities such as the water, gas and electricity companies to the private sector, sometimes at artificially low prices. Privatisation takes many different forms and is a portmanteau term that needs to be carefully unpacked to understand which parts of the luggage apply to a particular activity. Opponents of privatisation of social services argue that its main aim is to reduce expenditure and services; that it encourages the growth of profit-making commercial organisations that have no valid place in social services; and that it undermines collectivist-based welfare systems.

Warning that discussions of privatisation too easily lose their way from the outset because of too narrow an approach or lack of clarity, Munday S. (1996) refers (p.60) to privatisation as 'an attempt to increase the role of market forces', with three distinct aspects to privatisation policy:

1. A transfer of ownership from the public to the private sector;
2. Liberalisation: an attempt to permit and to promote competition in areas where previously there was no competition;
3. Franchising or contracting out: allowing and encouraging private firms to make bids to run services that were exclusively run by the public sector.

As this chapter shows, since 1990 privatisation in UK social services has involved partially all three aspects. O'Higgins (1989) similarly refers (p.157) to privatisation in the British context as 'a mechanical process that can be clearly defined as a decrease in the proportionate or relative role of one or more of state production, finance, or regulation in the supply of a good or service'.

O'Higgins makes a crucial distinction between privatisation as *instruments* and privatisation as *ideology*. The former meaning focuses on changes in methods and procedures which should be judged essentially on outcomes, the extent to which the privatisation methods achieved policy goals. This is important to bear in mind with privatisation as instruments in social services. The alternative view does not accept the validity of this narrower interpretation of privatisation. O'Higgins cites commentators from the political Left and Right who argue that different methods in social policy are based on conflicting values and can have profound impacts on societal values at large.

Walker (1984, p.41) is quoted by O'Higgins (p.158) as representing a traditional socialist welfare perspective:

> Once one set of values based on values such as social integration and community is replaced by another reflecting different values, such as self-interest, the nature of the service and its social consequences will have been transformed.

Walker (1984, p.27) condemns privatisation 'as one manifestation...of the increased importance given to individualistic values'. Right wing views of welfare (e.g. Murray, 1984) criticise 'the welfare state' for undermining people's willingness and ability to help themselves and one another, whereas privatisation 'promotes values of self-reliance and of individual and family responsibility', which are seen to be the only foundation for lasting prosperity and social well-being (O'Higgins, 1989, p.159). O'Higgins argues that there is an important aspect of privatisation that is not covered in either the instruments or ideology approaches to privatisation. His 'third way' will be discussed in the conclusion of this chapter.

Mixed Economies Of Social Services

As Higgins observes, the reality is that in the UK there has always been a 'mixed economy of welfare' of state and private provision in social services, but until the late 1970s there was a widespread and incorrect view that social services equalled public services. Following Higgins, the shift towards forms of privatisation in social services can be better understood using a simple framework that is very useful in comparative studies of social welfare and social services.

In any country the total social services or social care system comprises four sectors:

1. *Informal*: Family, friends, colleagues, neighbours. Care and support is normally unpaid and to varying degrees is still the main source of help for individuals in need. Widespread social and demographic changes (eg. ageing populations, smaller families) are having a major impact on families' ability to provide care.
2. *State agencies*: Publicly owned and financed social services agencies, usually at local or regional government levels. In the UK local government has substantial legal responsibilities to provide social services for elderly people, children and families and people with disabilities.
3. *Not-for-profit*: This sector ranges from small self-help groups without paid staff, to agencies with substantial budgets employing many professional staff. Although 'non-governmental' in status, many NFP agencies receive large payments from state social services agencies, increasingly through purchase-of-service-contracts.
4. *For-profit*: This includes companies paying dividends to share holders and smaller enterprises operated as profit-making businesses e.g. many privately owned residential homes for elderly people of which there are many in the UK.

Each country will have its own particular mix of social care from the four sectors above. For example, former-communist countries of Central and Eastern Europe relied almost entirely on sectors one and two for social care provision. The German tradition has been to rely heavily on large welfare organisations in sector three to provide services, but with substantial public funding. This has also been the case in the Netherlands.

A policy of privatisation in social services, as in the UK since 1990, attempts to reduce the role of the state sector in direct provision of services, along with reducing public expenditure. Through legislation (see below), policy initiatives and other devices, government attempts to place maximum responsibility for social care with the three non-governmental sectors. The motivation for this has been both ideological and economic, the latter because of cost increases associated with demographic factors such as ageing populations and increased longevity.

We now move on to examine in some detail the privatisation of social services in the UK since 1990, and how this links with the diffusion of NPM in British public services.

The 1989 Government White Paper 'Caring for People'

The White Paper and legislation a year later marked a watershed in the history of social services in the UK. As already indicated, Britain always had a mixed system rather than a state monopoly but since the implementation of the Beveridge Report social services have been loosely equated with public services. The White Paper has changed both the perception and the reality of UK social services, with post-1990 implementation of a privatisation policy relying heavily on doctrines and methods from NPM.

The context for 'Caring for People' included mounting concern over escalating costs and over use of residential care for elderly people, a system that produced 'perverse incentives' to use residential care when home based care could often be a preferred and cheaper option. So, key objectives of government's proposals for change included 'the development of domiciliary, day and respite services to enable people to live in their own homes wherever feasible and sensible' (p.5). The influence of NPM was evident in three other objectives (p.5) 'to promote the development of a flourishing independent sector alongside good quality public services; to clarify the responsibilities of agencies and so make it easier to hold them to account for their performance; and to secure better value for taxpayers' money...'.

A clear responsibility was placed upon local authorities to develop a social services market by using services of not-for-profit (NFP) and for-profit (FP) agencies where this represented a cost-effective service choice. In line with privatisation and NPM orthodoxy the role of the local authority in social services was to shift progressively from that of provider to one of acting as an *enabling authority*. This change in role is fundamental to the subsequent privatisation process.

Certain specific benefits for service users (and providers) should result from these changes: greater choice of services for users; innovation and greater flexibility in services; better value for money and improved cost-effectiveness in services resulting from the introduction of markets and competition. Later in this chapter we examine to what extent these benefits are being achieved in the new systems.

The White Paper specified ways for local authorities to establish a full mixed economy of care: clear service specifications and arrangements for tenders and contracts; developing the external provider market; identifying local authority in-house services to suitable to 'float-off' as self-managing units. The Government decided against extending compulsory competitive tendering – as required with some services in health and education – to social services and has not done so since. It considered that the greater use of service specifications, agency agreements and contracts would '...have the beneficial effect of requiring authorities to define desired outcomes; to be more specific about the nature of the service they are seeking to provide to achieve those outcomes; and to define the necessary inputs' (p.23).

The local authorities were expected to continue with some but significantly reduced direct service provision. As is illustrated later, a critical question in the new era of quasi-markets has been how a local authority decides just what services to continue to provide itself. 'Caring for People' expected local authorities to retain the capacity to act as providers in services for people with high dependency levels, or particularly challenging forms of behaviour. Local authorities were concerned that they would become a pre-welfare state agency of last resort, providing minimal services for groups of users seen as too problematic or financially unattractive for non-state agencies. That concern remains but may have lessened since the election of a government more sympathetic towards social services.

Early reactions to the White Paper and the 1990 legislation were predictably mixed. Opponents dismissed it as the latest and perhaps most ominous development in a Right-Wing government's ideologically driven programme of wholesale privatisation, regardless of how appropriate privatisation was to the field of social services. The fear was that there would be a rapid and unplanned growth of the private-for-profit sector, concerned only with profits, reducing costs and quality at the expense of the vulnerable service user. Any 'marketisation' of social services was seen as wholly inappropriate given the nature of the producer-consumer relationship, the lack of purchasing power of the consumer and severe limitations on real choice.

More sanguine commentators accepted the need for a controlled development of the existing mixed economy of social care, emphasising the potential for benefits from regulated markets, greater budgetary control and the need for systems to target scarce resources on citizens most in need. In other words, NPM was seen to have much to offer to this new world of UK social services where only a partial form of privatisation i.e. 'quasi-privatisation' was to be introduced. The research based account of developments in the post-1990 semi-privatised UK social services now follows.

Developing Quasi-Markets in Social Services

In reviewing the research on post-1990 privatisation developments in the UK, three basic questions have to be addressed:

1. What principal methods and procedures have been used in this process and how far have they been developed?
2. What issues have arisen with implications for the form and scale of privatisation that is appropriate to social services in the UK?
3. What evidence is there concerning the effects of the privatisation programme e.g. in implementing the goals of policy and legislation?

The following discussion draws heavily on published research (Wistow et al., 1994 and 1996) commissioned by central government. The research was conducted mainly by staff from the Personal Social Services Research Unit and the Nuffield Institute for Health. It must be emphasised that this research tells only part of the story of privatisation in that it was concerned primarily with developments and experiences of local authority social services departments – increasingly the 'purchasers' rather than 'providers' of social care. The experience and evaluation of the non-state service providers and – crucially – the question of outcomes for service users were not a significant part of the brief for this research.

The Early Stages of post-1990 Social Services Privatisations

The first published research (Wistow et al., 1994) examines the early stages of local authorities' promotion and development of mixed economies of social care, specifically in community care of adults. Early on in their account of post-1990 developments Wistow et al. define privatisation as a move away in funding from direct public expenditure based on taxation; and in service provision to 'delegation of service provision to non-public agencies via contracting-out or other means, or to individuals by passive neglect or active support of family and other carers' (p.36).

Local authorities were strongly encouraged by Government to take steps to separate the functions of *purchasing* and *providing*, a distinction seen as essential to the creation and working of an effective mixed economy of social services. The pre-1990 tradition had been for local authorities to both fund and provide most services, but within a mixed economy of social services. In future they should only provide services themselves when there were compelling reasons (e.g. cost-effectiveness) to do so. The perceived advantages of purchaser-provider separation included clarification of objectives, reduction of provider vested interests and benefits for supply-side competition.

A Mixed Economy of Supply

A major task for local authorities in facilitating forms of privatisation with quasi-markets has been to ensure there would be a sufficient number of acceptable independent suppliers. In the immediate post-1990 period there were financial incentives to set up fully or partially independent Trusts to take over responsibility for residential care homes. Trusts were often based in Housing Associations. Many local authorities saw this as preferable to selling elderly persons Homes to the private sector because they retained some influence in the work of Trusts. Trusts had the advantage of protecting residents' security of tenure, avoided staff redundancies, and local authorities were less exposed if Trusts ceased to operate.

In the early stages there was little evidence of enthusiasm for privatisation devises such as management or staff buy-outs, workers' cooperatives, or employee share ownership schemes. Local politicians – depending to some extent on their political persuasion – were opposed to schemes which they considered unethical, open to fraud or at the very least were financially risky. It was safer to keep to quasi-privatisation devices that enabled local authorities to retain sufficient control in a service so that it could be brought back under their control; to keep a proportion of the service within the authority; and to externalise only services for the less dependent users.

Research showed that in the early stages there was very little active encouragement for commercial for-profit suppliers of social services. A not-for-profit agency tended to be more acceptable because, unlike commercial agencies, it could not distribute profits to owners and share holders, as with private companies. There was, and remains, a fear that commercial operators will 'cut corners' on quality and use other unacceptable means to drive down costs e.g. exploit care staff through low wages and poor conditions of service.

There is a widespread view that in a very competitive social services market the only way open for private suppliers to make an acceptable profit is to reduce costs. Nevertheless, the better private suppliers could have an advantage because of price efficiency, or greater willingness to respond to public sector requirements. Wistow *et al.* conclude that 'other things being equal, local authorities might prefer the supplier who comes closest to meeting their quantity and quality requirements at an affordable price' (p.89).

Service Specifications and Contracts

Contracting of often a loose form was evident in English social services well before 1990. Local authorities traditionally made grants to voluntary organisations with only a general agreement of what the voluntary organisation would provide. Local authority control might amount to no more than representation on agencies' committees and a perusal of the annual report and accounts. Changes since 1990 have been designed to tighten and strengthen the relationship between the sectors and ensure that the local authority receives 'value for money'. The 'contract culture' is now well established in social services, not altogether to the liking of the voluntary sector. Smaller, more radical agencies engaging in advocacy for marginalised groups have either lost completely or had their local authority funding seriously reduced.

Arguments for the move to formal contracting include: reductions in costs; increased efficiency; reduction in bureaucratic procedures; by-passing trade union restrictions and political patronage; increased user choice; increased specialisation in services; and greater likelihood of innovative service arrangements. Arguments against contracting include: high administrative costs for both purchasers and provider agencies; loss of traditional independence and autonomy of many independent agencies, lower wages, employment insecurity in provider agencies; reduced accountability and lower quality of services; less risk taking and innovation by external providers.

It is too early to come to a clear conclusion on these classic arguments concerning contracting. Early on local authorities were warned that, based on American experience, they should retain a significant degree of direct service provision to avoid the danger of large, powerful independent organisations moving into a near monopoly position in a social services market. The consequence for competition and prices would be obvious. Some local authorities have heeded that warning more than others.

Local authority social services staff have progressively used NPM methods to become more skilled and sophisticated in developing and managing quasi-markets in social services. Service specifications in contracts are more tightly drawn than previously, specifying in some detail the quantity and quality of service inputs and outcomes. These include improvements in users' situations, the precise amount of service to be delivered and the standards to be achieved. There may also be requirements concerning suppliers' equal opportunities policies, complaints procedures, staff salary scales and conditions of service. At times service specifications are so detailed that suppliers complain of excessive bureaucracy.

Compulsory competitive tendering has not been introduced as part of the privatisation programme, nor is it ever likely to be. Instead, local authorities use more collaborative rather than competitive approaches such as 'select list tendering' which allows approved agencies to tender. This helps to guard against both low cost-low quality suppliers gaining contracts, and the danger of poorly resourced suppliers collapsing after gaining contracts. Local authorities also use single supplier and extant supplier negotiation as a means of working with reliable agencies – at an affordable price. Purchasers have found that the administrative and staff time costs of contracting are high, so that alternative ways of securing affordable quality services are very attractive in times of increasing budgetary pressure on local authorities.

When social services contracts are negotiated they are normally of three kinds. *Block contracts* are similar to the former grants to voluntary organisations in that they enable a local authority to buy access to facilities without necessarily specifying the number of users to be served. '*Cost and volume contracts* specify the total cost or budget and the volume of service to be provided (the clients to be served) but not the welfare outcomes or quality of care' (Wistow *et al.*, 1994, p.90). A disadvantage of these contracts is that fewer services may prove to be needed than have been purchased, so money has been wasted. '*Cost per case contracts* pay an agreed amount per client or unit of output on delivery (retrospectively). Spot

Privatisation of Social Services in the United Kingdom 275

purchasing by care managers is an example of this kind of contract, with purchases tailored to the needs of individual clients. Administratively they are the most costly for both purchasers and providers' (Wistow *et al.*, 1994, p.90).

Wistow *et al.* draw some general conclusions from their first period of research into the UK's experience of quasi-privatisation in social services. This includes a discussion of the question of to what extent social services are different from other privatised services. There was little enthusiasm and support for competition and markets in social services, the post-1990 changes being interpreted more in terms of managing a mixed economy of care i.e. evolution rather than revolution in UK social services.

The White Paper's notion of the local authority's 'enabling role' is central to the question of to what extent social services may be different. Enabling was seen as 'a role for social services authorities based less on the direct provision of their own services and more on shaping and influencing the wider range of resources available within the communities they serve' (Wistow *et al.*, 1994, p.135). This enabling role could be interpreted as community development and/or market development. The former, with its emphasis on working with local groups and organisations to help them to develop their caring capacities, was seen as more in line with established social services values.

The emphasis in the White Paper on enabling as market rather than community development was seen by the great majority of local authorities as in line with the values underpinning the NPM but quite contrary to traditional social work and social services values.

> That so many respondents, of all political persuasions, emphasised that social care is different in kind from other public services can be seen to raise questions about the limits of markets and/or the discrepancies between the traditional values and assumptions of social work and the personal social services, and those underpinning the 'new public management' (Wistow *et al.*, 1994, p.137).

There were also technical or feasibility questions concerning the introduction of markets into social services. It was acknowledged that in certain conditions markets may produce a socially efficient allocation of resources, but there were structural imperfections to overcome. A major problem was, in many areas, an insufficient number and range of alternative suppliers of services, particularly in domiciliary care. For market conditions to exist there has to be an adequate number and range of non-statutory service providers. A related issue was the under-development of suppliers, with too many too small not-for-profit agencies.

Nevertheless, the research suggested that NPM was gaining a firm foothold in post-1990 social services, despite the uncertainty and problems in establishing markets in this sector.

> The investment in management development and information systems will enable the new public management to establish a stronger foothold in the personal social services and lead to a shift from administration to management and from direct provision to internal cost centring and external contracting (Wistow *et al.*, 1994, p.145).

The important question to be addressed in the follow up research was whether the developing quasi-markets, with their NPM principles and methods, were proving effective in producing outcomes for service users as set out in the White Paper, namely independence, choice, cost-effectiveness and innovation. This will be considered in the next section of the chapter.

The Effectiveness of Quasi-Markets in Social Services

As Balloch (1997) states (p.23), privatisation in UK social services has developed most in residential care.

> In the residential sector, since the Registered Homes Act 1984, private (i.e. for-profit) homes have more than doubled in number and voluntary homes have increased by a quarter, while local authority homes have decreased by one third.

Privatisation is much less developed in domiciliary care, although there been significant changes since 1990. In 1992 only 2 per cent of home help and home care contact hours were provided by private organisations, increasing to 29 per cent by 1995. It is very tempting for local authorities under budgetary pressure to externalise their home care services, with expectations of reducing the cost of the service by at least 30 per cent. Most have opted for only partial privatisation of the service because of concerns that there is no regulatory body to check standards in this service; the supply side of the market is characteristically under-provided compared with residential care; and a general political sensitivity towards radical change in how the service is provided.

Balloch is only one of many critics of what is seen as the cost-cutting motivation behind privatisation in social services. This may be less marked under a new Labour government but the drive to keep public funding of social services under firm control remains as part of an election commitment not to raise personal taxation. Consequently, local authorities have introduced and/or increased charges for some social services and restricted eligibility for community care services to reduce demand. In these fiscal circumstances the cost-effective imperative rates highly in local authorities' decisions about which services to provide themselves and which ones should be privatised.

Is the Market Working?

The second phase of the Government commissioned research (Wistow *et al.*, 1996) into the working of the post-1990 changes in social services for adults addresses this question. Unlike the earlier research, this work does take into account the perspectives of independent suppliers as well as those of the local authorities surveyed in the first stage.

Wistow *et al.* identify several levels at which the success or otherwise of market outcomes may be assessed i.e. political, economic and social goals of the new reforms. It must also be emphasised that there are various groups of stakeholders in this social services system, with perhaps very different criteria for assessing success or failure in social services markets.

Principal goals of the White Paper were to promote and extend *choice, innovation, and cost-effectiveness* in community care.

> The creation of social care markets was primarily advocated on the grounds that it would promote gains in choice, cost-effectiveness and innovation. These criteria of success are essentially features of service systems believed to improve outcomes for users. As such they are best regarded as intermediate rather than final outcomes and, thus, as proxy rather than real indicators of the successful operation of social care markets in terms of their social goals (Wistow *et al.*, 1996, p.124).

The evidence on *choice* – a much vaunted goal – has been mixed, with choice being reduced rather than extended in some respects. User choice has a price attached to it in that a user's preference for one service rather than another is often restricted by a local authority's willingness/ability to pay the cost of a higher price service. A particularly controversial example concerns local authorities increasingly only being willing to provide domiciliary services to a very dependent user up to the point where the cost is no more than that of residential care for that person. The concern is that some users may be forced into residential care for cost saving reasons when they would much prefer to stay at home.

Nevertheless, Wistow *et al.* quote the Audit Commission (1993) for evidence of attitudinal change in respect of choice. In their survey the Commission found that the great majority of local authorities provided potential residents of homes with a list of options, with the opportunity to visit homes before a final decision. Staff in a high proportion (84 per cent) of authorities provided staff with guidelines on how to offer choice. These are important developments but far short of the experience of choice available to the consumer in the High Street when equipped with purchasing power to chose between goods offered by rival supermarkets.

With the *cost-effectiveness* goal of privatisation, the chief concern has been over the dangers of sacrificing quality for cost savings, particularly in a context of constant budgetary cuts and restraint. Some local authorities referred to 'quality thresholds' and seeking the best price above that required to secure a quality threshold. Select list tendering is also used to attempt to secure acceptable quality levels at the lowest price.

Local authorities have been most successful at keeping costs down in residential care where over supply in the market has benefited the local authority purchaser. One private care home owner complained that the problem now is that local authorities demand the quality of a Rolls Royce while only being prepared to pay for a Ford Escort! Recent media attention was given to the closure of private homes in one large local authority because the authority paid a quite uneconomic price for residents it was responsible for. This is now a common complaint. The situation is rather different with domiciliary care where there are less suppliers and less competition.

Finally on the question of cost-effectiveness, Wistow *et al.* question the longterm value of targeting resources on the most dependent users. This may be cost-effective in the short to medium term but if preventative work is largely abandoned there may well be serious longer term cost consequences.

The research evidence on the *innovation* criterion is modest and mostly impressionistic. The researchers reported that several authorities acknowledged the value of the market in stimulating innovation e.g. placing direct services into an external trust; the sometimes imaginative packages of services in care management; and the introduction of internal trading accounts. Where the post-1990 reforms have been more demonstrably effective is in diverting people from entry into residential care. Wistow *et al.* refer to a minimum diversion rate of 20 per cent reported by the Association of Directors of Social Services, despite the limited contribution made to this change by the independent service sector.

Conclusion

Wistow *et al.* underline some important conclusions from their research into the introduction of privatisation and quasi-markets in British social services:

1. Local authorities became less anti-market and more 'market pragmatists' (p.162)

    A crude anti-commercialism was being replaced by a more cautious recognition that social care markets could offer potential benefits and opportunities for users and carers, as well as problems which would still have to be overcome. Thus sixteen of our twenty-five authorities saw overall advantages in developing markets.

    Contrary to many expectations, profit-maximisation was not the overwhelming motive of the private sector. This was most evident with large suppliers, often multi-home owners.
2. The celebrated purchaser-provider separation was arguably the lynch-pin in the development of social care markets, a radical departure for local authority social services departments from their traditional mainly provider role. This separation was designed to strengthen previously weak functions such as needs assessment, service specifications and performance review; 'to weaken the influence of providers' vested interests...' (Wistow *et al.*, 1994, p.169); to make providers more responsive to users' needs. Experience has shown that purchasers have overestimated the combatitive element in commercial purchaser-provider relationships, with the need for a more collaborative relationship in social care. Purchasers in social services have needed to take a firm stance with providers in representing the needs of relatively powerless, dependent service users.
3. Post-1990 experience has shown

    ...that many social care needs are such that they imply long-term contracts between service users and service providers in which the quality and continuity of personal relationships, no less than the environment in which care is provided, are important aspects of their effectiveness (Wistow *et al.*, p.171).

This differs significantly from much contracting in the business and commercial worlds.
4. Earlier we referred to how British government reforms have introduced NPM into the field of social services, thereby changing the culture of these services. Rhodes (1995) distinguishes between two separate strands in this development, namely managerialism and new institutional economics, the latter becoming the dominant influence after 1988. Concerning the future, Wistow *et al.* and others argue that markets in some form in social services are here to stay, the task is to discover the most appropriate form(s) consistent with social services policies and objectives. Social services are different and this must be recognised in the particular form that privatisation takes in the future.

Why Not Privatise All Social Services?

Some years ago a highly provocative, futuristic paper suggested that the logic of post-1990 developments in UK social services was a local authority social services department reduced to a handful of staff whose sole function was to negotiate and monitor contracts with the independent sector. These staff would not be social work trained but MBA graduates highly skilled in IT. More realistically senior management in the same authority produced a 'core services' paper for local politicians which suggested criteria for deciding which services should continue to be provided solely or partially by the local authority, rather than being contracted out.

This large local authority has been only one of many trying to cope with increasing demand and reduced funding for social services. The Audit Commission together with the central government's Social Services Inspectorate carry out inspections and publish reports on the performance of individual social services departments. The Guardian newspaper reported (18.11.98, pp.8-9) of a highly complimentary report on Wolverhampton social services – but they now have to reduce their budget by 10 per cent over the next three years.

The much larger local authority proposed to deal with its serious budgetary problem and implement government policy by introducing the 'core services' strategy, and reducing costs by staffing reductions and increasing charges to users. Core services were defined as those social services which it is essential that the local authority has available to it, although it is not essential that the authority directly provides these services.

The core services strategy is a policy of reducing local authority service provision to the minimum, and is a partial response to the question 'why not privatise all social services?'

The following criteria were advanced for the authority retaining at least a partial position as a director service provider:

1. Services which the local authority has a legal duty to provide itself: These are relatively few in number and include investigation and assessment in cases of child abuse; and other types of assessment, inspection and registration. However, legal requirements to be the service provider are not fixed forever, future changes making it possible for local authorities to purchase even some of these services from the independent sector.
2. Services which for one reason or another the external market is unable or unwilling to provide to an acceptable standard or price: Reference was made earlier to for-profit providers' reluctance to provide services for people with high levels of dependency or particularly difficult patterns of behaviour. A local authority must retain the capacity to provide services for these groups.
3. Where it is wise for the local authority to provide a proportion of the service because of the possibility of unanticipated exits from the market by external suppliers, or the danger of cartels: This danger is evident in the provision of domiciliary care where the market is under-developed and there are some very big suppliers.
4. Where public expectation and consumer choice requires public provision in the mixed economy of services: It is difficult to cite specific examples here. In some local authorities it may be politically unwise to withdraw completely from providing certain services (e.g. residential care for older people) because of traditional views.

The question posed at the head of this section cannot be adequately addressed here. Its economic and other complexities require much fuller treatment. Nevertheless, the question does prompt some re-thinking and clarification of 'received wisdom' concerning who should provide what in social services in any country, not only the UK.

Conclusions

O'Higgins' (1989) argument is that both ideological and instrumental approaches to privatisation ignore the importance of contexts in which changes take place. His preference (pp. 159-60) is for a third way.

> A strategic approach that is more sensitive to the political economy of social welfare than instrumental approaches, but less deterministic than ideological approaches. It draws upon a number of features of the existence of both a mixed economy and a mixed polity of social welfare and in so doing indicates the inadequacy of the other two approaches.

Features of this approach include a dynamic policy environment where a past optimal balance may no longer exist. In the case of social services there are now an increasing number of relatively affluent pensioners who not only have private pensions but are also able to afford to pay at least a proportion of their social care costs. A second related modern context feature is a shift to systems that increasingly puts money into the hands of service users for them to buy services of their choice from a variety of service providers.

But O'Higgins sounds a note of caution over possible consequences of the non-state sector becoming too big. He quotes (pp.161-2) Klein (1986, p.28):

> Much of the attraction of the private sector depends on its marginality. To the extent that the private sector replaces the public sector, there is a risk that it may also reproduce its weaknesses, its rigidity, its unresponsiveness and its administrative costs – with the bureaucracy of regulation taking the place of the bureaucracy of management.

This is a timely warning for the UK – and already a feature of the German social care system with its huge non-state welfare bureaucracies. In the UK there is no doubt that a developing form of privatisation in social services is here to stay, with uncertainties over a form that is appropriate in the special field of social care i.e. that will deliver outcomes consistent with policy and users needs. An important government White Paper on social services is awaited that should address this central issue. Its thinking and language can be expected to show the continuing influence of NPM in British social services.

References

Audit Commission (1993), *Taking Care: Progress with Care in the Community*, Health and Personal Social Services Bulletin No 11, Audit Commission, London.

Balloch, S. (1997), 'Counting the Cost', *Community Care (20-26 February)*, p. 23.

Department of Health (1989), *Caring for People: Community Care in the Next Decade and Beyond*, HMSO, London.

Hood, C. (1991), 'A public management for all seasons', *Public Administration*, vol. 69, pp. 3-19.

Keen, L. and Scase, R. (1998), *Local Government Management: The Rhetoric and Reality of Change*, Open University Press, Buckingham.

Klein, R. (1984), *Privatization and the Welfare State*, Lloyds Bank Review, January, London, pp. 12-29.

Munday, B. and Ely, P. (eds) (1996), *Social Care in Europe*, Prentice Hall, Hemel Hempstead.

Munday, S. (1996), *Current Developments in Economics*, Macmillan Press, Basingstoke.

Murray, C. (1984), *Losing Ground: American Social Policy 1950-1980*, Basic Books, New York.

O'Higgins, M. (1989), 'Social Welfare and Privatization: The British Experience', in S. Kamerman and A. Kahn, *Privatization and the Welfare State*, Princeton University Press, Princeton.

Rhodes, R.A.W. (1995), *Prime Minister, Cabinet and Core Executive*, St. Martin's Press, London.

Walker, A. (1984), 'The Political Economy of Privatisation', in J. LeGrand and R. Robinson (eds), *Privatisation and the Welfare State*, Allen and Unwin, London.

Wistow, G. and Knapp, M. *et al.* (1994), *Social Care in a Mixed Economy*, Open University Press, Buckingham.

Wistow, G. and Knapp, M. *et al.* (1996), *Social Care Markets: Progress and Prospects*, Open University Press, Buckingham.

14 Social Service Delivery by Private and Voluntary Organisations in Germany

ROLF G. HEINZE AND CHRISTOPH STRÜNCK

Introduction

There are two things that have shaped social service delivery in Germany since the Weimar Republic, the dominance of non-profit organisations, the so-called *Wohlfahrtsverbände* (welfare associations) and the political doctrine of subsidiarity. The only thing that has widely changed is the overall financial participation of the state. Nevertheless, one can see several new paths of development, e.g. increasing competition between commercial and non-profit suppliers or a management-driven change within non-profit organisations. These paths of development will be discussed later. However, the text refrains from discussing the health sector because this has developed quite separately with its strong medical profession, the state-orientated insurance organisations and additional business interests (see Bönker and Wollmann in this volume).

Germany belongs to the group of welfare states in which voluntary organisations are strong pillars of the institutional system of welfare provision. They have always had the difficult task of co-operating closely with public authorities in the provision of standardised mainstream services and being responsible for answering new needs and providing services. This is different to Britain where many of the ordinary social services are provided by the municipalities and in contrast to Sweden where the role of civic organisations is largely reduced to advocacy and campaigning. The result has been a strong prevalence of their first role which has always helped in consolidating and developing services.

In addition, *corporatist arrangements* have had a long tradition in Germany:[1] (a) at the *central* level and in the respective policy sectors (health, social assistance, youth policy including nursery school services) when it comes to negotiating standards for social services and institutions and centrally prescribed levels of remuneration for services rendered; here the big five welfare associations usually take part; (b) at the *local* level of daily municipal policies concerning social services, (mainly services for the elderly, for youth and family help and nursery schools); here the representatives of the associations take part in planning the type and levels of public provision as members of the local committees linked with the local parliaments (e.g. in the committees which are obligatory in the area of planning facilities for children and youth). Given the close relationships between the representatives of the municipalities, the political parties, the social insurance schemes and the voluntary organisations and their boards, it is no wonder that the accounting system resembles cameralism and that trust and negotiation play a big role in governing the mutual relationships.

A Special Kind of 'Associative Democracy': The Rise of Corporatism in the German Social Service Sector

A central point of departure for the German system of social service delivery was the flourishing of numerous charities and self-help organisations in the second half of last century, organised by local citizens in the context of the (Roman)-Catholic or Protestant churches or in the context of the organised forms of the labour movement (Evers, 1995). Peak organisations mainly followed tasks and problems instead of ideological camps and only at the end of the last century were the predecessors of the present-day large voluntary organisations founded. Even before the end of the last century the provision of social services in German cities developed in the framework of a corporatist system, with municipal representatives on the boards of the local (non-profit) welfare associations and sensitive mechanisms were established for the mutual adaptation of the priorities of municipalities in the social field and the concerns of the voluntary organisations that were pioneering services and seeking municipal support (Sachße, 1993).

The path from a rich diversity of initiatives towards an organised landscape with a limited number of big organisations was paved mainly in the Weimar Republic (Tennstedt, 1992). The establishment of a Ministry of Labour marked the emergence of the state as a central partner for issues of both social help and services. Its legislation and political culture of centralised bargaining such as in industrial relations favoured central bargaining throughout as well as having centralised umbrella organisations as bargaining partners. The initiative to organise on a peak level was especially facilitated by the voluntary within the two big churches – the *Diakonie* (Protestant) and the *Caritas* (Catholic), alongside the smaller Jewish agency and a further welfare association, known today as the *Deutscher Paritätischer Wohlfahrtsverband* (DPWV).

They felt threatened by the strong social-democratic/state ambitions towards transforming the dual structure which had developed within the municipalities, turning co-operation with voluntary bodies into a form of 'municipal socialism' with services run by the public authorities themselves. The developing welfare associations pursued a strategy of centralisation and concentration to avoid loss of power (Neumann, 1989).

Within the labour ministry – a new creation of the Weimar Republic whose collective identity has influenced every such ministry up to the present day – a group of civil servants existed with close links to the Catholic *'Zentrum'* party. With the principle of subsidiarity being a part of Catholic social teaching, they favoured voluntary organisations and forced the revenue-strapped municipalities to accept the dominance of non-profit organisations (Tennstedt, 1992). Thus, the specific shape of the German welfare state was determined in the Weimar era, where the 'organisation of welfare associations became the associational complement of the centralised welfare state' (Tennstedt, 1992, p.352). In fact, the real legislation process in social welfare reinforced the 'dual system' of public purchasing and private provision which had already developed.

The third sector organisations therefore developed a strong position both through their national organisation and their joint national association, the *'Liga'*, as well as by the step-by-step extension of their role as primary partners alongside the development of social services at the local level. The *Arbeiterwohlfahrt*, the voluntary organisation associated with the social-democratic movement, had to join the national *'Liga'* in the latter part of the 20th century and to co-operate within the given culture of state/third sector relationships. These were marked by the increasing role of the municipalities and the health insurance schemes as financing bodies. The *Arbeiterwohlfahrt* also took part in negotiations about concepts and standards with the established non-profit organisations as the privileged partners when it came to carrying out and providing a service (Kaiser, 1993).

Following the Nazi regime with its forced etatisation of the organisations, the newly founded Federal Republic resumed and continued along the path which had already been established in the inter-war period. In a number of social laws (concerning social assistance, services for youth and in the area of help and care), voluntary organisations were given a special public status and a privileged role as service providers; they had to be the preferred contractors whenever a new public-funded social service or institution was to be set up. Given the strong influence of the (Catholic) church, the dual system was often interpreted as the practical realisation of the principle of subsidiarity (Sachße, 1995). In a legal sense, the principle of subsidiarity has been enforced within the income support law of 1961.[2]

There are two core dimensions of subsidiarity in German social policy. First, subsidiarity declares the tax-financed and means-tested system of income support to be subordinate to the social insurance system as the 'final net' in the welfare system. Second, it privileges voluntary organisations compared to public or commercial suppliers. By doing so, public authorities are pledged to support social support measures for youth, the disabled and the elderly. They are allowed to delegate the execution of these measures to voluntary organisations, which they often do in practice.

The priority given to non-profit organisations, encouraged by subsidiarity, has however grown into a strong financial and organisational collaboration between the state and NPOs. This has been described as a shift from subsidiarity to corporatism, the latter being rooted in the Weimar Republic (Heinze and Olk, 1981, 1984a,b). This shift has been marked by the following elements:

- Peak organisations at the federal and *Länder* level take part in the formulation and implementation of policies. At the local level their representatives even sit on political bodies charged with social planning (Thränhardt, 1984);
- The supply of services is financed by grants which are fixed in negotiations between state and NPOs. The internal wage structure of the NPOs is nearly the same as in the civil service sector. The whole organisational structure widely copies the principle of state administration (Neumann, 1993; Brauns, 1994);
- The NPOs have been increasingly co-financed by public money (Spiegelhalter, 1990; Goll, 1991). During growth periods the relation between public money and their own resources from contributions or

donations has dramatically changed in favour of public money (Thamm, 1995).

This development on the other hand has neglected non-organised interests and projects in the social sphere, an effect which German corporatism has always been criticised for (Heinze and Olk, 1981). In fact the state provides the leading peak associations with a guarantee to maintain a form of monopolistic representation, combined with generous subsidies (Sachße and Tennstedt, 1988). This model shaped the social service sector until the beginning of the 1990s, although there were changes that are still taking place (see below).

Welfare Associations as Suppliers: Figures and Developments

The cultural changes of the late 1960s brought about the formation of a number of local initiatives, associations and self-help groups which either did not join one of the big voluntary associations or were only loosely organised in the *DPWV* – the welfare association which is less powerful than the others, but which is more willing to take a modest role as a mere umbrella organisation. As a result, one can find in Germany 'two cultures' made up of a traditional and a new generation of associations and service-providing organisations. In the meantime, however, these new institutions have themselves often been in operation for more than 25 years. In some sectors – such as in the area of nursery groups organised by parents – they have succeeded in achieving the same status concerning contracts for economic support as the other older providers. In other sectors – especially where the service concepts gave innovative answers to conflictual issues which were difficult to resolve with the culture of the majority, such as many services for drug addicts and miss-treated women – it became much more difficult to gain the same reliable and considerable level of public support given to traditional voluntary organisations.

Self-help organisations, which flourished in the 1980s as a counterpart to the bureaucratic services of the big welfare associations, have in the meantime mostly been integrated into the traditional organisations. Each has an average of 19 to 20 members. Nearly one third of the groups is engaged in care for the elderly, one quarter in family and youth support. They are followed by drug addiction, health, psychiatry (15-20 per cent), migration issues (10 per cent), feminism (8.5 per cent), and the disabled (5 per cent) (see Braun, 1994).

Their quantitative dimensions are difficult to estimate. Recent research suggests that there are nearly 25,000 self-help groups with 375,000 individual members (Teichert, 1993), whereas a survey organised by the federal Ministry of Family Affairs shows that there are about 50,000 groups in West Germany, compared to 5,000 in the former GDR (Braun, 1994). As providers of professional social services, they are nevertheless clearly dwarfed by the big welfare associations and their service units, many of which have themselves integrated a large number of self-help groups.

In contrast to the second wave made up of small local associations, the organisational features of these big voluntary associations are more complex. Until now, five non-profit organisations have dominated the social service sector: the *Deutscher Caritasverband* (DCV; Catholic), the *Diakonisches Werk* (DW; Protestant), the *Arbeiterwohlfahrt* (AWO; social democratic); the *Deutsches Rotes Kreuz* (DRK; German Red Cross), the *Deutscher Paritätischer Wohlfahrtsverband* (DPWV; a loosely linked association strongly influenced by self-help organisations) and the *Zentrale Wohlfahrtsstelle der Juden in Deutschland* (ZWSt; Jewish). These five national organisations are organised according to a double ratio:

On the one hand they see themselves as organisations which support societal goals and values, defending the interests of underprivileged and weak groups; accordingly, the formal command structures are run by persons who do this work on a voluntary basis and come from church or other related organisations. Each organisation encourages a different creed and outlook. On the other hand, they have never established themselves as organisations of members (except for the *Arbeiterwohlfahrt*) but as organisations made up of serving members and help-providing (local) associations. Even if they are concerned with the problems of the groups they work for, they are not committed to them by organisational relationships.

In fact, their main task is the provision of specialised social services, which demand the employment of many different professions in addition to the voluntary members. The main fields of work can be found in:

- health (mainly running hospitals),
- social help for youth,
- family support,
- care of the elderly,

- care of the disabled,
- advice to fringe groups,
- vocational training for professionals,
- lobbying and public relations in the field of social policy.

Focusing on the most important fields of social services, the following welfare associations' share of total supply can be estimated:

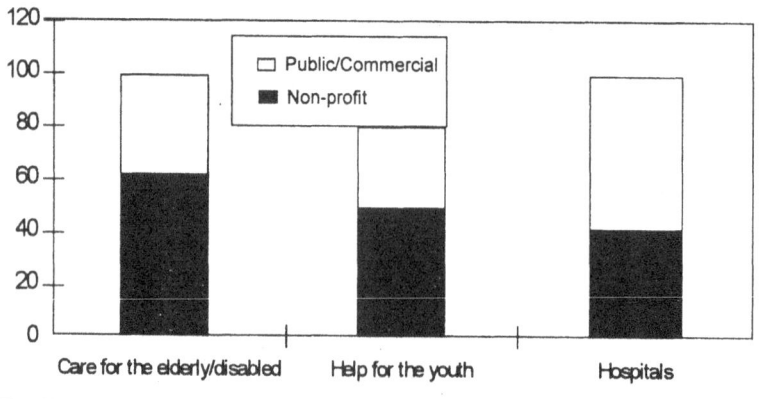

Figure 14.1 **Welfare associations as suppliers, numbers in percentages**
Source: BAGFW, 1997, p.8

Each association is formally ruled by a voluntary body, whereas the services are carried out by professionals. In addition, each association employs a professional management at the top. The political impact, the legal privileges and the economic base of these welfare associations are judged to be unique by international comparison (Schmid, 1996). The size of the workforce is also very impressive, even when compared to other branches of business. With 1.1 million employees in the year of 1996, it exceeds sectors such as textile production, the catering trade or the coal mining sector.

Social Service Delivery by Private and Voluntary Organisations 291

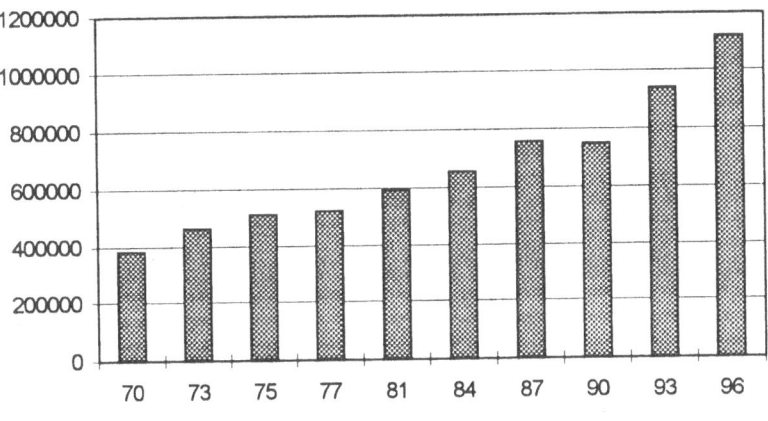

Figure 14.2 Growth of employment within welfare associations 1970-1996
Source: *BAGFW, 1997, p.11*

German reunification helped the establishment of massive welfare associations in the former East. This has additionally boosted employment in this sector. The majority of employees are employed in the well-established fields of hospitals, youth work and care of the elderly.

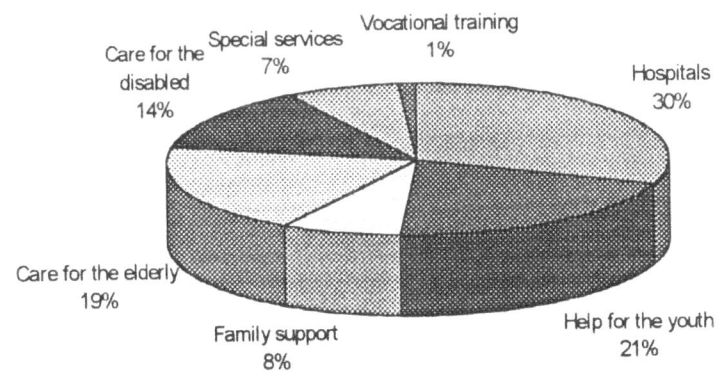

Figure 14.3 Shares of employment in main fields of activity
Source: *BAGFW, 1997, p.10*

Concerning places for clients the welfare associations have also shown a growth in recent decades. Some changes in the law have also fuelled this development.

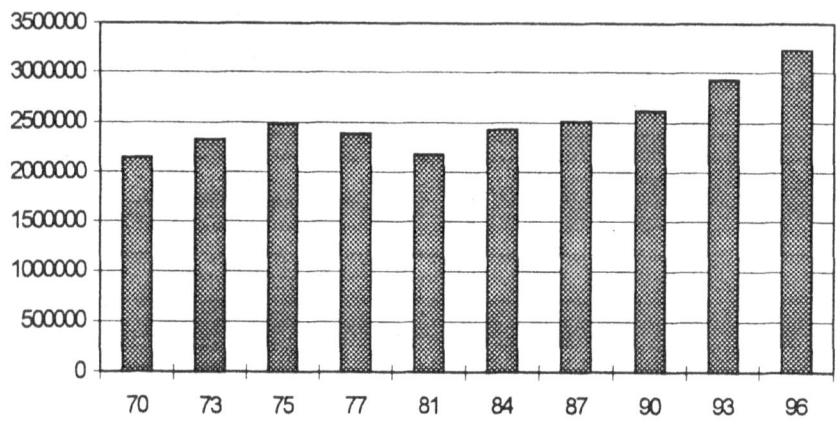

Figure 14.4 Places for clients 1970-1996
Source: *BAGFW, 1997, p.11*

Two levels have to be distinguished. Peak associations are mainly charged with political and advisory tasks, while the other units are mainly responsible for the supply of actual social services. These units have shown considerable growth and as a result have strengthened their influence and relative independence from the peak associations.

The structure of revenues mirrors the strong role of the state in financing social services. Here, however, one has to rely on estimates since most of the voluntary organisations do not publish uniform data. According to an estimation by Goll (1991), about 11 per cent comes from public subsidies, while about 80 per cent of the total turnover of DM 46bn is made up of reimbursements for services rendered; nearly 5 per cent comes from donations and membership fees and 4 per cent from the churches.

Subsidies can come from all state levels; they mostly take (a) the form of a one-off initial investment by a ministry of one of the *Länder* or by a district or a municipality in the construction of a nursery school or a care centre which is then run by the respective voluntary body; or (b) it can mean subsidising the institution while in operation; this happens often in the framework of a time limited public programme or by a grant paid from the budgets of the municipality. Subsidies typically have no clear relationship involving a reverse commitment by the recipient to give a certain level of service.

Reimbursements are related to designated numbers and types of services rendered. To a minor extent, they can come in the form of fees paid by the clients themselves. The vast majority, however, are distributed by the social insurance funds (health and care insurance), the social assistance agencies and, where there is a clear contractual relationship with service-performance, from (municipal) public budgets. Negotiated and fixed sums per service rendered or per day/place/hospital bed are paid for care given in nursing homes or shelters. The negotiations about the terms and levels of reimbursement for care rendered have therefore by tradition crucial for the vast majority of the institutions and services run by the welfare associations, and it is therefore important that the associations and providers are able to take part in these negotiations.

There is a variety of subsidy and reimbursement types. Some reflect local traditions, others mirror the peculiarities of a specific administrative and policy field; e.g. some service-providers are paid nearly entirely from the local funds for social assistance, others get the bulk of their resources from municipal grants which have to be (re)stated every year, and others get their money predominantly from the health and care insurance funds. The fact that many service providers rely on budgets which represent a mix of subsidies and reimbursements from different sources makes this area even more complex.

Recent Changes and Core Challenges

In spite of the established functions of the German welfare associations they are facing new challenges which threaten their power and influence. Some experts even suggest a 'turning point' in the relationship between government and welfare associations. The landscape of social service suppliers is said to have become more 'pluralistic' which may lead to the end of corporatist arrangements in the long run (Backhaus-Maul and Olk, 1994, 1996). Indeed, recent re-formulations of the law have encouraged a decline in the applied principle of subsidiarity. Competition between private/commercial suppliers and the non-profit-making welfare associations has been supported at least in law. On a local level, however, the status quo remains and new projects are even forced to join the traditional umbrella associations, typical of German political governance (Heinze and Strünck, 1998).

The growing importance of business administration is mirrored by a growing number of management consultancies in the social sector.[3] As a result, new management vocabulary is being floated within the welfare associations, which puts pressure on their traditional organisation and outlook (Strünck, 1996). Among these issues are:

- Fiscal crisis forces welfare associations to implement new models of rationalisation;
- Public criticism increasingly concentrates on the lack of transparency, efficiency and flexibility of non-profit providers;
- Volunteering as an important resource is becoming rare. Social change leads to new patterns of civic involvement which do not fit into the strictly organised modes of welfare organisations. Consequently, a shadow has been cast on a crucial argument in favour of the peculiarites of non-profit compared to for-profit providers (Bäcker, Heinze and Naegele, 1995; Heinze and Bucksteeg, 1995; Olk, 1987);
- Recent changes in the law demand a higher level of transparency and comparability of supply. The need for handling *a priori* fixed budgets has grown (Heinze and Strünck, 1996). In the long run the traditional principle of automatic reimbursement will be replaced by budgets, with some exceptions remaining;
- New market mechanisms, such as compulsory competitive tendering, have been introduced, both in long-term care insurance as well as at the local level;
- European integration has made the transfer of social services less difficult and aims to achieve comparable conditions. The unique tax-privilege of German non-profit suppliers is thus also threatened (Loges, 1994).
- The recruitment patterns of employees have changed. Social change shrinks the traditional 'milieux'. The growing number of employees who have been trained outside the welfare associations' culture and have often undergone an education in business administration have a strong impact on organisational culture (Strünck, 1996);
- By being virtual 'quangos', the German welfare associations are automatically involved in the debate on new public management (Naschold, 1995). Changes in public administration, therefore, also affect the principles of their organisational structure. At least the

organisational myth of isomorphism, that they ought to reform, is widespread;
- Additionally, there has been a generational change among leading civil servants. In the whole field of social policy, the post-war generation which kept to the integrating principle of subsidiarity and maintained close political networks is reaching retirement (Heinze, Schmid and Strünck, 1999).

It is remarkable that questions about the legitimate roles of welfare associations have disappeared. This was the main topic in the 1980s that fuelled discussions about self-help organisations.[4] Instead, the appropriate economic competence as well as the relation to user's choice are now at the core of the debate.

Competition and New Contractual Relationships in Long-Term Care Insurance

The introduction of the 'fifth pillar of social insurance', the long-term care insurance, in 1995, is the most prominent example of recently changed environmental (Evers, 1998; Goetting, Haug and Hinrichs, 1994). Now there is also a prescriptive social insurance solution for the care question also exists. The insurers are the existing health insurance schemes, but the new branch is formally independent, with each health insurance now having an additional care insurance section (Alber, 1996).

Until 1995, the providers of institutional and home care services (municipal, non-profit and commercial associations) received their reimbursements either from the care-dependent persons themselves or, in case these were dependent on social assistance, in the framework of contracts with the municipal social assistance offices. In addition, the municipal and non-profit organisations received additional grants mainly for investments and maintenance, while the commercial providers usually had to operate without such money (Garms-Homolova, 1994).

There were two main reasons for introducing an insurance-based solution. On the one hand, it was seen as unfair that many people had to resort to social assistance in the case of care dependency, especially institutional care, with its high costs of around DM 6,000 per month and with more than 80 per cent having to be paid for or helped by social assistance. On the other hand, the municipalities, which had to bear the bulk of social assistance costs (which made up two-thirds of all social assistance payments), were eager to be rid of them by introducing an insurance solution.

The most important element in the new reform regarding contract culture is the introduction of a quasi-market system with very restricted rights and incentives for future political intervention by public authorities. Legislators have been 'courageous' (Schulin, 1994, p.303) insofar as they have removed the ancient special and favourable conditions for the non-profit welfare associations as providers. Much more than in the health sector, a system of competitive tendering has been installed. Each provider which fulfils some professional premises has to be allowed to offer institutional or home care as a provider licensed for insurance reimbursement; commercial providers are now explicitly put on an equal footing with providers which work within the framework of the big voluntary agencies (as corporate members and non-profit organisations). Municipally-based organisations are to be given quasi-commercial or non-profit status. In order to safeguard equality for competing providers, public authorities are no longer allowed to give continuous grants to a special group of providers (such as previously to non-profit organisations).

Finally, what is quite remarkable is the fact that the municipalities and the *Länder*, which after the reform have fewer possibilities to intervene in the care field, feel somewhat freed from obligations rather than bereft of rights and responsibilities. They are glad to be able to restrict their part to a minimum (e.g. additional social assistance payments) and to point to the responsibility of a self-regulating system of financers and providers where seemingly no politics at all are needed, because under the new law even the total care budgets are capped. Altogether, the insurance funds are not allowed to exceed income by more than a fixed and unchangeable 2.75 per cent share of insurance contributions.

Management-Driven Change

The majority of German welfare associations have implemented new mechanisms of business administration in order to cope with the new economic pressure. Above all, the long-term care insurance with its focus on efficiency and quality control, forces them to develop their economic skills. But it is not only that external pressure makes professionals feel more management-orientated. Fed by new generations of professionals, their organisational self-confidence relies more than a few years ago on economically successful behaviour. Thus, some groups within the welfare associations instrumentalise external factors in order to modernise the internal structure of their own organisations. Indeed. This has also produced a clash of culture (Strünck, 1996).

Besides the introduction of controlling measures, the debate on 'corporate identity'[5] and the growing need for management skills, the 'outsourcing strategy' has been the most prominent development (Heinze, Schmid and Strünck, 1997). The motives for outsourcing units such as catering or cleaning are complex. On the one hand, rationalisation looks much easier. On the other, the volunteers who formally govern will lose power if a strong management above the outsourced units acts more freely than before. Additionally, the liability of the umbrella organisation is thus restricted, an advantage in an age of growing economic threat and fewer financial responsibilities of the state.

Another motive for outsourcing reveals further details of economic pressure. By following this strategy, overall wage regulation can be avoided and some units made cheaper regarding to labour costs. Moreover, outsourced units such as financial consultancies can earn additional revenue on the free market by selling products to competing commercial suppliers. This, too, makes the distinction between the third sector and commercial suppliers less convincing. When considering forthcoming change, it could be argued that it no longer makes sense to speak of single 'welfare associations' but to speak of 'brands' of social service.

Of course, there are several problems hidden behind this. Volunteering to serve in a much more diversified organisation is not easy, although voluntary work continues to be an important feature of non-profit welfare associations. Furthermore the integration of such complex organisations becomes much more difficult when the economically most important parts claim to act more independently of the former umbrella organisation (Heinze, Schmid and Strünck, 1997).

The recent trends of marketisation and internal change strengthen the function of professional service provision and weaken the advocacy function of welfare associations (Rauschenbach et al., 1995). Nevertheless, this latter function remains to be rediscovered as an important element of a modern corporate identity of welfare associations. The impact of new market mechanisms clearly shows ambivalent effects which cannot be discussed here (see Bönker and Wollmann in this volume).

Europe and the Two Germanys: Consequences of Divided Development

Even at the European level a trend towards economisation has developed from the point of view of German welfare associations. Integration of NPOs into a common social policy is dominated by the French creed of '*économie sociale*' (Kuper, 1990). The provision of social services comes first in this concept (Schmid, 1994b). Driven by this concept, criticism of the tax privileges of German welfare associations has grown within the European Union (Loges, 1994). At the moment it is not altogether clear whether European integration actually stifles competition in the social service sector. Competition has already increased in the financially attractive field of in-patient treatment as well as in the field of outpatient treatment in former borderline areas.

Another national peculiarity lies in the social service provision in the former GDR. A rapid and broad institutional transfer implemented all the features from the West, although there was no developed culture of voluntary work in the East because of the anti-religious policy and the prescribed involvement of the ruling socialist party. The majority of social services were provided by the state-owned *Volkssolidarität* (people's solidarity), today a member of the loosely linked *Paritätischer Wohlfahrtsverband*. The Red Cross acted rather as a centralised mass organisation (Schmid, 1994a).

Obviously the state has tried to compensate for the missing infrastructure of organised solidarity by massive injections of financial and infrastructural aid. As a result, the welfare associations in east Germany act rather as quangos, fulfilling almost all public functions in the field of social services and focusing on an efficient provision of services. This 'learning process in quick time' (Angerhausen *et al.*, 1994) has led to a semi-public status for welfare associations and has weakened the organisational capacity for self-organisation and membership-orientation.

This development gives no support to the crucial argument that welfare associations matter because of their status between the market and the state. It can even be imagined that this 'modernisation by catching up' on the part of the eastern welfare associations will turn into a 'modernisation by overtaking'. The resulting emphasis on 'social enterprise' would then be able to speed developments in west Germany. The core question remains whether all the different welfare associations will turn into similar providers by processes of *isomorphism* and marketisation (DiMaggio and Powell, 1991). This does not lead necessarily to a uniformisation of services somewhat connected to bureaucratic and less responsive organisations. Many of the forthcoming options still depend on the institutional framework for user's choice, a widely neglected topic in the German model of social service provision (Evers et al., 1998). Thus, the floor is open for political benchmarking.

Notes

1 There has always been a debate in Germany about whether the peculiarities of the German social service sector fit into the analytical framework of neo-corporatism, which was primarily constructed with regard to trade union-state-employers tripartism (Beyme, 1991). However, one of the 'celebrities' in the debate on corporatism recently admitted publicly that the social service sector indeed represents a kind of 'sectoral corporatism' (Lehmbruch, 1996).
2 Referring to the complex phenomenon of subsidiarity (see Heinze, 1986; Münder and Kreft, 1989; Sachße, 1994 and Waschkuhn, 1995).
3 Many of these consultancies are a product of sourcing-out policies by the welfare associations. In addition, companies exist which have close personal links to welfare associations. At the same time, pure management consultancies have discovered the social sector as an additional field of revenue. Even the more welfare-orientated consultancies offer their support to commercial suppliers. As a result, the demarcation line between profit and non-profit has become increasingly blurred.
4 The pressure was also reduced because a vast majority of self-help-organisations had been integrated into traditional welfare organisations, above all into the loosely linked *DPWV*.
5 This debate clearly signals that the former corporate identity, namely the outlook and political/denominational creed, no longer integrates new generations of professionals.

References

Alber, J. (1996), 'The Debate About Long-term Care Reform in Germany', in OECD: *Caring for Frail Elderly People. Policies in Evolution* (Social Policy Studies 19), Paris, pp. 63-87.

Angerhausen, S., Backhaus-Maul, H. and Schiebel, M. (1995), 'Nachwirkende Traditionen und besondere Herausforderungen: Strukturentwicklung und Leistungsverständnis von Wohlfahrtsverbänden in den neuen Bundesländern', in T. Rauschenbach, C. Sachße and T. Olk (eds), *Von der Wertgemeinschaft zum Dienstleistungsunternehmen. Jugend- und Wohlfahrtsverbände im Umbruch*, Suhrkamp, Frankfurt a. M., pp. 377-403.

Bäcker, G., Heinze, R.G. and Naegele, G. (1995), *Die Sozialen Dienste vor neuen Herausforderungen*, LIT, Münster.

Backhaus-Maul, H. and Olk, T. (1994), 'Von Subsidiarität zu "outcontracting": Zum Wandel der Beziehungen von Staat und Wohlfahrtsverbänden in der Sozialpolitik', in W. Streeck (ed.), *Staat und Verbände. PVS-Sonderheft 25*, Westdeutscher Verlag, Opladen, pp. 100-35.

Backhaus-Maul, H. and Olk, T. (1996) 'Vom Korporatismus zum Pluralismus? Aktuelle Tendenzen in den Staat-Verbände-Beziehungen am Beispiel des Sozialsektors', in L. Clausen (ed.), *Gesellschaften im Umbruch. Verhandlungen des 27. Kongresses der Deutschen Gesellschaft für Soziologie*, Campus, Frankfurt a. M., New York, pp. 580-94.

BAGFW (Bundesarbeitsgemeinschaft der Freien Wohlfahrtspflege) (1997), *Gesamtstatistik der Einrichtungen der Freien Wohlfahrtspflege*, BAGFW, Bonn.

Beyme, K.v. (1991), *Theorie der Politik im 20. Jahrhundert. Von der Moderne zur Postmoderne*, Suhrkamp, Frankfurt a. M.

Braun, J. (ed.) (1994), *Praxishandbuch für Selbsthilfekontaktstellen*, Erstellt im Rahmen des Modellprogramms 'Förderung der sozialen Selbsthilfe in den neuen Bundesländern' des Bundesministeriums für Familie und Senioren, Third Edition, ISAB, Leipzig, Köln.

Brauns, H.-J. (1994), 'Die Wohlfahrtsverbände müssen ihre Orientierung am Staat aufgeben. Finanzierungsformen prägen Organisationsstrukturen – Was sich ändern muß', *Blätter der Wohlfahrtspflege*, vol. 9, pp. 161-63.

DiMaggio, P. J. and Powell, W. W. (1991), 'The Iron Cage Revisited. Institutional Isomorphism and Collective Rationality', in W.W. Powell and P.J. diMaggio (eds), *The New Institutionalism in Organizational Analysis*, University of Chicago Press, Chicago, London, pp. 63-82.

Evers, A (1995), 'Part of the Welfare Mix: the Third Sector as an Intermediate Area', *Voluntas*, vol. 5., pp. 159-82.

Evers, A. (1998), 'The new Long-Term-Care Insurance Program in Germany', *Journal of Aging & Social Policy*, vol. 10, pp. 77-98.

Evers, A., Haverinen, R., Leichsenring, K. and Wistow, G. (eds) (1998), *Developing Quality in Personal Social Services. Concepts, Cases and Comments*, Ashgate, Aldershot.

Garms-Homolová, V. (1994), 'Comprehensive Health for the Aged and Initiatives for an Insurance in Germany', *Zeitschrift für Gesundheitswissenschaften*, vol. vol.2, pp. 26-38.

Goetting, U., Haug, K. and Hinrichs, K. (1994), 'The Long Road to Long-Term Care Insurance in Germany', *Journal of Public Policy*, vol. 14, pp. 285-309.

Goll, E. (1991), *Die freie Wohlfahrtspflege als eigener Wirtschaftsfaktor. Theorie und Empirie ihrer Verbände und Einrichtungen*, Nomos, Baden-Baden.
Heinze, R.G. (ed.) (1986), *Neue Subsidiarität. Leitidee für eine zukünftige Sozialpolitik?* Westdeutscher Verlag, Opladen.
Heinze, R.G. and Bucksteeg, M. (1995), 'Modernisierung der lokalen Sozialpolitik – Potentiale freiwilligen Engagements im Wohlfahrtsmix', in W. Fricke (ed.), *Jahrbuch Arbeit und Technik*, Dietz, Bonn, pp. 208-18.
Heinze, R.G. and Olk, T. (1981), 'Die Wohlfahrtsverbände im System sozialer Dienstleistungsproduktion. Zur Entstehung und Struktur der bundesrepublikanischen Verbändewohlfahrt', *Kölner Zeitschrift für Soziologie und Sozialpsychologie*, vol. 33, pp. 94-114.
Heinze, R.G. and Olk, T. (1984a), 'Rückzug des Staates – Aufwertung der Wohlfahrtsverbände? Verbandliche Wohlfahrtspflege und "neue Subsidiarität"', in R. Bauer and H. Dießenbacher (eds) *Organisierte Nächstenliebe. Wohlfahrtsverbände und Selbsthilfe in der Krise des Sozialstaats*, Westdeutscher Verlag, Opladen, pp. 173-88.
Heinze, R.G. and Olk, T. (1984b), 'Sozialpolitische Steuerung. Von der Subsidiarität zum Korporatismus', in M. Glagow (ed.), *Gesellschaftssteuerung zwischen Korporatismus und Subsidiarität*, ASJ, Bielefeld, pp. 162-94.
Heinze, R.G. and Strünck, C. (1996), 'Kontraktmanagement im Windschatten des "Wohlfahrtsmix" ? Neue kommunale Steuerungsmodelle für das System der Wohlfahrtsverbände', in A. Evers and T. Olk (eds), *Wohlfahrtspluralismus. Vom Wohlfahrtsstaat zur Wohlfahrtsgesellschaft*, Westdeutscher Verlag, Opladen, pp. 294-322.
Heinze, R.G. and Strünck, C. (1998), 'Wohlfahrtsverbände, Selbsthilfe und private Anbieter – neue Rollenverteilung auf lokaler Ebene?', in D. Grunow and H. Wollmann (eds), *Lokale Verwaltungsreform in Aktion: Fortschritte und Fallstricke*, Birkhäuser, Iller, Boston, Berlin, pp. 103-19.
Heinze, R.G., Schmid, J. and Strünck, C. (1997), 'Zur Politischen Ökonomie der sozialen Dienstleistungsproduktion. Der Wandel der Wohlfahrtsverbände und die Konjunkturen der Theoriebildung', *Kölner Zeitschrift für Soziologie und Sozialpsychologie*, vol. 2, pp. 242-71.
Heinze, R.G., Schmid, J. and Strünck, C. (1999), *Vom Wohlfahrtsstaat zum Wettbewerbsstaat. Arbeitsmarkt- und Sozialpolitik in den 90er Jahren*, Leske + Budrich, Opladen.
Kaiser, J.C. (1993), 'Freie Wohlfahrtsverbände im Kaiserreich und in der Weimarer Republik', in K., Teppe (ed.), *Jahrbuch Westfälische Forschungen*, vol. 43, Westfälisches Dampfboot, Münster, pp. 26-75.
Kuper, B.-O. (1990), 'Économie Sociale – eine Herausforderung an die freie Wohlfahrtspflege?' *Nachrichten des Vereins für öffentliche und private Fürsorge*, vol. 70, pp. 307-09.

Lehmbruch, G. (1996), 'Der Beitrag der Korporatismusforschung zur Entwicklung der Steuerungstheorie', *Politische Vierteljahresschrift*, vol. 37, pp. 735-51.
Loges, F. (1994), 'Wohlfahrtsverbände als Unternehmen', *Theorie und Praxis der sozialen Arbeit*, vol. 2, pp. 58-72.
Münder, J. and Kreft, D. (ed.) (1989), *Subsidiarität heute*, Votum, Münster.
Naschold, F. (1995), *Ergebnissteuerung, Wettbewerb, Qualitätspolitik, Entwicklungspfade des öffentlichen Sektors in Europa*, Edition Sigma, Berlin.
Neumann, V. (1989), 'Der Verband der freien Wohlfahrtspflege als Rechtsbegriff', *Beiträge zum Recht der sozialen Dienste und Einrichtungen*, vol. 4, pp. 1-30.
Neumann, V. (1993), *Freiheitsgefährdung im kooperativen Sozialstaat. Rechtsgrundlagen und Rechtsformen der Finanzierung der freien Wohlfahrtspflege*, Heymanns, Köln, Berlin, Bonn, München.
Olk, T. (1987), 'Das soziale Ehrenamt', *Sozialwissenschaftliche Literatur Rundschau*, vol. 14, pp. 84-101.
Rauschenbach, T., Sachße, C. and Olk, T. (eds) (1995), *Von der Wertgemeinschaft zum Dienstleistungsunternehmen. Jugend- und Wohlfahrtsverbände im Umbruch*, Suhrkamp, Frankfurt a. M.
Sachße, C. (1993), 'Frühformen der Leistungsverwaltung: die kommunale Armenfürsorge im deutschen Kaiserreich', *Jahrbuch für europäische Verwaltungsgeschichte*, vol. 5, pp. 1-20.
Sachße, C. (1994), 'Subsidiarität: Zur Karriere eines sozialpolitischen Ordnungsbegriffes', *Zeitschrift für Sozialreform*, vol. 11, pp. 717-38.
Sachße, C. (1995), 'Verein, Verband und Wohlfahrtsstaat: Entstehung und Entwicklung der 'dualen' Wohlfahrtspflege', in T. Rauschenbach, C. Sachße and T. Olk (eds) (1995), *Von der Wertgemeinschaft zum Dienstleistungsunternehmen. Jugend- und Wohlfahrtsverbände im Umbruch*, Suhrkamp, Frankfurt a. M., pp. 123-49.
Sachße, C. and Tennstedt, F. (1988), *Geschichte der Armenfürsorge in Deutschland, vol. 2: Fürsorge und Wohlfahrtspflege 1871-1929*, Kohlhammer, Stuttgart.
Schmid, J. (1994a), 'Der Aufbau von Wohlfahrtsverbänden in den neuen Bundesländern. Gesellschaftliche Selbsthilfebewegung oder quasistaatliche Veranstaltung?', in J. Schmid, F. Löbler and H. Tiemann (eds), *Organisationsstrukturen und Probleme von Parteien und Verbänden: Berichte aus den neuen Ländern*, Metropolis, Marburg, pp. 181-99.
Schmid, J. (1994b), 'Der Wohlfahrtsstaat Europa und die deutschen Wohlfahrtsverbände. Zur politisch-ökonomischen Dialektik zwischen europäischer Integration und verbandsorganisatorischer Differenzierung' in V. Eichener and H. Voelzkow (eds), *Europäische Integration und verbandliche Interessenvermittlung*, Metropolis, Marburg, pp. 453-83.

Schmid, J. (1996), *Wohlfahrtsverbände in modernen Wohlfahrtsstaaten. Soziale Dienste in historisch-vergleichender Perspektive*, Leske + Budrich, Opladen.
Schulin, B. (1994), 'Verträge mit den Leistungserbringern im Pflegeversicherungsrecht (SGB, vol. XI)', *Vierteljahresschrift für Sozialrecht*, vol. 22, pp. 285-307.
Spiegelhalter, F. (1990), *Der dritte Sozialpartner. Die Freie Wohlfahrtspflege – ihr finanzieller und ideeller Beitrag zum Sozialstaat*, Lambertus, Freiburg i.Br.
Strünck, C. (1996), 'Von Macht, Mythen und paradoxen Effekten. Betriebswirtschaftliche Reformen in der freien Wohlfahrtspflege', *Zeitschrift für Sozialreform*, vol. 11/12, pp. 715-25.
Teichert, V. (1993), *Das informelle Wirtschaftssystem. Analyse und Perspektiven von Erwerbs- und Eigenarbeit*, Westdeutscher Verlag, Opladen.
Tennstedt, F. (1992), 'Die Spitzenverbände der Freien Wohlfahrtspflege im dualen Wohlfahrtsstaat. Ein historischer Rückblick auf die Entwicklung in Deutschland', *Soziale Arbeit*, vol. 10/11, pp. 342-56.
Thamm, D. (1995), 'Geld statt guter Worte: Zur Finanzierung freier Wohlfahrtspflege', in T. Rauschenbach, C. Sachße and T. Olk (eds) (1995), *Von der Wertgemeinschaft zum Dienstleistungsunternehmen. Jugend- und Wohlfahrts-verbände im Umbruch*, Suhrkamp, Frankfurt a. M., pp. 356-76.
Thränhardt, D. (1984), 'Von Thron und Altar zur bürokratischen Verknüpfung. Die Entwicklung korporatistischer Beziehungen zwischen Wohlfahrtsverbänden und Staat in Deutschland', in R. Bauer (ed), *Die liebe Not. Zur historischen Kontinuität der "Freien Wohlfahrtspflege"*, Beltz, Weinheim, Basel, pp. 164-71.
Waschkuhn, A. (1995), *Was ist Subsidiarität? Ein sozialphilosophisches Ordnungsprinzip: Von Thomas von Aquin bis zur 'Civil Society'*, Westdeutscher Verlag, Opladen.

15 Trends in the Marketisation of British Social Services

MICHAEL HILL

Introduction

This chapter explores the extent to which three key sectors in British social policy – personal social services, social housing and primary medical care – have involved mixed economies at various points in time. It has been written to parallel the chapter on similar policy sectors in Germany by Bönker and Wollmann. That chapter stresses the extent to which the German policy sectors were always in various senses mixed economies and therefore the considerable continuity in policy in that country. This chapter will show that the British story has been rather different for two reasons. First, the emergence of a state role in the personal social services and social housing has been very much dominated by services run by local government, subsidised and supervised by central government. The case of primary care was a little different, because general medical practitioners were able to preserve the right to continue as self-employed practitioners, working under contract when the National Health Service was set up, but this too was scarcely a 'mixed economy' in the sense in which it is normally used.

Second, a series of policy changes in the 1980s and 1990s partly ended the relatively simple pattern of state run services. In two of the three services to be considered (with again the story with regard to primary care a rather different one) there are good grounds to speak of a Thatcherite revolution. However that revolution did not involve the simple replacement of public services by private ones, but rather the evolution of new kinds of mixed economies. Hence in Britain recent developments have injected a marked discontinuity into social policy.

1890-1945

Personal Social Services

The modern statutory social services only really emerged after the Second World War. That is not to say however that earlier generations were altogether indifferent to those social care problems which families could not, or would not, handle unaided. The Poor Law only offered a very basic system of institution based relief for those without the means, or the families, to care for them. In any account of the Poor Law social care, income maintenance and health care emerge as (by modern standards) very much mixed together. The Poor Law's origins lie in the 16th century, but it was legislation in 1834 that established a system that was to survive until the 1940s. The central concern of the 1834 legislation was to try to restore the principal, which had been undermined by extensions of cash relief, that help for the poor should only be given in institutions (work-houses) where all able bodied persons were required to work for their keep yet not achieve a standard of living superior to that of the poorest class of free labourer. At the same time it was recognised that both children and disabled elderly people would need to be treated slightly differently to the able-bodied poor. Thus workhouses provided a form of institutional social care. But they also began to develop as hospitals for the poor.

The second half of the 19th century saw an enormous flowering of charitable ventures. Many of these sought to add domiciliary care and social work to the institution based efforts of earlier organisations (Thane, 1982). Concerns for the welfare of elderly people tended to take the form of the recognition of the case for income enhancement, leading eventually to demands for state pensions (see Gilbert, 1966). By contrast – perhaps because of the dominance of the view that parents should normally work to support their children – charitable concerns about children began to focus on issues of neglect and ill treatment rather than cash deficiencies within families. Doctor Barnardo's, founded in 1869, together with denomination based children's societies, pioneered the development of institutional care for children. But perhaps more important in the long run was the role the National Society for the Prevention of Cruelty to Children (NSPCC) began to play in 1884 as a pioneer of interventions to prevent the ill-treatment of children. The NSPCC secured the passing of child protection legislation in 1889, 1904 and 1908 and played an important role in its enforcement

(Hendrick, 1994). It is important to note that, whilst legislation was important for this voluntary activity, there was very little public funding.

But there were other public policies which began to shape the services we now regard as the personal social services. Legislation was enacted to provide institutional facilities for the mentally ill and for the mentally handicapped. The main public response was to provide secure institutions (Jones, 1972). These hospitals were made the responsibility of local government.

Local authorities also had a range of community health care responsibilities. These came from 19th century public health legislation, which en-abled authorities to take preventative responsibilities to deal with infectious diseases and to provide hospitals for the mentally ill. Early 20th century legislation creating some community health services – community midwifery and health visiting in particular – added to the local services set up in the counties and county boroughs under the leadership of 'medical officers of health' (Lewis, 1986). Indeed, a flurry of legislation concerned with the conditions of Britain's children, in the first decade of the 20th century, provided two alternative approaches to replace or supplement the care offered by the Poor Law and by charities. The community health services were one such, working through health clinics and health visitors. The other alternative was the Boards of Education, which had secured powers to provide health care for children and to supply them with meals.

Until 1929 the Poor Law was administered by elected Boards of Guardians in individual parishes or groups of parishes, under the surveillance of the central government appointed Poor Law Board. The expenditure of Boards of Guardians were funded out of a local tax on property, the 'poor rate'. In the 1920s the decentralised arrangement for the funding of the poor law came under attack from Boards of Guardians in poor areas that faced heavy demands on their funds but had a low tax base (Gilbert, 1970; Branson, 1979).

Legislation in 1929 brought the Poor Law under the control of local government. After the 1929 Act Britain seemed to be travelling along a path followed by other countries, of constructing an integrated social care and social assistance system. But legislation in 1934, setting up a national body for the administration of social assistance for the unemployed, started a process of separating 'cash' and 'care'. Further legislation in 1940 and 1948 completed that process. Local authorities were left with the old 'workhouses' to run, as care homes for elderly and handicapped people whose families were unable to care for them.

To sum up, by 1945, Britain had begun to develop a system of local government run personal social services but most of the services involved were very rudimentary and still dominated by 'Poor Law principles'. Services were free but the rigorous family means tests of the Poor Law rationed access to them to the very poor (except where incarceration was deemed necessary for the protection of the community). The vast flowering of voluntary social care organisations and institutions during the later part of the 19th century was recognised by governments inasmuch as they provided them with a legislative framework within which they could carry out their activities. That recognition did not extend to public funding.

Housing

There were some important social housing ventures in the late 19th century. Philanthropists were encouraged to provide money, or to lend it at low rates of interest, for housing projects to improve the living conditions of the poor (Tarn, 1973; Burnett, 1985). But these ventures secured no support from the government. Public health legislation enabled local governments to clear slums but this activity was of minimal importance before 1914. What is also significant about this very early period is that the main self-help activity in the housing field had as its aim not the provision of co-operative forms of rented housing but the provision of loans to enable moderate in-come people to buy their own houses. The building societies, which remain the main source of funds for house buyers today, originated as mutual aid organisations taking in small savings and providing long-term loans for individual house buying (Boddy, 1980).

During the 1914-18 War rent control was introduced to try to curb inflation and appease unrest about escalating rents. By the end of the war there was evidence of a serious under-supply of houses. One of the first pieces of post-war legislation was a Housing Act that provided government subsidies to local authorities to build 'for the working classes'. This Act while not the first legislation to allow local authority house-building, was the first to subsidise it. It effectively initiated a programme of council house building that continued, albeit subject to regular modification as governments changed the subsidy arrangements, until the late 1970s.

The central subsidies reduced the cost of housing for tenants, but were often (particularly in the early period) insufficient to bring council housing within the reach of the very poor. By the 1930s some authorities began to experiment with 'differential rent schemes' which would enable some greater targeting of help to their poorest tenants.

What is clearly one of the historical puzzles of this period is that this subsidised house building did not result in a mixed social housing sector, comprising many private and voluntary sector owners as well as local government ones. There was a little subsidised house building by private builders but this was for sale to owner-occupiers (Bowley, 1945) and thus could not ultimately be classified as social housing. But the curious fact is that the voluntary associations which had been so prominent as pioneers of social housing did not significantly participate in the development of housing policy in this period. In 1939 there were only about 75 thousand dwelling units owned by housing associations.

Out-Patient Health Care

In the late 19th century low income people might obtain free or cheap medical services in one of four ways. They might go to the outpatient departments of voluntary hospitals set up by charitable foundations. They might obtain rudimentary medical services from the Poor Law. If they suffered from fevers or were mentally ill they might go to, or perhaps rather be sent to, hospitals set up by local authorities under the Public Health legislation designed to try to protect the public. Finally they might be able to get primary care services from doctors employed by the 'friendly societies' or trade unions, for which they paid subscriptions.

In 1911, very influenced by German developments, the Liberal government set up a social insurance scheme providing sick benefits and health care for wage earners. This scheme provided access to free primary health care for manual workers, but not for their dependants. In this way the British system reinforced an institutional distinction between primary (often described in Britain as general medical practice or just general practice) and secondary care (provided by practitioners working in hospitals but not necessarily requiring their patients to be admitted to a bed). It was given a strong institutional form by the establishment of the National Health Insurance panel system in 1911, which was further reinforced when the National Health Service was set up in 1948. Since 1948, except in medical emergencies (usually the consequence of accidents) British people have become accustomed to only being able to access the hospital system (for outpatient as well as inpatient treatment) via primary care practitioners.

Contributions under the 1911 Act were required from workers and their employers. These were collected by the government. But health benefits were provided through 'approved societies' chosen by the workers themselves. These societies were friendly societies, trade unions, industrial insurance companies or employers' provident associations. They were reimbursed by the government, drawing upon the National Insurance fund, for approved health care and sickness benefit expenditures.

Doctors were unwilling to be, as they had been under many of the previous voluntary schemes, the employees of the approved societies. They secured agreement that they would be paid 'capitation fees' for the patients they took on their 'panel' under the National Insurance scheme and therefore could operate as self-employed practitioners free to take on private work (note the resemblance here to the Berlin Agreement of 1913 described by Bönker and Wollmann).

After the 1911 Insurance Act those outside its protection – particularly the families of the employed – had to continue to seek help where they could (with the options outlined above). This situation continued until the establishment of the National Health Service in 1948.

The reason why the mixed economy provided through the insurance system did not survive the further extension of public health care in the 1940s will be explored more later. On the face of it, as Gilbert says, 'the network of collector salesmen had given the industrial insurance industry the power to force its way into' the health service (Gilbert, 1970, p.259). In fact there were substantial divisions between the different kinds of approved societies, and the various enquiries into ways of extending health care carried out in the 1920s and 1930s were given conflicting and often conservative evidence by these bodies. They did not seem able to articulate a clear case for the extension of their activities. The industrial societies were more interested in the private insurance they could sell on the back of their National Insurance duties than in the notion that they could have a bigger role in an enhanced system. As early as 1926 the Royal Commission on National Health Insurance concluded that the medical service should be in due course 'divorced' from the insurance system (HMSO, 1926, pp.65-6).

Comparative Assessment

The period 1850 to 1945 could have been broken down further between the largely *laissez-faire* period from 1850 to 1906 and the period after that date, during which significant social policy developments took place. In 1906 a government was elected with a large Liberal majority and support from the emergent Labour Party.

In the pre-1906 period government activity in the three social policy sectors was minimal. Social reform movements, very dominated by the middle class group who ran organisations like the Charity Organisation Society and the many housing and social service charities, were largely concerned to seek government sanction for their activities (legislation to enable them, for example, to 'rescue' children without being accused of kidnapping). There was however an extensive overlap between this group and others who, through bodies like the Fabian Society, were trying to secure more effective state action (Gilbert, 1966; Thane, 1982).

The social insurance idea made inroads into the health care system and it is relevant to note that the development both in the 1911 National Insurance Act and in legislation in the 1920s, of social insurance benefits for old, sick and unemployed people played their part in the demise of the Poor Law. What is relevant about that is the relatively centralised and weak form this development took – limited benefits paid by the state and not (except in the case of sickness benefit) involving any form of partnership with voluntary organisations or trade unions. In other words, other than local government, new participants in the social policy system were not emerging and little was being done to strengthen those already involved. The exceptions might seem to be in the field of health care, but what then is significant about the behaviour of the 'approved societies' is that they did little to court political popularity or to advance their claims as participants in the emerging 'welfare state'.

The local authorities developed one important new role, as the providers of social housing. The 1929 Act might seem to have given them an opportunity to move into a central role in both health care and social care as well. As far as health was concerned the key countervailing events lie outside the period with which this section is concerned. With regard to social care, the removal of most social assistance responsibilities in 1934 and 1940 fractured the nature of the policy package inherited from the Poor Law. The reasons for this cash/care split (in many ways peculiar to Britain) cannot be analysed in the space available here. Briefly, in the context of a weak social insurance system, issues of territorial justice and equity in taxation arrangements were regarded as of key importance. But perhaps the dominance of central government in this unitary state helps particularly to explain this outcome.

In sum, all three policy areas were, by 1945, ripe for the assertion of public sector dominance: health because the public/private compromise of 1911 had not worked very well; social housing because a strong local government system subsidised by central government had already been established; and social services because it was the two tiers of government jointly which had picked up the pieces of the collapsing Poor Law rather than the voluntary sector.

1945-79

Personal Social Services

Personal social services changes were made necessary by one of Labour's political commitments in 1945: to sweep away the last vestiges of the Poor Law. Whilst it saw this as principally a measure to reform social assistance, it had to deal with the fact that the Poor Law authorities had care responsibilities too. The key measures were two pieces of legislation: the Children Act and the National Assistance Act. Both were enacted in 1948. These set up separate local authority departments for children's and welfare services.

The new statutory departments were initially very small. Their resources and powers were limited, the continuation of voluntary activities was important for social welfare. As suggested in the discussion of the period before 1945, charitable organisations had become active in both childcare policy and in other areas of social welfare. With the new legislation of the 1940s it was possible for voluntary organisations to take on statutory functions as agents of the local authorities. The National Society for the Prevention of Cruelty to Children had its own network of inspectors who might carry out investigatory duties for local authorities. There were childrens' homes run by voluntary bodies, generally with religious connections, which could accept children placed 'in care' by Children Departments. Specialist voluntary organisations for blind or deaf people took on tasks for the new welfare departments. In some areas there were voluntary committees which organise services for elderly people. In practice voluntary organisations played only a small part in subsequent social services growth.

The evolution of services was slow. In the field of adult welfare there continued to be a high dependence upon voluntary organisations – providing services like meals in the home, day centres and sometimes supportive visiting (Means and Smith, 1994). But further legislation in 1962 gave local authorities the power to be direct providers of meals services and in 1968 they were given a 'general power to promote the welfare of the elderly'.

Payments for residential care for adults were subsidised through the use of a stringent means test. What this meant was that this form of care continued to be regarded – as under the Poor Law – as a last resort for poor people unable to make alternative arrangements for themselves (Townsend, 1962). Local authorities varied considerably on what they would do about charges for domiciliary services. Some supplied them free, some imposed limited standard charges whilst others used means tests to determine their charges.

In both children and welfare departments growth began to occur as wider activities were taken on in the 1960s. This involved an increase in the numbers of local authority staff providing direct services. The voluntary organisations did not wither, but there was no particular interest in using them as 'providers' of statutory services. It is difficult to get good figures for this period, but by 1979 only 8 per cent of local authority expenditure in England was going on payments to private and voluntary organisations.

In the 1970s childrens and adult welfare services were integrated in local authority social services departments. These established themselves as much bigger actors in the local government scene than their predecessor departments. A measure of this can be seen in their growth relative to other local government functions. In 1955 their total expenditure was only about 0.2 per cent of GNP. By 1987-8 personal social services expenditure had reached 0.9 per cent (Hills, 1990, pp.217-8).

There was another development across the later part of this period that did produce its own peculiar kind of mixed economy of care. A strong movement towards deinstitutionalisation occurred in relation to the care of neglected children, people with learning difficulties and people who were mentally ill. As far as children were concerned there was a great growth of fostering, with arrangements developing in which paid surrogate parents were hired by local authorities. In the case of the other two groups there was a development of small hostels and board and lodging arrangements so that people could live as far as possible 'in the community'. Whilst fostering was directly supported by money from the social services departments much of the support for the care of the adult groups came from social assistance funds (assisted by grants from either social services departments or health departments). Here then was the development of kinds of public/private partnerships in which care activities were undertaken by private households, small landlords and voluntary organisations with support from public funds.

Housing

The Labour government of 1945-51 substantially extended the subsidies to local authority housing departments. When the Conservatives won power in 1951 one of the central planks in their electoral manifesto was a promise to increase the rate of house building, both public and private. The period 1951-1964 was a boom period for house building. During this time two kinds of tenure began to dominate in Britain, owner-occupation and local authority tenancy. The decline in the privately rented sector was rapid, towards the later part of this period accelerated by slum clearance.

When they came to power in 1970 the Conservatives decided that public expenditure on local authority housing needed to be curbed. By that date the arrangements for the subsidy of council housing had become very complex, a legacy of the rolling forward of a succession of subsidy programmes for local authority house builders since 1919. They were all, however 'bricks and mortar' subsidies, towards the building of houses rather than support programmes for specific low income tenants. Nevertheless governments had, since the late 1960s, encouraged local authorities to devise schemes which concentrated housing support upon their poorer tenants (Malpass, 1990). The Conservatives' Housing Finance Act of 1972 set out to force local authorities to increase the rents for their houses bringing them closer to 'economic' levels. The Act determined that there should be a national means-tested rent rebate scheme, rationalising the variety of local schemes that had been set up over the previous decade, to offset the costs of the general rent rise for poorer tenants.

The period 1945 to 1979 thus saw continuation of the subsidy of public house building by both political parties. They differed on the balance they wanted to achieve between public sector and private sector building, and at the end of the period the Conservatives began to look for more direct ways of subsidising poor tenants than the general subsidisation of public house building. But both parties accepted the role of the local authorities as the primary providers of houses for people unable to buy houses for themselves. There was some slight interest at the very end of the period in the encouragement of an alternative provider, non-profit making housing associations, but as the statistics in table 15.1 show their contribution was minimal.

	Owner occupied	Housing Assoc.	Local authority	Private rented
1950	29.0	-	18.0	53.0
1961	42.3	-	25.8	31.9
1971	50.6	-	30.6	18.9
1981	56.6	2.2	30.3	10.9

Table 15.1 **Percentages of houses in various tenures in Great Britain 1950-81**
Source: Balchin, p.6 - using figures from the Department of the Environment Annual Report 1993

Out-Patient Health Care

The legislation creating a National Health Service (NHS) in 1948 brought hospitals under the direct control of Government appointed management committees, who would employ all staff including doctors. But primary care was treated rather differently.

The arrangements for general practitioner services involved their operation under the surveillance of local committees (Executive Councils), with strong practitioner representation. Doctors were remunerated by means of a capitation fee (based upon the numbers of patients they took on). Their right to buy and sell practices was ended. Doctor-dominated Medical Practice Committees were to control entry to new practices in order to deal with problems of maldistribution.

Hence the NHS started with two peculiar characteristics as far as primary care was concerned: the separation of its managerial arrangements from those for the hospital sector and a self employed status for general practitioners. There were related contractual arrangements for dentists and opticians, which will not be considered here.

Under the new NHS general practitioner (and hospital services) were provided free for everyone. The NHS was funded out of general taxation, though a small element of payment for the health service remained in the National Insurance contribution, creating a confusing illusion that this was what paid for the whole service. The notion of a totally free service did not last for long. Very soon Chancellors of the Exchequer, exploiting concern that demand for services was much greater than expected, secured first small payments for spectacles and dental treatment, and then prescription charges, as ways of raising revenue. Whilst the proportion of these costs recovered from patients rose steadily over this period no effort was made to extend cost-sharing in other ways.

Whilst general practitioners were allowed to take on private patients few did so. A survey in 1952 showed that 97.7 per cent of the population were registered as NHS patients (Mencher, 1967). It is important to bear in mind that a general practitioner can refer his or her NHS patient to private secondary care. Such growth as there has been of private medicine in Britain has been largely in the use of private consultants to get access hospital treatment (in private hospitals and also in the private beds of NHS hospitals). This is particularly likely to occur with treatments for which there is a waiting list. Private insurance companies have developed to support this phenomenon.

At the end of the 1960s governments explored ways to give greater unity to the structure of the health service. The Executive Councils were replaced by Family Practitioner Committees, bodies which perhaps could be said to be marginally more 'managerial', but the independent arrangements for general practice were not ended.

Before ending this section a comment is appropriate on a 'missing actor' – local government. One small part of the health service system went to local authorities in 1948 but was taken away in 1974 when the preventative community services were integrated with the hospital service. In 1948 local government made a bid for the NHS but the hostility of doctors to that option seems to have been crucial for its rejection (Pater, 1981; Webster, 1998).

Comparative Assessment

Webb and Wistow write of

> the surprisingly cohesive and widely accepted 'pure doctrine' of state welfare which underpinned the development of the post-war welfare state. The most effective and acceptable response to social problems was seen to involve comprehensive state social services, which were necessarily large bureaucracies, and which operated through paid employees – ideally with professional training and status (Webb and Wistow, 1982, pp.58-9).

Social services and social housing were largely delivered by the local authorities. While technically general practitioners had a self-employed status in many respects they were in practice also employees of the health service.

However the social insurance system and other key areas of public social policy often provided far from adequately for social needs. What emerged then was, however, not a public/private partnership to fill the gaps, but rather a range of private expedients. Many of these were private in the market sense rather than the voluntary sense – pensions, health insurance, owner-occupied housing. Others, particularly in the social care sphere, were private in a family sense – relatives filling gaps left by inadequate public services. There was a fear – explored in various reports about the role of the private sector (see the discussion in Webb and Wistow, 1982) – that deals between public agencies and private providers would result in the implicit substitution of private for public expenditure and the undermining of the independence of voluntary organisations. These fears were realised in the period after 1979.

Absent contender for participation were the trade unions and the churches. The former settled for a combination of industrial roles with (they hoped) a direct political influence upon the Labour Party rather than any part in the direct provision of other services. The latter were, by this time, a declining force in British society.

The local authorities were the key partners in two of the three policy areas, but as suggested above their involvement had been largely secured at the end of the inter-war period. They advanced rapidly as partners in housing developments at the end of the 1940s and they were well placed to take off as providers of social care services in the 1970s, but they failed to advance into health policy.

Since 1979

Personal Social Services

In the early years of the Thatcher governments the growth of local authority social services that had occurred in the 1970s continued, with local authorities protecting them to some extent from the general attack upon local government resources (Webb and Wistow, 1982; Hills, 1990). The personal social services were left almost untouched by legislative change until two major measures were enacted some ten years after Thatcher first came to power. One of these was the Children Act 1989, the other the Health Services and Community Care Act 1990. The latter initiated dramatic changes to the organisation of services and the public/private mix for the various adult care services, and particularly to the largest of the activities of local authority social services departments, the care of older people.

The antecedents of the 1990 Act were significant. The rapid increase in the numbers of the old, and particularly the very old was increasing the need for both residential and domiciliary care. With that rise came the use of a variety of private homes by those who could afford to pay (or whose relatives could afford).

The emergence of private care homes obviously reduced the burden upon statutory care providers. They made it easier for local authorities to maintain an adequate supply of residential places. Before 1980 the central social assistance authority was, in general, unwilling to help low-income people pay the fees for such homes. Then the rules were relaxed and local office managers were given considerable discretion to subsidise charges through means-tested benefit payments. The Conservative Secretary of State was placed in a dilemma between his commitment to the development of the private sector and his concern to keep income maintenance expenditure under control. In 1983, he imposed national limits upon expenditure. These were nevertheless much higher than those that had prevailed before 1980, when commercial home charges were rarely met. There followed a dramatic growth of private sector homes (see table 15.2) but a decline in the use of such homes by local authorities (since they could leave the social security authorities to foot the bill). That growth extended to nursing homes, doing very much what had hitherto been considered to be the work of the NHS and charging higher fees than care homes. A special high social assistance rate was allowed for these.

	Local authority	Private and voluntary with l.a. funding	Private	Voluntary	Total
1980	102.9	15.9	28.8	25.5	173.1
1983	103.6	11.9	42.1	26.5	184.1
1986	101.7	5.1	77.6	25.1	209.5

Table 15.2 Residents in various types of homes 1980, 1983 and 1986
Source: Hills, 1990, based upon DHSS statistics

A report on community care by the Audit Commission highlighted the 'perverse effects of social security policies' in these areas of private care. It pointed out that anyone entitled to means-tested benefit 'who choses to live in a residential home is entitled to allowances' up to the limit imposed by the benefit rules. Some of those people might be better, and/or more cheaply, cared for through a package of domiciliary services. Yet these could not be provided by the social assistance system.

The Audit Commission was very concerned about the extent to which this income maintenance subsidy of residential care distorted the pattern of care in the country as a whole. It noted the extent to which private homes were unevenly distributed geographically, commenting on their high incidence in the relatively prosperous parts of England. The consequences of this was, it said, that 'while central government attempts to achieve equitable distribution of public funds across the country, through the use of complex formulae within the NHS and local government, the effects can be largely offset by Supplementary Benefit payments for board and lodging' (Audit Commission, 1986, p.3).

After the Audit Commission report, the government commissioned a wider investigation by Sir Roy Griffiths (1988). Griffiths suggested that there should be a system under which local authority social services departments decided on social, not income, grounds that care was necessary and then had a responsibility to ensure that individuals obtained that care, either from the public or private sector. If individuals were unable to pay the care costs from the social insurance benefits or from other income, it would then be the responsibility of the local authority to provide a subsidy.

The government accepted these recommendations and embodied them in the 1990 Act. In doing so it also moved towards the partial privatisation of all existing local authority services in the area of community care. It aimed to ensure that the relative role of local authorities as the direct providers of care (both in residential homes and community services) would decline in favour of the private sector. Local authorities were to become the 'buyers' of packages of private care for low-income people, while their role, as suppliers, of such care declined. The local authorities were required to spend 75 per cent of the 'new' money granted to them as the social security system closed down its contribution to social care on the purchase of private or voluntary sector services.

The implementation of the 1990 Act, which mostly started after 1993, therefore forced local authority social services departments to support a more mixed economy of care. This pressure came from both the '75 per cent' rule and from the increased difficulties local authorities faced in sustaining and justifying public provision wherever private equivalents could be obtained more cheaply. It is debatable whether these private provisions were inherently more efficient, but lower wages levels and sometimes lower standards, certainly tended to make them cheaper. Whilst few local authorities privatised domiciliary care services very many found that it was expedient to sell residential homes. These sales were to a variety of owners – including voluntary organisations and companies formed by former local authority employees as well as ordinary for-profit companies.

	1993	1997
Local authority owned homes	77,596	58,651
Independent residential homes	19,270	111,444
Independent nursing homes	Nil	65,988
Total	96,866	236,083

Table 15.3 Elderly and handicapped people in residential care supported by local authorities in England by type of home
Note: 'independent' means 'voluntary and private'
Source: *Health and Personal Social Services Statistics 1997 edition (1998) Table C6, p. 59*

Table 15.3 charts the implementation of the 1990 Act showing the dramatic shift in local authority spending on residential care from funding places in their own homes to supporting people in private and voluntary homes. It also shows the emergence of a new category of local authority funded resident, persons in nursing homes who would hitherto have been in hospitals.

Social Housing

The Conservative reversal after 1979 of the consensus over social housing had three elements (a) the selling of council houses to their occupiers, (b) a much stronger attack upon general subsidy of social housing than that started by the previous Conservative government in the early 1970s and (c) efforts to find new social landlords to replace local authorities. The first of these was a central plank in their 1979 manifesto and was taken up through the 1980 Housing Act. The second involved a slow policy evolution. The third was more difficult to achieve and as a policy followed a tortuous path from the late 1980s to the present day.

In 1979 the Conservatives included a commitment in their election manifesto to provide a statutory 'right' for council tenants to buy the houses they were renting. The Housing Act of 1980 provides that right to buy – at market prices less a discount based on length of tenancy. Later legislation extended these provisions. A million and a half local authority tenants bought their homes during the 1980s (HMSO, 1992). It has been suggested that this measure did a great deal to enhance support for the Conservative Party amongst manual workers in the south of England. This is certainly a conclusion which the Labour party has drawn, abandoning its former opposition to the policy.

The sale of 'good' houses to better off tenants has enhanced social polarisation in housing (Forrest and Murie, 1988). The longstanding problem for cities of a gap between the 'good' estates and the 'bad' has been exacerbated. The measure reinforces the tendency for public sector housing to be housing for the poor. By 1986-87 almost two-thirds of local authority tenants were on means-tested benefits (figure from a Parliamentary answer quoted by Forrest and Murie, 1988, p.69).

The tendency for all who could buy to do so and for those left behind to be dependent on benefits was reinforced by central government changes to the way social housing was subsidised. The Conservatives cut subsidies to council house rents by requiring, with each successive settlement of the subsidy figure for local authorities, high rent increases. By the middle of the 1980s only about a quarter of all local authorities were still getting a general subsidy (Malpass, 1990, pp.147-8). In the 1990s further changes to the subsidy arrangements reinforced this development.

The Thatcher and Major governments also severely limited local authority building of new houses. In the late 1970s local authorities in the United Kingdom had built a little over 100,000 dwellings each year. In the 1980s and early 1990s the government made more money available to housing associations than to local government. In 1994 only 1680 public sector houses were completed. That figure (under 1 per cent of the total house completions) was dwarfed by the number of completions for housing associations (33,817 or 19 per cent of the total).

At last the housing associations seemed to be establishing themselves as alternative social landlords. However, even their growth was inhibited by the Conservatives' reluctance to spend money on social housing. Housing associations vary widely in size, scope and character. Some differ little in their characteristics from private companies, these have grown in size recently absorbing some smaller associations along the way. Others have distinct charitable aims and objects, and many are specifically local in their coverage. A small number are co-operatives.

Table 15.4, if compared with table 15.1, provides a statistical portrait of the implications of the measures taken by the Thatcher governments. The long growth of the local authority sector was at last ended, instead the sector began to shrink. The table shows the growth, albeit slow, of the housing association sector. Data on the two sectors which this account has not been concerned to look at – owner occupation and private renting – is included to illustrate the continuing growth of the former (fuelled by council house sales) and the static position of the latter.

	Owner occupied	Housing Assoc.	Local authority	Private rented
1987	62.7	2.6	25.1	9.6
1991	66.0	3.2	21.2	9.6
1995	67.1	4.0	19.5	9.7

Table 15.4 Percentages of houses in various tenures in Great Britain 1987-95
Source: Annual Abstract of Statistics 1998 Table 3.7, p. 53

Out-Patient Health Care

In the early 1980s the Conservatives did little to change the NHS. There were some further rearrangements to the management structure of the service, without implications for general practice. Then in the later 1980s demands began to emerge from the Conservative Right for bolder action against 'socialised medicine', reinforced by continuing concerns about rising costs. However, recognition of the NHS's continuing popularity with the electorate, restrained the government from following the outright privatisation ideas very far. Eventually the Government decided to further restructure the management of the service by moving towards a split between 'purchasers' and 'providers'. Legislation passed in 1990 allowed for the setting up of NHS Trusts. These are semi-autonomous bodies, ultimately answerable to the Secretary of State which are able to manage their own finances, appoint their own staff and plan a package of services which they 'sell' to the Health Authorities. The latter are required to act as purchasers of services on behalf of the patients in their area. They may make those purchases from the Trusts (that is individual hospitals or groups of hospitals) in their area and elsewhere, or even from private providers (though this is in practice rare).

In addition general medical practices were allowed to apply to become 'fund holders' able to make independent purchases from hospital providers for the needs of their own patients. A renegotiation of the general practitioner contract in 1990 also involved a much more directive stance by the government on the duties of primary care doctors, backed up by financial incentives for preventative work. Then in 1996 the separate organisations for the administration of general practitioner services were at last abolished. The general practitioners became direct contractors to the health authorities. Legislation in 1997 also allowed for the possibility of direct salaried employment of general practitioners.

In a way therefore the quasi-market reforms of the Conservatives in 1990 contributed to reducing the independence of general practitioners both by getting rid of the independent arrangements for the management of their services and by offering them the opportunity to tie themselves into the secondary care purchasing system. The new Labour government has taken that a stage further by moving to abolish purchase by fund-holders and replace it by the more collective participation of general practitioners in local purchasing activities through 'primary care groups'. General practitioners remain mostly self-employed but are now very tied into the organisational arrangements for the NHS.

Comparative Assessment

In analysing the period after 1979 some difficult distinctions need to be made between service cuts and forms of privatisation. The former affected all three sectors, but fell much more heavily on social housing than on the other two sectors. In social housing the fall in public investment and the sale of council houses to their occupiers was accompanied by a radical shift in the way social housing was subsidised, from what may be described as 'bricks and mortar' subsidies to the subsidy of low income people through the housing benefit system. That last development had a fundamental impact on the public/private divide since tenants of private market oriented landlords are also entitled to housing benefits. Britain is therefore moving towards a situation in which all landlords – local authority, housing association and private – have to make their rent setting decisions using market assumptions, leaving their low income tenants to seek benefit support.

Privatisation of social care provision emerged from what is widely regarded as a careless political decision affecting the use of the social assistance scheme. When subsequent rationalisation occurred, however, the advancement of a mixed economy of provision was strongly pushed by the government.

Health reform seemed to involve privatisation too. But in practice the absence of private health providers limited the impact of health privatisation, instead Britain experienced the quasi-market experiment of publicly owned 'trusts' competing for NHS business. This, however, had no bearing upon the privatisation of primary care. General practitioner services had always in some respects been contracted out. What was unusual about the implications of the 1990 legislation for them was that they were invited to become the purchasers of the quasi-marketised services of the hospitals. The aftermath of that development seems likely to be much greater incorporation of general practitioners into health planning at the local level.

The developments in housing and social care involved to a considerable extent an attack upon local authority provision. The housing legislation of the 1980s not only forced local authorities to sell council houses but also strictly limited their capital spending and regulated their rent setting powers. The 1990 community care changes forced authorities to consider bids from private providers. The Conservatives' public spending curbs as a whole had a very strong impact on local authority autonomy.

Conclusions

This account of British policy has shown that the three periods seem to have very different characteristics in respect of marketisation. The period 1850 to 1945 was one of low levels of state activity in the three policy sectors examined, and therefore a period of high levels of provision by private and charitable bodies. It should be added that in social services the restriction of access to limited public services was by way of means testing, associated with the Poor Law, for much of the period. This was also true of primary health care, except that after 1911 workers had access to social insurance financed health care. In the housing area the limiting factor was rather more low supply, and indeed means-testing was not used to limit access. However, once social housing emerged, it was almost exclusively supplied by public authorities and even in the area of social care there was very little government funding of the large voluntary sector.

In the period 1945-79 local authorities took over, and dramatically increased, the social care services originally developed under the Poor Law, the NHS made free primary health care universally available and the local authority 'council housing' sector was systematically enlarged. There was rationing through means tests for the more expensive local authority social care services (residential care). General housing subsidies to local authorities were used to keep down the cost of council houses, though towards the end of the period targeting support through means-tested rents became increasingly important. Primary health care was entirely free throughout the period, except that there were charges for prescriptions and for dental and optical services. What is particularly interesting about the second period is the strong stance – apparently supported across the main political parties – against the involvement of private service providers.

Then after 1979 marketisation was on the march. But its implications were very different for the three sectors. The personal social services remained rationed in much the same way, the dramatic change was the stimulus given to private provision by first the social security funding of social care between 1982 and the implementation of the 1990 Act and second the way the government demanded that the implementation of the 1990 Act should involve the development of a purchaser/provider system with many voluntary and private organisations amongst the providers.

Local housing authorities were squeezed by both the sale of council houses and the pressure from central government to raise rents. That squeezing forced the council house sector into becoming essentially the provider of welfare housing for the poor, a very high proportion of its tenants needing mean-tested housing benefits to enable them to pay their rents. Housing associations were encouraged as alternative providers, making some inroads into local authority domination. Also – in a sense – the sale of council houses to their tenants was a form of marketisation.

But what is interesting to note is that marketisation actually had very little impact upon primary health care (as opposed to hospital care). While the upward drift of prescription charges (and the other ancillary charges) continued, there were no efforts to impose other forms of cost sharing on patients. The general practitioners, on the other hand, moved increasingly into the main stream of state health policy.

The contrasts between Britain and Germany offered through these parallel case studies are perhaps surprising. In many respects Britain only really discovered marketisation after 1979. Then, whilst that led to dramatic changes to housing policy its impact upon always rather residual social care provision was quite modest, whilst the treatment of primary health care went in certain respects against the trend.

References

Audit Commission. (1986), *Making a Reality of Community Care*, HMSO, London.
Balchin, P. (1995), *Housing Policy*, Routledge, London.
Bowley, M. (1945), *Housing and the State*, Allen and Unwin, London.
Burnett, J. (1985), *A Social History of Housing 1815-1985*, David and Charles, Newton Abbott.
Department of Health (1998), *Health and Personal Social Services Statistics 1997*, HMSO, London.
Forrest, R. and Murie, A. (1991), *Selling the Welfare State*, Routledge, London.
Gilbert, B. B. (1966), *The Evolution of National Insurance in Great Britain*, Michael Joseph, London.
Gilbert, B.B. (1970), *British Social Policy 1914-39*, Batsford, London.
Griffiths Report (1988), *Community Care: Agenda for Action*, HMSO, London.
Hendrick, H. (1994), *Child Welfare: England 1872-1989*, Routledge, London.
Hills, J. (ed.) (1990), *The State of Welfare*, Oxford University Press, Oxford.
HMSO (1926), *Report of the Royal Commission on National Health Insurance*, HMSO, London.
HMSO (1992), *Social Trends 22*, HMSO, London.

HMSO (1998), *Annual Abstract of Statistics*, HMSO, London.
Holmans, A. (1987), *Housing Policy in Britain: A History*, Croom Helm, Beckenham.
Jones, K. (1972), *A History of the Mental Health Services*, Routledge, London.
Lewis, J. (1986), *What Price Community Medicine?*, Wheatsheaf, Brighton.
Malpass, P. (1990), *Reshaping Housing Policy*, Routledge, London.
Means, R. and Smith, R. (1985), *The Development of Welfare services for elderly people*, Croom Helm, Beckenham.
Mencher, S. (1967), *Private Practice in Britain*, Occasional papers in Social Administration 24, Bell, London.
Pater, J. E. (1981), *The Making of the National Health Service*, Kings Fund, London.
Tarn, J. N. (1973), *Five Per Cent Philanthropy*, Cambridge University Press, Cambridge.
Thane, P. (1982), *The Foundations of the Welfare State*, Longman, Harlow.
Townsend, P. (1962), *The Last Refuge*, Routledge and Kegan Paul, London.
Webb, A. and Wistow, G. (1982), *Whither State Welfare*, RIPA, London.
Webster, C. (1998), *The National Health Service: A Political History*, Oxford University Press, Oxford.

16 The Rise and Fall of a Social Service Regime: Marketisation of German Social Services in Historical Perspective

FRANK BÖNKER AND HELLMUT WOLLMANN

Introduction

In Germany, as in other OECD countries, social services are currently undergoing massive changes. In this paper, we aim to put these changes into a broader, comparative-historical perspective. We do so by elaborating upon two themes. First, we ask whether there is such a thing as a particular social service regime that has traditionally characterised the provision of social services in Germany.[1] To deal with this issue, the paper features a comparative analysis of three different types of social services – personal social services, health care and social housing. What emerges from this analysis is that such a regime did in fact exist. In spite of all cross-policy differences, the three fields under analysis have traditionally shared important features. In particular, they have been characterised by a peculiar 'mixed economy' combining state responsibility and involvement with the incorporation of private actors and a large amount of private provision. These institutional arrangements have set Germany apart from most other OECD countries.

We combine this comparison of different fields of social services with a comparison over time, that is, we look for continuities and discontinuities in the three areas. Our analysis shows that the institutional arrangements that have characterised social service provision until recently date back to the second half of the 19th century and took their basic shape in the Weimar Republic. Unlike in other countries, most notably the UK, the end of the

Second World War did not lead to a clear break with pre-war social policy. Nor did the post-war expansion of the welfare state or the 1969 and 1982 changes in government result in fundamental changes in underlying institutional arrangements. As for social services, the German welfare state has been a frozen one, until recently characterised by a high degree of institutional stability and, to use a fashionable term, path dependence. It is against this background of stability that the ongoing changes must be discussed. We show that the current move towards marketisation denotes a far-reaching departure from the traditional institutional arrangements. Yet, we also argue that there is an important element of continuity, so that changes can alternatively be interpreted as a (mere) 'modernisation' of traditional institutions.

The chapter proceeds in three steps. The first part deals with the formative period between the late 19th century and the 1930s in which the regime that governed social service provision until the late 1980s emerged. The second part focuses on the restoration of this regime after 1945 and its remarkable stability and persistence until the 1990s. Finally, the third part of the chapter covers the current changes in social services and examines to what extent these changes amount to a break with the past. The three parts share a comparative design. While emphasising common trends and patterns, they also pay attention to the differences between personal social services, health care and social housing.

The Rise of a Social Service Regime: German Social Services From the 19th Century to the 1930s

Whereas the foundations of German social insurance were laid in the 1880s with the introduction of health, accident and pension insurance, the institutional arrangements that have traditionally governed social services in the Federal Republic basically date back to the Weimar Republic. It was during this period that the institutions as we know them today took shape. In all three fields of social services under analysis the rise of the welfare state was associated not with the replacement, but an incorporation of the private associations that had sprung up since the mid-19th century. Instead of simply being substituted by state institutions and services, these associations and associational forms became part of a rather complex 'mixed economy' that combined state responsibility for social services with limits to direct state provision, just as the Bismarckian model of social insurance combined a high level of transfers with weak redistribution. The evolving regime reflected a historical compromise between the different social actors. It accommodated the aspirations of the labour movement to the reservations of the upper classes, state claims to the autonomy of the churches and the professions and the interests of the federal government to the interests of the other tiers of government. The forging and the relative stability of this compromise were encouraged by religious heterogeneity, as well as by institutional features such as federalism and the predominance of coalition governments.

Personal Social Services

Today's personal social services basically stem from two sources – municipal poor relief and private charitable activities. In the 19th century, public responsibility for the poor and needy rested with the municipalities. In Prussia, this traditional responsibility was codified by the 1794 Common Law (*Allgemeines Landrecht*), the 1808 Municipal Charter (*Städteordnung*) and the 1842 Law on Poor Relief (*Gesetz über die Armenpflege*). As in other German states, prevailing legal provisions largely confined themselves to putting municipalities in charge of poor relief, but hardly regulated its contents and design. New federal legislation after the formation of the German Reich in 1871 basically confirmed this situation. Until the First World War, both federal government and the states essentially refrained from regulating and funding personal social services.

Initially, municipal poor relief largely relied on workhouses. In the course of the second half of the 19th century, this traditional system began to evolve gradually into a more differentiated system with specialised services for different groups (Sachße, 1996, pp.150-9). The introduction of a social insurance system in the 1880s improved the material situation of the working class and increasingly left the municipalities with the non-working poor and service issues. At the same time, a strong movement of social reform, concerned with social disintegration and driven by the idea of bourgeois social responsibility, fought for the expansion and professionalisation of social services (vom Bruch, 1985). New forms of social services for children, young people, families, single parents, the unemployed and the like were established. These activities were still limited in scope and highly paternalistic. Until 1919, recipients of public assistance payments were still deprived of their voting rights.

Closely intertwined with these changes was the rise of private social welfare. The social problems associated with the rapid industrialisation and urbanisation also led to a mushrooming of private charitable activities (Sachße, 1996; Backhaus-Maul and Olk, 1994, pp.101-5). Besides municipal poor-relief, a dense net of private – confessional and non-confessional – associations emerged. Initially, these activities were highly decentralised and uncoordinated. Parallel to the ongoing changes in municipal poor relief, however, a process of reorganisation began. The confessional associations formed peak associations in 1848 (*Innere Mission*) and 1897 (*Caritas*); other charitable associations began to work together in a host of national reform associations, such as the German Association for Poor Relief and Charity (*Deutscher Verein für Armenpflege und Wohltätigkeit*). At the local level, first attempts at co-ordinating public and private welfare were undertaken. At the turn of the century most bigger German cities saw the creation of Central Charitable Agencies (*Centralen für private Fürsorge*) in charge of providing information about the available local social services.

During the First World War, the Government of the Reich began to intervene in the provision of social services (Sachße, 1996, pp.159-62). New forms of assistance for soldiers and their dependents were introduced, activities of private charities were put under state supervision and local governments started the systematic subsidisation of charities. The move to democracy in 1918 brought a further increase in state involvement. Confronted with mounting social problems and huge expectations, the Government of the Reich and the States substantially extended their role in the regulation and financing of personal social services. These changes found their legal expression in the adoption of national laws on social assistance and youth welfare in the mid-1920s which, for the first time, subjected social assistance and personal social services to a uniform regulatory framework.

The new interventionism did not lead to a 'socialisation' of personal social services, as advocated by many Social Democrats. While public social services were expanded in many municipalities, the mixed public-private system that had emerged in the second half of the 19th century essentially survived, although in a transformed variant. Private associations continued to provide a major share of personal social services. However, the composition of these private associations changed, with local bourgeois philanthropy being increasingly replaced with centralised and cartelised welfare associations (Backhaus-Maul and Olk, 1994, pp.102-5; Kaiser,

1995; Sachße, 1996, pp. 166-9). This rise of the welfare associations as key providers of social services had already begun before the First World War with the creation of the two confessional associations (*Innere Mission*, *Caritas*). It accelerated with the setting up of a number of other welfare associations between 1917 and 1924. In order not to leave the field to others, even the Social Democrats, though still believing in public provision, founded their own welfare association (*Arbeiterwohlfahrt*). The new social service legislation of the 1920s increasingly recognised the role of the welfare associations and what was now called 'independent welfare'.

This transformation of private welfare had different sources. War, inflation and political change had severely undermined the very basis of the old-style philanthropy. In contrast, the centralised organisation of the welfare associations corresponded much better with the new political environment and the 'politicisation' and 'nationalisation' of politics after the First World War. Moreover, the welfare associations had powerful allies. The leading confessional associations were not only backed by 'their' churches, but could also rely on support by conservatives and liberals who saw them as bulwark against left-wing attempts at 'socialising' services. Finally, they benefited from institutional conflicts between the different tiers of government, as the newly created Reich Ministry of Labour, dominated by the Catholic *Zentrum* party, regarded the welfare associations as a natural ally against the States and the municipalities.

Social Housing

Part of the 'social question' of the 19th century was the 'housing question'. Rapid urbanisation went hand in hand with a great housing shortage and disastrous housing conditions. As with personal social services, it was the municipalities and private associations which first reacted to these problems (Wollmann, 1983). Private initiatives took two forms: limited-dividend housing corporations established by reform-minded bourgeois groups and housing co-operatives formed by workers. While the quantitative impact of these activities remained negligible until 1918, they nevertheless helped to develop instruments of housing policy which were later used on a larger scale. Parallel to the limited-dividend housing corporations and housing co-operatives, some municipalities started to engage in housing policy, partly by making building plots or low-interest grants available, partly by providing municipal housing. In contrast to these initiatives, the Reich

Government and the States practically refrained from dealing with housing policy issues and confined their legislation to measures against epidemic and fire hazards well into the First World War. In Prussia, for example, a Housing Act was not adopted until the spring of 1918 – almost 20 years after deliberations had begun (Niethammer, 1979).

The First World War and the move to democracy resulted in increased state intervention into the housing sector (Frerich and Frey, 1993, pp. 235-41; Drupp, 1987; Ruck, 1987; Wollmann, 1985, pp.134-36). After the 1918 revolution, a socialisation of housing ownership and construction was briefly considered, but soon dismissed. Instead, housing policy concentrated on rent controls and the public subsidisation of private investments. In contrast to the minimal public involvement before the War, roughly 75 per cent of all housing units erected between 1924 and 1938 were publicly subsidised. Subsidies were largely financed by a special tax levied on house owners (*Hauszinssteuer*). As the states and municipalities preferred to subsidise non-profit organisations, subsidisation was accompanied by the expansion of co-operatives and limited-dividend housing corporations, partly in municipal ownership. The institution of social housing through limited-dividend housing corporations (*Wohnungsgemeinnützigkeit*) was codified by law between 1930 and 1940. Limited-dividend housing corporations were granted substantive tax-exemptions in exchange for the commitment to provide rental housing for low-income households on fixed conditions.

Health Care

Along with the 'social question', health care also became an issue (Frevert, 1984). Again, responses took different forms. As part of the transformation of their traditional poor-relief responsibilities, local governments began to build up a municipal health service in charge of controlling sanitary conditions and the health of schoolchildren as well as of offering medical advice to mothers. In addition, municipalities ran hospitals. Initially mainly meant for the poor, these hospitals became increasingly available for all citizens. Parallel to these developments, private activities flourished. On the one hand, churches and religious orders resumed their traditional role in health care. Having lost most of their hospitals after the French Revolution, they again established a number of confessional hospitals. On the other hand, health insurance funds were founded by unions, individual employers and professional associations in order to cover the costs of medical treatment.

In the case of health care, central government intervened relatively early. As early as in the mid-19th century, most German states authorised local authorities to introduce their own health insurance funds and to force local employers to establish funds. As part of the Bismarckian social insurance legislation, health insurance was made obligatory for the bulk of workers in 1883. The new system built strongly upon the existing structures in that both a highly fragmented system of funds and the funds' self-government arrangements were retained. Moreover, the new law did not affect the relations between the funds on the one hand and physicians and hospitals on the other. Until the end of the Weimar Republic, the structures of provision did not take the shape that characterised health care in the post-1945 Federal Republic.

At the outset, the health insurance funds enjoyed a rather strong position. They were officially put in charge of guaranteeing medical care and were allowed to choose particular physicians and hospitals for their members. In addition, they could also run their own facilities. All this gave them a strong bargaining position vis-à-vis physicians and hospitals. It goes without saying that physicians strongly opposed this system. In their struggle against it, they could rely on the support of conservative elites who were eager to restrict the position of the health insurance funds because of the strong role of the labour movement in the self-governing funds. Against this background, the years from 1883 to 1935 saw the adoption of a number of measures that weakened the position of the health insurance funds and tipped the balance in favour of the physicians (Alber, 1992, pp.46-55). The 1913 Berlin Agreement, enshrined in law in 1923, ruled out exclusive contracts between the health insurance funds and individual physicians and reduced the health insurance funds' leverage over the admittance of physicians. In the early 1930s, measures by both the Brüning and the Hitler governments led to a further strengthening of the physicians' position. In particular, physicians were granted the exclusive right to offer out-patient health care and, thus, no longer had to compete with hospitals and health centres run by the health insurance funds. At the same time, the corporatist elements were strengthened by the setting up of quasi-public representative organisations of the physicians (*Kassenärztliche Vereinigungen*). Enjoying an organisational monopoly, these organisations became responsible for negotiating services, fees and the admittance of physicians with the funds.

With the reforms of the early 1930s, a health care system came into being in which medical treatment was provided by self-employed physicians, municipal or confessional hospitals, financed by self-governing health insurance funds and regulated both by the state and by negotiations between the funds and the physicians. Besides this system, a small, subsidiary municipal health service continued to exist.

Comparative Assessment

In all three fields, the institutionalisation of service arrangements followed a similar pattern and took the form of an incorporation of what had initially been private, independent associations. This applied to welfare associations and limited-dividend housing corporations as well as to health insurance funds and physicians. The incorporation that took place had two sides: On the one hand, the state refrained from a pure public provision of services and delegated responsibility to at least partly autonomous associations. On the other hand, these associations lost their earlier independence and autonomy. By gaining quasi-public status, they also became dependent upon state money and subject to state regulation. What emerged were thus 'mixed' systems in which public and private elements not only coexisted, but were densely interwoven and interlocked.

While these commonalities indicated the existence of a single, overarching social service regime, institutional arrangement differed in detail. This is clearly shown by a closer look at the three main dimensions of public services – regulation, financing, provision:

Regulation: In the case of personal social services and health care, state regulation was supplemented by strong 'corporatist' elements. The welfare associations were officially enmeshed in decision-making structures at the local, State and Reich level. In the case of health care, a form of self-regulation existed with the health insurance funds and the physicians being authorised to decide important issues themselves. From a comparative perspective, the role of housing associations was clearly the weakest. Contrary to the other organisations, they had no formal say in regulation.

Financing: The financing of health care testified to its special position. The health insurance funds had their own, independent budgets and were financed by earmarked contributions. In contrast, personal social services – public as well as subsidised private ones – were funded from general tax revenues (and the far from negligible own funds of the welfare associations). In the case of housing, the assignment of revenues from the tax on houseowners implied a weak form of earmarking.

Provision: Public provision of services was most limited in the case of health care. Out-patient health care was primarily – and, eventually, exclusively – provided by self-employed physicians. In contrast, municipalities and welfare associations ran the bulk of hospitals. As for personal social services and social housing, non-profit organisations dominated the scene and were supplemented either by the municipalities or, in the case of social housing, public housing corporations.

These differences in the extent and form of incorporation were closely related to differences in the strength of providers. Self-government in the health sector reflected the strong position of physicians and health insurance funds. The former represented a well-organised and politically influential profession; the latter were already widespread before the introduction of obligatory health insurance and could claim to speak on behalf of the insured. As has been shown, welfare associations were likewise highly organised and able to capitalise on their ties with the churches. Moreover, the private provision of personal social services could be justified by confessional and ideological diversity. In contrast, the position of the housing associations was weaker. They were much smaller in number before 1918 and could less easily invoke professional or ideological arguments to claim a role in regulation and decision-making.

The Persistence of a Regime: German Social Services from 1945 to 1990

The new social service regime as it evolved during the Weimar years was transformed under the Nazi regime. While the institutions of social insurance remained largely unchallenged between 1933 and 1945, social services were subject to important changes (Frerich and Frey 1993, pp. 85-170; Sachße and Tennstedt, 1992; Hammerschmidt, 1998). On the one hand, the complex system that had emerged was brought under strict party control. Organisations affiliated with the new regime's opponents were dissolved and the autonomy of the health insurance funds and the surviving confessional welfare associations curtailed. A central party organisation, the National Socialist People's Welfare (*Nationalsozialistische Volkswohlfahrt, NSV*), took over key functions from the municipalities and welfare associations and became the main player in the field. Parallel to these organisational changes, social services became increasingly governed by NS ideology.

In Germany, like in other countries, the breakdown of the Nazi regime and the end of World War II stirred a broad debate about social policy reform. However, the traditional social policy arrangements were basically restored. All attempts at replacing the Bismarckian social insurance system with a Beveridge-type system, as advocated by the political left and parts of the allied powers, failed (Abelshauser, 1996; Hockerts, 1980; Ritter, 1991, pp. 156-9). Germany retained a dual system combining a status-oriented social insurance system with a residual means-tested social assistance run by local governments. As for social services, the Weimar arrangements with their characteristic 'mixed economy' were likewise reintroduced. The private provision of a large share of public services continued; welfare associations, limited-dividend housing corporations as well as health insurance funds and physicians retained their strong positions. From an international perspective, the Federal Republic continued to be characterised by corporatist structures in personal social services and health care and a high share of 'third sector' activities in social services (Schmid, 1996; Zimmer, 1998).

The post-war restoration was pushed through by a conservative political majority. In their struggle against more far-reaching reforms, the adherents of the status quo ante benefited from the fact that the twelve years of Nazi rule had discredited 'statist' solutions. The developments in the GDR provided further material to warn against a 'socialisation' of social services. Finally, reforms smacked of foreign interference and were particularly unpopular in the field of social policy where many Germans were used to seeing their country as a frontrunner and international model.

Once restored, the new-old institutions proved to be remarkably stable and resilient. Neither the reform debates in the late 1950s and early 1960s nor the 1969 and 1982 changes in government resulted in major institutional changes. The secular expansion of public services and the policy changes that did occur left the basic institutional architecture intact. Partly responsible were the well-known obstacles to reform that are built into the political system of the Federal Republic, including federalism and coalition governments (Katzenstein, 1987; Schmidt, 1996). Moreover, the prevailing arrangements of service provision put a premium on institutional stability by giving rise to highly organised provider interests and dense and stable policy networks.

Personal Social Services

Post-war reform of personal social services took place in two steps: The 1953 amendments to the provisions on social assistance and youth welfare basically confined themselves to removing NS elements from the law. In 1961, new laws were adopted. While the Act on Youth Welfare was but a slightly modified version of the original 1922 law, the new Federal Social Assistance Act brought a significant modernisation of social assistance in that it established an explicit legal entitlement to social assistance. It also sought to rid social assistance of its poor law connotations and called for a reorganisation of the whole system of social assistance benefits. At the same time, both acts corroborated the privileged role of the welfare associations as had emerged in the Weimar years, by giving them clear priority in service provision and by codifying their role in policy formulation. Challenged by municipalities and Social Democrats, these provisions were further confirmed by the Constitutional Court in a seminal ruling in 1967 (Backhaus-Maul and Olk, 1994, pp.105-8).

During the heydays of welfare state expansion in the late 1960s and early 1970s (which coincided with the coming to power of the Social Democrats in 1969), the position of the welfare associations was weakened (Bönker and Wollmann, 1996, pp.447-50). Local governments managed to increase their leverage over social services by extending their share and by means of standard-setting and social planning. At the same time, however, welfare associations retained their legal privileges and remained by far the single most important service provider. While their share in overall personal social services declined, absolute staff and service numbers increased in the course of the general expansion of social services. With the social service reforms of the late 1960s and early 1970s coming to a halt, the position of the welfare associations even stabilised. Confronted with massive fiscal stress and growing discontent with service quality, social policy 'rediscovered' the alleged virtues of 'subsidiarity'. In contrast to the early 1970s, many municipalities now sought, where possible, to delegate social services to the welfare associations. Moreover, the new Christian Democrat - Liberal coalition government which took over in 1982 stressed its commitment to 'subsidiarity'. The continuing predominance of the welfare associations is highlighted by the very fact that estimates for the early 1990s still put their average share in personal social services at about two-thirds.

Social Housing

Post-war housing policy largely relied on concepts and instruments already applied in the Weimar period (Frerich and Frey 1996, pp.128-36, 365-94; Wollmann, 1985, pp.135-52; Jaedicke and Wollmann, 1991). Confronted with an unprecedented housing shortage at the end of the Second World War, Christian Democrats and Social Democrats initially agreed upon the need for an active housing policy. Again, the idea of state or municipal ownership in housing or direct state involvement in home construction was dismissed. Instead, housing policy continued to rely on a combination of rent controls and subsidies, partly to house owners, partly in exchange for the provision of regulated low-rent housing. Limited-dividend housing corporations retained the tax privileges introduced in the 1930s. Departing from the Weimar practice, however, the 1950 Federal Housing Act made subsidies available to all, even commercial, investors. Nevertheless, limited-dividend corporations remained the main provider of low-income housing (Frerich and Frey, 1996, p.376-7). Between 1949 and 1978, they built more than four million dwellings, more than a quarter of all new housing. In the 1950s and 1960s, their share in new rental housing was even higher and reached 40 per cent. At the end of 1986, limited-dividend corporations still owned about 3.4 million housing units.

With the end of reconstruction, the consensus on housing policy showed first signs of erosion. Christian Democrats began to call for a retreat of the state. Initially, however, controversies largely focused on rent control, security of tenure and the privatisation of dwellings. In contrast, the need for and the instruments of social housing were less controversial. The subsidisation of limited-dividend housing corporations continued to play an important role irrespective of the parties in government, yet gradually lost importance with the general shift from the provision of low-income rental housing. Housing policy began to put more emphasis on promoting owner-occupied housing by a number of tax relief measures. At the same time, direct support of low-income tenants by means of the new housing allowance (*Wohngeld*), originally introduced in 1965, gained importance.

Health Care

Two laws in the early 1950s brought about the restoration of the health system that had – although but briefly – already existed in the early 1930s (Alber, 1992, pp.55-57; Hockerts, 1980, pp.146-50). In 1951, the autonomy of the health insurance funds was re-established along with the traditional self-government. In line with old age and unemployment insurance, however, the composition of contributions and boards changed. Employers now had to pay half of the health insurance contribution and were granted half of the seats on the boards of the health insurance funds. In 1955, physicians officially retained their monopoly in the provision of out-patient health care. At the same time, the official representation of physicians and the institutional framework for bargaining between the health insurance funds and the physicians was restored.

Health care has proved difficult to reform ever since (Rosewitz and Webber, 1990; Bandelow, 1998, pp.177-97). In the 1960s, still under the Christian Democrat-led government, early reform initiatives which aimed at increasing co-payments by the insured and at weakening the position of physicians failed due to the fierce resistance of physicians and rifts within the government. The coming to power of the Social Democrats in 1969 brought an expansion in benefits, but left the basic institutional structures of out-patient health care unaltered. In 1972, however, the financing of hospitals was placed on a new basis. The federal government and the Länder took over the capital costs of hospitals which had so far been covered by local authorities or included in the treatment charges (*Pflegesätze*) to be reimbursed by the health insurance funds.

Ever since the mid-1970s, health policy became essentially characterised by desperate attempts at containing the 'cost explosion' and the rise in health care contributions. As in the boom years, however, no fundamental institutional reforms were undertaken. From the 1977 Cost Containment Law to the 1988 Health Reform Law, the adopted measures combined cuts in benefits and increases in co-payments with ceilings on spending growth and a strengthening of the 'corporatist' elements (Döhler and Manow-Borgwardt, 1992). The change in government in 1982 had no major impact on health care reform either. While the programmes of Social Democrats and Christian Democrats somewhat differed, the dense policy network associated with self-government and the enduring participation of the Free Democrats, with their affinity to the interest of physicians and the pharmaceutical industry, guaranteed a high degree of structural continuity (Döhler, 1991).

Comparative Assessment

While all three fields of social services were thus characterised by a restoration of the institutional structures that had emerged during the Weimar Republic, as well as by the resilience of those restored structures, the particular patterns of development showed some differences. As shown by the opposition against the subsidiarity clauses in the Federal Social Assistance and Federal Youth Welfare Acts, the return to Weimar was most controversial in the field of personal social services. In contrast, restoration of the old institutional arrangements governing health care and, even more, social housing were less contested. In the course of these events, this changed. Once the least controversial, housing policy gradually became a field of conflict. At the same time, the personal social services and the health care regime proved to be remarkably stable and survived the expansion of the welfare state as well as the 1969 and 1982 changes in government.

Again, these different patterns reflected differences in actor constellations. In personal social services and health care, the involvement of more (and more powerful) actors and the existing corporatist structures of interest mediation resulted in dense and stable policy networks frustrating unilateral reform moves. Moreover, a positive-sum game prevailed in that the secular expansion of services for a long time allowed the accommodation of conflicting interests. Social housing differed on both counts. The incorporation of limited-dividend housing corporations was substantially weaker, and they faced strong 'outside' opposition by commercial housing corporations. Moreover, with increasing economic prosperity and the overcoming of the post-war housing problem, the very rationale for social housing became increasingly less obvious.

The Move Towards Marketisation: Social Services in the 1990s

The 1990s have brought far-reaching changes in the provision of social services. The three fields under analysis have seen major reforms which will transform the German welfare state as we know it. In line with the developments in other OECD countries, a large part of these multifaceted changes can be subsumed under the heading of marketisation.

Personal Social Services

Changes have been particularly drastic in the case of personal social services (Bönker and Wollmann, 1996, pp.452-6). Here, a greater pluralism and more competition in service provision have gone hand in hand with a partial expansion of the state's role in financing services. While social assistance and the existing personal social services have suffered from fiscal consolidation, two major reform initiatives have increased the state's role. In 1992, Parliament established a legal entitlement to a kindergarten place for every child aged three to six years. As a consequence, more than 300,000 new kindergarten places have been created since 1992. Even more important, however, was the passaging of the law on care insurance in May 1994 (Götting *et al.*, 1994). This law introduced a fifth 'pillar' of social security which has provided for compulsory insurance against the risk of requiring long-term care and has fuelled the booming market for care for the frail and elderly. Both reforms aimed at closing the notorious German gap in personal social services (See Alber, 1995, Bönker and Wollmann, 1998, pp.2-5; Häußermann and Siebel, 1995).

Since the mid-1980s, the welfare associations have increasingly lost their virtual monopoly as non-state providers of personal social services (Backhaus-Maul and Olk, 1994, pp.111-130). On the one hand, rival providers have flourished. In spite of the traditional privileges of the welfare associations, both self-help groups and commercial providers have gained ground. Commercial providers have been particularly successful in the growing market for ambulatory care, where barriers to entry are relatively low. In larger cities, commercial providers now hold about 50 per cent of that market segment. Parallel to this marketisation 'from below', a couple of legal reforms have gradually levelled the playing field. The official recognition of self-help groups as service providers in the 1990 Children and Youth Assistance Act has rendered local government support of self-help groups easier and has made self-help groups less dependent on co-operation with the welfare associations. However, the main engine of change has been the law on care insurance. It no longer grants any privilege or priority to the welfare associations, explicitly puts welfare associations and commercial providers on an equal footing and imposes major organisational reforms upon the welfare associations.

A final impetus for the marketisation of personal social services has stemmed from the far-reaching administrative reforms upon which German local governments have begun to embark (Reichard, 1997; Wollmann,

1996). In line with international developments, the envisaged reforms provide for new forms of public management. Within local government, the traditional bureaucratic and cameral model is replaced with performance-oriented contracts between the administrative centre and the different administrative departments. The same applies to the relations between local government and the welfare associations which are likewise becoming governed by new forms of contracts (Hartmann, 1997; Manderscheid, 1997). Again, these changes have contributed to more plural structures of provision and a greater commercialisation of the welfare associations (for some caveats, see Heinze and Strünck, 1998).

All these changes would not have been possible without a preceding erosion of the traditionally strong position of the welfare associations within local and national policy networks. A number of developments have conspired in weakening this position. For a start, the milieus in which the welfare associations have historically been embedded have suffered from the ongoing secularization. Not only has the shrinking role of the churches reduced the political clout of the welfare associations. They have also faced increasing problems in attracting volunteers, donations and even confessionally committed staff. With the erosion of these traditional assets of the welfare associations, however, their differentia specifica have become unclear.[2] At the same time, the welfare associations have increasingly come under fire for their bureaucratisation and their vast inefficiencies (Seibel, 1992).

Social Housing

The gradual retreat of the state from subsidising the construction of low-rent housing accelerated in the course of the 1980s (Jaedicke and Wollmann, 1991; Frerich and Frey, 1996, pp.380-94). What has traditionally been the chief strategy of housing policy became further discredited, as construction costs rose to prohibitive levels and as the access of the truly needy to the existing social housing was increasingly blocked by tenants whose income had, in the meantime, risen above the eligibility ceiling (*Fehlbeleger*). Moreover, the reputation of the limited-dividend housing corporations, the traditional providers of low-rent housing, suffered a heavy blow in 1982 when a scandal about financially corrupt top managers of the Neue Heimat mammoth, a trade-union owned limited-dividend housing corporation, hit the headlines.

As a consequence, public subsidisation of low-income rental housing has been gradually phased out since the mid-1980s. The 'special market' for social housing will be swiftly decimated within the next ten years. With little new accommodation for renting and the 'old' low-rent commitments of the investors gradually expiring, the number of low-income tenancies fell from 4.2 million in 1975 to 2.4 million in 1995 and is expected to dwindle further to a mere 0.8 million in 2005. The retreat from the traditional strategy of housing policy was eventually accompanied by the abolition of the institution of tax-exempt limited-dividend housing corporations in 1990 (Jenkis, 1994). At that time, the Christian Democrat - Liberal government faced little resistance to the abolition of what was once the backbone of social housing policy. It was not only that the Neue Heimat scandal had brought the whole sector into disrepute. More importantly, the bulk of the limited-dividend housing corporations, including many of the municipal-owned, only half-heartedly resisted to the government plans. Keen to abolish the traditional restrictions and to be able to operate as commercial enterprises in the future, most of them in fact welcomed the opportunities associated with commercialisation.

Health Care

While health care has featured prominently on the reform agenda since the mid-1970s, it took the 1992 Health Structure Law to introduce major structural reforms (Perschke-Hartmann, 1994; Reiners, 1993; Wilsford, 1994, pp.258-62). The new law combined stop-gap measures, such as the temporary imposition of a tight ceiling on the overall prescription budget with medium- and long-term structural reforms. Unlike its 1977 and 1988 predecessors, the new law has weakened the role of the peak associations in health care and has restored the role of the state and the market. The main innovation associated with the 1992 reform has been to put competition between the health insurance funds on a new footing. Traditionally, the choice of health insurance funds by the insured had been highly restricted in that only white-collar workers could freely choose between funds. This had led to distorted competition among the funds which, among other things, has weakened their position vis-à-vis physicians. The new law abolished the existing restriction in order to improve the health insurance funds' responsiveness, as well as their bargaining position. Since the beginning of 1997, all those insured have been permitted to choose their health insurance funds freely.

The passage of the Health Structure Law was facilitated by favourable political conditions. Short-term financing problems, the obvious failure of the 1988 reforms, a new minister and a new SPD majority in the powerful second chamber of parliament (the *Bundesrat*) opened up a temporary 'window of opportunity'. From a longer-term perspective, certain shifts in the actor constellation proved to be conducive to the forcing through of more radical measures (Döhler and Manow, 1997). In particular, the position of the physicians and their organisations has suffered from an increasing internal differentiation and a greater autonomy of the two big political parties.

Comparative Assessment

While all three fields have seen a tendency towards marketisation, this marketisation has taken different forms. Roughly speaking, marketisation can come in two variants which might be dubbed *external* and *internal* marketisation. External marketisation is equivalent to the privatisation of the *financing* of social services. In this case, reforms lead to the state ridding itself of financial responsibilities and to citizens paying for services or part of services themselves. In contrast, internal marketisation stands for the marketisation of service *provision*, that is, for reforms aiming at the intensification of competition between providers.

Starting from this distinction, the changes in the three fields can be summarised as follows: In the case of out-patient health care and social housing, internal marketisation has gone hand in hand with external marketisation. Health care reform since the mid-1970s has resulted in a reduction in benefits and an increase in co-payments and prescription charges. Likewise, the federal government and the *Länder* have scaled down expenditure on social housing. In contrast, marketisation of personal social services has been associated with the state increasing its role in financing services. Internal marketisation has likewise taken different forms. In the case of personal social services, there has been an opening up of the old system and a move towards more competition between a broader group of service providers. In the case of social housing, internal marketisation has largely been confined to the transformation of limited-dividend into commercial housing corporations. Finally, health care reform has introduced competition in an existing system of health insurance funds.

From a politics perspective, reforms in the three fields show similarities as well as differences. A closer examination would reveal that the success of the three main legal changes – the Law on Care Insurance, the abolition of limited-dividend housing corporations, and the Health Structure Law – has been highly contingent, hinging upon the exploitation of rather specific conjunctures. Nevertheless, a few general factors that have induced reforms can be identified. The reform attempts have without exception benefited from the enduring fiscal stress, aggravated by the costs of German unification. Thus, it is not coincidental that reforms have occurred after 1989. Fiscal stress has been felt most strongly in the case of health care where financial problems have automatically translated themselves into pressure on contributions. Paradoxically, fiscal considerations have also mattered in the case of personal social services, as one of the driving forces behind the introduction of Care Insurance has been the municipalities' social assistance burden.

Reforms have further been favoured by changes on the provider side that have undermined the former balance of power and the stabilising power of the traditional policy networks. In all three fields under analysis, key actors of the old regime have either suffered from an erosion of their position (welfare associations, physicians) or have redefined their interests over time (limited-dividend housing corporations). These structural changes suggest that the post-war social service regime is now definitively has come to an end.

Revolution or Modernisation? A Post-Script

Our analysis has stressed the revolutionary character of the ongoing changes. The current wave of marketisation amounts to a far-reaching departure from the institutional arrangements that have characterised German social service provision for more than 50 years. However, this is but one perspective. Seen from a different angle, important continuities can be identified. With its separation of regulation, financing and provision, the traditional regime, in a way, has always been 'modern' and has somehow 'anticipated' the guiding ideas behind current changes (Wollmann, 1996).

Against this background, these changes might better be interpreted as a 'modernisation' of social service provision.

Notes

1. Our notion of a social service regime both draws on and deviates from the idea of a welfare state regime as introduced by Esping-Andersen (1990). We share with Esping-Andersen a perspective that looks beyond state programmes and is interested in the links between the public and the private sector. At the same time, we confine ourselves to the analysis of social services.
2. German unification has further aggravated these problems (Angerhausen *et al.*, 1998). Owing to the different social and cultural settings, all efforts to replicate the 'proven' west German system of social service provision have not prevented the transformation of welfare associations in the East. The new welfare associations in east Germany are much closer to commercial service providers than their west German 'parents'. Both within and outside the welfare associations, the apparent viability of such 'lean' welfare associations has provoked the question as to whether the original west German model is out of date.

References

Abelshauser, W. (1996), 'Erhard oder Bismarck? Die Richtungsentscheidung der deutschen Sozialpolitik am Beispiel der Reform der Sozialversicherung in den Fünfziger Jahren', *Geschichte und Gesellschaft* vol. 22, pp.376-92.

Alber, J. (1992), 'Bundesrepublik Deutschland', in J. Alber and B. Bernardi-Schenkluhn, *Westeuropäische Gesundheitssysteme im Vergleich. Bundesrepublik Deutschland, Schweiz, Frankreich, Italien, Großbritannien*, Campus, Frankfurt a. M./New York, pp. 31-176.

Alber, J. (1995) 'Soziale Dienstleistungen. Die vernachlässigte Dimension vergleichender Wohlfahrtsstaat-Forschung', in K. Bentele, B. Reissert and R. Schettkat (eds), *Die Reformfähigkeit von Industriegesellschaften*, Campus, Frankfurt a. M./New York, pp. 277-293.

Angerhausen, S., Backhaus-Maul, H., Offe, C., Olk, T. and Schiebel, M. (1998), *Überholen ohne einzuholen. Freie Wohlfahrtspflege in Ostdeutschland*, Westdeutscher Verlag, Opladen.

Backhaus-Maul, H., Olk, T. (1994), 'Von Subsidiarität zu "outcontracting"': Zum Wandel der Beziehungen von Staat und Wohlfahrtsverbänden in der Sozialpolitik', in W. Streeck (ed.), *Staat und Verbände*, Westdeutscher Verlag, Opladen, pp. 100-35.

Bandelow, N. C. (1998), *Gesundheitspolitik. Der Staat in der Hand einzelner Interessengruppen? Probleme, Erklärungen, Reformen, Analysen*, Leske + Budrich, Opladen.

Bönker, F. and Wollmann, H. (1996), 'Incrementalism and Reform Waves: The Case of Social Service Reform in the Federal Republic of Germany', *Journal of European Public Policy*, vol. 3, pp. 441-60.

Bönker, F. and Wollmann, H. (1998), 'Von konservativen Wohlfahrtsstaaten, institutionellen Restriktionen und Reformwellen: Einige politikwissenschaftliche Überlegungen zu den gegenwärtigen Veränderungen im Bereich der sozialen Dienste', in T. Olk and H.-U. Otto (eds), *Soziale Arbeit als Dienstleistung*, Luchterhand, Neuwied, Darmstadt, pp. 1-15.

Bruch, R. vom (1985), 'Bürgerliche Sozialreform im Deutschen Kaiserreich', in R. vom Bruch (ed.), *Weder Kommunismus noch Kapitalismus. Bürgerliche Sozialreform in Deutschland vom Vormärz bis zur Ära Adenauer*, Beck, München, pp. 61-179.

Döhler, M. (1991), 'Strukturpolitik versus Ordnungspolitik. Ein Vergleich sozialliberaler und christlich-liberaler Reformen im Gesundheitswesen', in B. Blanke and H. Wollmann (eds), *Die alte Bundesrepublik. Kontinuität und Wandel*, Westdeutscher Verlag, Opladen, pp. 463-81.

Döhler, M. and Manow, P. (1997) *Strukturbildung von Politikfeldern. Das Beispiel bundesdeutscher Gesundheitspolitik seit den fünfziger Jahren*, Leske + Budrich, Opladen.

Döhler, M. and Manow-Borgwardt, P. (1992), 'Korporatisierung als gesundheitspolitische Strategie', *Staatswissenschaften und Staatspraxis*, vol. 3, pp. 64-106.

Drupp, M. (1987), 'Gemeinnützige Bauvereine im Wohnungswesen der Weimarer Republik', in W. Abelshauser (ed.), *Die Weimarer Republik als Wohlfahrtsstaat. Zum Verhältnis von Wirtschafts- und Sozialpolitik in der Industriegesellschaft*, Steiner, Wiesbaden, Stuttgart, pp. 124-46.

Esping-Andersen, G. (1990), *The Three Worlds of Welfare Capitalism*, Princeton University Press, Princeton, N. J.

Frerich, J., Frey, M. (1993), *Handbuch der Geschichte der Sozialpolitik in Deutschland, vol. 1: Von der vorindustriellen Zeit bis zum Ende des Dritten Reiches*, Oldenbourg, München/Wien.

Frerich, J. and Frey, M. (1996), *Handbuch der Geschichte der Sozialpolitik in Deutschland. vol. 3: Sozialpolitik in der Bundesrepublik Deutschland bis zur Herstellung der Deutschen Einheit*, Oldenbourg, München/Wien.

Frevert, U. (1984), *Krankheit als politisches Problem 1770-1880: Soziale Unterschichten in Preußen zwischen medizinischer Polizei und staatlicher Sozialversicherung*, Vandenhoeck & Ruprecht, Göttingen.
Götting, U., Haug, K. and Hinrichs, K. (1994), 'The Long Road to Long-Term Care Insurance in Germany', *Journal of Public Policy*, vol. 14, pp. 285-309.
Hammerschmidt, P. (1998), *Die Wohlfahrtsverbände im NS-Staat. Die NSV und die konfessionellen Verbände Caritas und Innere Mission im Gefüge der Wohlfahrtspflege des Nationalsozialismus*, Leske + Budrich, Opladen.
Hartmann, H. (1997), 'Neue Steuerung in der öffentlichen Verwaltung: Anspruch, Wirklichkeit und Perspektiven', in W. Hanesch (ed.), *Überlebt die soziale Stadt? Konzeption, Krise und Perspektiven kommunaler Sozialstaatlichkeit*, Leske + Budrich, Opladen, pp. 111-36.
Häußermann, H. and Siebel, W. (1995), *Dienstleistungsgesellschaften*, Suhrkamp, Frankfurt, M.
Heinze, R. G. and Strünck, C. (1998), 'Wohlfahrtsverbände, Selbsthilfe und private Anbieter - neue Rollenverteilung auf lokaler Ebene?', in D. Grunow and H. Wollmann (eds), *Lokale Verwaltungsreform in Aktion: Fortschritte und Fallstricke*, Birkhäuser, Basel, Boston, Stuttgart, pp. 103-19.
Hockerts, H. G. (1980), *Sozialpolitische Entscheidungen im Nachkriegsdeutschland. Alliierte und deutsche Sozialversicherungspolitik 1945 bis 1957*, Klett-Cotta, Stuttgart.
Jaedicke, W. and Wollmann, H. (1991), 'Wohnungspolitik und Regierungswechsel', in B. Blanke and H. Wollmann (eds), *Die alte Bundesrepublik. Kontinuität und Wandel*, Westdeutscher Verlag, Opladen, pp. 420-36.
Jenkis, H. (1994), 'Die Aufhebung des Wohnungsgemeinnützigkeitsgesetzes - eine wohnungspolitische Fehlentscheidung?', in P. Eichhorn and W. W. Engelhardt (eds), *Standortbestimmung öffentlicher Unternehmen in der Sozialen Marktwirtschaft*, Nomos, Baden-Baden, pp. 101-15.
Kaiser, J.-C. (1995), 'Von der christlichen Nächstenliebe zur freien Wohlfahrtspflege: Genese und Organisation konfessionellen Sozialengagements in der Weimarer Republik', in T. Rauschenbach, C. Sachße and Thomas Olk (eds), *Von der Wertgemeinschaft zum Dienstleistungsunternehmen. Jugend- und Wohlfahrtsverbände im Umbruch*, Suhrkamp, Frankfurt, M., pp. 150-74.
Katzenstein, P. J. (1987), *Policy and Politics in West Germany. The Growth of a Semisovereign State*, Temple University Press, Philadelphia.
Manderscheid, H. (1997), 'Neue Steuerung in der öffentlichen Verwaltung: Anspruch, Wirklichkeit und Perspektiven', in W. Hanesch (ed.), *Überlebt die soziale Stadt? Konzeption, Krise und Perspektiven kommunaler Sozialstaatlichkeit*, Leske + Budrich, Opladen, pp. 137-52.

Niethammer, L. (1979), 'Ein langer Marsch durch die Institutionen: Zur Vorgeschichte des preußischen Wohnungsgesetzes von 1918', in Niethammer, L. (ed.), *Wohnen im Wandel*, Hammer, Wuppertal, pp. 363-86.
Perschke-Hartmann, C. (1994), *Die doppelte Reform. Gesundheitspolitik von Blüm zu Seehofer*, Leske + Budrich, Opladen.
Reichard, C. (1997), '*Neues Steuerungsmodell*: Local Reform in Germany', in W. J. M. Kickert (ed.), *Public Management and Administrative Reform in Western Europe*, Elgar, Cheltenham/Lyme, pp. 61-82.
Reiners, H. (1993), 'Das Gesundheitsstrukturgesetz – "Ein Hauch von Sozialgeschichte"?', *Jahrbuch für Kritische Medizin*, vol. 20, pp. 21-53.
Ritter, G. A. (1991), *Der Sozialstaat. Entstehung und Entwicklung im internationalen Vergleich*, Oldenbourg, München.
Rosewitz, B. and Webber, D. (1990), *Reformversuche und Reformblockaden im deutschen Gesundheitswesen*, Campus, Frankfurt a. M., New York.
Ruck, M. (1987), 'Der Wohnungsbau - Schnittpunkt von Sozial- und Wirtschaftspolitik. Probleme der öffentlichen Wohnungspolitik in der Hauszinssteuerära (1924/25-1930/31)', in W. Abelshauser (ed.), *Die Weimarer Republik als Wohlfahrtsstaat. Zum Verhältnis von Wirtschafts- und Sozialpolitik in der Industriegesellschaft*, Steiner, Wiesbaden, Stuttgart, pp. 91-123.
Sachße, C. (1996), 'Public and Private in German Social Welfare, the 1890s to the 1920s', in M. B. Katz and C. Sachße (eds), *The Mixed Economy of Social Welfare. Public/private Relations in England, Germany and the United States, the 1870s to the 1930s*, Nomos, Baden-Baden, pp. 148-69.
Sachße, C. and Tennstedt, F. (1992), *Geschichte der Armenfürsorge in Deutschland. vol. 3: Der Wohlfahrtsstaat im Nationalsozialismus*, Kohlhammer, Stuttgart, Berlin, Köln.
Schmid, J. (1996), *Wohlfahrtsverbände in modernen Wohlfahrtsstaaten. Soziale Dienste in historisch-vergleichender Perspektive*, Leske + Budrich, Opladen.
Schmidt, M. G. (1996), 'Germany: The Grand Coalition State', in J. M. Colomer (ed.), *Political Institutions in Europe*, Routledge, London, New York, pp. 62-98.
Seibel, W. (1992), *Funktionaler Dilettantismus. Erfolgreich scheiternde Organisationen im 'Dritten Sektor' zwischen Markt und Staat*, Nomos, Baden-Baden.
Wilsford, D. (1994), 'Path Dependency, or Why History Makes It Difficult but Not Impossible to Reform Health Care Systems in a Big Way', *Journal of Public Policy*, vol. 14, pp. 251-83.
Wollmann, H (1983), 'Entwicklungslinien kommunaler Wohnungspolitik - eine wohnungspolitikgeschichtliche Skizze', in A. Evers, H.-G. Lange and H. Wollmann (eds), *Kommunale Wohnungspolitik*, Birkhäuser, Basel, Boston, Stuttgart, pp. 92-106.

Wollmann, H. (1985), 'Housing Policy: Between State Intervention and the Market', in K. v. Beyme and M. G. Schmidt (eds), *Policy and Politics in the Federal Republic of Germany*, Gower, Aldershot, pp. 132-55.

Wollmann, H. (1996), 'Verwaltungsmodernisierung: Ausgangsbedingungen, Reformläufe und aktuelle Modernisierungsdiskurse', in C. Reichard and H. Wollmann (eds), *Kommunalverwaltung im Modernisierungsschub?*, Birkhäuser, Basel, Boston, Stuttgart, pp. 1-50.

Zimmer, A. (1998), 'Modernisierung des Staates und der Nonprofit Sektor', in D. Grunow and H. Wollmann (eds), *Lokale Verwaltungsreform in Aktion: Fortschritte und Fallstricke*, Birkhäuser, Basel, Boston, Stuttgart, pp. 120-44.

17 Explaining Success in Administrative Reform

B. GUY PETERS

Introduction

The chapters in this book have examined the nature of the State and of administrative reform in Germany and the United Kingdom. The outcomes of the processes of change over the past several decades are, to some extent, the antithesis of what might have been expected from the usual characteriza-tions of politics in these two countries. The conventional stereotype of Britain has been of a pragmatic political system, changing little except through gradual adaptation. On the other hand, Germany generally has been portrayed as operating in a Continental, and more ideological manner and as being capable of changing itself rather completely when the need for change is perceived. While both of these views are stereotypes, they have been constructed because they contained at least some element of truth about politics in the two systems.

The experience in administrative reform appears to be exactly the opposite of those stereotypes. It has been the United Kingdom that has undergone the thorough, and almost revolutionary, transformation of its administrative system, to the point that what one finds at the turn of the millennium would be hardly recognizable to someone who had last observed the system in, say, 1979. On the other hand, the German system, when viewed from a sufficient distance, appears hardly unchanged, and such changes as have occurred have been incremental adjustments within a familiar and effective framework. One is here reminded of my late colleague, Douglas Ashford, and his book on 'British Dogmatism and French Pragmatism'. The stereotypes we have of political systems may be useful for some purposes, but they are often deceptive when used in place of more genuine analysis.

The observed differences between the expectation and the reality in these two administrative systems raises a more general question: what can explain the success or failure of administrative reform, especially large scale administrative reform such as that undertaken since the late 1970s? Just like the British/German comparison there are other seemingly analogous observations about the relative success of different systems. For example the United States, often taken as the heartland of private sector thinking and a natural for adopting market-based reforms of the public sector, actually has undergone much less change than other systems such as Britain, New Zealand and Australia (Peters, 1996a). Likewise, the Scandinavian countries have adopted more of the managerialist variety of reform than might have been expected, given the historical power of the state in these systems (see Olsen, 1991; 1996) and the social-democratic commitment to the use of state power to achieve egalitarian ends. What can explain these somewhat unexpected findings concerning administrative reform in a number of countries?

We will argue that there are four sets of factors that can explain the success or failure of reform efforts. First, there is a marked difference in the reform ambitions of different countries; some countries have reformed less simply because the leaders of these countries, and perhaps also the public bureaucracies themselves, have been less interested in change. From the above observation it might appear that Britain has succeeded while Germany had failed, but a good part of the difference may simply be the ambitions of the leaders. Further, the type of change that the reformer considers desirable is another relevant form of ambition. Altering structural arrange-ments that benefit certain powerful groups, for example, is less likely to succeed than changing internal procedures of a government.[1]

A second set of factors explaining the degree of success in reform is structural. We can identify comparatively a number of obvious differences among political systems, but analytically the question of structure will revolve around the number of formal and informal barriers that confront any advocate attempting to impose change on the administrative system. In the terms devised by one version of the new institutionalism, change is easier when there are as few 'veto points' – points at which autonomous actors can make decisions – as possible in the system that might hinder attempts at change (Immergut, 1990). Everything else being equal, complex systems with multiple veto-points will be more difficult to change, even given an equal desire on the part of all parties involved to change, than will simpler systems.[2]

Third, there are situational factors that can affect the ability to implement administrative reforms. Some of these factors are political, having to do with the leadership style and strength of leaders, and even their tenure in office (Hood, 1996). Other situational factors may be a function of the climate of opinion in a country and the perceived need to change the system. Still other situational factors may be a function of external shocks to the political system, and a sense that the political economy of the country has been failing (Boston *et al.*, 1991). Likewise, a strong economy may disguise the need for fundamental changes in the administrative system (Nakamura, 1999).

Finally, the strategies chosen to implement the reforms may influence the ability of a government to make those reforms actually function as expected. The questions of strategy, and of implementation more generally, are often ignored as politicians and their supporters attempt to change the public sector, but they do so at their peril. The same reform, if implemented differently may be more or less successful in being accepted and, then in achieving, its stated goals. A number of alternatives exist for producing change in organizations (Peters, 1998) but these are often not explored fully in the reform process.

Factors Explaining Administrative Reform

We will now proceed to discuss the above three forms of explanation for successes in reform. We can distinguish these three sets of factors analytically, but in reality they often interact. A strong desire to produce reforms in administration may not actually generate those changes if there is a sense that the political and economic systems are actually performing well (Nakamura, 1999). Likewise, a strong leader may be able to alter a complex administrative system containing multiple veto points only so much, no matter how much skill and political clout he or she may possess. As we will point out several times in the course of this paper, the German system is sufficiently complex that the incremental reforms we have observed are perhaps all that could have been expected from such a complex administrative and political arrangement (Benz and Goetz, 1996). We should, therefore, think of the success or failure of reforms in terms of contingencies, and identifying the combination of factors that appear to produce desired results (Peters, 1996b).

Ambitions

The first thing that can explain how well a reform effort succeeds is the degree of ambition, and the degree of commitment, of the political leadership. Some of that commitment may be the result of ideological commitments, especially the belief that the existing form of government is incapable of providing adequate service to the public. This pattern of belief was especially evident among neo-liberal leaders during the 1980s and 1990s. The Reagans and Thatchers of the period (Savoie, 1994) were committed to the idea that the then existing administrative systems were fundamentally flawed, and could be corrected primarily through the introduction of market-like mechanisms into the political system.

Similar degrees of commitment to administrative change could be found during the Carter administration, although stemming from very different reasons. President Carter appeared convinced that there was a technical solution to problems of bureaucracy and that greater efficiency in government could be obtained through reform (Szanton, 1981). The ambition to produce those outcomes was largely thwarted by the familiar difficulties of changing bureaucracies, and some poor choices of strategy. Still, there were certainly strong ambitions to change government, and the implementation of a number of changes, not least the Civil Service Reform Act of 1978 (Ingraham and Ban, 1984).

These strong commitments to reform can be contrasted with the seeming indifference of political leaders in some Continental European countries. While some of the same problems that motivated change in Britain could be seen in Germany, Austria and especially Italy, for example, there was not the ambition to address the problems through systemic change (Derlien, 1996b). In these cases there were either more important issues on the political agenda (reunification in Germany for much of the period), or these problems were of insufficient concern politically to motivate politicians to engage in the political struggles that would be required to implement a reform, or simply the individual leaders did not have sufficient interest in the topic to press it onto the agenda.

We have to this point stressed the reform ambitions of senior political leaders, but members of the public bureaucracy may themselves have some desires to change, as well as ideas about how to make those changes. For example, although granted the political space within which to do so by political leaders, the National Performance Review in the United States (the Gore Commission) reflected the desire on the part of many members of the career civil service to change their own structures and procedures (Peters and Savoie, 1995). Similarly, although the (strong) initial pressure for budgetary change came from political leaders, the process of Programme Review in Canada during the Chretien government has been driven to a substantial degree by public servants (Aucoin and Savoie, 1998).[3] Civil servants are often stereotyped as defenders of the status quo, and they often do defend their departments and programmes. That having been said, public servants often do have sincere ambitions to change the administrative systems within which they work. The initial reforms in the United Kingdom were driven by political leaders, but once the process was under way the torch was taken up by career public servants who have continued to drive the process.

Ambition is closely related to the situational factors to be discussed below. A politician who is not him or herself very keen on administrative reform may develop a great passion for the subject if there is an apparent political 'profit' to be made from campaigning for the change. Or if there is a general climate of opinion that the public sector is failing in meeting its goals there may be a greatly enhanced interest in reform by a number of politicians and parties. Again, analytically we can distinguish these two sets of variables, but in practice the distinctions tend to become rather murky.

Structural Factors

Even if all political leaders had the same level of ambition to reform their governments, they would be faced with vast differences in the political and administrative structures, and hence equally vast differences in their capacity to produce change. Some of these differences may arise from the familiar differences between presidential and parliamentary systems (Weaver and Rockman, 1995; Von Mettenheim, 1997). The basic argument is that the complexity of presidential systems and the need to get both legislature and executive to agree on a change will make reform less likely.

The capacity of Mrs. Thatcher to push through a series of rather dramatic administrative reforms in Britain, for example, reflects in part the capacity of leaders in parliamentary systems to impose their ideas on government. Not all parliamentary systems are alike, however, and majoritarian systems such as the United Kingdom are easier to change than are consensual systems such as the Scandinavian countries or the Netherlands (Lijphart, 1984). Some parliamentary systems may function almost like presidential systems and will require a great deal of coalition building if any significant legislation is to be adopted.

The familiar difference between presidential and parliamentary systems can be understood through the concept of 'veto points' mentioned above (Immergut, 1992). More complex political systems are characterized by more independent actors with the capacity to block action, if not always to promote action. Although the implementation literature has demonstrated that there are a number of effective ways to circumvent these blockages in policy-making systems (Bowen, 1982), still the complexity of some structural arrangements requires an investment of political skill and energy that would not be necessary in more streamlined political structures.

It is not only the simple distinction between presidential and parliamentary systems that may make a difference in the ability to push through administrative reforms. The German case of federalism, and the relative autonomy of the *Länder* in the system is an important example. On the one hand, the ability to transform administration may be limited by the autonomy of the governments, even though the legal basis of the personnel system is relatively unified. On the other hand, the presence of multiple autonomous governments does create an opportunity for innovation, and then for possible learning (Derlien, 1996a). As in the United States, subnational governments in Germany have tended to be more innovative in public administration than has the federal government, so that the learning that occurs is often vertical as well as horizontal.

More informal characteristics of the public sector also may make reform more difficult. For example, Katzenstein's (1987) characterization of Germany as a 'semi-sovereign state' may be overstated, but it does point to the number of societal connections that may limit the ability of the government to reform quickly. Some of those same connections, e.g. the strength of public sector unions, may have long inhibited change in Britain at one time but the rather radical transformations of the Thatcher years have reduced many of those constraints. Although not part of the structure of government itself, these social actors and their formal and informal powers create just as effective veto points as do the needs to get formal institutions to agree on reform (see Blais, Blake and Dion, 1998).

Finally, the nature of the bureaucracy itself may present structural barriers to reform. Different administrative structures accord greater responsibility to organizations existing below the level of the ministry. When, as in the United States, many of those organizations are powerful then changing the system becomes more difficult. Further, the status that the public service enjoys in society will affect the willingness of political leaders to attempt to implement major changes. The long-established status of *Beamten* in Germany, as well as their political linkages, makes imposing reforms more difficult than it might be in other systems. On the other hand, however, the political power of the civil service may provide it the latitude to engage in its own versions of piecemeal reform.

Following from the above discussion, one round of structural change may make any subsequent rounds of reform more difficult. For example, the British government was able to deconcentrate its ministries into a number of relatively autonomous organizations. Having done so, however, they have created a set of organizations that are developing relatively clearer linkages with social groups and may have the potential to be 'captured' by those organizations. Even the formally quasi-independent status granted to agencies may make subsequent changes more difficult. Likewise, granting greater autonomy to public servants through a process of internal deregulation (DiIulio, 1994) may make any later attempts to control these officials all the more difficult.

In summary, the structure of government and its relationships with civil society can have a profound influence over the capacity of an administrative system to reform itself. These structural factors are important individually, but taken together they can comprise a profound influence over the capacity of political actors to produce change. That having been said, the United States as one of the more complex systems extant has been able over the past several years to produce a good deal of change. Much less complex systems such as Norway appear to have changed more than expected on an ideological basis, but still to have encountered difficulty in so doing (Olsen, 1996).

Strategies

The final explanation for differential success and failure at reform is the strategy adopted by the reformers, both when constructing the reform and when implementing it. The 'how' element of reform often has been a forgotten component of analysis, as politicians rush to announce their (presumably) new ideas for making government work better and to gain as much political recognition as possible for their efforts. In some ways the announcement itself may be valuable, by making it evident to members of the public sector that there may be a need for change.[4] Still, having gone to the trouble of devising a set of plans for reform, it would be nice to implement them in something like the manner intended.

There are several interesting strategic questions that arise in administrative reform. For example, how quickly should the reforms be implemented? On the one hand, the New Zealand government was extremely successful in implementing a radical reform plan in the space of only a very few years (Boston *et al.*, 1991). On the other hand, the equally radical collection of reforms in the United Kingdom was implemented over the course of over a decade – over a decade and a half if one includes the Major government. The Gore Commission also expects its reforms to require at least ten years to be implemented fully. The 'short, sharp shock' strategy of New Zealand may work in a perceived crisis situation, but may fail in the face of complacency or bureaucratic resistance. On the other hand, the attenuated process of reform in the United Kingdom may have failed unless there had been the political continuity to keep the pressure on the public sector.

Another strategic question is whether the emphasis in the reform should be from the top down, or from the bottom up. Another way of asking this question is whether the emphasis in the process should be on political commitment or bureaucratic involvement and 'ownership'? One strategy would require reform to be driven from the very top of government, from presidents and prime ministers, in order to overcome the resistance to change inherent in any large organization. The alternative strategy would argue that the only way to produce really meaningful and enduring change is to involve the members of those organizations and to co-opt[5] them into the change process.

A related strategic question is whether 'one size fits all', or whether there can be the possibility for more differentiated reforms depending upon the nature of each organization in government. For example, a public organization that has the 'machine' characteristics described by Mintzberg (1979), with a large number of lower-skilled workers performing repetitive tasks (the post office perhaps), may require a very different set of reforms than will an organization dominated by professionals engaged in highly differentiated types of work (research laboratories, or a government legal office). Still, the advocates of a unified approach to reform might consider any such differentiation as allowing too much room for individual organizations to disregard the purposes of the reform and to continue to do what they always have done.

I would argue that a 'bottom up' strategy permitting some differentiation among organizations is likely to be the more successful approach. Empirically there is evidence that such strategies have been successful. For example, we can contrast the relative initial success of the National Performance Review in the United States and Programme Review in Canada with the relative failure of the Grace Commission and the Nielsen in the same two countries (Peters and Savoie, 1994). In the earlier reforms there was a top down strategy with little or no involvement of the career personnel. In the latter there was an initial thrust from the political level, and continuing expressions of commitment to the project, but also a large degree of involvement by the career personnel. There is, of course, some contrary evidence, as in the case of New Zealand and Australia (Halligan, 1999).

We could continue to identify a number of other strategic questions that arise when considering the design and implementation of reform. The most interesting question, however, becomes determining when particular strategies will be effective and when they will not. As noted already, this determination may require thinking about the interactions among the various factors we have been discussing, rather than thinking about them on a piecemeal basis. The extremely rapid success of the New Zealand reforms, for example, may be a result of the deep feeling of crisis at the time, and attempting to make these changes so quickly without that sense may have been disastrous. Further, New Zealand at the time[6] of the reforms was one of the most clearly majoritarian parliamentary systems existing, so that one party was able to seize control of government and implement its radical programmes of change with relative ease.

Summary

This paper has almost certainly not solved the problem of explaining success and failure. It has, however, noted some paradoxical cases of success and failure, and also pointed to a number of factors that may help in understanding the outcomes of a process of reform. The catalog presented here is incomplete, and we could certainly have cited a number of additional factors within these four broad categories. While that enumeration may satisfy a need for tidiness and completeness, it will probably do little to enhance our understanding further.

What does appear necessary is to begin a more sustained quest for understanding the contingencies of reform. Developing at least the beginnings of an ability to advise would-be reformers that if there is one set of circumstances then he or she should expect the following outcomes, or should adopt the following strategies, would make a great contribution to the utility of public administration in the advising about the practical problem of generating institutional change. As it is, the intuition and political commitment of the reformer may be as useful as anything the discipline has to offer by way of advice.

There are some substantial methodological problems in developing these statements, not least of which is the relatively small number of cases on which to draw when making generalizations, not to mention the strong role that national particularities play in producing any set of outcomes. Looking carefully at two countries such as Britain and Germany provides very detailed information on those two countries, but may not be particularly useful in building more general theories about reform. Still, the two cases, and especially the somewhat unexpected nature of the reforms may provide several more data points in the accumulating file of evidence about how and why governments can reform their public bureaucracies.

Notes

1 President Carter found this to be the case when he attempted to move some programmes from the (then) Veteran's Administration into the Department of Health and Human Services and into the Department of Education. He lost.
2 The logic is similar to Pressman and Wildavsky's idea (1976) about

'clearance points' in implementation. They argued that the more autonomous choices there were in the process the greater the likelihood of implementation failure.
3   This was a comprehensive review of public spending with the ambition (generally achieved) of substantial reductions in public spending.
4   Most civil servants have, however, heard much of this before and may simply wait out the current wave of reform as they have others before it. Indeed, one important reform task is finding a way to overcome the deeply ingrained scepticism of long-sitting officials.
5   Cooptation often has a pejorative connotation. It can, however, be seen as simply another organizational process to involve members of the organization.
6   Subsequent electoral reforms have produced a multi-party system and something much more like a consensual parliamentary democracy in New Zealand.

References

Aucoin, P. and Savoie, D. J. (1998), *Programme Review in Canada*, McGill, Queens University Press, Montreal.
Benz, A. and Goetz, K. H. (1996), 'The German Public Sector: National Priorities and International Reform Agenda', in A. Benz and K. H. Goetz (eds), *A New German Public Sector?*, Dartmouth, Aldershot, pp. 1-26.
Blais, A., Blake, D. and Dion, S. (1998), *Politics, Elections and Public Employment*, University of Pittsburgh Press, Pittsburgh.
Boston, J. et al. (1991), *Reshaping the State*, Oxford University Press, Auckland.
Bowen, E. (1982), 'The Pressman-Wildavsky Paradox', *Journal of Public Policy*, vol. 2, pp. 1-22.
Derlien, H.-U. (1996a), 'Piecemeal Reforms in Germany: The Intelligence of Bureaucracy in a Decentralized Polity', in J. P. Olsen and B. G. Peters (eds), *Lessons from Experience*, Scandinavian University Press, Oslo.
Derlien, H.-U. (1996b), 'Patterns of Post-War Administrative Development in Germany', in A. Benz and K. H. Goetz (eds), *A New German Public Sector?*, Dartmouth, Aldershot, pp. 27-44.
DiIulio, J. J. (1994), *Deregulating Government*, The Brookings Institution, Washington, DC.
Halligan, J. A. (1999), 'Paradoxes of Reform in the Antipodes', in J. J. Hesse, C. Hood and B. G. Peters (eds), *The Paradoxes of Reform: Soft Theory and Hard Cases*, de Gruyter, Berlin.

Hood, C. (1996), 'Of Shocks and Long Tenure: Reform in the United Kingdom', in J. P. Olsen and B. G. Peters (eds), *Lessons from Experience*, Scandinavian University Press, Oslo.

Immergut, E. (1990), 'Institutions, Veto Points and Policy Results: A Comparative Analysis of Health Care', *Journal of Public Policy*, vol. 10, pp. 391-416.

Ingraham, P. W. and C. Ban (1984), *Legislating Bureaucratic Change: The Civil Service Reform Act of 1978*, State University of New York Press, Albany.

Katzenstein, P. (1987), *Germany: A Semi-Sovereign Political System*, Temple University Press, Philadelphia, PA.

Lijphart, A. (1984), *Democracies: Patterns of Majoritarian and Consensus Government in Twenty-One Countries*, Yale University Press, New Haven.

Nakamura, A. (1999), 'Japan', in J. J. Hesse, C. Hood and B. G. Peters (eds), *The Paradoxes of Reform: Soft Theory and Hard Cases*, de Gruyter, Berlin.

Olsen, J. P. (1991), 'Modernization Programs in Perspective: An Institutional Perspective on Organizational Change', *Governance*, vol. 4, pp. 125-49.

Olsen, J. P. (1996), 'Norway: Reluctant Reformer, Slow Learner, or the Triumph of the Tortoise', in Olsen and B. G. Peters (eds), *Lessons from Experience*, Scandinavian University Press, Oslo.

Peters, B. G. (1996a), *The Future of Governing*, University Press of Kansas, Lawrence.

Peters, B. G. (1996b), 'What Works: The Antiphons of Administrative Reform', in B. G. Peters and D. J. Savoie (eds), *Taking Stock: Two Decades of Administrative Reform*, McGill-Queens University Press, Montreal.

Peters, B. G. (1998), 'Producing Sustainable Organizational Change', in P. W. Ingraham and R. Sander (eds), *Transforming Government*, Jossey-Bass, San Francisco.

Peters, B. G. and Savoie, D. J. (1994), 'Civil Service Reform: Misdiagnosing the Patient', *Public Administration Review*, vol. 54, pp. 418-25.

Pressman, J. L. and Wildavsky, A. (1976), *Implementation*, University of California Press, Berkeley.

Savoie, D. J. (1994), *Reagan, Thatcher, Mulroney: In Search of a New Bureaucracy*, University of Toronto Press, Toronto.

Szanton, P. (1981), *Federal Reorganization: What Have We Learned?*, Chatham House, Chatham, NJ.

Von Mettenheim, K. (1996), *Presidential Institutions and Democratic Politics*, Johns Hopkins University Press, Baltimore.

Weaver, R. K. and Rockman, B. A. (1995), *Do Institutions Matter? Government Capabilities in the United States and Abroad*, The Brookings Institution, Washington, DC.

Index

Academies of Public Administration *see Verwaltungsakademien*
accident insurance *see Unfallversicherung*
Adenauer, K. 96, 102
administrative courts 7, 45, 61, 135, 167
administrative culture 132–49, 150, 152, 166, 200–204
administrative integration 56, 57
administrative law 6, 7, 32, 49, 51, 135, 137, 145
administrative state 32, 47–63
administrative transformation 56–58
agencies 12, 39, 113, 133, 135, 139–41, 144, 148, 160, 163, 164, 165, 227, 230
agencification 165, 225
Allgemeine Ortskrankenkassen 104
Allgemeines Landrecht 329
Allied Control Council 90
American Zone of Occupation 120
Angestellte (im öffentlichen Dienst) 52, 156, 162, 174, 184, 185, 187, 188, 191, 192
Anschütz, T. 33
Arbeit statt Sozialhilfe 256

Arbeiterwohlfahrt 286, 289, 331
Arbeitslosenversicherung 58, 213, 245, 248, 339
ARD, *Arbeitsgemeinschaft der Rundfunkanstalten Deutschlands* 99
Armenpflege 329, 330
associative democracy 285
asylum-seekers 256
Audit Commission 238, 278, 280, 318
authoritative acts *see hoheitliche Befugnisse*

Bafög 251
Bains Report 183, 186, 190
Bank of England 48
Barnett formula 78
Beamte 49, 51, 56, 90, 134, 147, 156, 162, 165, 167, 174, 182–88, 191–93, 208, 286, 357
Beamtenrecht 42, 55, 135, 162, 164, 184
Benefits Agency 225–32, 238, 264
 cultural change 228
 districts and areas 228, 231
Bentham, J. 30

Berlin Agreement of 1913 309, 333
Bertelsmann Foundation 156
Besitzstandsmentalität 43
Beveridge Report 269
Bichard, M. 226, 228, 229, 230
Biedenkopf, K. 155
big government 53, 209, 210, 218
Bismarck, O.v. 2, 86–98, 87, 245, 261, 328, 333, 336
Blair Government 39, 71
Blair, T. 40
block contracts 274
Boards of Education 306
Boards of Guardians 225, 306
boroughs 110, 111, 113, 306
bottom-up approach 229, 248, 257, 358, 359
Brandt, W. 102
British Zone of Occupation 120
building societies 307
Bundesangestelltentarif 99
Bundesbank 4, 42, 100, 163
Bundesknappschaft 249
Bundesrat 4, 9, 42, 86–103, 344
Bundesrechnungshof 249
Bundessozialhilfegesetz 244, 251, 252, 253, 254, 337, 340
Bundestag 42, 86, 87, 102, 103, 155, 158
Bundesverfassungsgericht 4, 37, 42, 45, 50, 92, 337
Bundesversicherungsanstalt für Angestellte 248, 249
Bundesverwaltungsamt 160
Bündnis 90/Die Grünen, Alliance 90/the Greens 4, 155
bureaucratisation 52, 200, 342
Bürgergeld 260
bürgernahe Verwaltung 52, 121

cadre-type administration 55

care management 235, 278
Carter administration 354, 360
cash/care split 233, 306, 310
Catholic churches 285, 287
CDU, Christian Democrats 3, 14, 89, 96, 101, 102, 103, 338, 339
celtic periphery 67, 69, 70, 72, 80, 82
Central Charitable Agencies *see Centralen für private Fürsorge*
Chancellor of the Exchequer 315
Change Programme 230, 231, 232
charities 285, 305, 306, 308, 311, 321, 324, 329, 330
Charity Organisation Society 310
Child Benefits Section 232
Child Support Agency 232
Children Act of 1948 311
Children Act of 1989 233, 317
Children and Youth Assistance Act of 1990 (Germany) 341
Children Departments 311
Chretien government in Canada 355
Christian Democrat - Liberal coalition 337, 339, 343
citizen-oriented administration *see bürgernahe Verwaltung*
Citizens' Charter 140, 141, 146, 167, 228, 230
civic involvement 294
civic service culture 51
civic-culture 47, 204, 205, 207, 218
civil service 39, 68, 79, 132–49, 133, 134, 135, 138, 144, 158, 159, 163, 164, 182, 208, 226, 355, 357
Civil Service College 141, 147, 158, 191

civil service culture 47, 229
civil service ethics 138, 139, 142
civil service law *see Beamtenrecht*
civil service neutrality 165
Civil Service Reform Act of 1978 354
civil service reform commission 153, 162
Civil Service Reform Law of 1997 (Germany) 188
Civil Service Select Committee's Report on the Civil Service 159
civil society 5, 218, 357
Cold War 51
College of Applied Sciences for Engineering or Social Work *see Fachhochschule für Technik or Fachhochschule für Sozialarbeit*
College of Public Administration *see Fachhochschule für Verwaltung*
Commission on Local Government 173
Common Law 4, 6, 29, 30, 33, 199
Common Law of 1794 *see Allgemeines Landrecht*
Commonwealth 29, 33, 151
communes *see Gemeinden*
Community Benefits Council 229, 231
community care 233, 234, 235, 271, 277, 306, 318, 319, 324
Community Care Act 233
Competition for Quality programme 141, 230
compulsory competitive tendering 13, 17, 18, 113, 114, 137, 140, 141, 145, 159, 167, 187, 270, 274, 294, 296
Congress of Vienna 91, 97

Conservative government 9, 13, 19, 20, 35, 39, 70, 112, 114, 132, 139, 145, 147, 149, 179, 224, 225, 227, 313, 320, 321, 322, 324
Conservative Party 38, 77, 112, 314, 320
consociational democracy 3–4
constitutional engineering 85, 86
constitutional patriotism 51
consultative authoritarianism 55
contract culture 273
contract management 59, 163, 165
contracting out 17, 137, 179, 237, 259, 260, 266, 272, 323
contracting state 147, 234
control of legality *see Rechtsaufsicht*
controller concept 155
co-operative state 54
corporatism 285, 287, 288, 293, 299, 333, 334, 336, 339
cost accounting 155, 176
Cost Containment Law of 1977 339
counties 14, 70, 81, 109, 111, 112, 126, 127, 177, 228, 306 *see also Kreise*
Crown 2, 4, 8, 28–34, 48, 70, 108, 109, 134, 137, 140, 162
CSU, Christian Social Union 101
cultural change 199, 204, 229, 265, 278, 280, 288
customer care initiatives 229
customer orientation 61, 139, 141, 146, 148, 230, 259, 260, 265
Customer Service Manager 229
cutback measures 259
cybernetics 96

data protection officers 155
de-bureaucratisation 136, 140, 154,

155, 158
de-bureaucratisation hearing (1980) 153
decentralisation 69, 70, 74, 79, 85–103, 114, 123, 125, 126, 160, 163, 176, 178, 186, 188, 226, 227, 228, 244, 249, 259, 260
deconcentration 68, 79, 260, 357
democratic centralism 55
Department of Health 235, 236
Department of Health and Social Security 225
Department of Social Security 225, 227, 232
deregulation 52, 155, 158, 161, 357
Deutsche Angestelltengewerkschaft, DAG 185
Deutscher Beamtenbund, DBB 185
Deutscher Bund 88, 89, 98
Deutscher Caritasverband (DCV) 244, 286, 289, 330
Deutscher Gewerkschaftsbund, DGB 99
Deutscher Paritätischer Wohlfahrtsverband (DPWV) 286, 288, 289, 298, 299
Deutscher Verein für Armenpflege und Wohltätigkeit 330
Deutsches Reich 330
Deutsches Rotes Kreuz (DRK) 289
devolution 8, 22, 69–76, 73, 82, 160, 228
Diakonisches Werk (DW) 244, 286, 289
direct democracy 14, 15, 21, 122, 126, 247, 259
Direct Line model 232
Direct Service Organisations 141
Disability Allowance 227

districts 14, 110, 111, 126, 177, 228, 231 *see also Regierungsbezirke*
dual polity 9, 12, 19, 23, 108, 117, 124, 125

Efficiency Scrutinies 140
Einheitlichkeit der Lebensverhältnisse 92, 93, 95, 99
elective dictatorship 2, 108
enabling authority 269, 275
Enabling State 147
English regional government 71, 74, 81
English regions 68–72, 78
Enquete-Kommission Verfassungsreform 96
equal opportunity commissioners 155
Ernst commission 153
European integration 294
European Monetary Union (EMU) 41
European Union 73, 140, 159, 298
evaluation 158
executive class *see gehobener Dienst*
Executive Councils 314, 315
executive leadership 164

Fabian Society 310
Fachaufsicht 118
Fachhochschule für Technik or *Fachhochschule für Sozialarbeit* 192
Fachhochschule für Verwaltung 192
Fachhochschulen für Verwaltung 193
Family Practitioner Committees 315

FDP, Free Democrats 3, 101, 339
federal audit office *see Bundesrechnungshof*
Federal Constitution *see Grundgesetz*
Federal Council *see Bundesrat*
Federal Housing Act of 1950 338
Federal Ministry of Family Affairs 289
Federal Social Assistance Act *see Bundessozialhilfegesetz*
federal statistical office *see Statistisches Bundesamt*
Federal Youth Welfare Act *see Jugendhilfegesetz*
federalism 3, 9, 13, 55, 59, 85–103, 246, 329, 336, 356
Financial Management Initiative 159
First World War 11, 49, 91, 117, 118, 124, 125, 307, 329, 330, 331, 332
fiscal federalism 86, 90, 92, 94, 95, 97
Franckensteinsche Klausel 94
Freiherr vom Stein 116, 151
French Zone of Occupation 120
friendly societies 308
Führer principle 49, 119
Fulton Report 132, 140, 158, 160, 166

gehobener Dienst 192, 193
Gemeinden 51, 56, 57, 59, 99, 118, 120, 121, 252, 254, 257, 258, 259
General Practitioners 233
generalists 7, 135, 136, 182, 183, 192, 193
Generationen-Vertrag 248
German Association for Poor Relief and Charity *see Deutscher Verein für Armenpflege und Wohltätigkeit*
German Confederation *see Deutscher Bund*
German Confederation of Labour Unions *see Deutscher Gewerkschaftsbund*
German Democratic Republic 2, 15, 21, 54, 55, 56, 57, 58, 123, 153, 247, 289, 298, 336
Gewerkschaft Öffentliche Dienste, Transport und Verkehr, ÖTV 185
Glorious Revolution 29
Gore Commission 355, 358
Goschen formula 78
government by committee 15, 110, 112, 115
Grand Coalition 89, 96
Greater London Council 113
Griffiths, R. 318
Grundgesetz 3, 9, 10, 15, 28, 37, 42, 51, 56, 85, 92, 98, 120, 154, 162, 167, 177, 252

Habsburg 87
Hardenberg 151
Hardenberg, K.A. 87
harmonisation 90, 92, 93, 94, 249, 256, 262
Hauszinssteuer 332
health care 18, 38, 111, 161, 233, 234, 236, 238, 305, 306, 308–9, 310, 314, 322, 324, 325, 327, 328, 332–36, 333, 334, 335, 336, 339, 340, 343, 344, 345
health insurance *see Krankenversicherung*
health insurance funds 104, 333, 334, 335, 336, 339, 343, 344, 345

Health Reform Law of 1988 339
Health Services and Community Care Act of 1990 317
Health Structure Law of 1992 343, 344, 345
Hegel, G.W.F. 31, 33, 116
higher civil service 133, 142, 143, 144, 148, 163
Hobbes, T. 29, 30
Hofstede's index 201
hoheitliche Befugnisse 162
hollowing out the state 161
Home Rule 69, 74
House of Commons 71
House of Lords 72
Housing Act (Britain) 307
Housing Act of 1918 (Germany) 332
Housing Act of 1980 (Britain) 320
housing associations 19, 272, 308, 314, 321, 323, 325, 334, 335
housing benefits *see Wohngeld*
Housing Finance Act of 1972 313
Hume, D. 29

IG Metall, Industriegewerkschaft Metall 99
Immerwährender Reichstag 86, 88
incrementalism 4, 40, 150, 151, 158, 160, 167, 351, 353
indirect state administration *see mittelbare Staatsverwaltung*
Individualism 202, 218
individualist society 36
industrialisation 32, 109, 117, 173, 174, 195, 245, 330
information technology 226, 229, 231, 232, 259, 280
Institute of Chartered Secretaries and Administrators, ICSA 191
Institute of Local Government in Birmingham, INLOGOV 190
Institute of Municipal Treasurers and Accountants 173
Institute of Town Planning 173
institutional decentralisation and procedural integration 90
institutional legacies 161
intelligence of bureaucracy 151, 152, 155
interdepartmental task force for government reform (1969-1975) 153
interlocking policies *see Politikverflechtung*
internal rationalisation 60, 176, 179
International Institute of Administrative Sciences 154
Irish Republic 76
isomorphism 298

Jellinek, W. 33
Job Seekers Allowance 230
Joint Negotiating Committee for Chief Executives and Chief Officers 185
Jugendhilfe 251, 252, 330, 337
Jugendhilfegesetz 340
Juristenmonopol 8, 136, 157, 174
Justices of the Peace 109

Kaiserreich 2, 9, 32, 86, 88, 89, 91, 94, 100, 104
Kassenärztliche Vereinigungen 333
Kleinstaaterei 91, 98
Kohl government 44, 158
Kohl, H. 87, 103, 155

Kommunale Gemeinschaftsstelle, KGSt 154
Krankenversicherung 209, 213, 245, 246, 248, 250, 258, 286, 293, 295, 328, 333, 339
Kreise 10, 14, 17, 51, 59, 118, 120, 121, 122, 123, 127, 177, 185, 193, 252, 259
Kultusministerkonferenz 93

Laband, P. 33
Labour government 8, 12, 14, 34, 35, 39, 70, 71, 77, 114, 125, 145, 149, 225, 232, 238, 240, 277, 313, 322
labour movement 285, 329, 333
Labour Party 40, 70, 71, 77, 80, 132, 310, 311, 316, 320
Lafontaine, O. 103
Länderfinanzausgleich 95
Landesbanken 101
Landesversicherungsanstalten 248
Landrat 14, 123, 178
lawyers' monopoly *see Juristenmonopol*
lean administration 60
lean state 6, 59, 151, 155, 161, 198
Lean State commission 155, 157
legalism 6, 7, 55, 61, 109, 184, 194, 202, 208
Liberal government 308, 310
Liga 286
Lilley, P. 230
limited-dividend housing corporations 331–46
Local Authorities Conditions of Service Advisory Board, LACSAB 185
local authorities' associations 177, 185
local democracy 114, 122, 126

local government 7–23, 59, 67, 68, 71, 79, 81, 94, 99, 104, 107–27, 133, 135–45, 151–59, 164–67, 171, 177, 233, 238, 244, 252–55, 258, 265, 268, 304–12, 315–21, 330, 332, 336, 337, 341
Local Government Act of 1972 111, 175
Local Government Act of 1985 113
Local Government Management Board, LGMB 185, 187
local government service 112, 132, 137, 138, 143, 144, 148, 171–95
Local Government Training Board 191
Locke, J. 29
London boroughs 177
London mayor 115

Magistrat 116, 178
Major government 228, 230, 358
Major, J. 140
majoritarian democracy 3–4
management by objectives 164
management consultancies 153, 155, 156, 157, 294
managerialism 60, 61, 135, 139, 146, 147, 148, 152, 155, 159, 167, 200–204, 218, 233, 237–40, 280, 294, 296, 352
mandarins 132–34, 136, 142, 144
market testing 140, 145, 230
marketisation 18, 19, 20, 175, 178, 231, 233, 234, 235, 265, 269, 270, 297, 298, 304–25, 328, 340–46
Marxist-Leninist ideology 55
Masculinity vs. Femininity 203
Mathison, I. 226, 230

Matrikularbeiträge 94
Mayer, O. 33
mayor (*Bürgermeister*) 14, 16, 21, 104, 120, 123, 126, 127, 157, 164, 178
mediation committee *see Vermittlungsausschuß*
Medical Practice Committees 314
Metal Workers' Union *see IG Metall*
Metropolitan Councils 113
metropolitan developmental planning 158
Mill, J.S. 29, 30
ministerial accountability 159, 165, 168
ministerial bureaucracy 57
Ministry of Finance 260
Ministry of Health 40, 225, 262
Ministry of Labour 285, 331
Ministry of Labour and Social Affairs 262
Ministry of Social Security 225
Ministry of the Interior 153, 156
Ministry of Youth, Family and Health 262
Mischverwaltung 95
mittelbare Staatsverwaltung 117
mixed administration *see Mischverwaltung*
mixed economy of welfare 234, 236, 237, 240, 267, 270, 271, 272, 275, 281, 282, 304, 309, 312, 319, 323, 327, 328, 334, 336
Montesquieu, C. 7
Municipal Charter of 1808 *see Städteordnung*
Municipal Corporation Act of 1835 109
municipal socialism 118, 286

myth-creating function of management models 166

National Assembly at Frankfurt 88
National Assistance Act of 1948 225, 227, 311
National Association of Local Government Officers 173
national curriculum 39
National Health Insurance panel system 308
National Health Service 34, 40, 67, 111, 158–60, 167, 174, 181, 212, 233, 234, 239, 304, 308, 309, 314–18, 322–24
Trusts 238, 322
National Insurance Act of 1911 310
National Joint Council for the Administrative, Professional, Technical and Clerical staffs, APT & C 185
National Performance Review 355, 359
National Socialist People's Welfare *see Nationalsozialistische Volkswohlfahrt, NSV*
National Society for the Prevention of Cruelty to Children, NSPCC 305, 311
National Training Organization for Local Government, LGNTO 191
nationalist parties 69, 70
Nationalsozialistische Volkswohlfahrt, NSV 335
Nazi Germany 9, 49, 51, 88, 91, 104, 119, 125, 287, 333, 335
needs led vs. resource led 235
negative income tax 260

Neue Heimat 342
new institutional economics 280
new institutionalism 352
New Labour 240
New *Länder* (eastern Germany) 56, 97, 119, 123, 150, 155, 159, 162, 177, 180, 200, 247, 250, 259, 291, 298, 346
New Public Management 17, 20, 50, 58, 59, 60, 113, 122, 139, 151, 156, 160, 166, 167, 175, 176, 178, 190, 198, 203, 208, 218, 225, 227, 239, 259, 261, 264, 265, 266, 269–71, 274, 275, 276, 280, 282, 294
New Right 139, 147, 237, 240
New Steering Model 59, 61, 160, 190, 193, 259
Next Steps programme 135, 141, 160, 164, 225, 227
non-napoleonic group of Western states 81
non-profit organisations 17, 18, 20, 53, 122, 138, 143, 193, 284, 286, 287, 289, 294, 295, 332, 335
non-state welfare bureaucracies 282
Norddeutscher Bund 86
North German Confederation *see* *Norddeutscher Bund*
Northern Ireland 67, 127
Northern Ireland Agreement 76
Northern Ireland Assembly 67, 75, 79
Northern Ireland Secretary 75
not-for-profit agencies 272, 276
Nuffield Institute for Health 271
nursing care insurance *see* *Pflegeversicherung*

Obrigkeitsstaat 33

occupation powers 2, 9, 36, 50, 85, 88, 90, 92, 94, 97, 100, 119, 246, 336
öffentlicher Dienst 48, 49, 52, 53, 59, 104, 137, 150–68, 152, 153, 154, 155, 156, 161, 163, 165, 167, 174, 176, 183, 184, 189, 193, 194, 287, 295
Offices for Scotland and Wales and Northern Ireland 67, 73–80
Ollenhauer, F. 102
ombudsman 155
opportunity structure 150
Ordnungspolitik 37
outsourcing 297, 299
over-bureaucratisation 256
over-centralization 68
over-economisation 256
over-regulation 59, 256

Parlamentarischer Rat 9, 90
Parliament 1, 2, 4, 6, 7, 12, 19, 22, 28, 29, 30, 33, 48, 56, 72, 74, 76, 77, 108, 109, 110, 113, 134, 140, 165, 177, 208
Parliamentary Sovereignty 2, 8, 72, 82, 108
participation 68, 116, 164, 205, 206, 208, 247
party democracy 52
path-dependency 10, 11, 20, 21, 22, 57, 86, 126, 151, 256, 261, 328
PDS, Party of Democratic Socialism 4
pension scheme *see* *Rentenversicherung*
people's solidarity *see* *Volkssolidarität*
performance indicators 146, 164
performance measurement and pay

163–64, 167
performance related pay 141, 142, 156, 163, 188, 209
Permanent Conference of Ministers of Education *see* Kultusministerkonferenz
Permanent Diet *see* Immerwährender Reichstag
personnel management 171, 172, 177, 184–93, 194
Pflegeversicherung 19, 248, 257, 293, 295, 296, 341, 345
policy planning 158
Political Action study 209
political culture 167, 198, 199, 204–9, 214
politics-administration dichotomy 159, 164
Politikverflechtung 43, 91, 95–97, 96, 97
polytechnics 179
poor law 18, 118, 224, 225, 227, 230, 305, 306, 307, 308, 310, 311, 312, 324, 337
Poor Law Boards 109, 306
poor rate 306
Poor Relief *see Armenpflege*
postwar reconstruction 36
Power Distance 201, 203
PPBS 154, 156
prefectoral system 67, 74, 79
Preussische Städteordnung 116
primary medical care 304
primary vs. secondary care 308, 314
principal agent approach 59
private associations 330
Private Finance Initiative 231, 232
Private Sector Partnerships 231
private, for-profit sector 233, 255, 258, 260, 264, 266, 268,

270, 272, 279, 281, 293, 295, 296, 319, 341
privatisation 13, 19, 39, 52, 60, 62, 113, 141, 147, 154, 155, 158–61, 163–67, 217, 231, 237, 260, 264–83, 319, 322–24, 338, 344
producer-consumer relationship 270
professionalisation 112, 173, 175, 182, 183, 190, 227, 237, 250, 253, 257, 260
Programme Review in Canada 355, 359
Protestant churches 285
Prussia 32, 87, 174
Prussian County Charter of 1872 118
Prussian Municipal Charter *see* Preussische Städteordnung
public employees see Angestellte (im öffentlichen Dienst)
public sector employment 6, 161, 171, 208
  female 180
  part-time 180, 188
  training 189–93
public sector ethics 136, 137, 138, 167
public sector share of the GNP 5
public sector unions 157, 162, 184, 356
public service 136, 137, 355, 357
public utilities 173, 174, 266
public/private partnerships 313, 316
purchaser/provider relationship 141, 231, 233, 272, 279, 286, 322, 325

Quangos 79, 113, 127, 294, 298

quasi-markets 61, 62, 236, 265, 270–80, 296, 322, 323

Rahmengesetzgebung des Bundes 184
Rayner's efficiency unit 158
Reagan, R. 354
Rechtsaufsicht 118
Rechtsstaat 7, 28, 33, 37, 49, 51, 205
recruitment 144, 152, 163, 187–89, 192, 294
Red-Green coalition 103
referendum 8, 14, 15, 115, 122, 123, 126, 127
Regierungsbezirke 51, 292
Regierungspräsidium 121
regional planning 52, 68–69
regionalisation 21, 71, 100, 101, 102, 114
regionalism 67–82
Registered Homes Act of 1984 276
regulated autonomy 239
Reichsreform 87
Reichstag 3, 9, 88, 89, 91, 94
reinventing government 58, 132, 139, 157
Rentenversicherung 213, 245, 248–50, 262, 328
representative organisations of the physicians *see Kassenärztliche Vereinigungen*
residential care 276, 277, 278
responsive administration 249, 259, 261
Revolution of 1848 3, 12, 31, 88, 116
Roman Law 4, 5, 48, 199
Royal Commission on National Health Insurance 309
rule of law 3, 6, 29, 36, 47, 48, 193

Schmidt, H. 102, 155
Schröder government 44
Schröder, G. 87
Schumacher, K. 102
Scotland 8, 67, 127, 226
Scottish Grand Committee 77
Scottish nationalism 70, 73, 81
Scottish Parliament 8, 75, 114
Scottish Secretary 77, 80
Second World War 34, 100, 120, 173, 175, 224, 305, 328, 338
SED 96
select committee on constitutional reform *See Enquete-Kommission Verfassungsreform*
Select Committee on Welsh Affairs 77
self-help initiatives 253, 254, 257, 268, 288, 307, 341
self-help organisations 255, 257, 285, 288, 295, 299
semi-sovereign state 4, 98, 356
Senate principle 88
Senior Civil Service 79, 141, 142, 145, 168
separation of politics and administration 59, 227
SES concept 154
shires 109, 177
Simonis, H. 155
skeleton state 147, 161
small-state-ism *see Kleinstaaterei*
social assistance 225, 226, 227, 229, 306, 311, 313, 318, 323
social care 224, 233–38, 240, 265, 268, 271, 275, 277, 279, 282, 305, 306, 310, 316, 319, 323, 324, 325

Social Democratic-Liberal coalition
    102, 121
social federalism 8, 67–82
social housing 11, 18–19, 20, 111,
    119, 304, 307–8, 310, 311,
    313, 316, 320, 323, 324,
    327, 328, 331, 335, 338,
    340, 342, 344
social insurance system 225, 229,
    245, 247, 252, 255, 285,
    287, 293, 295, 308, 310,
    311, 316, 318, 324, 328,
    329, 333, 335, 336
social planning 287, 337
social question 331, 332
social security 49, 58, 91, 224–32,
    240, 244, 245, 246, 247,
    250, 317, 318, 319, 325,
    341
social security service 226
social services departments 224,
    233, 236, 238, 264, 265,
    271, 280, 312, 313, 317,
    318, 319
Social Services Inspectorate 238,
    280
social welfare law *see*
    Bundessozialhilfegesetz
social welfare office *see Sozialamt*
social workers 233, 237, 253, 264
Sozialamt 252, 253, 254, 258
Soziale Marktwirtschaft 247
Sozialgesetzbuch 246, 256
Sozialhilfe 246, 247, 250–55, 256,
    257, 259, 260, 261, 285,
    293, 295, 296, 330, 336,
    337, 341, 345
Sozialstaatsprinzip 167
Sozialwahlen 249
SPD, Social Democrats 3, 89, 96,
    102–3, 119, 156, 162, 245,
    330, 337–39
Speyer academy 154, 156
Städteordnung 329
state philosophies 167
Statistisches Bundesamt 160
Stein, Carl Freiherr vom und zum
    87
Steuerverbund 95
Stoiber, W. 155
Stormont 74, 75
Strauß, F.J. 103
subject culture 205, 208, 218
subsidiarity 18, 52, 122, 246, 248,
    254, 284, 286, 287, 293,
    295, 299, 337, 340

Taking forward Continuity and
    Change 159
Teltschick, H. 156
territorial reforms 13, 51, 111, 120,
    154, 158, 177, 259
Thatcher government 72, 177, 194,
    216, 266, 317, 321
Thatcher, M. 38, 70, 112, 125, 132,
    140, 144, 148, 158, 179,
    317, 354, 356
Thatcher 'revolution' 38, 114, 304
Thatcherism 70, 139, 147, 199,
    217, 218
third sector 159, 179, 254, 286,
    297, 336
Thirty Years' War 87
Thoma 33
top-down approach 229, 248, 358,
    359
trade union militancy 227
trade unions 18, 52, 185, 231, 232,
    273, 308, 309, 310, 316
Treasury 35, 78, 79, 80, 159
Treaty of Union 70
two chamber system 117

Ulbricht, W. 96
ultra vires doctrine 9, 108
Uncertainty Avoidance 202, 203, 218
unemployment insurance *see Arbeitslosenversicherung*
Unfallversicherung 245, 248, 328
ungovernability 53
unification 6, 9, 41, 44, 54–58, 97, 98, 101, 127, 150, 153–55, 166, 179, 200, 244, 247, 291, 345, 346, 354
unification vote 56
uniformity of living conditions *see Einheitlichkeit der Lebensverhältnisse*
unitary federalism 92, 93
unitary state 8, 67, 70, 71, 74, 81, 82, 88, 160, 167, 311
Unternehmen Freistaat Bayern 157
urbanisation 109, 110, 117, 173, 195, 330, 331
utilitarianism 5, 110

value for money 139, 140, 228, 234, 266, 269, 273
Vermittlungsausschuß 103
Verwaltungsakademien 191
veto points 160, 167, 352, 356, 357
Volkssolidarität 298
voluntary (not-for-profit) sector 233
voluntary organisations 112, 257, 264, 273, 284–89, 292, 307, 310–16, 319
voluntary sector 273, 294, 296, 297, 319, 324

Weimar Constitution 3, 85, 118
Weimar Republic 9, 15, 49, 51, 88, 89, 91, 101, 102, 104, 118, 165, 284–87, 327–40
welfare associations *see Wohlfahrtsverbände*
welfare mix 255
welfare 'monopolies' 236
welfare pluralism 236, 240
Welsh Assembly 8, 72, 114
Welsh Funding Council 73
Welsh Language Act 73
Welsh Language Board 73
Welsh nationalism 72, 81
Welsh referendum 81
White Paper Caring for People 234, 265, 269–71, 276, 277
White Paper 'Continuity and Change' 159
Whitehall 79, 108, 133, 142, 143, 162, 182
whole person approach 229, 253, 260
Wilson, W. 165
Wohlfahrtsverbände 6, 122, 181, 244, 245, 253, 254, 255, 257, 258, 260, 268, 284–99, 330, 334, 335, 336, 337, 341, 342, 345, 346
  culture 294
  membership-orientation 298
  peak organisations 287
  volunteers 297
Wohngeld 251, 252, 338
workhouses 305, 306, 329

Waffenschmidt commission 153
Wales 8, 67, 127, 226
Weber, M. 135, 157
Weberian bureaucracy 135, 136, 145, 146, 149, 151, 152, 177, 226, 230

ZDF Zweites Deutsches Fernsehen 100
Zentrale Wohlfahrtsstelle der Juden in Deutschland (ZWSt) 286, 289
Zentrum party 286, 331